(Blank Page)

This blank page represents everything I think I know about myself, recovery, this book, the meetings, my disease, and God, and unless a miracle occurs that causes me to have an open mind and a new experience with all these things, I shall never see the truth and cannot fail from remaining in my everlasting ignorance.

RECOVERY 5:12
Recovery Has a Name and Its Jesus

Copyright © 2023 by Gene Amons

All rights reserved. No part of this publication may be reproduced in any form, or by any means, electronic or mechanical, including photocopying, recording, or any information browsing, storage, or retrieval system, without permission in writing from the publisher.

Published in the United States by Ainsley & Hallie K. Publishers, 115 Day Rd., Deville, La, 71328

First Ainsley & Hallie K. Publishers Edition, 2023

Library of Congress Cataloging-in-Publication Data: 2023948341
Amons, Gene.
Title of the Book: RECOVERY 5:12
Sub Title: RECOVERY HAS A NAME AND ITS JESUS

ISBN 979-8-9893657-7-7 Hardback

ISBN 979-8-9893657-2-2 Paperback

ISBN 979-8-9893657-6-0 E-Book

Unless otherwise noted, all scriptures are from the
KING JAMES VERSION, public domain.

TikTok: @recovery5_12

Facebook: Recovery512

Instagram: recovery_512

Twitter: @RECOVERY_512

Handle: #RECOVERY512

Although this publication is designed to provide accurate information in regard to the subject matter covered, the publisher and the author assume no responsibility for errors, inaccuracies, omissions, or any other inconsistencies herein. This publication is meant as a source of valuable information for the reader, however it is not meant as a replacement for direct expert assistance. If such level of assistance is required, the services of a competent professional should be sought.

Unless otherwise indicated, all the characters in this book are fictitious. Any resemblance to actual persons, living or dead, is purely coincidental.

Dedicated to all those seeking recovery, in the Name of Jesus. May the life changing power of the Holy Spirit guide you on your journey in recovery. As you walk this path, remember that through faith and action, you too will find strength, healing, and a renewed spirit. The recovery community stands with you, offering support, love and unwavering faith in your journey towards recovery and salvation

CONTENTS

Preface 1

Introduction 3

The Stories 9

Powerlessness 25

Common Peril 39

The Great Obsession 49

Unmanageability 57

Step Two 73

Journey To Wholeness 93

The Requirement 99

Step Three 113

Step Four 121

Step Five 149

Step Six 191

Step Seven 219

Step Eight 235

Step Nine 249

Step Ten 277

Step Eleven. 291

Step Twelve 311

First Measure Of Faith 331

Second Measure Of Faith 351

Third Measure Of Faith 377

Fourth Measure Of Faith 403

Fifth Measure Of Faith 421

Faith In Action. 437

The Fellowship Of Prayer 461

Recovery 5:12 469

The Call	485
The Power Of Discipleship	493
Appendix: A	555
Discipleship In **Recovery 5:12:**	*555*
Frequently Asked Questions (Faq)	*555*
Appendix B	573
Groups: How It Works	*573*
Appendix C	575
Prayer Meeting: How It Works	*575*
Appendix D	579
Bible Study	*579*
Appendix E	583
The Beattitudes: Principles, Promises, And Fruit	*583*
Appendix F	595
What Is A Pastor?	*595*
Appendix G	599
What Is A Church Family?	*599*
Appendix H	603
Gifts Of The Spirit	*603*

Preface

In the realm of the spirit, we often find that our greatest journeys are those that take us from darkness into the light. This book, "RECOVERY 5:12," is precise directions to the powerful intersection of faith, recovery, and the life changing work of the Holy Spirit. It is an account of hope, healing, and the redemptive power that touches even the most troubled souls.

For many of us within recovery communities, we understand that salvation and recovery are not a one-time event but a continual journey. It is a journey that starts in the midst of despair and brokenness. In the depths of our wrestling and the throes of sin such as addiction and alcoholism, we feel a darkness that seems impenetrable. Yet, it is precisely in these darkest moments that the light of salvation has the opportunity to shine most brilliantly.

In this textbook, we embark on a profound exploration of recovery, beyond just a clinical process but as spiritual awakening. In our stories, we share that through faith and the power of the Holy Spirit, we have emerged from the depths of sin such as addiction and alcoholism into the embrace of salvation.

Jesus Name recovery celebrates the manifestation of the Holy Spirit in our lives, and this textbook is a testament to the reminder that, with faith, prayer, and action, we find the strength to overcome our darkest demons and rediscover the joy of salvation.

As you read these pages, we encourage you to open your heart as the Holy Spirit guides you on this life changing journey. May you find inspiration, encouragement, and the unwavering belief that no one is beyond the reach of God's love and salvation. We do recover.

In the spirit of recovery faith and the boundless grace of our Savior, let us embark on this journey together, from darkness to the light. Recovery has a Name and its Jesus.

INTRODUCTION

*"He sent from above,
he took me,
he drew me out of many waters."*
(Psalm 18:16)

In the end, we created this hell. We had run out of all ideas and there was no human power, including ourselves, that could help us. Only divine intervention could, and we hoped it would relieve us of this torture. We were addicts and alcoholics in need of saving. In the pages of this book, we found directions to a path of recovery that guided us from being bound by addictions to being recovered. The Power necessary to restore our lives is available to all who wholeheartedly seek it. Would it be made available to us who were just beginning? Of course, it would, provided we were willing to follow a few steps and incorporate the measure of faith required to abandon ourselves completely.

The background of this book lies within the journeys of many of us who have followed this Power out of the darkness of alcoholism and addictions through recovery into faith and been rewarded with a life like none that we could have ever imagined. It is a simple path but not an easy one. We will share in a general way what it was like.

One recovery journey began when I found myself at the end of my drinking and using careers. My life had met a bitter end. I found myself out of money, out of time, and out of luck. If not for a few good people, I would not have made it out alive. I found myself in the darkest hour of my life. But God!

God prepared a way out of the legal jam I had placed myself in after multiple DUI/DWI charges. I was bonded out of jail in the most unusual of manners and it is a story that is best saved for another day. Meanwhile, I found myself out of town, having given my truck away after a motor vehicle accident that was due to my drunkenness. Fortunately, there were no fatal injuries that occurred as a result. I had enough money for a few days in a hotel and that would translate to one last month's rent in a little house in the most rural of towns in the southernmost of states. It was bleak!

My daily life was once one of a high-profile executive and had now been reduced to a daily walk to the post office box, picking up a newspaper and slush drink at the local convenience store, and heading back home to another evening of disconnected cable static television and another pot of noodles. It wasn't gutter drunk or under the bridge tarpaulin living, but it was my lowest moment. However, things would begin to change.

I had been placed in a town where I knew no one other than the dysfunctional relationship that aided me. But three hundred and fifty-seven steps from the front door of the little rental property was a church. The type of church did not matter at all. Somehow, something just told me that church would be a good place for me to go. Following this advice, I was introduced to a preacher man and a group of people in a small church who would play the most integral parts in my recovery and salvation.

As I continued to obey God and follow the instructions of the preacher man, I also found myself thrust into a secular twelve-step program. There I ran across a man who would become my sponsor and who would take me through the twelve steps. Simultaneously, the preacher man was showing me the truth as it was found and outlined in the Word of God. These two spiritual giants were pouring their experience, strength, and hope into me.

Time would march on; I began taking the steps and following the Word of God. Immediately, I was introduced to prayer. My prayer life quickly grew, no, catapulted, from merely closing my eyes and speaking out to seemingly nothing to receiving revelations and directions from God. A relationship was formed out of prayer.

This prayerful life was based upon a tabernacle plan of prayer given to me through a sermon in Alexandria, Louisiana. This pattern of prayer began to reveal a series of steps that brought even more clarity to this spiritual journey I was on. I began to hunger and thirst for more as I was left to live life in steps ten, eleven and twelve. And this was a beautiful life. However, there was more.

Through prayer, faith revealed her measures, and these five measures of faith placed the missing pieces that my spirit had been yearning for. As I pursued these measures of faith, I found myself being of maximum service to God and so many other people. God would restore unto me everything I gave away for drugs and alcohol. God then abundantly gave to me until I found myself writing a book, creating recovery homes, and showing so many others this path. It was amazing.

This book was born. It's not another twelve-step program. It is a biblically based recovery path that can be utilized by all of society regardless of whether they are addicted or not. It provided a way for a broken soul and put it into direct connection with God. We have discovered that there is more after the "Our Father" that is prayed at the end of a meeting. The exact same thing can happen to anyone who wholeheartedly seeks God. Here is how we seek Him.

RECOVERY 5:12 is a spiritual recovery path that offers us a life-changing journey toward spiritual healing and wholeness by integrating a relationship with Jesus, spiritual practices, and a supportive community. It fosters spiritual growth, resilience, and a deep connection with the Power necessary for permanent recovery. Recovery is something we all need in some aspect of our lives, and for many of us, we need complete salvation. Recovery has a Name and it is Jesus!

The purpose of this book is to introduce others to God's plan for faithful recovery and how it can be applied to each of our lives. This book explores what that means and how it can be accomplished. It will share our experiences and outline the twelve recovery steps, including the five measures of faith, which are applicable to all sins such as addictions and alcoholism. These steps and measures include a principle that guided us out of our afflictions and, once taken, placed us in a life free from the bondage of sins such as addictions, alcoholism, and self. We have discovered five measures that provide a blueprint for living a recovered life. **RECOVERY 5:12** is a pathway to spiritual growth, maturity, and holiness, enabling us to become more like Jesus. In this book, we will explore how to apply the **RECOVERY 5:12®** approach to our spiritual journey. We have been delivered, but first things first. This is not a substitute for the Bible or the Gospel. Instead, **RECOVERY 5:12** takes those of us who were suffering in spiritual bondage and points us to the Good News.

RECOVERY 5:12 is a life-changing journey of healing, salvation, and spiritual growth. This book is a guide for individuals seeking a Power that can overcome their struggles with addictions, compulsive behaviors, and other harmful habits. This faith-based approach to recovery changed our lives. By exploring the life-changing principles of the Bible, this book facilitates a look toward the only path to inner peace, freedom, and wholeness in Jesus Christ. The journey of recovery in Jesus is not a one-time event but rather a daily commitment to walking in the light of His love and grace. Through surrendering to His will, seeking His guidance, and relying on the power of the Holy Spirit, we can experience a life beyond our wildest dreams. This book will provide practical tools, insights, and inspiration for anyone seeking to live a life of sobriety and spiritual transformation in Christ. This book is like the depths of the ocean. The different depths are designed for different people, skills, and creations. What we have found is that if you do what this book says to do, you will find yourself standing in the Gospel of Jesus Christ, recovered, and living by Biblical Principles. Let's get started!

First, we found that there were some preliminary questions that had to be answered and these could be asked in a myriad of ways. We were asked, "Do you have a problem?" If yes, then, "Do you want to do something about it?" If yes, then, "Do you need help?" When we finally were beaten to the point of reasonableness by drugs and alcohol, we quickly answered affirmatively to each of these questions. Until this point, very few will ever have the will to escape the hideous master, King Sin.

They then sat us down and began to qualify us in this manner. They asked, "Have you ever wanted to honestly quit drinking and using drugs?" If yes, then, "When you honestly want to, have you found that you cannot quit entirely?" This includes swearing off for a day, week, months, or even years only to find yourself doing the very thing that you did not want to do. Then they asked us, "If when in the throes of this sin such as addictions and alcoholism, do you find that you have little control over it, especially the amount?" Life injected with sins such as addictions and alcoholism had already convinced us of the affirmative to these qualifications. They told us that if we had been convinced by our own life stories of these qualifications, then we were suffering from the physical and mental symptoms of a spiritual illness that only a spiritual experience can conquer.

Initially, many of us had to address the spiritual illness, such as addiction and alcoholism, that was coursing through our bodies. Our flesh was on fire and unless we could add more of the drugs and alcohol to it, it would bend our minds into such a state of unreasonableness that truth was no longer identifiable. Unless we wanted to succumb to the insidious disease once again with more of the same, we had to get help! For some, this initial help came in the form of being locked up or hiring a bodyguard. Others sought hospitalization for detoxification from the substances. This four- or five-day period appears as hell on earth to our bent minds. But it was necessary to lift the mental fog enough to see the great wrestling our mind and flesh were caught up in.

The pages of this book enabled us to engage in a recovery path that changed our lives forever. It pointed to the effective seeking that is necessary for anyone who is facing life problems. It provided the necessary step-by-step directions for us, even though many of us already felt as if we were among the smartest people on the planet and for sure could figure out a solution to any problem before this one. Unlike other self-help books, we feel the message carried in these pages points to another Helper.

We discovered that this Power, which we could not previously receive because we could not see or know it, lives with us and shall be in you as it has moved into us. Sounds preposterous? It would mean that we would need to make decisions and express willingness to do anything to get out from under this spiritual oppression that had us so physically and mentally bound. This of course will mean that we will be talking about a measure of faith which, when sought, changed our very existence, and provided a life that was still incomprehensible but on opposite ends of the scale from the present incomprehensible pitiful demoralization that we were currently under.

Many of us revolted at such a proposition for it reminded us of such preconceived ideas about religion or the lack thereof from which we could never escape. We were reminded, "How is what you are currently doing or have done working for you?" The answer was obvious and if the answer was honest, we knew that we had reached some sort of bottom. We were out of ideas. But to follow this uncertain path still seemed daunting. Then they asked us, "What do you have to lose?" After all, if this path does not work, they could easily return all our current misery. This was logical enough for many of us to start this wonderful path that indeed changed our lives. Here are the steps we took and the faith by which we now live.

THE STORIES

*"Therefore,
if anyone be in Christ,
he is a new creature:
old things are passed away;
behold, all things are become new"*
(2 Corinthians 5:17)

They began to tell us a few of their stories and although different characters, times, and events, the same underlying issue was always there. We were tasked with looking for the similarities in our drinking and drug use. After reading and listening to other stories, we asked ourselves, "Did I drink or use drugs like them?" "Did I think like them?" If the answer is "Yes," then perhaps we suffer from the same thing they suffered with. And if we suffer from the same thinking, drinking, and drug usage, then perhaps if we take their solution, we too can experience the joy and freedom that is found on many of their faces.

Here are but a few accounts of our thinking as we drank and used drugs.

Sarah's Story - Shadowed Canvas: The Battle Against Addiction

In a bustling city, there lived a woman named Sarah. Sarah was a talented artist, but she had fallen into the clutches of addiction. Her drug of choice was heroin, a substance that promised euphoria but led her down a treacherous path. Sarah's addiction had consumed her life, affecting her thoughts, emotions, and actions. Her thinking revolved around one thing: obtaining and using heroin. From the moment she woke up until she went to bed, her mind was preoccupied with thoughts of the drug. Each day, Sarah would meticulously plan her drug use. She knew the exact time, place, and people she needed to be around to fulfill her addiction. Her calendar was filled with secret rendezvous, hidden in the depths of dimly lit clubs, secluded corners, and trap houses. She craved the rush, the temporary escape from the pain and emptiness that plagued her. The unyielding mental obsession and urges controlled Sarah's every move. As the clock ticked closer to her designated time, a wave of restlessness would wash over her. Before she ever put the drug into her body, she trembled with anticipation, her heart pounding in her chest. The urge to use became overwhelming, overpowering any rational thoughts or concerns about the consequences. She was already suffering from the mental obsession.

In her brief moments of sobriety, Sarah desperately attempted to break free from the grip of addiction. She knew the damage it was causing in her life, alienating her from loved ones, destroying her finances, and ravaging her health. Yet, her addiction seemed to possess a magnetic pull, luring her back time and time again. Sarah's rationalization and denial were constant companions. She convinced herself that she had control over her drug use and that she could stop whenever she wanted. She believed that her addiction was a personal choice and that it did not define her. She shielded herself from the reality of her situation, choosing to believe in a web of self-deception rather than face the truth. Using heroin became Sarah's escape and coping mechanism. Whenever she faced emotional pain or stress, she turned to the drug as a temporary respite. It provided a fleeting sense of relief, numbing her from the underlying issues that plagued her soul. But as the effects wore off, she would be left with an even deeper void of guilt, shame, and remorse, yet longing for another hit to fill the emptiness within.

As Sarah's addiction grew, she became isolated and secretive. She distanced herself from her friends and family, hiding her struggles behind a facade of normalcy. Her social life began to revolve solely around her addiction, leaving her with few genuine connections and a growing sense of loneliness. Sarah's addiction had transformed her into a shell of her former self. The vibrant colors of her art were replaced by a monochromatic haze. Her talent and potential were buried under layers of self-destruction, with each hit of heroin tearing her further away from the person she once was. But within the depths of her addiction, a glimmer of hope remained. Deep down, Sarah knew that she needed help, that she couldn't continue down this destructive path forever. And so, in her darkest hour, with a trembling hand, the flicker of determination in her eyes removed itself; the first step in recovery had taken her. She was powerless over the sin of addiction and her life as a sinner was spiritless. But she heard of a Power in recovery, so she began reaching out for the support and guidance she so desperately needed.

Sarah's journey would be arduous, filled with obstacles and setbacks. But she held onto the hope, knowing that there was something within her that promised the strength to overcome her addiction and rediscover the colors of her life. Here are the steps she took.

A Symphony of Redemption: Michael's Battle with Alcohol Addiction

Another one of our members in the heart of a small town was a man named Michael. Michael was a talented musician, but his life had spiraled out of control due to his addiction to alcohol. Day after day, his thoughts revolved around the bottle that consumed his existence. From the moment he woke up, Michael's mind would fixate on one thing: obtaining and consuming alcohol. It was a constant battle within his thoughts, a relentless desire that clouded his judgment and blurred his perception of reality. The allure of the bottle seemed to drown out the other aspects of his life, including his music, relationships, and personal well-being. The unyielding mental obsession and urges became the driving force behind Michael's actions. As the day progressed, a sense of restlessness or anxiety would wash over him, an insatiable craving for the numbing effects of alcohol. His body would tremble with anticipation, and his mind would become consumed by thoughts of satisfying the unrelenting "thirst" within him. His addiction was wreaking chaos upon his life – drunk or sober. His life was littered with broken relationships, missed opportunities, and self-destruction. Addiction held him in its clutches, trapping him in an insane cycle of rationalization and denial. The best he could do was to keep doing the same thing over and over while expecting different results.

Michael would convince himself that he had control over his drinking and that he could quit whenever he wanted. He would justify his behavior by blaming external factors, the pressures of life, or claiming that alcohol was his only solace in a world filled with pain. Deep down, he knew the truth, but admitting it would require confronting the depths of his addiction and the demons within him.

Alcohol had become Michael's escape, his solution for the hardships and emotional turmoil he faced. The moment the bottle touched his lips, he felt a temporary reprieve from his troubles. The weight on his shoulders seemed to lift, replaced by a fleeting sense of euphoria. But as the effects wore off, he found himself sinking deeper into a sea of despair, obsessing over the need for another drink to recreate that elusive moment of respite. As his addiction tightened its grip, Michael began to isolate himself from those who cared about him. His social life revolved solely around his drinking habits, which alienated friends and family who had grown tired of witnessing his self-destruction. The bottle became his constant companion, the only friend who never abandoned him, albeit one who was slowly taking everything he held dear.

Michael's talent as a musician began to fade into the background. The melodies that once flowed effortlessly from his fingertips were replaced by a discordant symphony of broken dreams. His artistry, once celebrated, now drowned beneath the suffocating weight of addiction. Within the depths of his despair, any flicker of hope was extinguished. Deep down, Michael knew that he couldn't continue down this destructive path indefinitely, but he no longer had a choice in drinking. And so, with trembling hands and a completely busted life of alcoholism, somehow, he was persuaded by the pain to seek help that he had never considered before, to reach out for the support that had eluded him for far too long.

Michael's journey toward recovery would be an uphill battle, filled with moments of doubt, temptation, and balks. But he clung to the glimmer of hope within him, knowing that what awaited him back in his alcoholism was destined to destroy him. Therefore, he pressed on with the simple directions he was given. Although they were weighty and not ideal, they were far better than the alternative.

Then there was a promise of a Power that could restore a life, music, and relationships better than those he had given away for alcohol. With each step he took, he embraced the daunting but necessary task of connecting to this Power, breaking himself free from the chains of addiction, redeveloping his passion, and composing a new melody for his life. Here are the steps he took.

Concealed Devotion:
Laurie's Battle with Prescription Pill Addiction

As we reviewed these experiences and heard others, we could see the similarity not only in these stories but with our own personal stories. The boundaries between different sins such as alcoholism and addictions are non-existent.

In another story, in the close-knit community of Alexandria, there was a woman named Laurie who seemed to embody the very essence of devotion. She was a pillar of the local church and was always seen with a warm smile, extending a helping hand to anyone in need. But behind her pious facade, Laurie battled a hidden demon—addiction.

Laurie's drug of choice was prescription pain medication. It started innocently enough, with a legitimate need for relief from chronic pain. But over time, her dependency grew, and the line between pain management and addiction blurred. As the pills took hold of her life, her thoughts became consumed by the next dose. Each day, Laurie would go about her duties as a devoted member of the church, her mind filled with conflicting thoughts. On one hand, she yearned for the comfort her pills provided, the temporary escape from the emotional turmoil she faced. On the other hand, her faith and her position within the church reminded her of the moral compass she should follow. She could not see that her moral compass was lacking the needed power to overcome her sin of addiction.

The obsession, cravings, and urges tormented Laurie, testing her resolve at every turn. During a church service, she would feel her body ache for the numbing relief of the medication. The pews became a battleground between her desire to worship and the relentless pull of her addictions. The struggle within her intensified, threatening to shatter the carefully constructed image she presented to her church family. Laurie's faith was intertwined with her efforts to hide her addictions. She was terrified of the judgment and condemnation that awaited her if her secret were to be exposed. Fear gripped her heart, and she became an expert at concealing her struggles, adept at masking her pain behind a smile that betrayed none of the turmoil within. She attended recovery meetings in neighboring towns, ensuring her involvement remained a secret from her church family. She would slip out during church gatherings under the guise of other commitments, attending clandestine meetings where she found comfort in the company of others fighting similar battles.

The irony of seeking redemption while hiding her struggle was not lost on Laurie. Laurie's rationalization and denial provided her with a false sense of control. She convinced herself that she had a handle on her addiction, that her faith alone would be enough to keep her on the straight and narrow path. She clung to the belief that if she kept her sin of addiction hidden, she could continue to serve as an example of unwavering faith to her church family. But addiction is a relentless foe. It erodes the very foundation upon which one's life is built. Laurie's facade began to crack, and the toll of her addiction seeped into her interactions with her church family. She grew distant, retreating into her own world of shame and secrecy, feeling the weight of her deception bear down on her soul. Within Laurie's heart, hope's flame darkened. She yearned for redemption, for the strength to overcome her addictions and rebuild the shattered pieces of her life. It was a journey she could not undertake alone, and the weight of her secret became too heavy to bear.

One fateful day, Laurie found the courage to confide in her pastor, baring her soul and exposing her hidden struggle. She expected judgment, but what she received was compassion, understanding, and a guiding hand toward the path of recovery. Her church family rallied around her, offering support, prayers, and a non-judgmental space for healing. Her church introduced her to **RECOVERY 5:12**. Once they saw the effects of this recovery path, they quickly investigated starting a **RECOVERY 5:12** program at the church.

Laurie's journey toward recovery would be challenging, marked by moments of doubt and temptation. However, with the love and support of her church family, she began to reclaim her life. Through **RECOVERY 5:12** and its recovery groups, along with a renewed connection with her faith, Laurie found that Jesus was not who she *thought* He was. She experienced Him and He confronted her sin of addiction, and she emerged from the darkness into a life filled with hope, forgiveness, and redemption as the rocks fell to the ground.

She now leads **RECOVERY 5:12** recovery groups at her church and the news spread that once the church folk came to "support" **RECOVERY 5:12**, they found themselves following the program's steps. Many of them took these steps and began walking in the measures of faith. They report a drastic improvement in their experience with the Holy Spirit and drive to search the Word more than they had ever considered. They thanked Laurie. Here are the steps they took.

Devoured by Darkness: Johnny's Battle with Food Addiction

This spirit of addiction consumes us in many forms. One of us is a young man named Johnny. He was an intelligent and ambitious individual, but behind his charming smile, he harbored a dark secret—Johnny was battling an addiction, an addiction to food. He suffered from an eating disorder that consumed his life, both physically and emotionally. Johnny's struggle began during his teenage years when he turned to food for comfort. Stress and anxiety became constant companions, and he found comfort in the temporary relief that eating provided. Initially, it started innocently, with occasional binges, but soon it spiraled out of control. Food became his drug, his escape from the harsh realities of life. As time went on, Johnny's addictions intensified. He would gorge himself on enormous amounts of food, unable to resist the urges that plagued him. The caloric addiction controlled him, dictating his every action and thought. He would isolate himself, spending countless hours in his room, indulging in secret feasts, ashamed and disgusted with himself. His relationships suffered too. Friends and family noticed the changes in Johnny's behavior, but he would deny any problem, hiding his addiction with lies and excuses. He became increasingly withdrawn, distancing himself from the world that had once brought him joy.

One day, as Johnny stared at his reflection in the mirror, he realized he couldn't go on like this. He had hit rock bottom. Determined to break free from the chains of his addiction, he sought help. He confided in his closest friend, Sarah, who had always been a pillar of support. Sarah, concerned for Johnny's well-being, encouraged him to seek professional assistance. Together, they researched treatment options and found a local support group for individuals struggling with eating disorders that followed the path of **RECOVERY 5:12**. It was there that Johnny met others who understood his pain, individuals who shared similar experiences. Through their stories, he discovered God's hope—a glimmer of light in his darkest moments.

The journey to recovery was far from easy. Johnny faced many setbacks, battling relapses and self-doubt. But he was determined that God could overcome his addiction and give him a beautiful life. With the support of his newfound community, therapy sessions, and a dedicated treatment plan, Johnny saw gradual progress. Throughout his recovery, Johnny began to understand the root causes of his addiction. Through **RECOVERY 5:12**, he delved deep into himself, confronting the underlying spiritual issues that had led him down this destructive path. He realized that the addiction was not simply about food but about finding spiritual comfort in a world that often seemed overwhelming. As the days turned into weeks, and the weeks into months, Johnny's strength grew. He developed healthier coping mechanisms. **RECOVERY 5:12** led him to surrender his reliance on food for reliance upon God. He discovered that God guided him in meditation and journaling. He learned to nourish his body with nutritious meals and appreciate food for its sustenance, not view it as a means to escape.

Slowly but surely, God began restoring him. Broken relationships were mended and restitutions were made with loved ones he had hurt along the way. The Lord placed desires into his heart as he pursued his dreams with renewed passion, utilizing the resilience he had gained through his battle with addiction.

Johnny's journey was a testament to the Power of God that provided him with perseverance and the strength of the Holy Spirit. God conquered Johnny's addictions, not without scars, but with a newfound appreciation for life's precious moments. As he stood at the threshold of a brighter future, he vowed to be an advocate, a source of inspiration for others who faced similar struggles. How could he not tell the world what only God could do in his life?

From that day forward, Johnny dedicated himself to raising awareness about **RECOVERY 5:12** and supporting those with eating disorders in spiritual need. He shares his story openly, offering hope and encouragement to individuals who feel trapped by their addictions. Through his vulnerability, he sparks conversations, shatters stigmas, and helps others realize that they are not alone and that God is the answer. Here are the steps he took.

Love Unchained: Tina's Journey from Relationship Addiction to Spiritual Freedom

Some of us struggled with addictions to relationships. One of our members is an older woman named Tina. She had lived a full and vibrant life, filled with accomplishments and cherished memories. However, deep within her heart, Tina carried a burden—an addiction to relationships. She became dependent on the validation and attention that came from being in a romantic partnership, and this addiction had begun to consume her.

Tina's addiction started in her early years when she experienced the joy and excitement of falling in love for the first time. The rush of emotions and the sense of belonging captivated her, leaving an indelible mark on her soul. As time went on, Tina found herself constantly seeking out new relationships, moving from one partner to another in an endless quest for that initial euphoria.

With each new partner, Tina believed she had found the solution to her loneliness and insecurities. But as the initial excitement faded, so did her happiness. She became restless and dissatisfied, seeking validation and love in all the wrong places. Relationships became a cycle of highs and lows, leaving her emotionally drained and empty. The addiction controlled Tina's life. She neglected her own well-being, pouring all her energy into maintaining these relationships. She lost touch with her passions, her friendships, and even her sense of self. The fear of being alone, of facing her own vulnerabilities, drove her to cling desperately to anyone who showed her affection. Tina's loved ones watched as she cycled through relationships, often ignoring warning signs and red flags. They tried to offer her advice and support, but she brushed them off, convinced that her happiness could only be found in the arms of another. She had become a prisoner to her addiction, unable to break free from the destructive pattern she had woven around herself.

One day, as Tina sat alone in her quiet apartment, she realized she needed to confront her addiction. The realization hit her with a wave of sadness and regret. She had sacrificed her own happiness and identity in the pursuit of love, only to find herself unfulfilled and lost. With a newfound determination, Tina embarked on a journey of self-discovery and spiritual healing. She sought **RECOVERY 5:12**. She listened to the stories of others who had walked a similar path, learning from their experiences, and finding comfort in their shared struggles. Through this path, Tina began to understand the underlying causes of her addictions. She discovered that manifestations of self came in the form of fear of abandonment and her need for validation and lack of self-worth. She realized that true happiness could only be found by cultivating a loving and nurturing relationship with God as He transformed her into a new creature.

As Tina took these steps, she began a spiritual work. She worked through her past traumas and insecurities; she could see God starting to give her life. She reconnected with long-lost friends, rediscovered her passions, and discovered God guiding her in self-care activities that brought her joy. Slowly but surely, God demonstrated His love, and she could accept this version of herself, understanding that her worth was not dependent on another person's affection but on God alone.

The road to recovery was not without its challenges. Tina faced moments of temptation when the allure of a new relationship would beckon to her. But armed with newfound strength and self-awareness, she resisted the urge to fall back into old patterns. She knew that her happiness depended on breaking free from the insane cycle of relationship addiction. Over time, Tina became an advocate for loving God's version of yourself and healthy relationships grounded in the Power that restores new life. She shares her story with others, knowing that God uses it to bring hope, inspiration, and empowerment to those who struggle with similar addictions. Through her vulnerability, she encourages others to prioritize their own well-being and find fulfillment from the Holy Spirit who now dwells within.

Tina's journey was a testimony to the resilience of the Holy Spirit. He has broken her free from the chains of addiction and she has emerged stronger and more self-assured. As she embraced her newfound dependence upon the Holy Spirit's Power, she vowed to live a life guided by His love, authenticity, and a deep appreciation for the beauty of solitude in Jesus Christ. From that day forward, Tina has become a shining example of how it is possible for God to overcome relationship addiction and give true happiness to those who seek Him. She dedicated herself to seeking God and helping others break free from the same cycle, reminding them that their worth was not defined by the presence or absence of a romantic partner. One can only rely upon a Power greater than themselves, and His Name is Jesus.

Tina's transformation is a beacon of hope, a reminder that it is never too late to embark on a spiritual journey of discovering God's version of yourself and claim a life beyond your wildest imagination. Here are the steps she took.

Untangling Love: A Family's Journey from Codependency to Spiritual Healing

Addictions even attack families! In a small town nestled amidst central Louisiana, there lived a devoted church couple named David and Emily. They were pillars of their community, known for their unwavering faith and commitment to their family. But beneath their seemingly idyllic life, a painful struggle persisted—one of codependency centered around their beloved son, Michael, who was battling the sin of addiction.

Michael had always been the light of David and Emily's lives. They had cherished him since the day he was born, showering him with love and protection. However, as Michael grew older, his experimentation with drugs took a dark turn, leading him down a path of addiction. David and Emily's love for their son morphed into a toxic codependency—a relentless need to save him from his own destructive choices. They enabled his addictions, covering up his mistakes and minimizing the consequences of his actions. They would bail him out of trouble, sacrificing their own well-being to shield him from the harsh realities of his addictions. Their lives revolved around Michael, neglecting their own needs as they desperately clung to the hope of his recovery.

One day, as David and Emily sat in a **RECOVERY 5:12** meeting for families of addicts, they listened to the stories of others who had walked a similar path. They heard about the destructive nature of codependency and the importance of detaching with love. A sense of recognition and guilt washed over them as they realized the detrimental effects their codependency was having on Michael's recovery. Their eyes met, and at that moment, they knew they needed to confront their own addictions and take steps toward healing. With the support of their church community, they sought guidance and began taking the path of **RECOVERY 5:12**. Through the Power of God, David and Emily embarked on their own journey of recovery. God began to set boundaries and prioritize their own well-being. They acknowledged the manifestation of themselves in their fears and insecurities, as they searched and tried to find the reasons behind their codependent behaviors. It was a painful soul-searching process, as they faced their own enabling patterns and began to untangle the web they had woven around their son.

As David and Emily started spiritually healing individually, they also sought spiritual guidance on how to support Michael's recovery without enabling his addictions. They attended **RECOVERY 5:12** meetings, where

God revealed effective communication skills and strategies which began to foster a healthy environment conducive to his healing. Michael, initially resistant to change, was taken aback by his parents' shift in behavior. He had grown accustomed to their enabling, but he soon realized that their new spiritual approach was an act of love. They loved him enough to no longer protect him from the consequences of his addictions. Tough? Indeed. Necessary? Absolutely! It was a painful realization for all involved, but Michael recognized that their actions stemmed from a deep desire to see him recover. With a newfound recognition of his powerlessness and spiritual disconnectedness, Michael began his own spiritual journey in **RECOVERY 5:12**. He sought treatment, attended **RECOVERY 5:12** meetings, and worked closely with someone who had also followed the path outlined in **RECOVERY 5:12**. He saw how they had received the Holy Spirit as the result of making Jesus Christ their Lord and Savior. It was a challenging road, marked by relapses and moments of despair from not admitting their unmanageability or spiritual disconnectedness, but his parents stood by his side, providing love, encouragement, and unwavering spiritual support without enabling his addictions.

As time passed, the dynamics within the family began to shift. David and Emily experienced God as He revealed the importance of individual relationships with Him, focusing on their relationship in Jesus Christ while still being present for Michael's journey of spiritual recovery. God reconnected them with their own passions, rekindled their relationship, and they found comfort in their faith. Although they had been in church their whole lives, the church community now witnessed David and Emily's transformation, inspired by their faith to confront their codependency, and support their son's recovery in a healthier way. The couple share their story openly, fostering discussions about addictions, codependency, and the Power of Christ's love in recovery. Emily often tells of being raised in church and being extremely active in church but never having truly experienced God.

David and Emily's journey is a testimony to the strength of a family's love, resilience, and the power of Jesus Christ. God led them as they detached with love, allowing Michael to take responsibility for his own recovery and relationship with God. With God, they experienced the road to spiritual healing, supporting one another through God's grace and unwavering faith. Here are the steps they took.

Finding Light in the Darkness: Pam's Journey to Overcoming Grief

In a close-knit community, there was a woman named Pam who had faced immense loss and struggled with her addiction to grief. Her life had been marked by deep sorrow and an insatiable need to dwell on the pain of her past. Pam's journey began with the realization that her addiction to grief was preventing her from moving forward and living a fulfilling life. She had experienced profound loss, the kind that shakes one's foundation and leaves scars that never truly fade. But instead of allowing herself to heal, Pam clung tightly to her grief, using it as a crutch and a way to stay connected to what was lost. But deep within herself, Pam knew that her addiction to grief was only perpetuating her pain. She longed for genuine healing and grief, a way to honor the memory of her loved ones while still finding happiness in the present.

With the support of her community and a newfound determination, she decided to embark on the **RECOVERY 5:12** path of recovery. Pam also sought the help of therapists, counselors, and her church's grief support group which specialized in grief and addictions. They helped her understand the destructive nature of her addiction and the importance of processing her emotions in a healthy way. Together, they unraveled the deep-rooted beliefs and patterns that had kept her stuck in the cycle of grief.

As she journeyed through the **RECOVERY 5:12** path, Pam learned to give herself permission to heal. Through the steps, she began to explore the full range of her emotions, embracing not only the pain but also the joy and love that still existed in her life. She discovered that God wanted her to honor her loved ones and gave her newfound happiness as she began living a life that they would be proud of. In **RECOVERY 5:12**, Pam surrounded herself with a support network of friends, family, and fellow grief survivors. They provided a safe space for her to express her emotions, share her stories, and receive the support and understanding she craved. Through their shared experiences, they offered guidance and encouragement, reminding her that she was not alone in her journey.

Recovery for Pam meant God redefining her relationship with grief. God gave her permission to feel sadness but also demonstrated the experience of His joy. Through the Holy Spirit, meditation, and engaging in **RECOVERY 5:12** groups, she began to experience fulfillment and peace. Over time, Pam began to notice God causing a shift within herself. She no longer identified solely as a person consumed by grief. She discovered God was demonstrating strength and resilience that she never knew she had. As she embraced **RECOVERY 5:12**, she found a renewed sense of purpose and used her experiences to help others who were also struggling with grief.

Pam's journey was not without its challenges. There were moments when the pull of her addiction threatened to drag her back into the depths of despair. But with each setback, she persevered, knowing that spiritual healing was a process, and that God had the strength to overcome the addiction to grief dwelling within her. In the end, Pam's recovery became a beacon of hope for others who were trapped in the same cycle of insanity. She became an advocate for acknowledging and processing grief, understanding that true spiritual healing means finding a balance between honoring the past and embracing the present. Her story inspires others to seek spiritual help and embark on their own journeys of recovery, reminding them that it is possible to find light even in the darkest corners of their hearts. Here are the steps she took.

CHAPTER 1

POWERLESSNESS

"We admitted we were powerless over sins such as addictions and alcoholism — that our lives had become spiritually disconnected."
(Romans 7:14-20)

"Who has woe?
Who has sorrow?
Who has strife?
Who has complaints?
Who has needless bruises?
Who has bloodshot eyes?"
(Proverbs 23:29)

Many of us did not like to begin this journey with so much talk of spiritual things. However, we were spiritually bound - enslaved and trapped in destructive patterns of sinful behavior, particularly in the context of sinful habits such as alcoholism and addictions. Before being delivered from sin such as addictions and alcoholism, we lived with this spirit of affliction as it pummeled our lives until we were indescribably ruinous souls. As a way of helping those who come this way, we will discuss many of the various manifestations of the spiritual bondage of sin such as addictions and alcoholism. We admitted the insidiousness of the disease coupled with a carnality that rendered us unable to help ourselves. We admitted that we were caught in a cycle of insanity and sin. We had become spiritually disconnected and therefore our lives had become completely out of control. We had only just begun. This was step one.

Who hath woe? Who hath sorrow? Who hath contentions? These vivid questions evoke a sense of the consequences that befell us as we indulged in alcohol and drugs to an extreme. By employing these vivid descriptions, we paint a picture of the entanglement and suffering experienced by those of us caught in sin such as addictions and alcoholism. We were in a constant state of restlessness, irritability, and dissatisfaction with or without alcohol and drugs. Whether it be through excessive drinking or a general state of restlessness, these are the detrimental symptoms that manifest when we stray from a spiritually connected path.

We had to admit a truth to our innermost selves: that we were powerless over this sin. We suffered from its unyielding grip, which progressively gets worse and never better. We would tarry long at alcohol and drugs; we would go on to seek mixed substances. This extended and intentional involvement with alcohol and drugs only leads to more problems and harm. We would look upon the alcohol and drugs when they were enticing, romancing them, and they seemed to answer back. We had lost all self-control and the ability to resist the allure of alcohol and drugs which led to overindulgence and its associated consequences. We could not, upon our own power, even look away from the captivating aspects of this sin. We had lost the power of choice and could not find the ability to avoid the pitfalls that arise from such an unhealthy fascination.

In the end, what once was a source of ease and comfort turned on us and bit like a serpent and stung like an adder. There was no longer a means of escape from the harmful effects of drinking and drug use, much less the consequences that always come with it. There was such a sudden and painful nature in the aftermath of the well-known spree which we all succumbed to in our drinking and drug use. Just as the venomous bite of a snake brings forth intense pain and suffering, the consequences of our drinking and drug use were equally devastating. Our lives were immediately filled with harm that arose from the complete loss of self-control that resulted from falling into the traps of addictions and destructive behaviors.

Our eyes beheld strange bed partners, and our hearts uttered perverse things. We went far beyond any warnings about the negative consequences of drinking and drug use. Under the influence of alcohol and drugs, our judgment and behavior became distorted – mind-altering. Specifically, we found ourselves drawn to promiscuous encounters with unfamiliar people. Our speech became corrupted, leading us to express perverse thoughts.

Yes, we were like someone who lies down in the middle of the sea, or someone who lies upon the top of a pole. Our minds were distorted! We were extremely disoriented and pitifully unstable every time we were intoxicated. Our lives were tossed and turned; we were unable to find stability. We had completely lost control and found ourselves in dangerous positions while we were consumed by the effects of alcohol and drugs.

Many times, we would come to and wonder who had stricken us and why we were so sick. We wondered who beat us, and why we did not even feel it. We wondered when we would ever wake up. Our mindsets were of someone trapped in the cycle of addictions and alcoholism. We knew of only one way to consume drugs and alcohol - which was excessively. Despite the experience of physical harm, such as feeling as if we had been struck or beaten, we would deny our sickness and exhibit a complete lack of concern for our well-being. We were powerless over the obsession to continue seeking out alcohol and drugs, longing for the next opportunity to indulge in our addictive behavior. Despite the preponderance of evidence, many of us were still unwilling to admit that we were powerless over our addictions and alcoholism. When we would awaken, we would seek it yet again.

In addition to this unyielding task master of drugs and alcohol, we were carnal under this sin. We were oblivious to the intense struggle between the desires of the flesh and righteousness. Being carnal or fleshly meant that our minds had lost the power of choice and followed the dictates of our flesh. We were bound and enslaved to it, the struggle of being spiritually disconnected and caught in the great wrestling of mind and body, left with only our sinful inclinations.

There was an internal struggle between sin and righteousness. We experienced internal frustration and inner conflict with our own actions. We acknowledge that we would find ourselves doing things that we did not approve of or desired to do. Despite our good intentions and desires to do what is right, we admit that we fell into patterns of behavior that we hated. We acknowledge that when we did things that we did not want to do, we were, in a sense, affirming the goodness of God's principle. By recognizing the discrepancy between our desires and actions, we affirm that the principle itself is good and serves as a standard of righteousness. Let us clarify that when we engaged in actions contrary to our desires, it was not our true selves that were responsible but rather the influence of sin such as addictions, alcoholism, selfishness, and self-centeredness dwelling within us. We distinguish between our innermost being, which desires to do what is right, and the indwelling sin that still exerts its power over us. We recognize the inherent weakness of our flesh, acknowledging that no inherent goodness resides in it. While our desire or will to do what is right is present, we lament the difficulty in consistently carrying out those good intentions. We were trapped in the human predicament of a great wrestling with the fallen nature and the ongoing battle against sin. We confess the frustration and paradox we experience in our spiritual journey. Despite our genuine desire to do what is good and righteous, we found ourselves falling into patterns of behavior that we knew were wrong. We continued to grapple with the struggle between our thoughts and actions.

We acknowledge that when we engaged in actions that we did not want to do, it was not our true self that is responsible, but rather the indwelling power of sin such as addictions and alcoholism. We distinguish between our innermost being, which desires to do what is right, and the ongoing presence of sin in our human nature. We recognized the existence of a spiritual law at work, where we encountered a recurring pattern: when we intended to do what was good, we still found the presence of evil within us, hindering our efforts. We were suffering from the flesh's relentless desire for alcohol and drugs coupled with the mind's obsession driving us to use drugs and drink. We were powerless. For if we had power, the solution would be as simple as telling ourselves to simply not think or drink. We chuckled at this preposterous proposition because we knew we were powerless to do either. Therefore, the insanity was revealed.

Once the deed was done, we found ourselves trespassers of God's law. There the flesh took control and took us on a well-known spree of debauchery and reveling. These sprees of iniquity often accrued consequences that ended in an overwhelming sense of guilt, shame, and remorse. At the beginning of our careers of sin, guilt, shame, and remorse were huge motivators that produced gaps between our using bouts. These motivators would quickly reduce in persuasion until they no longer had any power. But, in the beginning, they would result in great oaths sworn to our families, friends, and even ourselves that we would never repeat such incomprehensibly pitiful and demoralizing behavior again …only to find ourselves under the heel of life as it applied pressure to our spiritless souls which would foster a thought. This thought would fly into our broken brains, and we would think that it would be a good idea to commit the deed once again. Thus, an insidious cycle of insanity would be set off.

As stated, this cycle of insanity would continue until the first thing that would be forgotten would be the oath that we had sworn. Then, after a few more times around the wringer, we would give up on the guilt, shame, and remorse. Once this point had been reached, we were on such a tight cycle of insanity that contained only deed, trespass, flesh, debauchery, consequence, disconnected soul, thought …repeat. This would happen until the consequences no longer became relevant. It was just deed, trespass, flesh, revelry, disconnected soul, thought, repeat.

This reprobation was the last straw for many of our drinking and using careers. Our lives had been reduced to a cycle of mind, sin, flesh, debauchery, and disconnected soul. For once we reach this point, we are well beyond human aid and need saving.

This cycle of insanity could be drawn something like this:

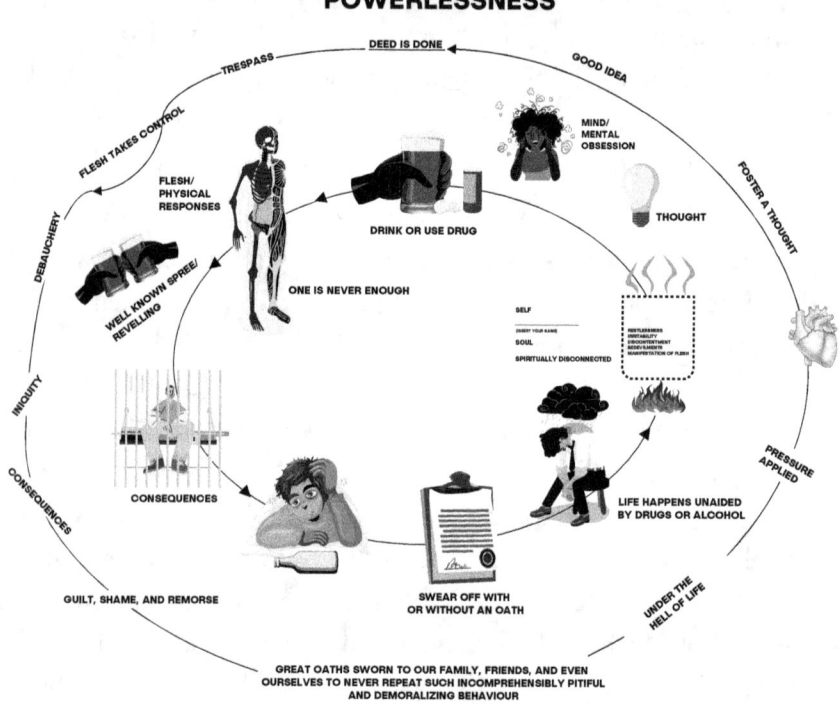

We were completely powerless and had no clue what to do. We were willing to do absolutely anything to get this monkey off our backs. We had run out of ideas and things became dark. Only a miracle could save us. Early on, that miracle came in the form of admission.

For you see, we had been living this life with an overarching truth to which we were oblivious. This truth was that we were indeed powerless over our minds and flesh. They were in a great wrestling because our souls had become spiritually disconnected. The proposition of being spiritually disconnected was hardest for those who had been in and around a church building all their lives. They felt as if they knew they were spiritually connected. After all, they made some life-altering decision at the age of twelve but then became blinded by the fact that they never took much honest action based upon that decision from that point.

The suspicion that we were spiritually disconnected was enough truth to admit into our minds. Once we accepted it into our minds, we discovered more truth! God replaced our hearts of stone with hearts of flesh, and we could finally let this truth into our innermost selves. We were indeed powerless. But there was more to learn from this problem with which we struggled.

Our souls had become spiritually disconnected, much like this example:

SPIRITUALLY DISCONNECTED
Unmanageability

ALL OF THESE ARE SYMPTOMS OF BEING SPIRITUALLY DISCONNECTED AND OPERATING IN THE FLESH. WITHOUT GOD'S AID, THERE IS NO WAY OF GETTING SPIRITUALLY CONNECTED TO THE HOLY SPIRIT

RESTLESSNESS
IRRITABILITY
DISCONTENTMENT
TORTURING THOUGHTS
(LISTED IN THE FOLLOWING PARAGRAPH)

MANIFESTATION OF THE FLESH
(GALATIANS 5:19-21)

We had to learn to fully concede to our innermost selves that we were lost. Although we may have once denied it, we had to admit that we were exhibiting a carnal life operating in the flesh. We began to see the symptoms! We were full of anxiety, depression, and unhappiness. We were restless, irritable, and discontented. We were plagued by bedevilments. Upon reading Galatians 5:19-21 and diving deeper into the meaning of the words, we saw very quickly that we were operating in the flesh. They told us that if we were operating in the flesh with any single one of these many symptoms, we are spiritually disconnected. And if we are spiritless, there is no way of getting spiritually connected to the needed Power without God's aid. When we began looking at the spiritual disconnectedness and self, it became apparent that until we became spiritually connected, that self and our disconnected soul would continue to play the origin in the cycle of the spirit of addiction's insanity. However, there was hope and we would experience it.

This revelation of our need to admit or let in the truth that had been overshadowing us did not come without great persuasion. And pain laced sin such as addictions and alcoholism is the great persuader. The first step to transformation was to admit that we were powerless over sin— that our lives had become spiritually disconnected. And we did so through the information we have just provided. However, this left us only with the problem, and having full knowledge of the problem only created a phenomenon that would eventually lead to backsliding or trying the old game once again. We needed some sort of solution.

The solution began for some of us with exposure to the religious side of life. I had lost everything and ran to the church because I had given my vehicle, family, and life away for drugs and alcohol. I crossed paths with a preacher man. The preacher man's unyielding support was something I had never experienced. The preacher walked shoulder to shoulder with this alcoholic addict through my dark time and saw God deliver me to freedom and salvation. Because of that, I asked this preacher to include his perception of us in the throes of this spiritual bondage.

Dear Friend,

I hope this letter finds you well. I wanted to take a moment to share with you some insights and experiences I have gained through my years as a pastor, particularly in relation to the spiritual bondage of addictions and alcoholism. It is my belief that at the core of these struggles lies a spiritual void that individuals often try to fill with substances.

I have witnessed firsthand the devastating effects of addictions on individuals and their loved ones. It is a battle that encompasses not just the physical and mental aspects but also the spiritual realm. I firmly believe that alcoholism is not solely a physical or mental disease but a spiritual condition that requires a spiritual solution.

While I recognize the importance of medical and professional support in the recovery process, I also emphasize the life-changing power of the Holy Spirit. God has the ability to heal and restore even the most broken and hopeless situations. Through a genuine spiritual connection with Him, individuals can find the strength and guidance needed to overcome addictions.

Prayer, Bible study, and fellowship with other believers play a vital role in the recovery journey. The sense of loneliness, fear, and guilt that often accompanies addictions can only be truly addressed through a spiritual solution. By turning to God and seeking His grace and mercy, individuals can find hope and healing in Christ.

RECOVERY 5:12 is supported by medical and treatment professionals who have witnessed the positive transformation of its members. I would encourage you to explore this restorative path and consider its principles and practices as a means of support and guidance in your own recovery journey. The testimonies shared in this book offer compelling evidence of the effectiveness of this approach.

Community and support are crucial in the recovery process. That is also why I want to bring your attention to this fellowship of RECOVERY 5:12. This community of individuals who have faced similar struggles provides the encouragement and strength needed for those spiritually bound to approach Jesus Christ who is the only one that can overcome their addictions. By sharing their experiences and supporting one another, they have become a beacon of hope for countless individuals seeking recovery in Jesus' Name.

I firmly believe that every person has inherent worth and the potential to bring about positive change for the Kingdom of God. It is never too late to seek spiritual help and embark on the path towards healing. Remember, you are not alone in this journey, and God's love and grace are available to guide you every step of the way.

As a pastor, I want to draw your attention to this book that I believe is of paramount importance to those who are afflicted with the spiritual bondage of alcohol and addictions. The subject matter of the book is covered in detail and with great mastery, and I believe that it has the potential to be of great help to those struggling with addictions.

The author of the book has been delivered by Jesus Christ from this hopeless state of mind and flesh and has spent many years in the treatment profession treating alcohol and drug addictions. Pastors have long known that spiritual deliverance is urgently needed to help alcoholics and addicts, but the application of such advice has been difficult.

Many years ago, this leading contributor to the book came under my pastoral care. While there, he acquired a spiritual revelation through prayer that he put into practical application right away. Later, he requested the privilege of being allowed to tell his testimony to others at the church, and with some misgivings, I consented. I followed the progress of this man as he shared this revelation with others and have been amazed at the results. The people who would come to church with him displayed an inspiring unselfishness, an entire absence of an ill motive, and a strong sense of fellowship. They believed that Jesus Christ could pull them back from the brink of death. I saw repentance, baptisms, and the infilling of the Holy Ghost.

To achieve the utmost effectiveness, it is essential to address the physical cravings experienced by individuals struggling with addictions. Before embarking on a journey of spiritual healing, it is crucial to liberate alcoholics and addicts from their overwhelming physical dependency on drugs and alcohol. I firmly believe that those battling addictions face an intensified physiological reaction to substances compared to the average person. Once trapped in the cycle of addictions, their self-assurance wanes, and they find themselves beyond human solutions. As a result, their challenges accumulate, presenting formidable obstacles that appear insurmountable.

I conclude by saying that the message that can interest and hold these spiritually enslaved people must have depth and weight. In every case, their ideals must be grounded in the Holy Spirit, if they are to experience a transformation of their lives. I admit that as a pastor, I have felt my own inadequacy when faced with the spirit of alcoholism and addictions. Although I give all that is in me, it often is not enough. Only God can produce this essential deliverance and transformation for these spiritless people.

I urge you to read this book and to take its biblical message to heart. My insights are based on many years of experience in pastoring, and I believe that these souls who have been delivered by the Name of Jesus have the message to help those struggling with alcohol and addictions to find a new life in Jesus Christ.

If there is anything I can do to support you or provide additional resources, I encourage you not to hesitate to reach out to RECOVERY 5:12. You are in my thoughts and prayers as you navigate this challenging but hopeful journey toward recovery and salvation.

With love and blessings,

Preacher Man

As the preacher alluded to, we were spiritually disconnected, as evidenced by a symphony of restlessness, irritability, and discontentment. Any one of these would have been enough to diagnose a disconnected soul. However, there are more manifestations of a disconnected soul such as having trouble with personal relationships, not being able to control our emotional natures, feeling like prey to misery, depression, and anxiety, being unable to make a living, having a feeling of uselessness, feeling full of fear, feeling unhappy, and being unable to be of real help to other people, much less to oneself. Our brother Paul told us that what we suffered from was flesh and to be in the flesh was to be spiritually disconnected. He gave us clear symptoms of being in the flesh and therefore spiritually disconnected. We found ourselves in adulterous relationships, we were mindless slaves to fornication, uncleanness and pornography consumed our activities of daily living, we chased after things instead of God, we were manipulating others, we hated those who were getting in our way, senseless arguments plagued us, we developed bitterness when others were being favored, we threw temper tantrums, stayed in angry quarrels, only thought of ourselves, were in love with our own opinions, were downright envious of the blessings of others, we were character assassins, and all other similar behavior - was not a basic solution for these torturing thoughts of a spiritually disconnected soul important? Of course, it was. When we saw others solve their problems by a simple reliance upon the Holy Spirit, we had to stop doubting the Power of the Holy Ghost. Our ideas did not work. But God did.

In this journey of **RECOVERY 5:12**, there exists a profound and extraordinary fellowship that finds its strength in the Name of Jesus. It is within this fellowship that the remarkable potential for rapid growth and transformation resides. As we delve into the stories and testimonies of those who have experienced deliverance from addictions, we are confronted with the undeniable truth that Jesus holds the key to salvation. This well-known pastor, in his heartfelt letter, shed light on the extraordinary possibilities that lie within this fellowship, acknowledging the remedy it offers to countless individuals facing similar struggles. It is a testament to the power of Jesus in healing and redemption, as these people speak with unwavering honesty and integrity about their journeys. Trusting in the hope found in Christ and embracing the authentic support of fellow believers, we embark on a path of healing, guided by the love and grace of our Lord. Together, we become living testimonies to the life-changing power of Jesus, who shines a light in the darkness of addiction and offers hope to those still seeking deliverance and salvation.

In the letter provided by the pastor, a profound understanding of addiction and its complexities is revealed. It emphasizes the significance of recognizing and addressing the physical aspects of addictions alongside the mental and emotional components. The pastor acknowledges the experiences of those who have suffered from addictions and highlights the inadequacy of solely attributing it to maladjustment or mental deficiencies. Instead, the letter emphasizes the crucial role of addressing physical sickness within the body of an addict. By recognizing that addictions encompass a multidimensional struggle, we gain a more comprehensive understanding of their nature. It is through this holistic approach that we can begin to unlock the path to true healing and recovery.

It is evident that there is an unexplainable response in the body of the alcoholic or addict to drugs and alcohol. At best, the manifestation of this phenomenon can be described as an abnormal reaction to the substances when compared to average people. Although we find this abnormal reaction to alcohol and drugs to be quite intriguing, it also explains why every time we would trespass, this abnormal reaction primarily manifested in the flesh, led to a loss of control, and the inability to stop drinking, using drugs, and sinning. While our opinion may hold little weight, we can say that this explanation made enough sense to us, especially as alcoholics and addicts. It provided an explanation for many of the things we could not previously understand. While we approach the issue of recovery from a spiritual and altruistic standpoint, we believe hospitalization to be an effective option for those who are highly anxious or confused and in need of detoxification. In such cases, it may be necessary to clear the person's mind and provide a four- or five-day period of detoxification before approaching them with our message. By doing so, we increase the likelihood that they will understand and accept what we have to offer. One thing was for sure, we could not drink or use drugs without developing this phenomenon of craving from which there is no escape without God's aid. We admitted we were powerless over sins such as addictions and alcoholism — that our lives had become spiritually disconnected. Therefore, we latched onto recovery through Jesus' Name with the desperation of someone drowning. In the following chapter, we will review more of the **RECOVERY 5:12** path to recovery.

CHAPTER 2

COMMON PERIL

"We admitted we were powerless over sins such as addictions and alcoholism — that our lives had become spiritually disconnected."
(Romans 7:14-20)

*"The righteous cry out,
and the Lord hears;
and delivers them out of all their troubles.
The Lord is close to them that are of a broken heart;
and saves such as be of a contrite spirit."*
Psalm 34:17-18

As we continued with this first step, we had to discover some things in common. The first element in the powerful cement that binds us came when we realized that we all suffer the same hellish peril. In these next paragraphs, we go to exhaustive lengths to describe the darkness of our spiritual bondage. This is not to bring about feelings of remorse or self-loathing but rather to present a familiarity which is the band capturing our attention strongly enough to pursue entry into this wonderful path of **RECOVERY 5:12**. To the addict and alcoholic, these words along with our stories will resound as truth. To those who think they do not belong to this class of spiritual bondage, we invite you to replace the words addictions and alcoholism with your hurt, habit, or sin. Although potentially futile, we have an ulterior motive. That being, if you fancy yourself returning back to the vomit of addictions and alcoholism, we pray that you read this chapter and maybe, just maybe, it will stop one person from returning back to the vomit and instead persuade them to continue with this **RECOVERY 5:12** until they too experience this Power.

Our journey, like all who find themselves here, began during a time when we were utterly defeated and devoid of any hope. Despite our best efforts, we found ourselves unable to overcome the afflictions that plagued us, whether it be alcohol, drugs, gambling, or other forms of immorality. It wasn't until we looked at ourselves in the mirror that we realized the severity of our situations, which had been staring us in the face all along. We had battled with ourselves for so long, and even though we were once held in high regard, we had found ourselves alone and trapped by our addictions. Sin had taken on various forms, and we knew that it was hindering us from living a fulfilling life. We were left to cry all night long with tears streaming down our faces, as our former friends had abandoned us, and even our allies had turned against us. We were now slaves to our vices, with no place to call our own and no way to escape the relentless grasp of addictions and alcoholism.

We were utterly lost, drifting aimlessly in the treacherous wilderness of sin, devoid of any sense of purpose or guidance. We witnessed others who claimed to have found comfort in God, but we scoffed at them, arrogantly opting to pursue our own self-indulgent desires instead. Our hearts were hollow, and our souls were tormented, mercilessly consumed by the insidious grip of addictions. We knew deep down that we were harvesting the bitter fruits of our own actions, and the burden of our transgressions became an unbearable weight to bear. Our once cherished dreams lay shattered, our lives reduced to mere ruins. Our resolve crumbled, rendering us utterly powerless to resist the clutches of the enemy that had overtaken us.

We resembled a wounded and terrified animal, desperately fleeing from the excruciating agony inflicted by our addictive and alcoholic cravings, with no one to turn to for aid. We found ourselves abandoned, forced to confront the merciless repercussions of our actions, as our carnal desires devoured us from within. Our dignity was obliterated, and we were consumed by overwhelming shame and vulnerability in the sight of God. We moaned and lamented in the depths of our despair, completely bereft of any glimmer of hope for liberation. We were forced to confront the brutal truth that our own choices or the lack thereof had led us astray, plunging us into a state of moral decay and spiritual defilement. We had willingly surrendered to the seductive allure of alcoholism and addiction, entangling ourselves in a web of sinful indulgence, engaging in acts of adultery and fornication. Our impurity was unmistakable, evident to all who crossed our path, yet we remained blind to the imminent devastation awaiting us. Our carnal cravings held us captive, forging spiritual shackles that bound us tight.

In our desperate states, we cried out to our conception of God, seeking His mercy. However, our own fleshly desires stripped us of all that was precious to us. Even when we dared to step into the church, we felt unwelcome, believing that *our conception of God* had forbidden us from entering. We groaned as we searched for something to satisfy our physical cravings, and some of us were forced to trade our only possessions for alcohol or drugs just to survive. We cried out to *our conception of God*, imploring Him to see us in our misery. We sought validation from anyone who would listen, convinced that no one had ever experienced the same pain as us. We believed that *our conception of God* had brought this suffering upon us in a time of wrath.

In our misguided devotion to alcoholism and addictions, we strayed from the righteous path, mistakenly believing that God had ensnared us, subjecting us to endless suffering. The weight of our sins rendered us feeble and powerless as our fleshly desires consumed us. Our distorted perception mocked our cherished values, leaving us crushed and desolate. Seeking comfort, we turned to temporary relief in drugs and alcohol, only to find ourselves trapped in a vicious cycle. We felt surrounded by enemies and treated as unworthy of love.

From the depths of our struggle, we understand your pain and suffering if you too are battling alcoholism or addictions. We were once captives of our own fleshly desires and sins, reaching out for help to friends who turned us away. We grappled with the consequences of our disobedience, wrestling with self-condemnation. But know that you are not alone in this fight.

Many of us were prideful, thinking ourselves spiritually superior, only to find ourselves dying in the streets, searching for something to numb the pain and keep us alive. We cried out to *our conception of God* in agony, pleading for relief from the anguish of our souls. In the grip of addictions and alcoholism, we waged a war against our own souls, tormented by sorrow for the depths to which we had sunk. Our lives became battlegrounds of strife, with the specter of death ominously lingering at every turn. Our desperate cries for help fell on deaf ears, leaving us to confront our inner demons alone. The enemy within reveled in our pain, distorting our perception and obscuring the true essence of God.

We fell into the trap of believing that *our conception of God* was the only true one, and we sought revenge against those who had wronged us. We cursed the day when *our conception* would bring destruction upon our enemies, and we wished for others to suffer as we had suffered. Our hearts were sick and twisted, consumed by delusions of grandeur and grandiose self-loathing. We were completely disconnected from the divine, and *our conception of God* was flawed and incomplete.

Enveloped by the abyss of addictions and alcoholism, we were tragically convinced that it was the Lord Himself who had veiled our spirits with confusion. Blinded to the truth, we failed to acknowledge that our own choices had led us astray, witnessing in despair as our once luminous souls crumbled into desolation. With our magic-magnifying minds twisted by anguish, we fixated on destruction and chaos, sparing no mercy for those who dared stand in our way. We ruthlessly tore down defenses, leaving a wake of shame and devastation in our paths. Bitterness consumed us, rendering us incapable of extending a helping hand or finding comfort within ourselves. We burned with an uncontrolled fury, unleashing our wrath upon everything in our vicinity. Our distorted perceptions painted a world filled with enemies, callously pushing away those who brought us happiness and joy.

Anger and conflict consumed us, leaving our emotional states in chaos. We had become our own worst adversaries, as our strength and defenses lay shattered. Overwhelmed by perpetual sorrow and anguish, even the religious convictions that once offered comfort were obliterated in the haze of our intoxication. Regardless of our societal standing, the wrath we harbored spared no one, not even ourselves, causing us to reject the notions of sacrifice and abandon our core beliefs. We dismantled the walls of our naive understanding and shattered our own misconceptions, proudly establishing our sins where we once found comfort and happiness. Driven by a fierce determination, we sought to demolish the barriers surrounding our spirits, meticulously measuring their downfall. The protective walls and defenses that once shielded us now lay in ruins, burying our beliefs amidst the self-created rubble.

The eyes of those of us struggling with addictions and alcoholism were worn out with weeping, and our souls were in anguish. We were exhausted by grief at the destruction of ourselves, and our plans and designs were fading. Some of us were consumed with covetousness, crying out to others for help, falling wounded in the streets and slowly dying in their eyes. In our rebellion, we turned our backs on the truth and wandered aimlessly in the darkness. We refused to listen to the voice of wisdom and guidance, instead following the path of destruction. Our souls were plagued with unrest and turmoil, and we were consumed by the desires of the flesh. The chains of the spirit of addictions bound us tightly, and we were powerless to break free. We were responsible for adding every link to the chain of consequences with which our addictions would beat us. Our minds were clouded with confusion and our hearts with sorrow as we drifted further and further away from our true purpose. We were lost in the wilderness, searching for something to fill the emptiness inside. But our search was in vain, for we had rejected the one true source of fulfillment and joy.

We were the prodigals, recklessly squandering our inheritance in a whirlwind of self-destruction. Our rebellion against God led us to dwell in the depths of filth and hunger, forsaking the abundant blessings He had bestowed upon us. Blinded by our own pride, we became slaves to our addictions, chaining ourselves to the pursuit of our selfish desires. In our folly, we turned our backs on God's call, our heart hardened and was consumed by the flames of our insatiable cravings. We were prisoners of our own making, lost in a wilderness of darkness and obsession, beaten down by the whip of our sins. The weight of our chains grew heavier with each passing day, driving us deeper into the pit of despair, as we added link after link to our own misery.

As we cried out for help, it seemed as though our prayers fell on deaf ears. We stumbled and fell, with obstacles and temptations blocking every potential path. Our own selfish desires waited to ensnare us, like a bear in its den or a lion in wait. We had strayed from the path of righteousness and tore ourselves apart with our own delusions. We aimed our weapons at ourselves, inflicting deep wounds that left us broken and bleeding. Others mocked us and laughed at our misfortunes. We fed ourselves bitterness and suffering, forgetting the taste of true health and happiness. We were brought low, with our faces in the dirt and our teeth broken on the stones. We had lost all hope, and our spirits were crushed. The bitter poison of despair and hopelessness consumed our thoughts, and we felt the end approaching.

Lost in the darkness of our own selfishness, we were unable to find a way out. We cried out for help, but it seemed as if God was blocked or, worse yet, refusing to hear our pleas. As we continued to stumble and fall, we faced obstacles at every turn, while our own self-centeredness devoured us. We were broken and wounded, both physically and spiritually, and we had forgotten what it was like to experience health, satisfaction, and happiness.

Our hearts were heavy with sorrow when we realized what we had become. We were ensnared by the enemy within, and we had no one to blame but ourselves. Our selfish desires had led us down the path of destruction, and we found ourselves trapped in a pit with no way out. The waters of despair threatened to consume us, and we were drowning in our own misery.

As God's children, we were entrusted with the care of our own offspring, but we failed miserably. We neglected our duties as parents and left our children to suffer. Even animals have the instinct to nurse and feed their young, but we were so consumed by our sins that we couldn't provide for our own flesh and blood. Our little ones cried out in hunger and thirst, and we had nothing to offer them. We were once blessed with abundance and feasted on the finest delicacies, but now we were reduced to starving in the streets, our children withering away before our very eyes. Our indulgence in our addictions had stripped us of our humanity and left us lower than the animals. The consequences of our actions were severe, and we were left to wallow in the misery we had created for ourselves.

We were created in the image of God, pure and blameless. Yet, our sinful actions defiled us, and we became weak and sickly, with faces darkened by our spiritual death. Our bodies wasted away like dry wood on our bones, and we were worse off than those who died in battle. We unleashed the full force of our anger upon ourselves as if setting fire to the spiritual world and burning it down.

It was hard to believe that evil could penetrate the stronghold of our minds. However, sin and its destructive behavior allowed it to take root within us. Even in our supposed moments of righteousness, we still found ways to harm innocent people. As leaders, we stumbled around aimlessly like the blind, covered in the shame of our own guilt. People recoiled at our presence, shouting, "Unclean! Don't touch me!" We became societal outcasts, wandering from place to place, unwelcome and abandoned. No one cared for us anymore, and we were left to scatter.

We strayed from the path of righteousness, ignoring the wisdom of our faith, and rejecting the help of those who had found their way. We searched for salvation in all the wrong places, and when we could no longer see a way out, we cried out in despair. But the enemy within us had already ensnared us, and we were helpless to escape its grip. Our sin had become like a predator, stalking us relentlessly and catching us off guard. We had trusted in ourselves, our own strength, and our own understanding, but we had been deceived. Sins such as addictions and alcoholism had captured our very soul, the source of our being, and left us with no hope of rescue.

Laugh and be glad while you can, for a day of reckoning is coming. We once thought that suffering was reserved for others, but we were the ones experiencing shame and humiliation. We protested, "We have paid the price for our sins, surely God will have mercy on us and end our exile." However, we soon realized that it was not God who was punishing us, but rather the consequences of our own actions. Our own guilt and shame were exposed by the way we lived our lives.

Let us reflect on what we have brought upon ourselves. See our shame and disgrace. Our homes are now inhabited by strangers, and our possessions have been taken away. The enemy has destroyed our beliefs, and seemingly, we were cut off from the Holy Spirit. We forced ourselves to rely on self, and we found burdens of fear, self-pity, and self-centeredness. Our sin had been driving us like donkeys until we were exhausted and restless, with no relief from the consequences of our actions.

In our arrogant pursuit of our own desires, we stumbled down a destructive spiritual path, blinded by our carnal cravings. The consequences of our actions left us isolated and suffering. The spirit of alcoholism and addictions had us in its grip, rendering us powerless to break free. Chaos consumed our lives as we sought comfort in all the wrong places. Our souls hungered for fulfillment and stability, leading us further into self-destruction. Our once-strong characters were weakened and violated by feverish desires. Dreams shattered, burdened by a weight too heavy to bear. Happiness became a distant memory as self-pity and bitterness filled our hearts, and our pride crumbled to nothingness. Our spirits sickened, tears flowing freely as we faced the depth of our spiritual abandonment. Our minds became ruins, overrun by wild and dangerous thoughts. Ashamed, we hid our faces, mere shadows of our former selves. The physical component of this disease of powerlessness was too much to bear, slow down, or stop. We needed a power greater than ourselves to help us. We needed the Power.

Now we stop a minute to ask, once again, if any of the things we have discussed up to this point sound like your life at all. If this is the case, then you, like we once were, are suffering from a spiritual illness that only a spiritual experience can conquer.

In the midst of our bleakness, a glimmer of hope emerged. We turned to the One with the power to heal and transform our lives. Through faith, we found that He has the strength to overcome our sins such as alcoholism and addictions. We discovered the truth about this Power who offered unwavering love and mercy to all who believed in Him. Despite our doubts and fears, we would learn to trust in Him, surrendering everything. This Power walked beside us, offering love and support even when we felt undeserving. He understood our pain and suffering and offered redemption and healing. With repentance and humility, we turned back to Him, finding forgiveness and acceptance in His loving arms.

Though the journey was challenging, through the Power, He delivered the strength to escape the darkest times. Our identities were no longer defined by addictions or past mistakes but by the grace of the Power flowing through us. Tears of joy and gratitude filled our eyes as we realized we were not alone, but rather part of a community that shared our struggles and celebrated our victories. The Power heard our cries, reached down into the depths, and lifted us out of the mire. He showed us mercy and grace, offering a new chance in life. Despite our wrongdoings, He never abandoned us, promising to be with us through every trial and challenge. We were once burdened by abandonment and rejection, but we became convinced that there was One who had all the Power to restore us. We cried out to Him, knowing that only through His grace could we be brought back to the light. Recognizing our powerlessness over our addictions and alcoholism and our unmanageable lives, we wrestled and struggled, ultimately surrendering to find victory. And now, we walk this path, sharing our experiences with others, so that they too may find their way back to the Power.

We acknowledge that our first step towards recovery was to admit or let in the truth that we were powerless over our flesh and mind as they related to sins such as addictions and alcoholism, and that our lives had become unmanageable or spiritually disconnected. By accepting this truth, we recognized that we were poor in spirit and in need of divine intervention. The promise of this step towards salvation filled us with hope and happiness, knowing that through our surrender to God, the kingdom of heaven belonged to us.

Through the steps and measures that follow, we found a path to spiritual and emotional recovery, leading us to a deeper relationship with our Creator and a life of fulfillment and purpose. But we are not out of *step one* yet. Along with our fleshly cravings for sin, there was a mental obsession that was consuming us. Therefore, we are not finished with this step, so let's continue.

CHAPTER 3

THE GREAT OBSESSION

*"We admitted we were powerless over sins such as
addictions and alcoholism — that our lives had become
spiritually disconnected."*
(Romans 7:14-20)

*"There is a way which seems right to a person,
but the end thereof are the ways of death."*
(Proverbs 14:12.)

As those who struggle with sin such as alcoholism and addictions, we were plagued by a great mental obsession. We believed that we could somehow, someday, control and enjoy our lives on our own terms. We desperately clung to the idea that we were no different from others, physically or mentally. Our lives were marked by a series of futile attempts to prove ourselves and regain control. But this obsession was nothing more than a dangerous delusion, leading us down the path of insanity and death. We had to come to a place of fully conceding to our spirit that we were truly spiritually disconnected. It was not enough to simply acknowledge it intellectually; we had to allow this overshadowing truth to penetrate our thick heads then deep into our hearts. Only then could we begin the journey of recovery, smashing the illusion that we were like those who were truly spiritually connected. Chapter Three explores this great mental obsession and the hopelessness it brings, leading us to the necessity of discovering true connection with the Spirit.

We have come to realize that we cannot rely on our own conceptions to control our lives. We experienced fleeting moments of false control, only to fall back into deeper despair and depravity. We have come to believe that all of humanity is afflicted with a progressive spiritual disease that leads to a downward spiral of sin such as addictions and alcoholism. The only path to true recovery is by surrendering our minds and lives to the Power and relying on His guidance and strength. This is easier said than done. How were we to surrender our minds? First, we had to acknowledge our powerlessness over sin and that our lives were uncontrollable. Only then could we completely give ourselves away. Only then could we experience true freedom and an abundant life.

We recognized that our sins had left us with a spiritual illness that cannot be cured by human means. We tried every method available to us, but nothing made us feel truly connected. Even when we experienced temporary relief, we always ended up returning to our destructive patterns of behavior. We had to acknowledge that there is no human power that could make us spiritually whole. Only through surrendering our minds and lives to the Power could we find true spiritual healing and recover. We cannot become "normal" on our own, but with a Power greater than ourselves, we can become new creations in Him.

Despite our efforts to prove ourselves exceptions to the rule, many of us were truly separated from the Power, though we did not believe it at the time. We deceived ourselves in every way possible, attempting to live as if we were spiritually connected. However, no matter how hard we tried, we could not control our lives or think in a way that reflected our true spiritual state. If anyone who is struggling with sins can turn their life around and live for Christ, we applaud them. For we know from experience just how difficult and elusive that goal can be without Him.

When we were lost, we tried countless methods to regain control of our lives. We sought comfort in isolation or through avoiding being alone altogether. We tried to distract ourselves with constant activity, from partying to pursuing spirituality without religion. We made promises and oaths to ourselves to stop our sinful habits and tried everything from exercise to reading inspirational books to spas to treatment centers. We have even submitted to voluntary and involuntary commitment to behavioral facilities. Despite all these efforts, we remained unmanageable.

It is not for us to judge another person's heart. However, we can examine our own lives and see where we stand. If we are spiritually disconnected and attempting to live our lives according to our own will and power, the outcomes are plagued with the unyielding pursuit of just one good break. We try to control our actions, thoughts, and feelings through various means, but ultimately, it's all failure. The problem is that many of us are naturally incapable of turning from our destructive ways and seeking help while there is still hope for us. We hope that we all have the courage and humility to admit our need for saving and turn to the solution to overcome our struggles.

We must acknowledge that when backsliding or returning to a spiritually disconnected life after a period of being connected, we are quickly consumed once again by wickedness. If we truly desire to stop sinning, we must fully surrender and abandon any notion that we will someday be immune to temptation. We should not be fooled by the idea that we must suffer greatly or for a long time to be gravely affected by immorality. We have witnessed many individuals, who would be offended to be labeled as sinners, struggling to control their lives on their own. As those familiar with the spiritual symptoms of sin such as addictions and alcoholism, we see countless people all around us who are also suffering. It is our duty to guide them toward the truth of their situation and towards the Power, which is the only true way to recovery.

Looking back, we realize that we continued in our sinful ways for far too long, even if we had the ability to change through our own efforts. For those who are unsure whether they have entered this dangerous territory, let them try to leave their sins behind. If the sins are unmanageable, they will find no success, regardless of their efforts. In the beginning, we felt like we were in control of our lives, only to return to our sinful ways soon after. Even if we were able to maintain control for a while, we were still unmanageable in the end.

We believe that few who read these words can truly stay away from sin on their own. Some of us suffered mental consequences the day after making plans to quit, while most of us relapsed within a few weeks. We still feel it now in other moments such as when we tell ourselves that we are going too fast, and the flesh rears its ugly head and fights with its familiar voice. It tells us that we should wait until another day and reminds us of the special event that is coming up that will have great food. It will remind us of the great pie that we have left in the refrigerator. It will even tell us that a box of snack cakes is what we need right now because of the wonderful tart strawberry cream in its rolls. Although seemingly trivial now, this flesh once ruled us and used sin such as gluttony, alcoholism and addictions as its whip.

The question arises for those of us who are unable to control our thoughts and actions: how can we stop attempting to fulfill our desires on our own and instead turn to help? We assume, of course, that the reader desires to change their current way of living. But the idea that a person can change their sinful ways without a spiritual basis is as fanciful as the Easter Bunny and flying reindeer. Many of us thought we had a strong character and a great urge to cease our sinful behavior forever. Yet we found it mentally and physically impossible to do so. This is the baffling feature of sin as we know it - the utter inability to leave it alone, no matter how great our need or desire. We can render a greater service to people who are suffering this mental torture and are yearning for a better life. So, we shall describe some of the mental states that precede back-sliding to a life run on our own thinking, for obviously that is the crux of the problem.

The spirit of alcoholism and addictions occurs because of a person's separation from the Power. When we try to live our lives disconnected from the Power, we are easily influenced by sinful thoughts and behaviors that lead us down a path of destruction. Friends who try to reason with us after a debauch of living on our own terms do not understand the internal battle that we are facing. Our minds and hearts are blocked by the wreckage of sins, and we are unable to see the harm that our actions are causing to ourselves and to others. Such as when we repeatedly turn to alcohol and other addictive substances, we are seeking to fill a void in our lives that can only be filled by a relationship with the Power. It was as if we were trying to fill a God-sized hole within us. Addictions and alcoholism are only a symptom of deeper internal issues, including a lack of purpose and a sense of worthlessness.

We were warned against the dangers of giving in to our sinful desires and urged to seek the guidance and strength of the Power in all aspects of our lives. When we fail to do so, we fall prey to the temptation to indulge in various forms of wickedness. As a result, we find ourselves experiencing a curious mental phenomenon where our sound reasoning fails to hold us in check. We feel as if we have no control over our actions and wonder how it could have happened. We have knowingly engaged in sinful behavior, feeling justified by our selfishness, anxiety, depression, and other negative emotions. But we must acknowledge that our justification was woefully inadequate in the face of the devastating consequences that inevitably followed.

It's important to recognize that when we make decisions without seeking the Power, we're operating without His wisdom and guidance. Our premeditation may be lacking in serious thought about the consequences of our actions. To break free from addictions and find true healing, we must turn to the Power and seek His help. We must recognize that our own justification is insufficient and that we need the guidance and wisdom of the Power to make the right decisions in our lives. We must wait on the Power and seek it in every aspect of our lives, including our decisions about alcohol and other addictive substances.

Those of us who have endured immense trials acknowledge that the portrayal of being devoid of the Power accurately reflects our state. We recognize the absence of divine guidance in our lives. However intelligent we may be in other respects, where our sins such as addictions and alcoholism have been involved, we have been strangely insane. It's strong language but true; we were poor in spirit. Many of us think that we have control of our lives and that the negative consequences of our actions do not fully apply to us. We acknowledge that we have some mental symptoms, but we believe that we have not gone to the extremes that others have and that we are not likely to. However, the truth is that we are all disconnected from the Power when we live without seeking His guidance and wisdom. Without the Power, we will be unable to stop the insanity of our lives through our own knowledge. This is a point that we need to emphasize and re-emphasize, as it has been revealed to us through bitter experience. The wages of sins such as addictions and alcoholism are death, and this truth applies to everyone. None of us can escape the consequences of our sinful actions, no matter how much we may think we have control over our lives. We are hopeless when we rely solely on our own reasoning.

Whether we are regular churchgoers or not, the principle outlined for us is not intellectually difficult to understand. However, the actions we take towards recovery are often drastic and require a significant shift in our thinking. We must be willing to let go of our old beliefs and ways of living and instead embrace a new biblical principle. This is not an easy task, but the moment we make the decision to commit ourselves to the recovery process, we experience a feeling of relief. We are called to live a life that is centered on God and His teachings. This means putting aside our own desires and selfishness and instead seeking to follow His will for our lives. When we commit ourselves to this path of recovery, we experience the life-changing power of God. We can find healing from our brokenness, and we can be restored to a life of purpose.

The journey of recovery is not an easy one, but it is a journey that is well worth taking. As we turn to God and He guides us, we can find that He provides hope and strength as He overcomes the challenges that we face. We trust in His goodness and faithfulness, knowing that He will never leave us nor forsake us. With God's help, we experience the joy and freedom that comes from living a life that is centered on Him. It is important we discover that Jesus Christ solves all our problems. We are brought into a way of living infinitely more satisfying and more useful than the life we lived before. Our old manner of living may not have been a bad one, but we would not exchange the best moments in our old life without Jesus for the worst moments we now have with Him. We would not go back to a life without Jesus even if we could.

We hope **RECOVERY 5:12**'s steps and measures of faith strikes home to many like us. Many people only feel slightly injured by sins such as addictions and alcoholism. Most of us are badly mangled by them before we really begin to solve our problems. People like us are heartbreaking. There is no other solution than Jesus Christ. We have tried.

Once more: people like us at certain times have no effective mental defense against sins which is anything that blocks us from Jesus. Neither ourselves nor any other human being can provide such a defense. Our defense must come from being connected to the Comforter.

CHAPTER 4

UNMANAGEABILITY

"We admitted we were powerless over sins such as addictions and alcoholism — that our lives had become spiritually disconnected."
(Romans 7:14-20)

"…that at that time ye were without Christ, being aliens from the commonwealth of Israel, and strangers from the covenants of promise, having no hope, and without God in the world: but now in Christ Jesus we who sometimes were far off are made nigh by the blood of Christ."
(Ephesians 2:12 & 13)

"Without Jesus, we are lost in chaos and brokenness – spiritless."

Recognizing the difference between a life separated from God and a life rooted in Jesus Christ is of utmost importance. When we found ourselves struggling to break free from sin or lacking control over its presence, it signified a clear disconnection from Jesus Christ on a spiritual level. Overcoming this spiritual ailment can only be achieved through the power of the Holy Spirit. With great wrestling, have we wrestled with our mind and flesh, and we have prevailed.

We sincerely hope that we have conveyed this distinction effectively. It is through wholeheartedly offering ourselves to Jesus Christ and His Holy Spirit beginning to dwell within us that we triumph over the spiritual afflictions of addictions and alcoholism. Let us earnestly seek His abundant grace and unwavering strength to live a life that brings Him pleasure and honor.

For those who consider themselves atheists or agnostics, the idea of a spiritual experience may seem impossible due to intellectual pride. However, continuing the path of disconnection from Jesus Christ has only led and continues to lead to disaster, particularly if one falls into the category of being hopeless and unmanageable. The choice between being doomed to spiritual death while separated from Christ or living guided by the Holy Spirit was not an easy one for many of us to make. As we strive to overcome the grip of alcoholism and addictions, we find ourselves initially hesitant to consider the role of the Holy Ghost in our recovery. We cling to the hope that we are not truly spiritually disconnected, but eventually, we must confront this reality. We cannot live a fulfilling life without a spiritual foundation. We must acknowledge our need for the Power, for without it, we are doomed to a life of hopelessness and despair. It may seem daunting to embrace this spiritual way of life, but we need not be disheartened. Our experiences have shown us that we can find strength and comfort in the Holy Ghost. Simply adhering to a code of morals or a philosophy of life will not be enough to conquer our sins. Despite our best efforts, our human resources will inevitably fall short. We were lost in our addictions, and our own human willpower was not enough to overcome it. We needed power, a Power beyond ourselves, to restore us to sanity and give us the strength to resist temptation. We knew that there was one who had been given all power under heaven and earth, and we realized that we needed to turn to Him. But where could we find Him?

Well, that's exactly what this life-changing recovery path is about. The main purpose of this book is to guide you to Jesus and to experience the transforming Power of the Holy Ghost, which is the solution to all our problems. Our goal is to lead you to the Word of God for your renewed and recovered life. This means that we will be talking about Jesus Christ and the Bible, which can be difficult topics for those who are agnostic, atheist, or filled with intellectual pride and prejudice. As we share our personal struggles and fellowship with new individuals, we often see their hope rise. However, their hope quickly fades when we begin to discuss spiritual matters, particularly when we mention the Name of Jesus, as it can re-open a subject that they thought they had avoided or ignored altogether. Better yet, it may be a subject that they feel they are well versed in from their many years of churchgoing or their grandmother's concept of Him. However, they cannot escape their delusion enough to see that their lives have been one long history of sinfulness and disconnectedness.

In our desperation, we began to inquire about Him. We needed to know who Jesus really was and what He wanted for us. We asked people who knew Him and who had experienced His transforming power. We read the Bible and discovered that Jesus was not the one-dimensional figure we had imagined Him to be. He was not just a moral teacher or a historical figure, but the Son of God who came to save us from our sins – even addictions. As we learned more about Jesus and His teachings, we began to experience a change in our hearts. The things that once seemed impossible became possible through Him. We were no longer spiritless and lost but found our way back to God through the power of the Holy Ghost.

Now we see things differently. We see that our skepticism and intellectual pride were barriers to the true deep and effective experience of God and His power. We see that our rejection of Jesus Christ was a rejection of the very source of our salvation and freedom from the spirit of alcoholism and addictions. Through our experience, we have come to know that faith in Jesus Christ is not weak or cowardly, but rather a source of immense strength and courage. We have witnessed the transformation of countless lives through the power of the Holy Ghost, and we have come to comprehend the incomprehensible.

Our faith in Jesus Christ and the Power of the Holy Ghost grew as we continued this path of recovery. **RECOVERY 5:12** suggested that we pray and read the Word of God daily throughout the day. It was through these practices that we discovered that as we prayed and meditated on the Word of God, we were filled with a sense of peace and serenity that we had never known before. Our burdens were lifted, and our addictions were overcome, not by our own strength or willpower, but by the Power of God as we took these steps and lived in this measure of faith. We learned that the Holy Ghost is not just some abstract concept or theological idea, but a real and tangible Presence that we can experience in our lives. It is the same Power that raised Jesus from the dead and it is available to us if we only believe and ask for it.

The Holy Spirit began to work in us and transform our lives. We began to understand that the root of our addictions and alcoholism was not merely a physical or mental problem, but a spiritual one. We needed a spiritual solution to overcome our struggles, and that solution was found in Jesus Christ. He is not just a concept, but a living and present reality. We experienced His love, grace, and power in our lives, and we were able to watch Him overcome our addictions and find true freedom. Jesus says, "I am the way, the truth, and the life. No one comes to the Father except through me" (John 14:6). We have found this to be truth in our own lives. Through Jesus, we have been able to connect with God and experience His power and guidance.

Alcoholism and addictions are a problem that has plagued humanity since ancient times. We, therefore, carry forward the warning that was given to us of the dangers of drunkenness and addiction and encourage you to seek spiritual help and healing in the Name of Jesus. The spirit of drugs and alcohol is a mocker and a brawler; every time we are led astray by them, we are not being wise. The spirit of alcohol and addictions always leads us down a dangerous path and causes us to act foolishly. We are instructed, "Do not get drunk or use drugs, which leads to debauchery. Instead, be filled with the Spirit" (Ephesians 5:18). We should seek to be filled with the Holy Spirit rather than turning to alcohol or drugs for comfort. But we had no choice in the matter. We had lost the power of choice in sin.

We must admit our powerlessness and recognize that our lives have become spiritually disconnected. *Step one* requires us to humbly acknowledge that we cannot conquer our struggles alone, that we need power greater than ourselves, and that we must relinquish our ego-driven control. This step is the foundation upon which lasting transformation is built. This can only be done once sins such as addictions and alcoholism have brought us to a place of utter defeat. It was here the old man told us to *come on in, valiant soldier, you fought your best fight, lay your weapons down, you lost.* This was not meant to be humiliating. It was necessary to come to the complete understanding that all our great ideas have been exhausted and that there is a place we can come to where we are welcomed and cared for. That place is humility.

Unknowingly we had arrived in a place of repentance. We were poor in spirit, completely broken, and out of ideas. We had reached our bottom and we were amazingly still alive, and for what reason? God only knows. But here, in this realm of repentance, although we had no clue at this point in our journey, there was a promise already being applied to us. A promise that this *step one* was going to be a blessing the moment we could look back to this point. We were blessed at the precise moment that we realized we couldn't do anything separate from God. Only then were we truly submitting to His will. And to do His will is to receive the kingdom of heaven. But as the Lord knows, we could not see any of this from the vantage point of complete brokenness. Do not be discouraged, many of us passed through this unknowingly. Keep taking this step.

Before we even began taking this step, picked up this book, the Bible, or thought about God, we were called to this place and in this brokenness, there were spiritual realities being manifested. We saw this in each step and measure along the way. We found ourselves right in the middle of a great wrestling match between our flesh and mind. The prophecy foretold upon us in this state is that we would prevail. We could not see it at this point. There was still some action we needed to take from this humility.

ג NUN

Humility is our soul being bent to its knees in humble submission. There was no one with us. We no longer had our "six" covered. We were brought to our knees with no other plans or ideas. This powerful spiritual position of righteous submission was the very seed that was being planted in our hearts which contained Power beyond our wildest inclination. However, this seed would need to receive more action. In this moment, for many, this seed of humility is sown and some fall by the wayside; it is trodden down, and the fowls of the air devour it. Some fall upon a rock; and as soon as it is sprouting up, it withers away, because it lacks moisture. Some fall among thorns of distractions, and the thorns spring up with them and choke them. But for us, they fell on good broken ground, sprang up, and bore fruit beyond our wildest imagination. Here are the steps we took. Let's learn more of humility.

Humility paved the way for our healing. It invited us to shed our pride and recognize that our human limitations necessitate reliance on something greater than ourselves. It compels us to acknowledge that addictions, pain, and adversity have surpassed our ability to cope alone. Humility means the complete stripping of our self-centeredness! Humility is embracing vulnerability and surrendering our will to a higher purpose. It is essential to remember that humility does not equate to weakness. Instead, it embodies strength. Humility empowers us to seek help, to admit our mistakes, and to learn from them. It enables us to accept wisdom from those who have walked a similar path. When we humbly surrender, we open ourselves to the healing grace of God. These conditions invite His strength to work through us, which is vital, for this is what guides us towards a life of freedom. Humility allows us to acknowledge our brokenness while embracing the hope that comes from divine intervention even if we can't see it in the beginning.

There was much to learn about humility. This book could not contain all that needs to be understood about the humility that we are now experiencing as we are brought to our knees by a power outside of ourselves. We will share some of our lessons in humility with you. When we exalted ourselves, seeking to be the center of attention, craving recognition, and asserting our assumed superiority over others, we were bound to be humbled. This prideful attitude hindered our spiritual progress and prevented us from receiving the help and healing we desperately needed. On the other hand, as soon as we embraced humility and acknowledged our imperfections, we opened ourselves up to the possibility of being exalted by God. Humility doesn't mean thinking less of ourselves but rather thinking of ourselves less. It is about recognizing that we are part of a greater whole and being willing to surrender our ego-driven desires to grow and heal. When we allow false pride to take root in our minds, it always leads to disgrace. False pride blinds us to our own faults, inflates our egos, and distorts our perceptions of reality. It drove us to seek personal gain at the expense of others, to act arrogantly, and to disregard the counsel of those around us. Although we cannot see it now, humility reminds us of our identity as God's chosen people—holy and beloved. Humility is a powerful affirmation that despite our past mistakes, we are inherently worthy of redemption. This *step one* experience forms the foundation for our recovery journey, as humility teaches us to view ourselves through the lens of compassion. Humility then invites us to intentionally "clothe" ourselves with virtues that are essential in the process of spiritual healing. These virtues, although foreign to us, are contained within the seed of humility that has been planted within us which will manifest as compassion, kindness, gentleness, and patience. Humility encapsulates the essence of God's requirements for His people.

It serves as a guiding principle for our actions, attitudes, and relationship with God.

Humility is the doorway to *step one*. It is the understanding that we are not in control and that our lives have become unmanageable. It is the willingness to let go of our ego, to shed the mask of self-sufficiency, and to recognize our vulnerabilities. Humility empowers us to surrender to the truth, to seek help, and to accept that we cannot do it alone. But there is still more action needed, as the seed of humility needs watering.

פ PEY

We cried out. Out of our mouths came the words of faith that would change the course of our lives. Some say that the moment we opened our mouths and cried out there was faith that flowed into us. The physical temple we carried was filled with the light of faith for the very first time.

When we cry out, we express our heartfelt desperation for help. It involves acknowledging that we are facing difficulties that are beyond our own ability to handle. Crying out is offering our self-reliance and recognizing our need for divine intervention. We emphasize that when the righteous cry out, the Lord hears and delivers us from all our troubles. We can assure you that God is attentive to the cries of His people and is ready to come to our aid. In *step one*, crying out is instrumental in initiating the process of change. By recognizing our limitations and reaching out to God, who is the Power, we acknowledge that we cannot overcome these challenges alone. It is an act of humility, allowing us to seek strength beyond our own capacities. When we cried out, we unknowingly were aligning ourselves with the belief that God hears our cries and delivers us from troubles, which cultivated the seed of faith in the life-changing power of divine intervention. This provided a needed motivation to take the necessary steps toward change. We did not know it at the time, but we were trusting in God's assistance to be present throughout our journey.

This glimmer of faith that came the moment we cried out of humility introduced us to God, who created His people, calls us by name, and declares that we are His. It describes how God promises to be with us through challenging times, assuring us that we will be overwhelmed by a different kind of waters and consumed by a fire burning deep down in our souls. This crying out equipped us with the power of seeking. We were immediately encouraged to ask, seek, and knock, assuring us that if we ask, we will receive, if we seek, we will find, and if we decide to take action, the door is opened to us. As we cried out, we had unknowingly exhibited the faith to approach God's throne of grace with confidence, and we received mercy and found grace to help in this moment of need. There was power in this seed and once it was watered by our cry for help, the remarkable Power that once sacrificed Himself for us on a cross now surrounded us.

ת TAV

The cross. The power of the cross was not a foreign term to many of us. However, it was filled with mystique and misunderstanding in our prejudiced minds. These two crossed sticks marked the source of the necessary Power that is needed to restore the lives that He had intended for us. At the point where the two sticks cross lies the heart of God, Jesus Christ Himself. It would be from here that we would receive freedom from our captivity.

The power of the cross is the universal condition of humanity—everyone has sinned and fallen short of God's glory. It acknowledges that we are unable to attain righteousness on our own. However, the power of the cross, when applied to the initial stage of *step one* of our spiritual journey, is our first encounter with the redemptive work of Christ. The power of the cross in *step one* signifies the beginning of the process of salvation and the life-changing impact of the cross.

Through the power of the cross, God's grace is made available to all. The power of the cross lies in the redemption accomplished by Jesus

Christ. Redemption refers to the act of buying back from captivity. The cross represents the sacrifice made by Jesus to redeem humanity from the bondage of sin– even alcohol and addictions. In humility, we cried out to God. When we did this, we were unknowingly accepting Jesus' sacrifice on the cross and placing faith in Him, and we were unleashing the experience of justification. Justification is the act of being declared righteous before God, not based on our own merits or works, but through His grace . This justification is freely given to believers through faith in Christ Jesus which we watered with humility as we cried out to Him. The power of the cross lies in the fact that it offers salvation to all who believe, regardless of our past failures, shortcomings, or addictions. It assures us that our salvation is not dependent on our own merits or achievements, but solely on God's grace and our faith in Christ. We were reminded that while we were still sinners, separated from God and unable to save ourselves, God took the initiative to send His Son, Jesus Christ, to die for us on the cross. This act of sacrificial love demonstrates the depth of God's love and His desire to reconcile us to Himself. It offers forgiveness, freedom from sin's grip, a new purpose centered on righteousness, and spiritual healing.

By embracing the work of the cross, we begin a journey of ongoing transformation, where we are empowered by the Holy Spirit to live as followers of Christ. This Power within the seed planted firmly within our hearts has now been watered and is initiating our new life in Christ and the freedom it brings. This Power was needed to create a radical change in our lives and establish a new identity in Christ. This new identity in Christ contained within this *step one* phenomenon believes that the central importance of the cross is in initiating our relationship with Christ and our understanding of the Gospel. By crying out in humility, we were accessing a Power that would initiate our salvation and provide hope for the future. It began our recovery journey of repentance, forgiveness, and salvation. The power of this cross is the salvation of people from all walks of life. But this was just one of three great powers contained within this seed that had been planted within our hearts.

ל LAMED

The Good Shepherd. The Good Shepherd and His staff are the loving care, guidance, protection, rescue, salvation, and discipline that Jesus provides to us who follow Him. This staff signifies His role as the vigilant Shepherd who watches over His flock, ensuring our well-being and leading us into eternal life. *Step one* marks the beginning of our eligibility or act of betrayal. All it would take would be thirty dollars and a ride if we were not willing to take more action.

Unbeknownst to us, that which was contained in the moment that we cried out in complete humility was tremendous Power, that of the cross and the guidance of the Good Shepherd. The power of the Good Shepherd with His staff means that we have a loving and compassionate guide who is committed to our success. As we embark on the first step of this spiritual endeavor, we can trust in the Good Shepherd's provision as we take that initial leap of faith. The Lord becomes our strength, shield, and helper. We may encounter doubts, anxieties, or uncertainties about the path ahead. However, the power of the Good Shepherd's with His staff reassures us that we can move forward without fear. He is actively involved in our journey, leading, and guiding us, and providing the assistance we need. His hand steadies us, keeping us secure in moments when we stumble. The power of the Good Shepherd extending His staff towards us gives us confidence that even in those moments, we will not fall. He upholds us with His hand, offering support, strength, and protection. This coupled with its connection between the unseen and the seen prevents us from experiencing defeat as long as we seek Him, and these steps are how we seek Him.

The power of the Good Shepherd is manifested in His Word, which serves as a lamp for our feet and a light on our journey. Just as a lamp illuminates a dark path, God's Word provides the wisdom and clarity we need as we take the first step. We were reminded to rely on the power of the Good Shepherd's Word. We were encouraged to study and meditate on Scripture, seeking guidance and revelation for *step one*. As we took these steps with the principle found in God's Word, we walk with assurance, knowing that the Good Shepherd is leading us. Power was only potential to those who would not cry out or who would not be brought to the point of humility. But we were cautioned that although we may experience this redemptive Power early on, action is still needed.

YOD

The spark of God. Faith in *step one* is difficult for us to grasp. Therefore, the Holy Spirit reveals itself as the spark of God. It suddenly appears the moment God's Hand is applied to our lives, much like the power of art lies within the moment the artist applies the tip of their brush to the blank canvas. At that moment, and each similar moment that ensues, lies the complete Power of transformation. The artistry is in the moment, the spark.

This spark of God that was contained within the seed carried the power of willingness, which is the mustard seed of faith. Although these spiritual terms are foreign to us in the beginning, we quickly saw that this spark was the foundational building block and the essential element in every work that proceeded out of His mouth.

The spark of God contained commitment, trust, and action, all of which were "potential" concepts for us. We had never thoroughly performed any of them. *Step one* requires a commitment to embark on the path of spiritual growth and to initiate this process. In the beginning, it was sins such as drugs and alcohol that were the persuaders for this commitment. When we had cried out in humility, we were unknowingly committing our way to the Lord, committing ourselves to the task at hand, and surrendering our intentions and actions to His desired outcome for our lives. When we cried out, we exhibited a trust in the Lord's guidance and provision which would become the central theme of our journey. Our souls were connecting to a level of trust in God. Trusting in God and His guidance allowed us to approach *step one* with humble confidence and faith. Once we followed humility with action, we witnessed the spark of a promise that God will act. Our humble commitment and trust were not passive but were accompanied by active participation.

Seeing the power of God's spark being applied in *step one* encouraged us to take decisive action. As He demonstrated His creative power to initiate this spiritual process, we embarked on the journey toward spiritual maturity. We were blessed because we had become poor in spirit but in that moment, the kingdom of heaven was ours.

Blessed are the poor in spirit; for theirs' is the kingdom of heaven" (Matthew 5:3). This overarching beatitude covers this portion of our recovery walk. It did not make sense to us at this point in our journey, but we were guaranteed that if we were thorough and honest from the very start, we would look back on this portion of our recovery and in wonderful brokenness smile on the fact that Jesus was right there with us.

A principle is already at work in our lives through the *step one* process. We recognized our brokenness because of external scrapes, bruises, and scars. But we could also sense that there was another brokenness as the humility was watered by the cry for help. We recognize that there is a Love at work repairing that which we gave away due to sins such as drugs and alcohol. The promise sounds simple. There is a promise already covering us that we cannot possibly conceive of. The promise is for all of those who are poor in spirit. For theirs' is the kingdom of heaven. We are truly blessed when we realize we can't do anything without God. This is the poor in spirit that He speaks of. He recognizes our brokenness. The brokenness of our spirits. Only then will we submit to His will. We then see that the kingdom of heaven is ours. We see that it was given the moment we cried out. This is the moment we discover that we have actually submitted to His Will.

Love.

Admitting powerlessness over sin, addictions, and alcoholism is a crucial step in finding spiritual recovery and salvation. For Holy Ghost-filled recovered believers, the Holy Spirit plays a significant role in the process of surrender and repentance. Here are some Holy Ghost-filled spiritual actions we took to acknowledge our powerlessness over these struggles and seek spiritual reconnection. God humbled us before Him in prayer, as we admitted our powerlessness over sins such as alcoholism and addictions. We asked the Holy Spirit to take control of our lives and help us overcome these challenges. We learned through this process to confess our struggles and weaknesses to God and, if appropriate, to trusted fellow believers. Confession is a cathartic and repentant experience, allowing us to receive support and accountability. We sought inner healing through prayer ministry and deliverance sessions led by individuals experienced in these spiritual practices. We watched the Holy Spirit bring healing and salvation to brokenness in our lives. We asked the Holy Spirit to deliver us from the bondage of sin such as addictions and alcoholism. We then embraced the power of God's grace, which sets us free and renews our spiritual connection. We began dedicating time to fasting and prayer, seeking God's guidance and direction for our life. The Holy Spirit revealed His purpose and plan for our healing, service, and ministry. We found ourselves participating in Spirit-filled worship and praise gatherings. We engaged in heartfelt worship, creating an atmosphere where the Holy Spirit moved and brought freedom and breakthroughs. We began to cherish the moments that allowed us to meditate on scripture and soak in God's Word. We watched the Holy Spirit renew our mind and break us free from negative thought patterns and behaviors.

We recommend connecting with a supportive community of believers who can offer encouragement, prayer, and accountability as you walk through the recovery process. In cases of alcoholism and addictions, we suggest seeking those who have already received the gift of the Holy Spirit as the result of believing in Jesus Christ. The Holy Spirit works through Spirit-filled people to aid in our recovery. We must cultivate an attitude of gratitude, which is nothing more than an alarm reminding us to thank God for His love and faithfulness even in the midst of struggles. Gratitude opens our heart to the Holy Spirit's redemptive work.

Remember that overcoming sin, addictions, and spiritual disconnection is a journey that requires time and effort. But the actions are immediate. We were told to be patient with ourselves and rely on the Holy Spirit's power and guidance every step of the way. God's love and grace are always available to those who seek Him with a repentant heart.

If you or someone you know is struggling with the spirit of alcoholism and addictions, the Bible offers hope and healing. When we reached our careers' end of drinking and using drugs, we cried to the Lord in our trouble, and He saved us from our distress. He brought us out of darkness, the utter darkness, and broke our chains. When we cry out to God in our distress, He saves us and set us free from our chains of addictions and alcoholism.

The second component of the powerful cement that unites us is the profound truth that each one of us has found this shared solution. We have uncovered a pathway to freedom that we can wholeheartedly embrace and unite upon. Together, we can take cooperative and harmonious steps towards this common solution.

This book carries the wonderful message of hope to those who find themselves trapped in spiritual bondage. It reveals the great news that there is a way out, a path to being recovered that we can all embrace and find comfort in. Recovery has a Name and it is Jesus!

CHAPTER 5

STEP TWO

"We came to believe that Jesus is the way and the truth and the life — that no one comes to the Father except through Him."
(John 14:6)

*"And Jesus said unto them,
Because of your unbelief:
for verily I say unto you,
If ye have faith as a grain of mustard seed,
ye shall say unto this mountain,
Remove hence to yonder place;
and it shall remove;
and nothing shall be impossible unto you."*
(Matthew 17:20)

Step two in the deliverance process from the spiritual bondage of addictions and alcoholism is a critical and necessary step. We must confront ourselves with a simple yet profound question: "Do I truly believe, or am I even willing to believe, in a Power greater than myself?" This inquiry demands brutal honesty and humble recognition of our own powerlessness. We must acknowledge that we are incapable of conquering our sins such as alcoholism and addictions alone and must rely on a higher force for assistance. It is through this step that God has judged us, and has also heard our voice, and has given us His righteousness.

When confronted with this stone which we once rejected and wholeheartedly saying "yes" or showing a willingness to believe, we begin our journey to recovery. Through faith, we build a solid spiritual foundation with this Power as the chief cornerstone. Starting with simpler concepts, we can establish accessible spirituality without needing full comprehension upfront. Spirituality is a gradual journey where we can embrace more complex principles as we nurture our faith. Hindrances, like reluctance and stubbornness, can impede our growth, and genuine progress requires abandoning limiting beliefs and being open-minded. In times of crisis, we become receptive to spiritual practices. Letting go of old patterns brings a profound shift in our perspectives, leading to peace and purpose. True growth and healing come from humility and willingness, remaining open to the guidance of a higher power in our spiritual journey.

The reader may question why they should believe in a higher power. We believe there are compelling reasons to do so. Consider this: we have many theories about the workings of the natural world, such as wind. Despite not being able to see it, we accept its existence without hesitation. This is because we experience its effects and understand the practical applications of this unseen force. Similarly, the Holy Spirit is unseen, but its effects can be felt and manifested in our lives. Through the power of the Holy Spirit, we overcome our struggles with addictions and alcoholism, find peace in the midst of chaos, and experience a sense of purpose and fulfillment.

In the world of addictions and alcoholism, many of us struggle to accept the idea of a higher power. We had some sort of concept of it, and we thought we knew exactly what God wasn't. We read books and listened to arguments that convinced us we could manage our own lives. We thought we didn't need God to explain our existence or to find freedom from our addictions. As we continued in our addictions, however, the reality of our powerlessness and the need for a higher power became clear. We realized that the material world we see is not the full reality and that there must be a God who is the source of all things. Yet, our pride and stubbornness made it difficult to accept this truth. It was only after experiencing a brutal loss through wrestling with our doubts and fears that we began to experience faith-induced humility. We began to understand that our own ideas were limited, and that true freedom could only come from accepting the one true God. And as we surrendered to Him, we found that He had the strength to overcome our addictions and guide us into living a new life in Him.

Through our recovery in Jesus Christ, we have come to understand that there is a higher power at work, and that Power is God. We have come to recognize that our human intelligence, while valuable, is not the ultimate source of wisdom and understanding. We have learned to submit our will and our lives to the care of God, trusting in His guidance and direction. Through this surrender, we have found true freedom and peace. We began trusting in the Lord with all our heart and leaned not on our own understanding; in all our ways we submitted to Him, and He made our paths straight! We have learned to trust in God, to seek His will for our lives, and to follow His lead. And in doing so, we have found a new purpose and meaning in life, one that is far greater than anything we could have achieved on our own.

Through our recovery in Jesus Christ, we have discovered the true power of humility and faith. We have learned to put our trust in God and to let go of our own self-centered ways. And in doing so, we have found a new way of living, one that is truly fulfilling and life-giving. We picked up a wonderful principle early on. We lived a life full of developing answers before listening — that was folly and shameful. Therefore, we took the cotton out of our ears and placed it into our mouths. We quit making hasty decisions about spiritual matters and those who practice them. Our pride and arrogance blinded us to the Truth that was the only thing that could bring us purpose and direction in life. We must lay aside our prejudices and biases and humbly seek guidance and wisdom from those who have experienced the life-changing power of faith. We must not focus on the human frailties of those who practice religion, but instead look to the stability, happiness, and usefulness that faith can bring to our lives. Let us be open-minded and receptive to the spiritual side of life, for it holds the answers we have been searching for.

Through the Power of the Holy Ghost, He has overcome our addictions and delivered us into a new way of life. We have learned to rely on Him and seek His guidance in all aspects of our lives. We can do all things through Christ who gives us strength. This strength has allowed us to face the challenges of addictions and come out on the other side, stronger and more faithful than ever before. We have found purpose and direction in our lives through our relationship with Jesus, and we know that we are not alone in our struggles. God tells us, "Never will I leave you; never will I forsake you.'" (Hebrews 13:5) With the help of Jesus and the support of our fellow believers, we are able to live a life free from addictions and full of hope for the future.

We flatly declare that since we have come to believe in God, to take a certain attitude toward that Holy Spirit in Jesus' Name, and to do certain simple things, there has been a revolutionary change in our way of living and thinking. In the face of collapse and despair, in the face of the total failure of our human resources, we found that a new Power, Peace, Happiness, and sense of Direction flowed into us. This happened soon after we wholeheartedly took a few simple life-changing steps and began living in a measure of faith toward a new recovered life.

Once lost and struggling with the emptiness and despair of addictions, we finally came to understand the root cause of our suffering. It was not just the consequences of our sinful actions, but a deeper sense of dissatisfaction and disconnection from the Spirit. We discovered a way out through a spiritual awakening in Jesus Christ. We bear witness to the life-changing power of encountering God's presence in our daily lives. It is now the cornerstone of our recovery and the source of true joy and meaning. Without faith, it is impossible to please God because anyone who comes to Him must believe that He exists and that He rewards those who earnestly seek Him.

Over countless generations, the collective experiences of millions have offered proof of the existence of the Holy Spirit. Just as we believe in the existence of wind despite not being able to see it, we can believe in the power of the Holy Spirit despite not being able to physically see or touch Him. So, we fix our eyes not on what is seen, but on what is unseen, since what is seen is temporary, but what is unseen is eternal. Furthermore, we have come to recognize that our human intelligence alone is not enough to solve the problems of sin such as alcoholism and addictions. It is only through the guidance and strength of God that we are able to overcome our struggles and find true freedom. Let us therefore open our hearts and minds to the reality of the Holy Spirit and trust in the power of Jesus Christ to renew our minds and transform our lives.

After witnessing the life-changing power of God in the lives of those who embraced Jesus as their Lord and Savior, we could no longer deny the reality of the Holy Spirit. Everything became possible the moment we believed. We realized that our self-reliance and limited understanding had held us back. We were urged to trust in the Lord wholeheartedly and submit to His plan, assuring us that He would lead us on the right path. True peace and freedom from sin such as alcoholism and addictions could only be found through surrendering our will to God and embracing His will for our lives.

We value the use of logic and reason. Our God-given intellect is meant to seek truth and understanding. We do not blindly accept propositions, but rather examine evidence and make logical conclusions rooted in faith. Our belief in Christ is not a blind leap, but rather a reasoned and logical choice. Faith and reason are not contradictory, but complementary, offering clarity and meaning to our lives. We are called to always be ready to provide a reason for our hope with gentleness and respect (1 Peter 3:15).

When faced with a crisis beyond human aid, we confronted the binary proposition of God's existence. It compelled us to make a choice and declare it to others. God is everything or nothing to us! We arrived at a point where our own understanding had reached its limit, and we turned to trust in the Lord completely. We embraced the truth of Proverbs 3:5-6, placing our faith in God's guidance to illuminate our paths and provide a new life. We let go of our old identities and placed our full trust in Him.

We realized that our faith was misplaced, as we worshipped our own understanding instead of God. Surrendering to God and putting our faith in Him transformed our lives. We discovered true worship from the heart and found a new identity in Christ. Our faith became the substance of hope and evidence of the unseen. We let go of the idolatry of our sins such as addictions and alcoholism and turned to the one true God, finding the hope and assurance we sought in Him. Our reliance on our own reasoning led us astray, but through faith in Jesus, we found transformation and the power of God's love. We acknowledged our denial and pride, realizing that faith in Jesus was a reasonable and logical choice supported by biblical accounts. Opening our hearts to a spiritual life, we experienced spiritual freedom greater than any sin such as alcoholism and addictions could give us.

We recognized the Holy Spirit as the source of power that guided us and set us free from sins such as alcoholism and addictions. Faith in Jesus became the foundation of our existence. If our stories can inspire honest introspection and open-mindedness in others, they may choose to join us on this journey. Through surrendering to Jesus Christ, we experienced the truth and found healing. Now, we help others through our testimonies and the power of the Holy Spirit. With Jesus as our guide, we walk in His love, liberated from the chains of sin.

In our recognition of the allure of sin and its consequences, we came face to face with the bondage it placed upon us. We realized that our own efforts to stop sinning were futile, as we lacked the power to overcome it on our own. The temporary pleasure of sins such as addictions and alcoholism only led to insatiable cravings and destructive consequences, leaving our lives stained with filth.

In this realization, we turned to Jesus Christ, understanding His strength and power to overcome sin. We humbly admitted our need for His grace as sinners, acknowledging our powerlessness. We recognized that true freedom could only be found through the work of the Holy Spirit within us. By surrendering ourselves to Jesus, He began to work in and through us, breaking the chains of addiction and offering healing to those who earnestly seek Him.

We understood that the unmanageability of our lives was due to a deep spiritual disconnection. This disconnection manifested as restlessness, irritability, and discontent. Conventional diagnoses and treatments fell short of addressing the true root of our struggles. We recognized that our spiritual condition was reflected in these and other symptoms such as anxiety, depression, and unhappiness. We needed spiritual healing to find true recovery.

The devastation caused by sins such as addictions and alcoholism reached the depths of our souls, filling our minds with guilt, shame, and remorse. Despite our repeated attempts to quit, we found ourselves trapped in a cycle of destruction. It became evident to us that addictions were not solely a physical matter but had a spiritual component as well. Our disconnection from God drove us to seek temporary pleasures like drugs and alcohol to fill the void within us.

In acknowledging our powerlessness over addiction and the unmanageability of our lives, we recognized the need for spiritual healing and reconnection with God. We identified with the words of the Apostle Paul, understanding that our addictions stemmed from a spiritual sickness. This realization led us to rely on God for help and to seek a deeper connection with Him. We cried out for help, surrendering ourselves to a higher power, and understanding that our sins were a symptom of our spiritual disease.

As we humbly cried out, our souls began to grow, and we discovered that the solution lies in a Power greater than ourselves which is Jesus Christ. He became our guiding light, leading us out of the darkness of addictions and into a place of peace and joy. We learned that mere knowledge of the problem was not enough; true freedom required surrendering our will to God's and seeking His transformation in our lives.

Rejecting the belief that relapse is inevitable, we embraced hope and purpose in our newfound deliverance. Grateful and faithful, we entrusted our recovery journey to God's guidance each day. We understood that vacillating between the problem and the solution was futile—we needed to fully commit to Jesus for our deliverance. Without Jesus, our knowledge of the problem would lead us back to our destructive habits. We would remain trapped in addictions and sin until we released it all and let go of the false knowledge we once held.

Believing in a Power greater than ourselves, which is Jesus Christ, is crucial for our salvation. We acknowledge that our understanding of God is limited, and we recognize that our previous conceptions lacked the power to heal us. It is essential to set aside debates about different beliefs and focus on the shared understanding that a higher Power can guide us in overcoming addictions. We discovered, after all, that it is the Potter who molds the clay, not us who mold the Potter. Therefore, who were we to develop a concept of a Higher Power when it is the Power which develops us?

The *second step* involves admitting the possibility of a Power greater than ourselves. When we believe or are willing to believe in Him, we are on the right path. This belief in Jesus allows us to become part of God's household and we have the power to become His children.

Taking the *second step* is not the end, but rather the beginning of a new life in Christ. We must actively seek a deeper relationship with Him, and let faith be accompanied by action. Surrendering our will to God and relying on His strength and guidance in all aspects of our lives are crucial. Alcoholism and addictions are not solely physical or psychological problems; they have a spiritual dimension too. Recognizing this spiritual malady is important as it leaves us restless, irritable, and discontented.

We were not left to fight this battle alone. We were given the promise of a Power greater than ourselves which could restore us to sanity. This Power is God and His Name is Jesus. We found strength and hope in the words of scripture in 2 Corinthians 12:9, where it says, "My grace is sufficient for you, for my power is made perfect in weakness." Through our faith in Jesus Christ and our willingness to surrender to His will, we found the strength and courage to face our addictions. We found freedom from the spiritual bondage of self and the power to live a new life in Christ. We were no longer slaves to our addictions but children of God, redeemed by the blood of the Lamb. This sounded like a tall order for many of us, whether agnostic or believer.

In taking this step, in the face of uncertainty, it was recommended that we joined with a Holy Ghost-filled person and say this prayer as it is said for all who come this way. The task was simple, if appropriate; we joined hands to show unity, bowed our heads to give reverence, closed our eyes because He is Holy, and then listened to or said the following prayer:

Reviving Grace: A Prayer for Strength, Guidance, and Unfailing Love

(If appropriate, hold another person's hand, then as people bow their heads, closing their eyes in silence, someone reads this prayer over them)

Dear Lord,

We come to you in a state
of weakness, feeling discouraged and lying in
the dust. We feel ourselves fading away
and in need of your help. We
ask that you would revive us by
your Word, just as you promised you

> *would. May your Word be a beacon of light in our darkness, guiding us towards the path of righteousness. May it be a source of strength and encouragement as we face the challenges of our daily lives. We trust in your unfailing love and grace, knowing that you are always with us and will never forsake us. We thank you for your mercy and ask that you continue to pour out your blessings upon us.*

We have poured out our lives before Him, knowing that He has always been there for us. So now we ask:

<u>Guided by the Spirit: A Prayer for Understanding, Strength, and Faithfulness</u>

> *May Your Holy Spirit guide us as we walk the path of righteousness. Help us to understand Your ways and Your wisdom, and may we always meditate on Your splendor and Your wonders. In times of weakness and sorrow, give us the strength to carry on and to find comfort in Your words. Protect us from the lies and deceit of this world, and give us the grace to remain faithful to You. We surrender ourselves to You, Lord, and we trust that You will guide us on our journey towards recovery and wholeness.*

We have just made the choice to obey His truth and walk in the splendor of all that He teaches us as we pray:

Surrendered and Empowered: A Prayer for Guidance and Courage

*"Help us to surrender our wills to
You and follow Your guidance every day.
We know that we cannot do it
alone, but with You, all things are
possible. Give us the courage to face
our challenges and the humility to seek
help when we need it. Show us
Your mercy and grace as we walk
this path of recovery. Amen."*

From this point forward, we wholeheartedly embrace the teachings of Jesus and diligently follow them all. We pursue Him with joy in our hearts, as His instructions make us obedient with each action we take.

Once we admitted to our innermost selves that we were powerless and recognized that our lives had become spiritually disconnected, we were faced with the proposition that God either is or He isn't. *Step two* requires us to be willing to believe in a power greater than ourselves. This step is the chief cornerstone upon which lasting transformation is built. This can only be done once we acknowledge that there is a Power greater than ourselves. Just this acknowledgment unlocked a doorway through which were about to step and change our lives forever.

We were still standing in the place of repentance. We were poor in spirit. But here, in this realm of repentance, there was a promise being applied to us. A promise that these first three steps, which were repentance steps, were going to be a blessing the moment we could look back to this point and see. We were blessed at the precise moment that we were willing to believe in Jesus Christ. Only then were we truly submitting to His will. And to do His will is to receive the kingdom of heaven. But the Lord knows, we could not see any of this from the vantage point of complete brokenness. Do not be discouraged, many of us passed through this unknowingly. Keep taking this step.

Before we even began taking this step, picked up this book, the Bible, or thought about God, we were called to this place and in this brokenness, there were spiritual realities being manifested. We saw this in each step and measure along the Way. We found ourselves right in the middle of judgement. This judgement was concerning at first. However, we need not be disconcerted. This judgement was more about deliverance.

ד DALET

The door. The door whose threshold we are about to cross into freedom has been placed before humanity for centuries. God planned it long before our lungs breathed air. This entry is marked with the blood of sacrifice. It is applied to its doorposts and lentil. This is a sign and protection for us, indicating that we were to be spared. As we continue to take spiritual action toward being recovered, the spirit of addictions and alcoholism – sins – will pass over us because we have entered the door marked with the Lamb's blood. This is not a long- drawn-out process. We hastily enter this step. We need to be dressed in the garment of faith and ready to leave this old life behind. We are about to step through unto God's deliverance and protection. Taking this step liberates us from the slavery of sin such as addictions and alcoholism. This step will forever be a reminder of God's faithfulness to His covenant with us. This covenant requires obedience to God's instructions, the redemption and protection he provides, and the faithfulness of God in delivering us from the oppression of sin. It holds a central place in these steps and will continue to be celebrated, reminding us and others of the miraculous events that unfolded during these steps and through these measures.

Opening our hearts to Jesus invites His Presence into our lives. The moment we confess that God is everything, we are being led to spiritual growth. We are immediately experiencing the power of the Good Shepherd as He begins to guide and teach us. The power of the cross releases within us as we gain a deeper trust in faith. The entire *step two* process is a mind-transforming experience. This relationship empowers us to overcome challenges. It brings us comfort and purpose. We have a new direction. The spiritual door's power lies in this personal connection and communion with Jesus. This results automatically in positive changes in our lives. Through this relationship, we find spiritual nourishment and a sense of His presence.

Jesus declares Himself the door. He is the only one who can provide salvation. He is the only one who can bring us true fulfillment. Our lives had no purpose without Him. We accept Him as Lord and Savior, and in that moment we also embrace His teachings. Upon seeing His power, we surrender to His guidance. This relationship brings forgiveness and reconciliation with God, and therefore, promises of an eternal life if we stay close to Him and perform His work well. By crying out, we opened the gates of righteousness and began seeking this path of spiritual growth which deepens our relationship with God.

In *step two* of our spiritual journey, pursuing righteousness and aligning with God's will becomes crucial. **RECOVERY 5:12** – these steps are how we seek God in pursuit of righteousness. These measures of faith are how we align ourselves with God's will. Our intention is to take this step through the door with thanksgiving and praise the Lord. This participation indicates our willingness to follow divine principles, knowing that it's through this door that the righteous enter. Just what do we mean? Entering through the door involves seeking alignment with God's will. As we enter, we begin practicing virtues and reflecting His values. Additionally, *step two* includes praise and worship to deepen our connection with the divine and enhance spiritual growth.

We recognize the life-changing power of seeking spiritual guidance, wisdom, and understanding. We actively engage with God, seeking a deeper connection and persistently asking, searching, and knocking. Recognizing God as the ultimate source of power and knowledge, we understand that prayer, seeking, and effort yield divine guidance, insight, and blessings. Recovery entails humbly approaching God, expressing heartfelt desires, and seeking His will.

When the door was opened, we received an invitation to enter a place of safety and security. We were placed in His presence which provided access to deeper spiritual understanding in Christ. Opening the gates mentioned in Isaiah 26:2 grants us spiritual blessings, further deepening our relationship with God and benefiting from His presence and protection. *Step two* of our journey of being recovered focuses on cultivating righteousness and maintaining faith aligned with God's will. The power of the spiritual door in this step lies in recognizing the importance of remaining faithful and committed to God's ways. The door is open for those who keep their trust in God. This is the beginning of the seed of righteousness's growth that was planted from the bending of humility in the previous step.

NUN

The seed of righteousness from our *step one* experience is the seed planted by humility and watered by our crying out to God. It contains the wonderful power of the cross, the Good Shepherd's staff, and the spark of God. Next, we acted and began taking *step two* where we were willing to believe that there was a Power greater than ourselves. Once we were able to say yes and realized that the Power was not anything like our previous conception of it, we found ourselves at the covenant door. Once we crossed over the threshold of this door and began to believe in Jesus Christ as the only way, truth, and life, we sensed that the seed burst open and released the powers within. These resulted in His righteousness, which now began to take root within our hearts and spirits. The seed of humility from *step one* was now establishing itself as the seed of righteousness which would grow in and around us through the remaining ten steps, or until the moment that our spirits were drawn out into the *first measure* of faith. This all seems quite elaborate at this point, so let's back up a minute and talk more about His righteousness in this second step.

The pursuit of righteousness in *step two* signifies our desire to seek God's righteousness rather than relying on our own flawed attempts. We recognize that it is through Jesus' sacrifice and His righteousness that we can find true life, prosperity, and honor. In this step, we acknowledge our powerlessness to save ourselves and instead place our trust in Jesus, who is the embodiment of righteousness. We understand that our pursuit of righteousness is not based on our own efforts, but rather on our surrender to Jesus and His righteousness working in and through us. We were encouraged to seek God's kingdom as the central focus of our lives. It aligns with *step two* of recovery in Jesus' Name, emphasizing the importance of surrendering our own efforts, trusting in God's provision, and seeing His righteousness guide our paths. By seeking His righteousness above all else, we embark on a journey of transformation and experience the blessings that flow from living in alignment with God's will.

In *step two*, there is a definite transformation that occurs in the lives of those of us who came to believe and embrace Christ. We are no longer bound by the power of sins such as addictions and alcoholism but have been set free and are now under the influence and authority of righteousness. We were reminded of the shift in focus and allegiance that needs to take place to be recovered.

By acknowledging a higher power, we are essentially recognizing that we have been set free from the bondage of our addictions and struggles and are now aligning ourselves with righteousness with each action we take. Righteousness becomes the guiding principle and a source of strength for those in recovery. It represents a way of living in harmony with God's will and seeking to do what is right and good. Embracing righteousness involves embracing a new way of life that is no longer characterized by destructive behaviors and harmful patterns but is instead marked by transformation, integrity, and moral uprightness. In *step two* we seek to surrender our old ways, acknowledge our need for His assistance, and commit to living a life aligned with righteousness. We recognize that relying on our own strength alone is insufficient, and we choose to trust in Jesus to lead us on the path of healing and recovery.

Through faith, we are reconciled with God and granted the righteousness that comes from Him. We are not defined by our past mistakes or struggles but find a new identity in Christ, marked by righteousness and reconciliation with God. The concept of righteousness is closely tied to the second step. Righteousness is a state of being in the right relationship with God, where we see Him align our lives with His will and values. It involves pursuing a life of integrity, moral uprightness, and seeking to do what is right, all of which we cannot do without his aid.

We were encouraged to shift our focus from our own self-righteousness and insufficient attempts to earn salvation to embracing the righteousness that is a gift from God. True righteousness is not achieved by human effort alone but is received through faith and reliance on Christ. In our journey in these two steps, we come to terms with our powerlessness over our struggles of flesh and mind in spiritual disconnectedness and seek a higher power to lead us on the path of being spiritually recovered. We recognize the need to let go of self-reliance and instead place our trust in God's righteousness and guidance. We understand that true transformation and healing come from embracing the righteousness that is available through faith in Christ.

The spiritual principle of righteousness plays a vital role in *step two* by reminding us that our journey toward being recovered involves surrendering our own attempts at righteousness and instead relying on the righteousness that comes from God. It is the need to trust in God's grace and life-changing power rather than relying on failed personal efforts. It was a step we all had to take. Even if it had been fifty days since our last debauch, it was still a time of a grateful harvest in our lives when *step two* was fully realized.

Indeed, the second step means "deliverance" or "judgment." In the context of recovery, the second step holds special significance, representing the theme of deliverance from various struggles such as drugs and alcohol. This deliverance is needed for the successful consummation of recovery. *Step two* involves seeking deliverance from the grip of sins such as alcoholism and addictions. It is a process of breaking free from substance abuse and harmful behaviors and finding a path to recovery and salvation.

Many people in recovery seek deliverance from mental health challenges like depression, anxiety, or post-traumatic stress. Overcoming these challenges leads to a sense of liberation and newfound hope. The "judgment" of *step two* relates to the process of God examining our hearts and searching for our acceptance of His Spirit that occurs in recovery. Seeking inner witness of the Holy Spirit illuminates areas for service, ministry, and repentance. Recovery is about realizing that we are not in control over our lives or those of others. It involves making conscious decisions and facing the facts about our lives, leading to a sense of empowerment and deliverance from feeling powerless and spiritually disconnected.

We all find spiritual aspects in our recovery journey. The "deliverance" of step two is the sense of spiritual liberation and finding peace within ourselves. Recovery offers the opportunity for a profound life change. Like deliverance from old ways, it enables us to start anew, as God rebuilds our lives and creates the needed psychic change sufficient for permanent recovery. It's important to remember that each step holds spiritual significance, and not everyone who takes the second step will experience recovery in the same way. However, for those who find deliverance, it carries us from a state of wrestling to the covenant door of righteousness. There the Power encourages and motivates us throughout our recovery process.

As we have seen in our trek through unmanageability, the great teachings of the Beatitudes have been at work in our lives. This is a phenomenon that occurs in each step and measure along the way. Located under the umbrella of Matthew 5:3, we find the *step two* Beatitude which is "Blessed are those who mourn; for they shall be comforted" (Matthew 5:4). Until *step two*, we could not see why we were mourning. We thought it was the sacrifice of self that would be required. We thought the uncertainty of what would be left if we gave all of ourselves to Christ was what caused us to mourn. But as we found this recovery path of holiness, the principles and promises seemed to grow and change before our eyes.

Sure, early in this progress, there are so many obstacles of prejudice that we can't comprehend why our souls and spirits mourn. One mourns the complete loss of self and the other recognizes the true reason for the mourning, and so we mourn.

The second step's promise that follows this principle is one of the great promises. For we shall be comforted! A sense of ease and comfort is all that we had been looking for when sin became the master of our lives. And now the Master offers us the comfort of the kingdom of heaven. What a Mighty God!

Blessed are those whose hearts grieve because they have sinned. We recognize that our alcoholism and addictions were sins. Yes, we sinned. Yes, we recognize it has separated us from Jesus. This is the reason our spirits mourned!

However, the Lord comforted us. He consoled us. He is the One who provides comfort and strength to us. We come to rely on the power of the Holy Ghost to lift us up and encourage us in our faith journey and to refresh us along the way.

Joy.

In *step two* of recovery, we are among those who mourn. We grieve the loss of our old ways and beliefs, but we take comfort in His guidance towards a new life. Through our mourning, we learn to let go and surrender to a higher power. Our hearts were blessed as we acknowledged our powerlessness - unmanageability - and sought help, receiving the promise of comfort and a fresh start.

Trusting in Jesus, we continue taking the necessary steps towards complete recovery, knowing we are not alone. His presence brings us comfort and leads us to a fulfilling life. Righteousness and repentance become foundational principles in our struggle against addictions. In Jesus, we find hope, forgiveness, and a transformed mind.

We already see that there is action to take in these steps. Although it is difficult to conceive of us ever doing any of the spiritual actions that we see those who have completely recovered doing, we too will someday look up and see ourselves standing in many of these actions.

For those who have completely recovered, the Holy Spirit plays a central role in guiding and empowering our faith. To deepen our belief that Jesus is the way, the truth, and the life, and because no one comes to the Father except through Him, we suggest taking Holy Ghost-filled spiritual actions.

We seek the Holy Spirit's guidance through prayer, asking for revelation and understanding about Jesus' significance and His role in our lives and salvation. This is easier done with a Holy Ghost-filled believer than alone or with someone who may not understand.
We were told to get a King James Version (KJV) Bible and immerse ourselves in the scriptures, particularly the New Testament Gospels, to learn about Jesus' teachings, His life, and the profound impact He has on humanity. We entertained the notion of participating in Spirit-led praise and worship sessions. Then we watched ourselves be filled with the Holy Spirit's presence as we worshiped Jesus and magnified His Name. Most of us embraced the practice of speaking in tongues as a form of spiritual communication with God. We watched the Holy Spirit pray through us and open our hearts to a deeper communion of Christ's truth. We joined spiritual gatherings, such as revivals, conferences, and retreats. These events are centered around experiencing the Holy Spirit's presence and receiving spiritual revelations.

Regardless of how new we are to this walk, we share our faith journey and experiences with Jesus. By testifying to others about the life-changing Power of Christ, we strengthen our own beliefs in His way and truth. We pursue the manifestation of spiritual gifts as described in the New Testament, such as prophecy, healing, or discernment. These experiences deepen our awareness of Jesus' presence and power. It is suggested that we dedicate periods of fasting and prayer to draw closer to Jesus and seek

His will for our lives through watching the Holy Spirit lead and guide us during these times of consecration. We yield ourselves fully to the Holy Spirit's leadership and conviction, watching Him reveal Jesus' truth to us and transform our hearts and minds. Finally, we embrace Jesus' commandment to love one another as He loves us. Through acts of love and compassion, we experience His presence and witness His truth in action.

Remember that spiritual growth is a journey, and belief is strengthened through a combination of experiences, fellowship with other believers, and a sincere desire to know and follow Jesus. We keep seeking the Holy Spirit's guidance and watch Him deepen our understanding and conviction in Jesus as the way, the truth, and the life.

Accepting Jesus as our Savior plants a seed of His righteousness within us, overcomes our addictions, and gives us a life with purpose. We must seek Him, turning to His living Word for new life. We approach Him with gratitude for the progress made and seek His guidance for the steps ahead. Despite the challenges we may encounter, we persist on the path set before us, faithfully following His Word. In doing so, we discover God's strength and courage, overcoming addiction and becoming the person He intended us to be. The Bible shows us that failure is not the end of the story. Many individuals in Scripture have struggled and stumbled, only to be redeemed and restored through God's grace. And so shall we. Here are the steps we took.

CHAPTER 6

JOURNEY TO WHOLENESS

RECOVERY 5:12 - Steps and Measures for a Life Transformed by Christ

*"Do not conform to the pattern of this world,
but be transformed by the renewing of your mind.
Then you will be able to test and approve what God's
will is—his good, pleasing and perfect will."
(Romans 12:2)*

When it comes to recovery, the key is not to rely on our own strength and willpower. Instead, we must give ourselves completely to Jesus Christ and rely on His Power to overcome our struggles. If we are separated from the love of Jesus, we are indeed incapable of being honest with ourselves. But when we turn to Him and surrender our lives to His care, we can begin to experience the life-changing power of His love and grace. But exactly how do we give ourselves completely to Him? That's exactly what this path of recovery reveals.

We may suffer from emotional and mental disorders that make recovery more challenging. However, through Christ, all things are possible. We must have the capacity to be honest with ourselves, with Him, and with other human beings, even when it is difficult. We were not born to fail; we were born with the potential to become all that God created us to be. By relying on His strength and following His ways, He will overcome our addictions and we will experience the fullness of life that He intends for us.

Our testimonies are special messages that show how God's love changes lives in an amazing way. We tell our stories to give hope to others who are also struggling with sin such as alcoholism and addictions. We want them to know that God is good. If we truly want to have a positive change in our lives and have a relationship with Jesus Christ, we must be willing to go to any lengths for victory over sin such as alcoholism and addictions. We must let go of prejudices that keep us stuck in doing bad things. We need to be honest and open-minded with ourselves, admitting that we can't control our sin. We seek Jesus to take care of us. This means we must keep growing spiritually and help others too. The benefits we get from this kind of life are great. With Jesus, we are free from the things that hold us back and experience a happy life like He promises. When we become closer to God, we feel peace by following His ways.

When we were ready to start following Jesus, we learned that we had support from other people who believed in Him too. They were there to help us on our journey. With the help of God, we saw amazing things happen. He helped us overcome our own problems and the problems of others who were struggling with sins such as alcoholism and addictions. This led us to live a life of recovery and happiness, just like God planned for us.

Sometimes, as people, we don't like change. We want to keep doing things the same way we always have. But when it comes to recovering from addictions such as alcoholism, holding onto our old ways just makes things worse. The truth is that there's no easy way to beat sin, even alcoholism and addictions. We must be ready to try a new way of living, one that follows God's teachings. We can't just wish our addictions away; we must give ourselves to God and He will help us. That means we must be brave and give recovery our all right from the beginning. We must be willing to let go of what we think we know and trust that God will show us the right way to go.

Remember that we face a tough challenge when recovering from sins such as addictions and alcoholism. It can be tricky, requiring us to be patient which requires great strength! On our own, it's just too much for us to handle. But there is One who has all Power in heaven and on Earth; that One is God, and His Name is Jesus. May you experience His Power now!

Half measures avail us of nothing. We reach a moment when we must make a conscious decision to turn away from our old ways of living and embrace a new way of life in Christ. We must throw ourselves under His protection and care with complete abandon, trusting in His guidance and direction for our lives. This kind of surrender is not easy, and it requires us to face difficult truths about ourselves and our past.

Here is the path we took:

1. We admitted we were powerless over sins such as addictions and alcoholism — that our lives had become spiritually disconnected. (Romans 7:14-20)

2. We came to believe that Jesus is the way, and the truth, and the life — no one comes to the Father but by Him. (John 14:6)

3. We decided to follow Jesus, we denied ourselves, and took up our cross, and followed Him. (Matthew 16:24)

4. We searched and tried our ways, and turned again to the LORD. (Lamentations 3:40)

5. We confessed our faults one to another, and prayed one for another, that we may be healed. *The effectual fervent prayer of a righteous man avails much.* (James 5:16)

6. We humbled ourselves in the sight of the Lord, and He lifted us up. (James 4:10)

7. We humbly, on our knees, confessed our sins, God being faithful and just forgave us our sins, and cleansed us from ALL unrighteousness. (1 John 1:9)

8. We remembered those who had something against us and became willing to first be reconciled to them all. (Matthew 5:23-24)

9. We did unto them as we also have them do to us *except when to do so would injure them or others.* (Luke 6:31)

10. We continue to acknowledge our sin, expose our iniquity, confess our transgressions to the LORD; and He forgives the iniquity of our sin. Selah. (Psalm 32:5)

11. We rejoice evermore, pray without ceasing, and in everything give thanks: for this is the will of God in Christ. (1 Thessalonians 5:16-18)

12. We now teach others to observe all things whatsoever Jesus has commanded us: and, see, He is with us always, even unto the end of the world. Amen. (Matthew 28:20)

We therefore beseech you by the mercies of God, that as we have presented our bodies as a living sacrifice, holy, acceptable to God, which is our reasonable service. We are no longer being conformed to this world, but being transformed by the renewing of our minds, and we may prove what is that good, acceptable, and perfect will of God. We say, through the Grace given to us, to everyone that comes this way, not to think of themselves more highly than we ought to think but to think soberly, according as God has given to each of us the measure of faith which are designed to guide us in this new life. Once we have come this far, here are the measures of faith which align us to God's will:

First: *We experienced having our spirit drawn out, we grow in grace, and the knowledge of our Lord and Savior Jesus Christ. To Him be glory both now and forever. Amen* (2 Peter 3:18)

Second:	*We recognize the bittersweet steps of repentance, the sacrifices of God are a broken spirit: A broke and contrite heart, O God, You will not despise.* (Psalm 51:17)
Third:	*We were casted out in remission, we humbled ourselves under the mighty hand of God and He exalted us in due time: we cast all our care upon Him; because He cares for us.* (1 Peter 5:6 & 7)
Fourth:	*We were allied in restitution, truly, inasmuch as we do to one of the least of those in need, we do it unto Jesus Christ.* (Matthew 25:40)
Fifth:	*We no longer walk in darkness, Jesus Christ is the light of the world: we follow Him and no longer walk in darkness, but have the light of life.* (John 8:12)

Everything that is spoken to us through this recovery path is like joyous treasure, filling our lives with gladness! A pink cloud of grace and protection has seemingly surrounded us as we have determined in our heart to obey whatever He says, fully and forever! We immediately become convinced of three vital issues:

(a) That we are sinners and that our lives had become spiritually disconnected.
(b) No human power could relieve us of sins or save us.
(c) Jesus could and would if he were sought with our whole heart.

If you are not thoroughly convinced of these three vital issues, you ought to fall back on your face, search the scriptures, and re-read this book up to this point or else throw all of it away. This may seem harsh, however, we were told that we could continue to try our own ideas and then were asked, "How has that been working for you?" We knew there had to be something different so we pressed onward.

If you are completely out of ideas and convinced, we reached *step three*, which is where we decided to turn our will and lives over to the care of God. Just what do we mean by this and just what do we do? When we say that we turn our will and lives over to God, we mean that we turn over our thoughts and efforts or actions to God. This is a very serious matter. It is soul surgery if you will. Therefore, before answering the how and why of it, we had to first determine if we were properly prepared to make such a decision. We had to ask ourselves: will you be made whole?

CHAPTER 7

THE REQUIREMENT

*"Do not conform to the pattern of this world,
but be transformed by the renewing of your mind.
Then you will be able to test and approve what God's
will is—his good, pleasing and perfect will."*
(Romans 12:22)

At this point, we are only at *step three*. It is much like standing in line for a roller coaster at an amusement park. The ride is obviously full of thrills and excitement as evidenced by the screams and laughter of the riders that went before us. As the roller coaster comes to a halt, the previous riders collect their disheveled selves, the lap bar raises, and they exit the carts with wonderful reports and reviews. We then begin our final approach toward the carts and suddenly, a hand presses against our chest! The carnival ride director points at a large ruler and sign on the wall which reads, "Height Requirement is 48 inches." What does this mean? The answer is that if we do not meet the requirement, then we are not able to get on the ride. Taking these steps is very much the same way. Too many times, people will try all manner of self-deception to circumvent or run and jump through this step without fully comprehending the most basic requirements, which we shall now review.

The first requirement is that we be convinced that any life run on our own thinking can be a success. This is a very difficult task for those of us who often believe that we are the smartest people in the room or that we are the center of our universe. We are a people who would be in such a desperate state of needing help but would look help right in the mouth and tell it how to help us. On that basis of running our lives on our own thinking, we are always in collision with something or somebody, even though our motives are good.

How many times have we thought about the other person using drugs with us in the seedy motel room only to have the thought filled with our misconception of camaraderie and talk of loyalty? We too had become the very existence of that which society points at as they pass the lowliest of places. These old, abandoned structures which had long gone out of business were sources of excitement for us. We would get excited after finding an obscure entrance through an old air-conditioning vent. We were really living … or so we thought.

We try to live by self-propulsion. We are like a servant who wants to run the whole household, who is forever trying to arrange the lights, the table setting, the furniture and the rest of the staff and visitors in our own way. If our arrangements would only stay put, if only people would do as we wished, life would be great. Everybody, including ourselves, would be pleased. Life would be wonderful. In trying to make these arrangements we can be quite virtuous. We are kind, considerate, patient, generous, even modest, and self-sacrificing. Heck! We will give you the shirts off our backs. On the other hand, we may be mean, egotistical, selfish, and dishonest. As with most humans and snakes, we are likely to have varied traits.

Remember, we are trying to determine if you meet the requirements. Are you tall enough to get on the ride? A more relevant question is, "Did the previous paragraph sound like you at all?" If yes, then know that this is soul surgery and you have just been admitted. Because this is very serious, we will continue to check the requirements until we are certain.

In our journey, we may sometimes feel dissatisfied with the circumstances of our lives. We might start to believe that we are not receiving the blessings we deserve. As we continue to strive for more, we become increasingly demanding. However, this only leads to more frustration, and we can't figure out why. We acknowledge that we are partially responsible for our situations, but we are sure others are more to blame. We become angry, self-righteous, and even more self-pitying. Our core problem is our self-centeredness, even when we try to do good. We are under the delusion that we can find happiness and fulfillment by controlling the world around us. We crave things that we believe will bring us satisfaction, and we are willing to go to great lengths to obtain them. Unfortunately, our efforts only make others want to take advantage of us, leaving us feeling empty and unfulfilled. Are we not, even in our best moments, a producer of confusion rather than harmony? Even in our best moments, clean and sober! Our best moments!

Remember that we are about to continue onto serious spiritual business. Do you meet these requirements as described in the previous paragraph? Does this sound like you? If yes, let's continue with the procedure.

We are like the Pharisees and Sadducees who focus solely on their own self-righteousness and adherence to principles, while ignoring God and the needs of others. We are like the rich man who hoards his wealth and ignores the plight of the poor at his doorstep. We are like the prodigal son who demands his inheritance and squanders it on his own pleasure, without a thought for his father or others. We are like Saul, who seeks to destroy those who do not agree with his own beliefs and ideals, rather than seeking unity and understanding. Whatever our claims of righteousness or piety, are we not all consumed with our own desires, our own grievances, and our own self-absorption?

As we continue to prepare for this soul surgery, does this previous paragraph sound like you at all? Do you meet the requirements? Let's go a couple of more paragraphs just to be sure. The soul is not a simple thing to tamper with. And once we give it to Jesus and it's covered by His blood, there is no room for return without making it a bloody mess.

The root of our problems lies in the selfish spirit that resides within us. This self-centeredness is manifested by numerous forms of fear, self-deception, self-seeking, and self-pity. We often offend others with our efforts, and they retaliate in response. Sometimes, they hurt us, apparently without any cause. However, we eventually realize that we had made decisions with our broken brains which were based on our spiritless selves, which had put us in a position to be hurt by others.

Sound familiar? Still meeting the requirement? As it becomes more evident that we are meeting the requirement, this surgery is happening. Let's continue.

So, our troubles, we think, are basically of our own making. They arise out of ourselves, and the addict/alcoholic is an extreme example of our own thinking violently disturbing our own peace, though we usually don't think so. <u>*Above everything*</u> ... Wait! Stop for a second!

What is the meaning of "above everything?" Most of us interpret it as meaning "On top of or higher than." However, when we're new converts who haven't prayed the third step prayer yet, repented, and are still relying on our own *conception* of a "higher power," we ask if this means being above our loved ones or above our sins such as drugs and alcohol. The answer is typically "Yes." But does "above everything" mean being above ourselves? Those of us who are deeply self-centered take longer to respond, but eventually, we too answer "Yes." However, does "above everything" mean being above "God"? The rank sinner, who is ruled by extreme self-centeredness and currently playing God in their own life, vehemently says, "No." Why? Because the spirit of self that is controlling their life has them believing that the self is God. This selfish spirit is willing to sacrifice loved ones, turn to the old solution of alcohol and drugs, and even send ourselves to the flames but will resist acknowledging that anything is above it, the spirit of selfishness.

This exercise involves all levels of disconcertment. This always pushes people into their own minds in search of this spiritual dilemma. Many exhibit physical symptoms like getting angry, being moved to tears, jumping out of their chairs, pacing the room, and even leaving the room. They will do all this before they will admit that "above everything" means above "God". As soon as someone concedes and confidently says, "Yes" to being above "God", they meet the requirement.

We are reminded that in this moment of our journey, we are still holding onto our own personal *concept* of God, which is just a reflection of ourselves. We are the ones who created this *concept*, and it is an extension of us. It's a moment of realization that all along we have been praying to ourselves, our own created *concept*. It's no surprise that our prayers only worked about half the time.

When we see the flashing blue lights of a police car behind us, we pray that it's not for us, but sometimes it is. And when our prayers to our *concept* of God go unanswered, we make excuses like "God is testing us," "He is making us wait," or "He is angry with us." We fail to see that our *concept* of God is not separate from us, but is rather a reflection of our own selves. Therefore, it has never had any power or control.

There have been two instances where a potentially new convert would easily say, "Yes" when asked if "above everything" means above "God". The first scenario is when the person is still engaged in sins such as addictions and alcoholism, or the spirit has found a substitute for the sin and has no intention of stopping. In this case, the person no longer meets the requirement, as they are continuing to rely solely on medications, therapies, advice, and other human solutions. They still hold onto the arm of the flesh.

The second scenario arises when someone has repented of their sins in the past and has been living in God's hands for some time, but they continue to sin. Some of us fall into this category. When asked if "above everything" means above God, we readily admit that it has been quite some time since we have repented of our sins as we continue to give in to them. Here, we must acknowledge that those of us who have repented and then continued to live as unrepentant sinners are no better than a person who stands in the nail-scarred hands of Jesus and insults Him by disregarding His sacrifice and mocking the nail holes in His wrists. By continuing to play "God" in our lives, we have made a mockery of Christ and salvation. This revelation usually shakes us to the core and prompts us to repent at once.

Returning to the task of establishing if you meet the requirement … above everything, we sinners must be rid of the spirit of selfishness, for it will lead to our destruction. Only with God's help can this spiritually disconnected life be made into a new creation. Despite our numerous moral and philosophical convictions, we were unable to live up to them on our own. After all, it was plain to see that many of us were raised better than we turned out. It is through God's grace and guidance that the plague of selfishness is overcome.

We asked ourselves, "What percentage of self-centeredness am I?" Anything less than one hundred percent indicates that we are still playing God and have not fully connected with Him. We cannot reduce our self-centeredness through our own willpower or efforts. We must acknowledge the true instigator of our spiritual disease or sin, which is the sinner within. If we now understand this, then we meet the requirement to proceed with taking the necessary steps to be rid of this sinful bondage. We had to have God's help.

As stated previously, just what do we do? Well, this is how and why we made the third step decision: we had to stop playing God. It did not work. In the previous paragraphs, we prepared ourselves for soul surgery and realized that we had been playing God in our own lives without even realizing it. Self, a soul tyrant, demanded mental and physical attention from us, destroying us and leading us to sin. For those struggling with alcoholism and addictions, it was now apparent that this spirit was playing

God all along. We were praying to ourselves, and it is no surprise that our *concept* of Jesus had only a fifty-fifty success rate. We would pray for the consequences to pass us by, but when they didn't, we had to make excuses for why God did not answer our prayers. It never dawned on us that God does not need propping up nor defending. He is God all by Himself.

It was a crushing realization that our prayers did not go beyond our minds because the self would not allow it. We had been deceived by the god of self. It was self who poured alcohol down our throats, opened the pill bottle, supplied the drugs, looked at the pornography, placed the bet on the table, and the list goes on and on. We were disgusted by this Self and were ready to have it removed once and for all. Now, we were ready for this next step!

Next, we decided that hereafter in this drama of life, God was going to be the Shepherd; we are His sheep. He is the Teacher; we are His disciples. He is the Lord; we are His subjects. He is the Master; we are His servants. He is the Father' we are His children. Most good ideas are simple, and this simple understanding was the keystone of the new and triumphant spiritual arch through which we were about to pass to freedom.

When we humbly accepted the role of a sheep, disciple, student, subject, servant, or child, we were right-sized. Miraculous things started to happen. God became our new employer, and we became His employees. When people asked us what the job was, we responded with calmness, "I don't know." These three words were powerful flailing to our ego. We were encouraged to remain in this state for as long as possible. It was as marvelous as having a fully paid college scholarship and living with supportive parents. Being all-powerful, God provides everything we need if we remain close to Him and perform His work well. Just how do we do this? We seek Him. He is in the seeking. How do we seek Him? Here are the steps we took.

Established on such a footing, we become less concerned with ourselves, our small aspirations, and designs. Instead, we focus on how we could make a positive impact on life. Offering our lives to the Power of the Holy Spirit, we enjoyed inner peace and discovered He has the ability to cope with the challenges of our lives, as we become more aware of His presence. As a result, we begin to see that our fear of the present, future, and even the afterlife was overcome. This was a rebirth, a transformation, a complete psychic change sufficient to overcome the bondage of self and sins such as alcoholism and addictions.

The Power that leads to happiness had been so elusive, and we wondered where and how to find it. We knew we needed it and saw that others had already found it. The third step revealed the necessary action into this Power, which made us contemplate whether to turn back or move forward. We learned that walking in total integrity and in the light of God's Word was the only way to experience true joy. But we didn't know how to accomplish that. When we removed our religious intolerance and keen ability to only see the hypocrisy in others, we saw that those who wholeheartedly follow the ways of God are overwhelmed with joy and seemingly never do wrong. They are always choosing the Lord's path, but how? God shows us the right way to live, by obeying His instructions with all our hearts. We longed for our lives to bring Him glory as we followed His holy instructions. Those who had taken these steps were never crippled by shame, drawing their strength from His principle. We began to thank Him with a heart of truth. We were learning about His righteous principle and wanted to be faithful to all that His Word was revealing. So, we pleaded with Him to never give up on us.

Before taking the third step, we carefully considered if we were ready to commit ourselves completely to God and find true happiness. We examined the prayer we were about to say on our knees.

Third Step Vow

"God, I offer my Self to Thee— to guide me and use me according to Your will. Free me from the bondage of self, so that I may fully submit to Your will. Overcome my difficulties and use them to bear witness of Your strength and grace, so that those I seek to help may see Your Power, Your Love, Your Way of life at work in me. May I always follow Your will, Lord!"

God, I. We realized that the vow begins with God, not with our own understanding, conception, or idea. We spoke to God as our new Master and acknowledged ourselves as the other party in this covenant. We recognized that God, regardless of any previous conception we may or may not have had, is the Power behind it all, and that true joy is only found by walking in total integrity according to His Word. When we call upon God, not our conception, we start to walk in the light of His Word, which is total integrity. This third step prayer fills us with joy and a passion for seeking Him. We never again do what is wrong and choose to follow the path of the Lord if we remain under this covenant. How do we do this? This is the prayer we prayed.

This is how God prescribes the right way to live, by obeying His principle with all our heart. We long for our lives to bring Him Glory as we follow His holy principle! We are never ashamed because we draw strength from His principle. We give thanks to Him from new hearts of love and truth. Every time we learn more of His righteous principle, we will be faithful to all that His Word reveals, and we know that He will never give up on us.

Offer ourselves. The act of offering ourselves as a living sacrifice is a symbol of complete surrender to God's will. By offering ourselves to Him, we recognize that He is the one in control and we are willing to follow His lead. As we obey God's Word, we experience the life-changing power of His grace in our lives. We become more aware of His plans for us, and our hearts are filled with understanding. The Lord's grace is always available to us. It is by His grace that sin is overcome. We continue to live according to His principle.

This prayer also reminds us that God's ways are always simple but not always easy. There will be times when we witness others breaking His way of life. The tragic hypocrisy is that it may even be some of us. Regardless, it is important for us to remain steadfast in our commitment to God, even when others around us are not following His path. We can take comfort in the fact that we are His beloved, and He will always guide us in what is right in His eyes as we continue to seek Him.

The flames of this spiritual altar burned with fervor! It demanded one who would be devoted to His principle. We understood what it meant to be cast out of society. The haughty and powerful had oppressed us without reason, but we had no fear, only trembling awe, for we had discovered the miraculous words contained within this step. The fire was kindled by His promises, which became a wellspring of our joy; the revelation of this offering thrilled us like one who had discovered hidden treasure. As we approached the fire, we despised every falsehood and hated every lie that our selves told us, for we were becoming zealous for walking in His ordered steps. This fire, kindled in our bones, would soon cause us to stop and praise Him throughout the day, for His ways are perfect! Great peace and well-being come to those who love His principle, and we shall never stumble again. We hungered for His salvation even more, for an unquenchable desire to please Him had been kindled in us. This fire created an indescribable love for His principle; our innermost being longed to follow His perfect commands! We pledged to keep His instructions and heed His counsel; all our ways would be laid bare before Him.

"To guide and use me according to Your will." From the midst of the fiery altar, we cried out to the Lord, asking Him to create a new life and mold us according to His will. As He created this new creature, He would be the guide. He is the potter, and we are the clay. He is going to use us according to His will. We were quickened when we remembered that His will was His thoughts. He was going to use us according to His thoughts. What was He thinking?

"Free me from the bondage of self." We desired to be freed from these chains of sins such as addictions and alcoholism and selfishness so that we could fully live out His divine plan. We trusted that the Almighty One would remove any obstacles that stood in our way so that we could be a testimony to others of His power, love, and way of life.

"So that I may fully submit to Your will." Our hearts were filled with a deep longing to follow the Lord as we presented this prayer to Him as an offering. We begged for more insight into His Word and pleaded for His intervention to rescue us from our own destructive tendencies. We vowed to fully submit and offer Him our joyful praises for all that He is teaching us, as His marvelous words become our new anthem of worship. We now do these things so that we may fully submit to His thoughts.

"Overcome my difficulties and use them to bear witness of Your strength and grace." With fervent faith, we asked that He lay His strong and gracious hand upon us, for we had made the conscious decision to abandon ourselves and follow His ways without reservation. We eagerly intertwined with His deliverance, knowing that His truth would sustain us in every circumstance. And though we might sometimes wander off the path, we trusted that the Lord would come after us, for we were His beloved. Our lives were to become testimonies of His mercy and grace.

"So that those I seek to help." On the potter's wheel, we were presented with a concept we had never even considered. We were now going to be seeking. Not only God but seeking others to help. We would be new creatures indeed.

"May see Your Power, Your Love, Your Way of life at work in me." Faith in the Word of God was present, firmly standing in the heavens and anchored to eternity. His faithfulness would become the Power that endures from generation to generation, and all that He created firmly testifies to His Love. Everything stands at attention by His decree, for all that He has made serves Him. He is the Way. His words are our deepest delight, and they did not give up even when all seemed lost. The profound revelations He is teaching us are unforgettable works, as they have kept us alive more than once. We acknowledge God in this place and at work in our lives.

"May I always follow Your will, Lord!" We pause this covenant prayer asking that we always follow His thoughts. For He is the Lord!

We were then presented with the question. If we are to always follow His thoughts, then what is He thinking? We were stunned and speechless. Most of our immediate answers were "I don't know." Well, that was obvious, judging by the way our lives had been lived! The question remained, "What is He thinking?" We immediately retreated into our own minds for the answer, as this was the familiar place that we always ran to in service of a now disgruntled and fearful task master, self. Only this time, we found no answer on how to truly know what the Creator of the universe was thinking.

This spiritual question reminds us of the recent soul surgery of the "above everything" previously discussed in that it is uncomfortable each time we are drawn out of ourselves and into the spiritual. But how are we to know what Jesus is thinking? Many of the religious bring up the great standard Sunday school answers such as prayer, seek, ask, or church. However, powerful, we had no idea how to use them properly. We simply had no idea how to figure out what God was thinking. After reaching a true point of, "I really don't know," we find ourselves with one last action. We were encouraged to ask. With that simple suggestion, we asked. And He responded. We were aghast at the idea that we had never thought about asking God what He was thinking. Not what was He thinking about us, but simply what was He thinking. It would change our prayers for the rest of our lives.

We now began to understand those three pertinent ideas that we had to be convinced of. We then had to think about whether we met the requirements. We were challenged with "above everything" and saw that we were indeed overcome with a spirit of self which had been driving us as a master does his slave. We were presented with a prayer which will drive self out and replaced it with a new Lord. There was freedom brewing in the air. We were becoming anxious to make the prayer. To take the third step action.

At this point, we get with this Holy Ghost-filled person and ask them to speak this prayer over us as we prepare to enter our own covenant with the LORD.

<u>Total Surrender: A Prayer of Dedication and Gratitude</u>

Dear Jesus,

I am joining this child in preparation to surrender completely to You. They are making You their Savior and acknowledging that they belong to You. They are offering their heart, their mind, their body, and their soul to You. May Your love and grace fill us and guide us in all that we do. Thank You for the salvation You have given us, and for the sacrifice You made on the cross. Help us to follow You wholeheartedly, and to serve You in all that we do. We trust in You, and we know that You will lead us on the path of righteousness. Thank You, Lord. Amen.

We seek to live our lives pleasing Him. Even though evil waits in ambush to destroy us, we set our hearts before Him to understand more of His ways. We have learned that there is nothing perfect in this imperfect world except His words, because they bring such fantastic freedom into our lives! And if we continue to have a remnant of Self left, we can see how this is already panning out to be a better life than the one that ran us into here.

Those who recover, experience immediate growth through the Word. God's hands have molded and shaped us into who we are today. His revelation light has enabled us to learn how to please Him more. His devoted lovers witness how He treats us and rejoice, as His words are intertwined with our hearts. We know that His principle is always right, even when He judges us. He fulfilled His promise to comfort us, His servant, with a kiss of mercy. We prayed for His tender love to help us persevere, as we took delight in His life-giving Truth. Our pride and dishonesty were exposed, causing us shame. We now recognized how these things oppressed us, all because of our passion for His way of life. His devoted servants followed us as we followed the path of His instruction. We asked Him to make us passionate and whole-hearted in fulfilling His every wish, so that we would never be ashamed of ourselves again.

We concluded the vow by committing to always do God's will or thoughts. Unlike other prayers, there will be no "Amen" at the end of this vow. As our brother Paul taught us, we should pray without ceasing. This means that even after we rise from our knees after praying the third step vow, we are still walking in constant prayer. Through walking under this covenant, our life gives thanks in everything we do, for this is God's will for us in Christ Jesus. He gives us life and His attention when we pray and ask Him to rescue us from our misery. We will never forget what He reveals to us. He defends and redeems us in our sufferings, just as He promised. As rank sinners, we were once far from salvation and ignored His message of truth. But God showed us His tender mercies and gave us life through the revelation of His principle of deliverance.

We realized that having an understanding person like our spouse, best friend, or spiritual advisor by our side when taking this spiritual step would be beneficial. The prayer's wording can vary as long as the idea of offering ourselves permanently to Jesus Christ is conveyed without reservation. This prayer is just the beginning, but when we make it honestly and humbly, we will feel its significant impact immediately. Let us pray.

CHAPTER 8

STEP THREE

*"We denied ourselves, took up our cross
and followed Christ."*
(Matthew 16:24)

*"Humble yourselves in the sight of the Lord,
and he shall lift you up."*
(James 4:10)

We were now at *step three*. Here is how we took it: we got on our knees, bowed our heads in reverence to the Master Jesus Christ, and closed our eyes so there were no distractions as a Holy Ghost-filled person led us in the following vow and we repeated:

"God, I offer myself to Thee— to guide me and use me according to Your will. Free me from the bondage of self, so that I may fully submit to Your will. Overcome my difficulties and use them to bear witness of Your strength and grace, so that those I seek to help may see Your Power,

Your Love, Your Way of life at work in me. May I always follow Your will, Lord!"

The gospel burst upon the scene the moment we got down on our knees and offered our lives to His consuming fire. The prayer is taken and then usually followed with silence as the new convert is allowed as much time as they need with the Lord. Once this holy time has ended, they will rise from their knees and return to the task at hand, which is taking these steps. Happy are we, for the world will call us blessed!

This is a perfect time to introduce the new convert to Jesus Christ and not who they think He is. It is as simple as saying, "[new convert], meet Jesus Christ" and then turning to the Spirit in the room and saying, "Jesus, meet [new convert]." For, after all, we "be" merely facilitators, having placed their hands into God's.

As Psalm 46:10 says, "Be still, and know that I am God: I will be exalted among the heathen, I will be exalted among the heathen, I will be exalted in the earth." Bring to the attention of the new convert that God is breaking the spiritual bondage of their conceptions. At this moment, some leave their conceptions behind and never look back, while others struggle with them until they finally fall away. It is only through completely surrendering ourselves to Jesus and seeking Him that we can truly be set free from our own limited *conceptions*.

Upon taking the third step towards our spiritual recovery, we became aware of the mighty breath of His Power moving upon us from a place beyond ourselves. We felt the weight of the bondages of self being lifted as they were destroyed by His consuming fire the moment we offered ourselves to Him without reservation. In humble prayer, for the first time, we approached God without seeking anything for ourselves. Looking back, we recognize that God has breathed new life into us. He had come to rescue us from our misery and defend us in our sufferings. He had redeemed us and was reviving us, fulfilling His promises to us. In our wickedness, we were far from this salvation, but God's tender mercies gave us life again through these ordered steps and this third step prayer.

Though we faced many enemies who persecuted us, we made a covenant to remain steadfast in following this path of **RECOVERY 5:12**. We grieve over our past faithlessness and that of others, but we walk in God's promises now. We pray that God sees our love for His instructions, and we are grateful for His tender kindness in breathing life into us once more. All His words are true, and every one of His righteous steps will prove to be everlasting. He reached down from on high and took hold of us; he drew us out of deep waters. He rescued us from our powerful enemy of selfishness, from our foes which were our own character defects, who were too strong for us. They confronted us on the day of our disaster, but the Lord was our support. He brought us out into a spacious place; He rescued us because He delights in us (Psalm 18:16-19).

This third step covenant remains with us. We must deny ourselves, take up our cross, and follow Christ. *Step three* required us to turn our thoughts and efforts over to God with the intent to never pick them up again. This step is the keystone under which lasting change is experienced. This can only be done once we realize that we are the sinners who caused the sins such as addictions and alcoholism that brought us to a place of utter defeat. It was here that the old man told us that all our religious upbringing did not automatically equal a life-changing experience with the Holy Ghost, one in which the Holy Spirit enters, fills us, and endues us with Power from upon high. However, it was necessary to come to the complete understanding that all our great ideas of who we or our mother conceived of God could not save us. We were struck with the proposition that if our concept of God was no bigger than a fifth of whiskey or some traumatic life event buried in our past, then we perhaps needed to consider that there is a God beyond our conception. We had to consider that there is a place we could come to where we were welcomed and cared for. That place is the breath of God.

We continued the path of repentance through *steps one, two,* and now *three.* We were poor in spirit, completely broken, and out of ideas. We had reached the bottom and we were amazingly still alive, and for what reason? God only knows. But here, in this realm of repentance, although we had no clue at this point in our journey, there was a promise already being applied to us. A promise that *step three* was going to be a blessing the moment we could look back on this point and see it clearly. We were blessed at the precise moment that we realized there was a Power and this Power is God. Only then were we truly submitting to His will. And to do His will is to receive the kingdom of heaven. But the Lord knows, we could not see any of this from the vantage point of complete brokenness. Do not be discouraged, many of us passed through this unknowingly. Keep taking the next step.

As we began taking this third step, we were called to this place, and in meekness, spiritual realities began manifesting. We see this in each step and measure along the Way. Once we said this prayer and offered ourselves to God, we found ourselves right in the middle of happiness because we were experiencing a new Way, a new Truth, and a new Life. We were becoming spiritually connected to our new Lord and Master, Jesus Christ. We were plugging in. The prophecy foretold upon us in this state is that people would call us blessed and inspirations. We could not see it at this point, but there was some action being taken in our spirits.

א ALEPH

The Power. The Power that we experience in the third step is the very breath of God. The breath He takes before He even utters a word. The very breath that He used to create the heavens and the Earth out of a void. The same breath that He used to create man. And the same breath he used as He called out our names. We realized that we were the one out of the ninety and nine. There was no one with us. We no longer had anyone. We were brought to this place with no other plans or ideas. This powerful spiritual position of submitting to this Power was the very breath that was being breathed into our hearts, which contained Power beyond our wildest inclinations. This breath would take on more action.

We were reminded that the Lord is near to those who are brokenhearted and crushed in spirit. We reassure you that when we feel powerless, God is our strength. We trust in the Lord with all our hearts, recognizing that His wisdom surpasses our limited understanding. The Power of *step three* reflects a heartfelt plea to God for inner renewal. To access this Power, we had to surrender our will as God aligned us with His will. We had to be still and recognize the sovereignty of God. It reminds us that as we relinquish the control we thought we had and surrender to God's guidance, He will be exalted and His divine purpose will be fulfilled. By embracing a posture of stillness, we open ourselves up to the life-changing working Power of the Holy Spirit in our lives.

The Spirit. This consuming fire of the Holy Spirit is what we offered ourselves to once we met the requirement to recognize that we were the ones who were wrecking our own lives. Many who come this way are unwilling to admit that they are truly spiritually disconnected and although they may have had an extensive religious upbringing, they cannot see why their previous religious experiences did not provide the necessary transformation that can only come from the Holy Spirit. At the very mention of His Name, the agnostics and atheists slam all their doors and windows shut of any understanding and the religious accept Him only after He can perform a few prescribed criteria developed by people before us that are blindly accepted as truth.

This third step experience is life-altering for both the theologically inclined and theologically adverse. This is the only place that these two warring tribes can agree. Until a position of meekness is adopted, little or no explanation can break through such spiritual prejudices. But the moment we are meek, discarding all our old ideas and becoming willing to believe there is a God and His Name is Jesus, miraculous things happen. It is this fire that fuels the altar upon which we offer up the sinner in our lives and this consuming fire begins a mighty work as we are transformed into new creatures humble, mournful, and now meek. May you experience the awesome power of this consuming fire as you navigate this beautiful step in the spirit.

ר RESH

The Prayer. There is a reverence that we stand in as we enter this third step prayer. It is on bended knee with heads bowed low to the majestic King of Kings, Lord Jesus Christ. In this reverence, we experience the bridge between the seen and the unseen. It is here where we bring ourselves to the feet of Jesus. Our temple is brought with hands wide open to this bowed experience and the Power flows in as the Holy Spirit consumes that which is of old and God begins building with us anew. We are on our way to the life He had intended for us this whole time.

Prayer allows us to entrust our paths and decisions to the Lord, believing that He intervenes along the way. Prayer is submitting ourselves to the authority of God as He uplifts us and brings about positive change in our lives. Prayer connects us to Jesus. Without this connection, we are unable to witness Him bear fruit in our lives or achieve meaningful transformation in our recovery journey. Prayer is trusting in the Lord wholeheartedly and acknowledging His presence in every aspect of our lives. By praying, we are surrendering our own understanding and leaning on God so we can experience the clarity needed for our recovery journey. Prayer connects us to God's grace which is more than enough to sustain us. When we pray, embrace our vulnerabilities, and rely on Him, we become vessels for His life-changing work.

The third step is about blessedness. In the context of recovery, the third step offers the ingredient for finding happiness even after going through challenging times. Here's how the third step applies to the recovery journey. Recovery involves discovering joy in life. It is the process of learning to appreciate the small ways God reminds us of His love, finding pleasure in recovery activities, and experiencing a newfound sense of happiness in recovery and salvation. The blessedness of the third step cultivates gratitude during the recovery journey. Gratitude practices help us focus on God's provision in maintaining a life subject to Him. As we progress in our recovery, we discover a sense of fulfillment of His purpose. Overcoming challenges leads to a deeper understanding of God and opens doors to new opportunities for happiness, service, and ministry to others.

Recovery involves letting go of our prejudices and embracing a life in Christ. The happiness in the third step serves as a reminder to seek joy and choose God's will along the recovery path. Finding happiness in recovery is fostered through building meaningful connections with others. Engaging in recovery groups, ministry, and building healthy relationships contributes to a sense of happiness through belonging.

Recovery involves loving Jesus and treating others with kindness. Embracing the happiness of the third step is a gentle reminder to be compassionate toward ourselves and others during the ups and downs of the journey, knowing that God provides a way of escape from every sorrow. Each step forward in recovery is a blessing and a cause for celebration for what God is doing in our lives. Embracing the third step is about celebrating progress and achievements, no matter how small they may seem. It's important to acknowledge that the recovery journey for us all is the same, but our experiences are unique to each of us, and not everyone will experience happiness in the same way. However, the third step serves as a source of inspiration and hope for those seeking blessings in our recovery process. It also reminds us that happiness is attainable and within reach as we take steps towards healing and growth.

Peace.

We look back on this step. To deny ourselves, take up our cross, and follow Christ, as mentioned in Matthew 16:24, requires a deep commitment to living a life surrendered to God's will and guided by the Holy Spirit. As Holy Ghost-filled recovered believers, here are some spiritual actions we take to embrace this calling. We begin each day with prayer, surrendering our lives and desires to God, and asking the Holy Spirit to lead us as we take up our cross of acceptance and surrender.

We immerse ourselves in the teachings of Jesus and the Word of God, studying the Gospel to understand Christ's life, teachings, and example. We dedicate time to fasting and prayer to draw closer to God and seek His will for our lives. Fasting is the catalyst that develops spiritual discipline and dependency on the Holy Spirit. We practice discernment and attune our hearts to the promptings of the Holy Spirit. We observe the Spirit direct our decisions. We strive to obey God's commandments and follow Christ's teachings. Obedience is an essential aspect of denying ourselves and living in alignment with God's will. We follow Christ's example of selfless service with compassion. We look for opportunities to serve and love others in our recovery community and beyond. We continuously examine our hearts and seek repentance for any sins and shortcomings. We forgive others as Christ has forgiven us. We connect with a supportive faith community that encourages spiritual growth. We cultivate a spirit of humility or selflessness. We seek to put others' needs before our own and be willing to learn from others who are spirit-filled believers. We trust in God's faithfulness as He helps us persevere through challenges. We seek the Holy Spirit to strengthen our faith as we walk the path of discipleship.

Remember that denying ourselves, taking up our cross, and following Christ is an ongoing journey of life change. It involves daily surrender to the Holy Spirit's empowerment. We are encouraged to be open to the Spirit's work in our lives. We seek to live in a way that reflects Christ's love, grace, and truth.

The principle we gain at the feet of God in this step is meekness. The promise we receive is inheriting the life that God intended for us. Humility is the Fear of the Lord; its wages are riches and honor and life (Proverbs 22:4). We now realize how this principle is the same thing that brought us to *step one*: admitting our powerlessness and surrendering to God. However, we cannot rely solely on humility without further action. We must work on taking these ordered steps. Faith by itself, if it is not accompanied by action, is dead (James 2:17).

CHAPTER 9

STEP FOUR

*We searched out and examined our
ways and turned again to the Lord.
(Lamentations 3:40)*

As we embark on this course of vigorous action, let us remember to ask God to:

*"Search me, O God, and know my
heart; try me and know my anxious
thoughts; and see if there be any
hurtful way in me, and lead me
in the everlasting way.
Psalm 139:23-24*

We must humbly offer ourselves to the Lord, not just with words, but with a strenuous effort to rid ourselves of the things that have been blocking us. Remind the new convert that anyone who conceals their transgressions will not prosper, but those who confess and forsake them will find compassion (Proverbs 28:13). In other words, if they start this journey on a lie, then all they will achieve is a lie. Therefore, we must face our shortcomings and sins, confess them all to God, and seek His forgiveness. Only then can we inherit the life that God intended for us. Our sins such as addictions and alcoholism are but a symptom of the greater issue. So, we have to get down to the causes and conditions of our trespasses so that the Lord can add to us another righteousness.

We performed a quick survey of our lives. We opened the Bible up to Galatians 5:19-21. We used the King James Version. We made a checklist of the manifestations of the flesh. Next to each manifestation of the flesh, we placed Strong's Concordance Lexicon number associated with each word and then selected at least one definition. This seems intimidating, which is why it was imperative that we went through it with a Holy Ghost-filled believer who could aid us with obtaining and using these biblical resources. Then we scoured through the lexicon words for meanings that we could understand and labeled our lives where applicable. Then we placed a checkmark by each manifestation that we had or were currently committing. It looked something like this example:

	MANIFESTATION	STRONG'S	MEANING
✓	ADULTERY	G3430	FAITHLESS SEX
✓	FORNICATION	G4202	SHAMELESSLY IMMORAL SEX
✓	UNCLEANNESS	G167	IMMORAL THOUGHTS
✓	LASIVIOUSNESS	G766	EXCESSIVE SEX
✓	IDOLATARY	G1495	VICES
✓	WITCHCRAFT	G5331	DRUGS; MAGIC
✓	HATRED	G2189	HATEFUL
✓	VARIANCE	G2054	QUARREL
✓	EMULATIONS	G2205	JEALOUSY
✓	WRATH	G2372	INDIGNATION
✓	STRIFE	G2052	PROVOCATION
✓	SEDITIONS	G1370	DISAGREEMENT
✓	HERESIES	G139	DISUNITY; TEAR APART
✓	ENVYINGS	G5355	ILL-WILL; SPITE

✓	MURDERS	G5408	KILLING A PERSON; CHARACTER ASSASINATION
✓	DRUNKENNESS	G3178	INTOXICATION
✓	REVELLINGS	G2970	LETTING LOOSE

We then asked ourselves, who was committing these manifestations? We followed that with probably the same person who was placing the check marks. We discovered it was perhaps us. We would find out much more as we continued this path.

In *step four*, we examine ourselves to uncover the truth about our sins or shortcomings, and to rid ourselves of them promptly and without regret. We cannot deceive ourselves about the true nature of our wrongdoings, and we need the help of God to accomplish this. We approach God with the humility of the third step, acknowledging the seriousness of this step, and ask Him to search our hearts and reveal to us any of our ways that are offensive to Him. With God's guidance, we strive to follow the path of everlasting life. God begins searching us and knowing our hearts. He immediately begins trying us and knows our thoughts. He sees all the wicked ways in us and leads us in the way everlasting. Again, there was no "Amen" in that third step prayer. Therefore, we are currently experiencing what it means to walk in the covenant we have established in Christ.

ב BET

As we stood in repentance of the first three steps, in complete humility, we were aware of the stains of sins such as addictions and alcoholism on our lives. These sins were a part of our past and had a hold on us, causing us terror, bewilderment, despair, and frustration. In this fourth step, we were introduced to the concept that our bodies are temples. We now realized that our repentance was evidence that our bodies were being made into sacred temples, being prepared to receive the Spirit of Holiness. Through this miraculous experience, we were filled with the Holy Spirit, and we no longer belonged to ourselves, but to God, who purchased us with the precious blood of Jesus Christ. Therefore, we use our bodies, minds, souls, and spirits to bring glory to Him. Or do you not know that our body is a temple of the Holy Spirit within us, whom we have from God? We are not our own, because we were bought at a price. So, we glorify God in our body (1 Corinthians 6:19-20).

The true joy that we sought was hidden beneath the ruins of our past. We struggled to find a way to stay pure and holy. We would discover that we could only achieve this by living in the Word of God and walking in His truth. But we could not do this with all the wreckage of our pasts blocking the way. We longed for God with all our hearts, and He would be the one who would keep us on the right path. We began to treasure His Word in our hearts so that we would not sin against Him using alcohol and drugs. But we had to remove the refuse which filled our hearts. He is our great God, and we praised Him above all else once our hearts were purged of the remnants of our useless lives in sin. We prayed that He would continue to teach us His power through these steps and measures, and we spoke of His principle continually, reciting His counsel out loud. We found more joy in following His commands than in pursuing all the sinful riches of our previous lives. We set our hearts on His ordered steps and measures, paying close attention to all His ways. We delighted in His principles, and we walked in His words. His Word is a lamp at our feet and a light to our path (Psalm 119:105). In this way, we got to the action needed to remove this wreckage of our past.

ב NUN VS. נ NUN

We recognized that our desire to jump straight into righteousness without first humbling ourselves in this fourth step was misguided. Instead, God's plan from *step one* for us was to walk in humility before Him, to clean our temples, and to seek His righteousness. In humility, we learned that our true strength comes from being connected to Him and submitting to His will. We humbled ourselves before the Lord, and He lifted us up (James 4:10). Humility teaches us that fear of the Lord is the beginning of wisdom, and knowledge of the Holy One is understanding (Proverbs 9:10). Through humility and submission to God, we gained true wisdom and understanding. Then we could walk in His righteousness. Otherwise, we would have jumped right into our cluttered righteousness, felt our own "power", and then thought we had connected ourselves to humility with misplaced faith that would lead only to futility. This became revealed more and more as we cleared away the wreckage of our past.

י YOD VS. א ALEPH

The cleansing of our temple was reminiscent of the question we were asked at the beginning of this step, which revealed that we did not know that our bodies are temples of the Holy Spirit, who is in us, and whom we have received from God. We are not our own; we were bought at a price. A high price was paid: destruction of self. The *step one* experience flooded our minds. This is why we honor God with our bodies (1 Corinthians 6:19-20). As we cleaned our temple, we discovered the faith that the Holy Spirit is at work in us, and we were honoring God with our bodies. We discovered this because we would soon find that He is accomplishing things for us we could never do. It is not Power that we are seeking in here as in *step three*, but rather willingness.

מ MEM VS. ו VAV

This was a new discovery! This spark we experienced in *step one* came from the unseen. It was the willingness needed to save us from ourselves. He sent from above, and He took us, He drew us out of many waters (Psalm 18:16). Therefore, we immediately thought that we were connected to the unseen. But this had not happened yet. We would soon behold the glorious manifestation of the Almighty God once this step had been thoroughly and honestly taken! From the heavenly realms, He graciously descended upon us, reaching out with His mighty hand to rescue us from the vast tumultuous waters within that threatened to engulf us. With His divine power, He lifted us high above the waves of our defects of character, freeing us from the depths of our own despair. This could only lead to our rejoicing and offering praise to the Lord, for His unwavering love and deliverance had granted us salvation. This would overflow into our walk of faith. Therefore, the womb was open, and the overflowing would begin.

י YOD VS. נ NUN

As you see, our willingness to take the necessary steps to cleanse our temples was an act of faith. Now, willingness is confidence in what we hope for and assurance about what we do not see. As in our *step one* experience, we may not have seen the full picture of what lay ahead in this fourth step, but we had confidence in God's plan and were willing for Him to guide us. Humility was not the tool needed here. Once we became willing, there was only two things that stood in our way. Those two things were spirit and opportunity. Neither of these were designed to be obstacles. Therefore, we began putting forth the necessary effort in this step.

נ NUN VS י YOD

Once we went through this process of cleansing and building, our willingness was converted into faith before our very eyes. In this step, like in *step two*, we experienced God's righteousness, because it is in the heart of the gospel that the righteousness of God is revealed. It is a righteousness that is by faith from first to last, just as it is written: the righteous will live by faith (Romans 1:17). *Step one* resounds in our ears. Verily, I say unto you, without humility, willingness, and overflowing faith, our temple cannot be made clean. God opposes the proud but shows favor to the humble (James 4:6). Through righteousness, we come to understand the importance of willingness which is the size of a grain of mustard seed growing into an overflowing faith. Faith leads to His righteousness, which is prepared to fill our temple. Without faith, it is impossible to please God because anyone who comes to Him must believe that He exists and that He rewards those who earnestly seek Him (Hebrews 11:6).

Through our crying out in prayer of the first step, this spark of God or faith generates the needed humility. It was the unseen force that appeared as soon as we realized that we had been utterly defeated and bowed in reverence to the only one who could help us, the King of Kings. In the third step, we humbled ourselves, and therefore, under God's mighty hand, He lifted us up in due time (1 Peter 5:6). As the fifth step will soon demonstrate, faith transforms the once barren womb into a virgin womb, ready for new life. It was becoming apparent that these steps were our seeking. We could not experience one without the other. Thus, we were prepared to take the next step on our journey of spiritual growth.

We honestly took this fourth step, as we searched our hearts for any flaws that caused our failures. Through humility, we identified where our own selfishness manifested itself as bitterness, fear, and immorality. Our own selfishness had defeated us, and we were going to see its manifestations in our lives in these steps. Therefore, with the Lord's help, we tried to complete this fourth step examination as thoroughly and quickly as possible. We realized that without faith, we could not overcome these manifestations of self. All of us had become like one who is unclean, and all our righteous acts were like filthy rags; we all shrivel up like a leaf, and like the wind, our sins sweep us away (Isaiah 64:6). Thus, we knew that we needed God's help to see ourselves clearly and to be cleansed from our sins. So, we searched within and began to see some of the most common manifestations of flesh.

Bitterness is the number one offender of the manifestation of flesh. It is the root of many spiritual diseases that plague alcoholics, addicts, and all manner of sinners. In fact, it is the most destructive offender of flesh. From bitterness stem all forms of spiritual disease such as adultery, fornication, idolatry, drug use, hatred, variance, emulations, wrath, strife, seditions, heresies, envying, murders, drunkenness, reveling, and such. Our temple had been not only mentally and physically ill, but we had also been spiritually sick. We warn against the consequences of allowing bitterness to take root in our hearts. If we bite and devour one another, beware, or we will be consumed by one another (Galatians 5:15). We have seen the list of the fruits of the flesh and its manifestations (Galatians 5:19-21). To overcome this spiritual malady, we had to first recognize it and be willing to deal with it. Humility, not righteousness, was key in this process, as it required us to honestly examine ourselves and our actions. We had to set aside our pride and egos and ask God for help.

Some of us still balked at the idea of writing our sins down. If we had to be honest, we would say that we simply could not do the paperwork that was given to us. We may have felt like we could fill out the parts about who had hurt us, but when it came to who we had hurt, we just could not find the willingness. We were full of fear because it would bring up stuff that made us upset. Some of these traumas were so severe that they would conjure dreams about things that happened years ago.

We were quickly reassured that it is a tough road to walk but there is so much freedom the Lord wants us to have in Him. One of the things He showed us along this path is how much we hold ourselves hostage to events that are no longer occurring. It makes us shut them behind closed doors in our minds, yet they slip out from time to time. When they do, our minds recreate the events and without even knowing it, we feel as though the events from years and years ago are reoccurring in the present moment. This is a trick of the enemy. So, the Holy Spirit walks with us as we identify events that are no longer happening, and we bring them out of the closet and place them on paper. When we remove them from the dark corners of our minds and write them down on paper, we bring them to the Light.

In dealing with bitterness, it was willingness that enabled us to list them. We took our paper and created the first column by listing people, institutions, or principles with whom we were angry or bitter. Once we created this list, we made a second column and asked ourselves why we were angry, and the list overflowed. In most cases, it was found that our pride, self-esteem, security, pocketbooks, ambitions, personal relationships, and sexual relations were hurt or threatened, which composed the third column. So, we were sore, we were "burned up." Oh, did we make lists!

This would be our grudge list. Overall, bitterness is a dangerous spiritual disease that destroys us from the inside out. But with God's help and the willingness to confront it, He overcomes it and delivers healing for our temple.

On our grudge list we created a second column and set opposite each name our injuries. Then a third column was developed to identify the areas of our lives that had been affected by this bitterness. This column was broken into five sub-columns which allowed us to further examine whether it was our pride, self-esteem, security, pocketbooks, ambitions, personal relationships, or sex relations that had been interfered with.

Because this can be confusing to our fog-riddled minds, we were usually as definite as this example:

BITTERNESS INVENTORY: THE GRUDGE LIST							
Column One	Column Two	Column Three					Column Four
		Affects my:					Our own mistake:
		Pride or Self-esteem	Security or Pocketbooks	Ambitions	Personal Relationships	Sex Relations	
I'm Bitter at:	The Cause:						

Name	Description	1	2	3	4	5	6	7	8
Tim Brown	His attention to my wife, Melinda. Told my wife of my mistress. Tim Brown may get my job at the office.	X	X		X				
Tonia Jones	She's a nut—she snubbed me. She committed her husband for drinking. He's my friend. She's a gossip.	X		X					
My employer, Jerry, CEO of Seaside Hospital	Unreasonable—Unjust—Overbearing—Threatens to fire me for drinking and padding my expense account.	X	X						
My wife, Melinda Rogers	Misunderstands and nags. Likes Tim Brown. Wants house put in her name.	X	X		X	X			

Therefore, we heard this and followed this newfound willingness with action by doing what they suggested. We went back through our lives. We were building upon a foundation. If thoroughness was the mortar of our foundation, then honesty would be the sand. Considering this, nothing counted but thoroughness and honesty. Because without them both in following these simple instructions, we would be foolish and be building this house upon mortar or sand alone, and the rain will descend, and the floods will come, and the winds will blow and beat upon this house, and it will fall and great will be the fall of it! If you start this journey with a lie, then all you will end up with is a lie. The scent of righteousness began to grow strong.

Verily, when we finished writing our grudge list, we reflected upon it with great care. It was apparent that the first column contained a list of people, institutions, or principles with whom we held anger or bitterness. In the second column, we acknowledged that the world and its inhabitants were often unjust and in the wrong. However, in our self-righteousness, we failed to progress beyond this point. We were trapped with the bitter root that prevented us from moving on and we remained in a state of anguish. At times, we felt remorse, which we directed towards ourselves. In this examination, we realized that we must include ourselves in the first column and even our concept of God. We fought and struggled to have our own way, but this only worsened matters. It was as if we were in a war, and the victor only appeared to win.

False humility had us playing a game where one person would punch the other until they said, "Uncle." However, in this game, we were punching ourselves repeatedly in the eye until we cried out, "Uncle!" We lifted our bloody fists in triumph, but these moments were brief. Self-pity would soon interrupt our victories, reminding us of our flaws, which we were trying so desperately to overcome. Nonetheless, the essential spark of change still eluded us. We were reminded that each heart knows its own bitterness, and no one else can share its joy (Proverbs 14:10). We had to search ourselves further.

It is written that bitterness is like a root that grows deep and spreads wide, defiling many. It is said that bitterness causes trouble and defiles many others around us (Hebrews 12:15). We came to realize that our bitterness not only made us mentally and physically ill but also spiritually sick. We learned that a heart filled with bitterness could not receive the Holy Ghost and that harboring such feelings shut us off from the blessings of God (Ephesians 4:30-31). We found that to be bitter was to be in spiritual bondage to sins such as addictions and alcoholism, which leads to death (Romans 6:23). Therefore, we took heed of the warning given to us by the prophets of old, and included in our lists all bitterness, anger, and malice in our hearts, so that we might be renewed in our minds as we would cast these things out in the next step. We were told that if we sat with our anger for any length of time it would often reveal itself as grief. Then from grief to self-pity. From self-pity to self-delusion. Then self-delusion leads us right back to our life of sin and bitterness.

In these steps, we confessed our sins and then we asked God to cleanse us from all this unrighteousness. Through taking these steps, we forgave those who wronged us and prayed for those who despitefully used us, knowing that vengeance belongs to the Lord (Matthew 5:44). But not to worry, we will continue to walk alongside you. The anticipation is just too exciting not to tell of these steps.

As we humbled ourselves before the Lord through the first three steps and into this fourth step, we cast away all bitterness. In the following steps, we found that our minds were renewed, and our hearts were filled with the peace that surpasses all understanding (Philippians 4:7). We learned that the only way to overcome bitterness is through the Power of God's Love, which covers a multitude of sins (1 Peter 4:8). To live a life free from anger and bitterness, we must turn to the teachings of the Bible. We are advised to be swift to hear, slow to speak, and slow to wrath (James 1:19-20). This means that moving forward, we should take the time to listen to others before reacting, and not allow our anger to control us. We were told to take the cotton out of our ears and put it into our mouths. We were also instructed to put away all bitterness, anger, and malice, and instead be kind, tenderhearted, and forgiving (Ephesians 4:31-32). This reminded us that just as God has forgiven us through Christ, we should also forgive others. Listening became a virtue we had to painstakingly learn.

But how can we let go of the bitterness and anger that has taken root in our hearts? The answer was simple but not easy. We can do all things through Christ who strengthens us (Philippians 4:13). By turning to God and relying on His strength, we watched Him overcome even the most deep-seated bitterness and anger. In the next steps, we prayed for the Holy Spirit to fill us with peace and joy, and to help us let go of our anger and forgive those who have wronged us. Ultimately, we bore with each other and forgave one another if any of us had a grievance against someone else. We forgave as the Lord forgave us (Colossians 3:13).

To overcome bitterness, we had to turn to a different perspective and approach. We had to examine our grudge lists and recognize that the world and its people had dominated us, as evidenced by the second column. We realized that holding onto the wrongs done by others, whether imagined or real, had the power to destroy us. We needed to find a way to master these forms of bitterness, but it wasn't as simple as just wishing them away.

We resolutely looked for our own mistakes. We reviewed each piece of bitterness in our lives and asked ourselves, "Where was I selfish, dishonest, self-seeking, and fearful in this relationship?"

We referred to the example:

BITTERNESS EXAMINATION: THE GRUDGE LIST									
Column One	Column Two	Column Three					Column Four			
		Affects my:					Our own mistake:			
I'm Bitter at:	The Cause:	Pride or Self-esteem	Security or Pocketbooks	Ambitions	Personal Relationships	Sex Relations	Selfish	Dishonest	Self-Seeking; Self-Seeking; Seeking Gain	Fear
Tim Brown	His attention to my wife, Melinda. Told my wife of my mistress. Tim Brown may get my job at the office.	X	X			X	x	x	x	X
Tonia Jones	She's a nut—she snubbed me. She committed her husband for drinking. He's my friend. She's a gossip.	X			X		X	x	x	X
My employer, Jerry, CEO of Seaside Hospital	Unreasonable—Unjust—Overbearing—Threatens to fire me for drinking and padding my expense account.	X	X					x	X	X

| My wife, Melinda Rogers | Misunderstands and nags. Likes Tim Brown. Wants house put in her name. | X | X | | X | X | X | x | X | | x |

This fourth step, which includes the examining of our own faults and shortcomings, is in line with what the Bible teaches us. Jesus says, "Why do you look at the speck of sawdust in your brother's eye and pay no attention to the plank in your own eye? How can you say to your brother, 'Let me take the speck out of your eye,' when all the time there is a plank in your own eye? You hypocrite, first take the plank out of your own eye, and then you will see clearly to remove the speck from your brother's eye" (Matthew 7:3-5).

By looking at our own faults and shortcomings, we are taking the first step towards His righteousness, which is an important aspect of overcoming bitterness. Pride goes before destruction, a haughty spirit before a fall (Proverbs 16:18). When we are willing to examine ourselves and our own faults, we humble ourselves before God and before others which will be essential as we take these steps.

In searching, we notice that the word "fear" is identified in the grudge list alongside the difficulties with Mr. Brown, Mrs. Jones, the employer, and the wife. This simple word manages to permeate every aspect of our lives. It is a malevolent and destructive force, intertwining itself into the very fabric of our existence. Its presence sets off a chain reaction of events that lead us to experience undeserved misfortunes. Yet, if we examine our own actions honestly, did we not set this chain of events into motion ourselves? Fear should be viewed as akin to stealing from God, as it brings about even more trouble and turmoil in our lives. What are we to do with them?

We reviewed our fears thoroughly. We put them on paper, even though we had no bitterness in connection with them.

fear EXAMINATION		
Column One	Column Two	Column Three
List of fears		
Being Alone		
Relapsing		
Going to Jail		
Children Not Loving Me		

We asked ourselves, "Why do I have these fears?" and completed column two.

fear EXAMINATION						
Column One	Column Two	Column Three				
		Mark X if it did not relieve the fear				
		Self-Reliance	Self-Confidence	Cockiness	Trusting in Self
List of fears	Why do I have these fears:				
Being Alone	Every one of my relationships that I get in always ends up messed up.				
Relapsing	No matter how hard I try, I always relapse.				
Going to Jail	I am afraid that I will have to go to jail for the things that I have done.				
Children Not Loving Me	I have been a horrible parent to my children. I am not sure how they will forgive me.				

Did we not rely on ourselves for our very survival? We trusted in our own abilities and self-confidence, but it wasn't enough to conquer our fears. Even when we were at our most confident and self-assured, the spirit of fear still had a grip on us. We learned that self-reliance was good as far as it went, but it didn't go far enough. We began to mark an "X" in column three under each of the areas that we exercised daily for our very survival.

Up to this point, it was obvious that our past was filled with us relying solely on ourselves. That is never enough. In this light, we came to realize that we were egomaniacs with inferiority complexes, thinking we could solve our problems on our own while also waiting for help that was not coming. We suffered from grandiose self-loathing. Our great revelation was that this may have been our best efforts, and it still couldn't explain why we still had this list of fears. Therefore, we had no other action but what would later become our first, which is to trust in the Lord with all our hearts and lean not on our own understanding; in all our ways, we submit to Him, and He made our paths straight (Proverbs 3:5-6).

We are learning that it is better to take refuge in the Lord than to trust in humans (Psalm 118:8), even ourselves. We had to learn to rely on God and seek refuge in Him, rather than trusting solely in our own abilities. Therefore, we continued and were usually as definite as this example:

fear EXAMINATION					
Column One	**Column Two**	**Column Three**			
		Mark **X** if it did not relieve the fear			
List of fears	**Why do I have these fears:**	Self-Reliance	Self-Confidence	Cockiness	Trusting in Self
Being Alone	Every one of my relationships that I get in always ends up messed up.	x	x	x	X
Relapsing	No matter how hard I try, I always relapse.	x	x	x	x
Going to Jail	I am afraid that I will have to go to jail for the things that I have done.	x	x	x	x
Children Not Loving Me	I have been a horrible parent to my children. I am not sure how they will forgive me.	x	x	x	x

Perhaps there is a better way—we think so. More shall be revealed as we take these steps.

Meanwhile, what about sex? Sex is the sacred reserved act. It is a gift from God to be enjoyed. However, just like any other gift, it can be misused and become a source of temptation and sin. Flee from sexual immorality. All other sins we commit are outside the body, but when we sin sexually, we sin against our own body. We did not know that our bodies are temples of the Holy Spirit, who is in us, whom we have received from God! We are not our own; we were bought at a price. Therefore, we are designed to honor God with our bodies (1 Corinthians 6:18-20). This was a concept we thought we had neatly evaded or disregarded all together.

As humans, we are prone to temptation and sins such as addictions and alcoholism, and sex is no exceptions. It is important to exercise self-control and discipline in this area, and to overcome any struggles we may have. We cannot do any of this until our ideals become rooted in the Holy Ghost. We must also respect the sanctity of this gift and refrain from engaging in any sexual conduct without asking God.

This is where our egos and instincts immediately aligned with any source that spoke to the contrary. We searched for explanations and rationalizations galore. We explained instincts that we had only heard about and yet saw that our sex problems could not improve with any of these ideas. We had to have God's help. Without His help, we could only go into our own heads and guess what the creator of the universe would say about our sex problems. We would discover that it was not a matter of whips and chains or candy and games that God was interested in. He had the perfect plan and partner for us if we would only seek Him.

We treat sex as we would any other problem. Whom have we hurt, and was sex involved? We listed each sex relation. We reviewed our conduct involving sex over the years. In column one, we made a list of whom we hurt, and whether sex was involved. This was our sex relations list. Next, we asked ourselves, "What was my conduct involving this sex?" Much like the example below:

IMMORALITY EXAMINATION			
Column One	Column Two	Column Three	Column Four
Whom did we hurt and sex was involved? We list our sex relations:	What was our conduct involving this sex?		
Jo	Cheated on them		
Pat	Used them for sex, drugs, and money		
Jean	Lied to them, didn't really love them		
Shelby	Slept with their cousin		
Myself	Can't stop watching porn		

Column three, in these sex relations, we asked ourselves, "Did we unjustifiably arouse jealousy, suspicion or bitterness? Did we use our sex powers lightly or selfishly? Was our sex power despised and loathed?" We then marked an "X" under each applicable area as in this example:

IMMORALITY EXAMINATION						
Column One	Column Two	Column Three			Column Four	
		In these sex relations did we…				
Whom did we hurt and sex was involved? We list our sex relations:	What was our conduct involving this sex?	Unjustifiably arouse bitterness, jealousy, or suspicion?	Use our sex powers lightly or selfishly?	Despise or loath our sex powers?		
Jo	Cheated on them	x	x	X		

Pat	Used them for sex, drugs, and money	X	x	x				
Jean	Lied to them, didn't really love them	x	x					
Shelby	Slept with their cousin	x	x					
Myself	Can't stop watching porn	x						

We then asked ourselves, "Where were we at fault? Were we selfish, dishonest, or inconsiderate?" We then marked the answer accordingly.

IMMORALITY EXAMINATION							
Column One	Column Two	Column Three			Column Four		
		In these sex relations did we…			Where were we at fault? Were we…		
Whom did we hurt and sex was involved? We list our sex relations:	What was our conduct involving this sex?	Unjustifiably arouse bitterness, jealousy, or suspicion?	Use our sex powers lightly or selfishly?	Despise or loath our sex powers?	Selfish?	Dishonest?	Inconsiderate?
Jo	Cheated on them	x	x	X	x	x	X
Pat	Used them for sex, drugs, and money	X	x	x	x	x	X
Jean	Lied to them, didn't really love them	x	x		x	x	X
Shelby	Slept with their cousin	x	x		x	x	x
Myself	Can't stop watching porn		x		x	x	x

We got this all down on paper and looked at it. In this way, we would soon see how our pain and sorrow would be converted into our very testimony, one to never be added to nor taken away from. This testimony would be the very catalyst that would take us through the rest of our journey and become the soap box that we will climb upon to tell the world of the goodness of God.

We were on the cusp of experiencing true joy, but how could we remain pure in the eyes of the Lord? We knew that only by following His Word and taking these steps could we hope to resist the temptation of sins such as addictions and alcoholism. Our hearts burned with a passion for God, and we resolved to hold fast to His teachings and keep them close to our hearts. We knew that His Word was the greatest treasure and that it would protect us from the snares of the devil. We would soon see Him working in our lives as we continued working through these steps.

Blessed be the Name of the Lord, who has given us His counsel and shown us the steps to righteousness. We will not stray from His directions, but will instead recite His wisdom to ourselves constantly, so that we may be reminded of His goodness and grace. Through these steps, thus far, we are finding true joy in obeying the Lord and living according to His will, rather than in the fleeting pleasures of this world.

His Word is a lamp at our feet and a light to our path (Psalm 119:105), and we will soon have hidden His Word in our hearts so that we might not sin against Him (Psalm 119:11). We delight in the Lord and His ways, because in His presence there is fullness of joy; at His right hand are pleasures forevermore (Psalm 16:11). May we never forget this journey in His Word and may His Spirit always guide us.

Step four involves us taking a fearless and searching examination of ourselves, with the help of God's guidance. We become willing to face the truth about our faults and admit them to ourselves and to God in these steps. We recognize that we cannot change on our own and that we need the help of Jesus Christ. We also acknowledge that we have harmed others and become willing to make amends to them as we take these steps.

In *step four*, we took the time to reflect on our successes and strengths, recognizing that these are gifts from God. We learned to be grateful for all that we have and to use our strengths for His glory. As we continued this journey, we learned to rely on God's strength and wisdom. We realized they were never ours. We experienced true freedom and joy in living according to His will.

Step four was a turning point for us, as we realized the importance of identifying our sins and shortcomings. Taking these steps helped us confront the things that we had been avoiding or denying and face the facts of our actions. We now saw how these past behaviors affected ourselves and others, and we soon sought to make amends wherever possible in these steps. Through this process, we gained a deeper experience of God's character and His desire for us to live holy and upright lives. We have come to recognize the areas in our lives where we have fallen short, and we are striving to see our weaknesses overcome with God's help.

As we continue to walk in His ways, we are growing in our knowledge and love for Him. We are learning to trust Him more fully and to surrender our lives to His will. *Step four* is a humbling and life-changing experience, and we are grateful for the opportunity to bring these flaws to Him as we seek His forgiveness and healing.

Step four revealed to us our own weaknesses and faults. We were no longer blind to the areas of our lives that needed healing and transformation. But we took heart, knowing that God is faithful to complete the work He started in us. We were willing to lay down our pride and humbly submit to His leadership, knowing that His ways are higher than ours. By taking this step, we were also being equipped with a testimony to help others who may struggle in similar ways. We speak from experience and share the hope and healing that we have found in God's Word. We pray that all who come after us may also find the joy and freedom that comes from walking in His ways. We trust that as we continue to take these steps and measures, God will continue to guide us and transform us into the image of His Son. We are grateful for the privilege of knowing Him and serving

Him, and we give Him all the praise and glory as He separates us unto Him.

In the first step, our faith started as a small spark from God. Now, in this step, our faith has grown, and we have developed a willingness to follow His will. As we receive more revelation from Him, our faith overflows, and we learn how to serve Him better. It brings us joy to see how others observe God's treatment of us, and we firmly believe that His Word is becoming even more deeply rooted in our hearts. Through our faith, we come to understand that God's judgment is always right, even when it is directed at us. Nonetheless, we remain steadfast in our belief in His righteousness, which is embedded within us.

In this step, we humbly ask God to show us His mercy, and we have complete trust that He will comfort us as His devoted servants. We have faith in Him to fulfill His promises to us. This step strengthens our faith, as we know that God loves us tenderly and empowers us to continue. We find joy in His life-giving truth. We reject the arrogant lies we once told ourselves and the self-reliance that burdened us. We have faith that others will also follow this path of God's guidance. Through our faith, He ignites our passion! We wholeheartedly commit to fulfilling His every desire, and we will never feel ashamed again.

In the fourth step, we begin to see more of His righteousness, just as it was revealed in the second step. Righteousness is the shining light of truth. This concept has already taken hold in our hearts, and we are beginning to understand the seed that has been planted in us. It is becoming more and more clear that this seed has fallen on good soil. We have heard and fully embraced the message of the Kingdom. He is aligning our lives to bear His good fruit, and we see Him yield a harvest thirty, sixty, and even one hundred times greater than what has been sown deep within our hearts.

His righteousness is implanted in our hearts as the guiding light of truth, and it continues to direct our choices and decisions through these steps. It is a lifelong commitment, providing us with righteous rules to live by. In these steps, we acknowledged our brokenness and humbly surrendered to the living Word, which is breathing new life into us. What we once saw as an inventory of pain and sorrow is now being transformed into a testimony through these steps. We asked the Lord for guidance at the beginning of this step, and we are grateful for the revelations He has given us on how to best serve Him.

We are aware that if we do not complete this step, our lives will tilt back toward our old ways, but if we continue to follow what God teaches us, the balance will be weighed in our favor. The ungodly spirit has been trying to throw us off track, but we remain steadfast in our determination to obey God fully and forever. The steps and measures we have been given are like treasure, bringing joy and gladness to our lives. We are still enveloped in a pink cloud of grace as we remain committed to God's will. We are convinced of the third step's three vital issues that have brought us thus far, and we are grateful for His righteousness that is being established in our hearts, providing us with the guidance we need to see Him bear good fruit through us and allowing us to live a fulfilling life in service to Him.

This fourth step is not an easy one to take. However, if we are thorough and honest in asking God to reveal anything in our hearts such as bitterness, fear, or immorality that is blocking us from being useful servants to Him and others, then we would have written down a lot. Before and after each examination of bitterness, fear, or immorality, we asked God to intervene. Before, we asked God to bring into our minds any manifestation of flesh that stands in the way of our usefulness to Him and other people. Once we thought we completed each examination, we stopped in silence and asked God to please search our hearts and bring to the surface any manifestation of flesh that we need to address. It is in these moments that we are sure to quickly write down anything the Holy Spirit reveals to us, regardless of the value of the thought, even if it was a simple thought of how we once were five years old and we took a penny candy from the corner store and got caught. We could easily place little value on this thought and brush it away. However, we caution against such folly, for anything that the Holy Spirit deems worthy should be written down. Now, we took this searching examination and tried it. We tried it by sitting with someone who is Holy Ghost-filled and understands the errand that we were on. This brought us to the next step.

The fourth step's change from "pain and sorrow" to "strength" is the journey from a place of hardship, struggle, and pain to a place of inner strength and hope. We went into the fourth step with great "pain and sorrow" early in the recovery journey, where we confronted and acknowledged the depth of our struggles. In recovery, it's essential to be honest and open about our vulnerabilities and pain. This vulnerability is the steppingstone towards recovery and salvation. The fourth step acknowledges pain, along with the need for the Holy Ghost and His help during challenging times. In recovery, seeking support from friends and family is crucial. As we progress through our recovery journey, God gives us perseverance, learning to face difficulties with determination.

Do not be disconcerted, the journey from Benoni to Benjamin involves a deep seeking of the inner presence of the Holy Spirit. As we confront our pain, we uncover inner strengths and resources we never knew God had given us. Embracing the fourth step's strength represents the growth that occurs during recovery. Life changes from Benoni, which is pain and sorrow, to Benjamin, which is strength, signifies finding purpose in the recovery journey. It is the transition from pain and sorrow to a life with renewed strength. The name Benjamin is a source of inspiration for others who are going through their own challenging times. It shows that even in the midst of pain, there is strength for change. It signifies the emergence of a more resilient person. Benjamin can also be seen as an encouragement to build a supportive environment that fosters service, ministry, and recovery. Surrounding ourselves with positive influences is crucial for a successful recovery.

Overall, the transition from Benoni to Benjamin embodies the essence of recovery, where we confront our pain, seek support, and discover our God-deposited inner strength. While the journey is unique for each of us, the transformation creates healing, growth, and strength for recovery.

Leaving the realm of repentance in *steps one, two*, and *three*, we carried this new position into a realm of remission. We walked into the fourth step and immediately got to writing and capturing our sins in black and white. This was a daunting task. Now we took them into the next step and admitted them to God, ourselves, and another human being. Many of us balked at this step, feeling the pink cloud of grace from repentance, and started to move on with our lives only to find that Grace is not to be mocked by continuing sinning.

The overarching principle for *step four* changes from the being poor in spirit of the previous steps into a promise of mourning, which is much the same as that experienced in the second step. We couldn't see it then, but we were blessed because we mourn. Throughout *steps four, five*, and *six*, this would be the overarching principle that guided us. Anytime along the way that we did not feel comfortable, we recalled why we mourned, and He comforted us. If we took these steps as directed, then our hearts grieved because we sinned. Although the Lord promises to console us, we must never forget the mourning because He has already brought us a mighty long way.

Longsuffering.

As we look back on this step, to "search out and examine our ways and turn again to the Lord" as stated in Lamentations 3:40, we take spiritual actions to engage in self-reflection, repentance, and renewal. Here are some steps we take. We dedicate time to prayer and meditation, asking the Holy Spirit to reveal areas of our lives that need examination and repentance. We confess any sins or areas of disobedience to God. We repent sincerely, turning away from sinful behaviors and attitudes. We pray for the Holy Spirit's wisdom in understanding His ways and submitting ourselves to God's will. We study the Bible to gain insight into

God's character, His expectations for His people, and the example of Jesus Christ. We engage in fasting to seek God's presence and draw closer to Him. Fasting focuses our hearts and minds on spiritual matters. We begin considering engaging in Spirit-filled worship, praising God for His mercy, grace, and forgiveness. Worship becomes an expression of our desire to return to the Lord wholeheartedly. We pursue revival through times of consecration and seeking God.

We now are positioned to observe the Holy Spirit renew our hearts and rekindle our passion for God. We are at a point as we work through this process to begin sharing our journey with trusted believers who can support and hold us accountable in our spiritual walk. We demonstrate our commitment to turning back to the Lord by showing love and compassion to others and seeking opportunities to serve and care for those in need. We make searching and examining our ways an ongoing practice, regularly trying ourselves by seeking the Holy Spirit's guidance to keep our hearts and lives aligned with God's purposes.

Remember that seeking God's forgiveness and turning to Him is a continuous process. God's love and mercy are abundant, and He welcomes a repentant heart with open arms. We watch the Holy Spirit work in us, leading us on a path of service, ministry, and a changed life.

As we roll up our sleeves in *step four*, withholding nothing, we approach this searching examination with the hunger and thirst of a dying man. We are hungering and thirsting after the righteousness that was implanted into our hearts in *step two*. We want more! The heartfelt mourning coupled with hungering and thirsting after righteousness changes the fourth step searching into a craving for righteousness. As we approach this step with this mindset, the game changes and we are filled with promise. When we seek God's ways just as a starving and parched person seeks food and drink, if we seek God that much, we are always satisfied by His presence in Jesus' Name.

Now that we have our pain and sorrows written down, what shall we do about them? Here is the step we took.

CHAPTER 10

STEP FIVE

*"We confessed our faults one to another, and prayed one
for another, that we may be healed. The effectual fervent
prayer of a righteous man avails much."*
(James 5:16)

In *step five*, we confess our sins to God and to each other and pray for one another. This leads to healing. Let us reflect on our journey. In the fourth step, we examined ourselves and acknowledged our brokenness. But what comes next? Our goal is to seek a deeper and more effective spiritual experience with the Lord, one that will transform us into new creatures in Christ. We are seeking a transformation of the mind sufficient for permanent recovery. The Lord shall add to us another righteousness.

אALEPH

The Power. The Power we experienced in the *third step*, the very breath of God, is now being applied to our *fourth step* examination. His breath tries us. The breath He takes before He even utters a word. The very breath He used to create the heavens and the Earth out of a void. The same breath He used to create man. And the same breath He used as He called out our names. We now know that we were the one out of the ninety and nine and that He has come to save us.

For the next step, we had to have someone who was Holy Ghost-filled journey with us. We were no longer going through this alone. We were brought to this place after using all the efforts He supplied in the *fourth step*. None of these were our plans or ideas. This powerful spiritual position of submitting to this Power was the very breath that was being breathed into our hearts which contained Power beyond our wildest imaginations. This breath took on more action.

We were reminded that the Lord is near to those who were once brokenhearted and crushed in spirit. We reassure you that when we felt weak and powerless, we were reminded to stop and seek God. For He is the only one who grants us strength. We trust in the Lord with all our hearts, recognizing that His wisdom surpasses our limited understanding. The Power of *step five* reflects a heartfelt examination and trying of ourselves for God and inner renewal. To access this Power, we had to confess our faults as God aligned us with His will. We had to be still and recognize the sovereignty and mercy of God. It reminds us that we never had control, we only thought we did. We surrendered to God's guidance, He was exalted, and His divine purpose was fulfilled as we prayed for one another and were healed by His Power. By embracing a posture of stillness, surrender, and confession, we opened ourselves up to the life-changing working Power of the Holy Spirit in our lives.

The great truth is that this Holy Spirit experience created a new attitude toward life, other people, and the Name of Jesus. We also established a new relationship with God. This means we were absolutely certain that the Holy Spirit had entered into our hearts and lives in a way that was indeed miraculous. How could we be sure? Because we saw Him accomplish things in our lives that we could never achieve on our own.

This Holy Spirit experience is characterized by a significant emotional shift in us that displaces and rearranges our old ways of thinking. The ideas, emotions, and attitudes that once were the guiding forces of our lives were miraculously cast to the side and replaced by a new set of beliefs and motives. These new beliefs and motives rooted in Christ began to dominate us. Our pain and sorrow became our strength – a testimony is being built.

As we prepared to embark on the fifth step of **RECOVERY 5:12**, we were reminded of the importance of confessing our sins to God and to one another. This act of confession is rooted in Scripture; therefore, in the fifth step we confessed our sins to each other, prayed for each other, and were healed. The prayer of a righteous person is powerful and effective (James 5:16).

The names of the steps are revealed throughout. Each letter of each name can be seen in each step and measure. They are rooted within a tabernacle pattern of old. However, we don't get distracted by the deep. We return to the task at hand.

Through our fourth step examination, we identified the obstacles that stood in the way of our recovery. Next, we prepared to confess our sins; He is faithful and just and forgives us for our sins and purifies us from all unrighteousness (1 John 1:9). We had to acknowledge these sins. But how?

By taking this fifth step confession, we open ourselves up to the healing Power of God's grace and mercy. We read of the importance of confessing our sins: then we acknowledged our sins such as addictions and alcoholism to God and did not cover up our iniquity. We said, "I will confess my transgressions to the Lord." And He forgave the guilt of our sins such as addictions and alcoholism (Psalm 32:5). We remembered these words: Whoever conceals their sins does not prosper, but the one who confesses and renounces them finds mercy (Proverbs 28:13). Therefore, we confessed our sins and sought the mercy and healing that comes from a humble and contrite heart.

We may think that we have done enough by admitting our sins to ourselves, but we often need the accountability of another person. As iron sharpens iron, so one person sharpens another (Proverbs 27:17). By confessing our sins to a trusted Holy Spirit-filled friend, we removed the sin blockage in our hearts and God recovered us. He overcame our struggles. The main reason why we confess our sins to another person is that it helps us avoid backsliding. If we claim to be without sins such as addictions and alcoholism, we deceive ourselves and the truth is not in us. If we confess our sins, God is faithful and just and will forgive us and purify us from all unrighteousness (1 John 1:8-9). Confessing our sins to another person helps us stay accountable to our spiritual journey, and it allows us to receive forgiveness and healing from God.

Jesus warns about the dangers of leading a double life and putting on a false persona to deceive others. He says, "Woe to you, teachers of the principle and Pharisees, you hypocrites! You are like whitewashed tombs, which look beautiful on the outside but on the inside are full of dead men's bones and everything unclean. In the same way, on the outside you appear to people as righteous but, on the inside, you are full of hypocrisy and wickedness" (Matthew 23:27-28). As stated at the beginning of this journey, the apostle Paul also acknowledges the struggle of living a double life. We do not understand what we do. What we want to do, we do not do, but what we hate, we do. And if we do what we do not want to do, we agree that the principle is good. As it is, it is no longer we ourselves who do it, but rather sin such as addiction or alcoholism living in us. We know that nothing good lives in us, that is, in our sinful nature. We have the desire to do what is good, but we cannot carry it out. Now, if we do what we do not want to do, it is no longer we who do it, but it is sins such as addictions and alcoholism living in us that do it (Romans 7:15-20). This is insanity.

We cannot overstate the importance of the fifth step's scripture: confessing our sins to one another and praying for each other, as it leads to healing. The prayer of a righteous person holds tremendous power and effectiveness (James 5:16). Though it may be challenging, this step is vital for our recovery. We must be merciful both with ourselves and with others. When we conceal our sins, we hinder our recovery, but when we confess and renounce them, we experience divine mercy (Proverbs 28:13). Our secrets keep us sick. Without honesty about our struggles, we cannot live fulfilling lives in this world. It is crucial to choose a trustworthy Holy Spirit-filled individual to confide in, for it is better to have someone to help us up if we fall (Ecclesiastes 4:9-10).

Step one is where we first cried out. Now in step five, out of our mouths came the words of faithful confession that would change the course of our lives. Some say that from the moment that we opened our mouths and began to confess there was faith that flowed into and from within us. The physical temple we carried was filled with light for the very first time.

When we confess, we are expressing our heartfelt plea and desperation for help. It involves acknowledging that we are facing difficulties beyond our own ability to handle. Confessing is a form of surrendering our self-reliance and recognizing our need for divine intervention. We emphasize that when the righteous confess, the Lord hears and delivers them from all their troubles. We can assure you that God is attentive to the confessions of His people and is ready to come to our aid.

In *step five*, confessing is instrumental in initiating the process of change. By recognizing our limitations and reaching out to God and another Holy Ghost-filled human being, we acknowledge that we cannot overcome these challenges alone. It is an act of humility, allowing us to seek a solution beyond our own capacities. When we confess, we unknowingly align ourselves with the belief that God hears our confessions and delivers us from troubles, and we cultivate the seed of faith in the life-changing power of divine intervention. This provides a foregone motivation needed to take the necessary steps toward change. At the time of our confessions, we did not know it, but we were trusting in God's assistance to be present throughout our journey.

This glimmer of hope that came the moment we confessed introduced us to a God who created His people, calls us by name, and declares that we are His. The Word describes how God promises to be with us through challenging times, assuring us that we will be overwhelmed by a different kind of waters and consumed by a fire burning deep down in our souls. This confession equipped us with the power of seeking. We were immediately encouraged to ask, seek, and knock, assuring us that if we ask, we will receive, if we seek, we will find, and if we decide to put forth effort, the door will be opened to us. As we confessed, we had unknowingly exhibited the faith to approach God's throne of mercy with confidence unaware, and we received mercy and found mercy to help in this moment of need.

Having a reliable and understanding confidant to share our struggles with holds great value. Truly, there is immense power in confessing our sins to one another and praying for each other. By opening up and sharing our struggles with another person, we invite the mercy of God to flow into our lives, bringing recovery. The fifth step's scripture urges us to confess our sins to a trusted follower of Christ, through which we can gain fresh insights into our challenges and discover a way forward (James 5:16). This person can pray with us and for us, offering encouragement on our journey. Seeking an understanding disciple of Christ allows us to benefit from this mutual sharpening. Let us not fear confessing our sins to one another, as it leads to the healing that God graciously offers. Finding a follower of Jesus Christ who can provide a safe space for us to be honest results in genuine recovery. People stumble for lack of guidance, but victory is found in the abundance of counselors (Proverbs 11:14). Similarly, seeking support from a wise disciple of Christ helps us overcome obstacles. As we share our struggles and seek accountability with a trusted confidant in Christ, let us also extend mercy to others. Let nothing be done through selfish ambition or vain conceit. Instead, in humility, let us value others above ourselves

(Philippians 2:3). By holding ourselves accountable while treating others with kindness, we foster authentic relationships that support our recovery.

We must exercise discernment when selecting the right person to confide in regarding our sins. We have been warned about those who gossip and reveal secrets, advising us not to associate with babblers (Proverbs 20:19). It is crucial that the person we confide in can keep our confessions confidential. Furthermore, they should understand our intention to confess and seek healing. Plans fail without wise counsel, but with many advisors, they succeed (Proverbs 15:22). Therefore, before proceeding with our confession, we should prayerfully consider seeking advice from wise people. Our goal is not to seek approval or validation from others, but to find recovery through God's mercy and forgiveness.

The connections along the path were uncanny because when we were standing in *step four* searching ourselves, the humility of *step six* rushed in and provided the fuel for the rest of *step five*. These steps seemed to become one. When we humbled ourselves and acknowledged the need for confession, we wasted no time in finding a suitable person to share our story with. Most of these steps and measures work the same way.

We came to *step five* prepared with a written fourth step examination and were willing to engage in a long talk, explaining to our pastor or disciple of Jesus Christ who the Holy Ghost is upon why we must do this. It is an urgent matter of life and death, and we must approach it with utmost seriousness. Those disciples who are approached in this way will likely feel honored and privileged to be trusted with our confidence and will be glad to help us on our journey toward recovery and salvation.

What once was a barren life full of pain and sorrow was about to become a virgin womb overflowing with purpose. We pocketed our pride and went to it, illuminating every twist of character, every dark cranny of the past. We made the call and began removing the root of bitterness. This number one offender of the manifestation of the flesh was the first to begin to receive our blows of recovery!

We now got going with a prayer partner and disciple of Jesus Christ as we enabled *step five*. This was our course: we pulled out our Bitterness Examination or the grudge list and began testing it. We immediately realized that the people who wronged us were perhaps spiritually sick. Though we did not like their symptoms and the way these disturbed us, they, like ourselves, were unwell.

We were usually as definite as this example:

BITTERNESS EXAMINATION: THE GRUDGE LIST									
Column One	Column Two	Column Three				Column Four			
		Affects My:				Our Own Mistake:			
I'm Bitter At:	The Cause:	Pride or Self-esteem	Security or Pocketbooks	Ambitions	Personal Relationships	Sex Relations	Selfish	Dishonest	Self-Seeking; Seeking Gain	Fear
Tim Brown **(SS)**	His attention to my wife, Melinda. Told my wife of my mistress. Tim Brown may get my job at the office.	X	X			X	x	x	x	X
Tonia Jones **(SS)**	She's a nut—she snubbed me. She committed her hus- band for drinking. He's my friend. She's a gossip.	X			X		X	x	x	X
My employer, Jerry, CEO of Seaside Hospital **(SS)**	Unreasonable— Unjust — Overbearing — Threatens to fire me for drinking and padding my expense account.	X	X					x	X	X

| My wife, Melinda Rogers (SS) | Misunderstands and nags. Likes Tim Brown. Wants house put in her name. | X | X | | X | X | X | x | X | | x |

It was shocking to see that most of the people on our grudge list were indeed spiritually sick. What were we to do about these people? Jaws dropped when it was suggested that we pray for these spiritually sick people. Therefore, we placed this list of the convalescent before us and in that instant, God took our grudge list and converted it into a prayer list right before our eyes. We agreed to ask God.

We were directed that anytime we ask God that it should be done so out loud for we were familiar with the power of crying out to the Lord from our *step one* experience. With the list of spiritually sick people before us, we prepared for our prayer. We were told when we said this prayer that God inclined His ear towards us, and the inhabitants of heaven stop and turn their direction towards the Lord's interest. Therefore, we prayed for each spiritually sick individual on our prayer list out loud, knowing that this powerful action was going to change everything for these people's lives along with ours. This was so serious an action that should we stumble during the prayer for any one of these spiritually sick people, that we should immediately correct ourselves and begin the prayer again. Not because we were seeking some sort of perfection but because we knew that the remnant of sins such as addictions and alcoholism would cause us to stumble on some of the more difficult individuals on our prayer list. Furthermore, we made note of those people who caused us to stumble in our prayer. These would be the very persons who would remain in our prayer life until we are released from this burden by God.

We had to ask God to help us because we had no idea how to be helpful to these spiritually sick people. He had to show us because we had no experience from which to draw how to show spiritually sick people anything other than the grudge, we had previously held for them. We named the person individually. This eliminated words like mom, dad, family etc. We had their names listed and now we had to pray for them individually. Unless it was an institution or concept, then we would name them directly. We were asking God to help us show these spiritually sick people the same tolerance, pity, and patience that we would cheerfully grant a sick friend. We had to learn of these ideas and concepts.

First, we had to be educated on what tolerance was. Paul teaches us that we should recognize that as we have embarked upon this spiritual journey that we have become a prisoner of the Lord and are walking in the manner worthy of the calling with which we have been called, with all humility and gentleness, with patience, showing tolerance for one another in love, being diligent to preserve the unity of the Spirit in the bond of peace. Tolerance of these spiritual sick people meant being diligent about preserving unity regardless of who they are or what they did. Paul turned up the heat as he admonishes us that we have no excuse, every one of us who passes judgement, for in that which we judge another, we condemn ourselves, because we who judge practice the same things. And we know that the judgement of God from *step two* rightly fell on us who once practiced such things. But be sure that when we pass judgement on those who practice such things and do the same ourselves, do we think that we will escape the final judgement of God? Or do we think lightly of the riches of His kindness and tolerance and patience, not knowing that the kindness of God is what has led us through repentance? As the Lord heals us through this process, we are no longer spiritually sick and no longer suffer stubbornness and an unrepentant heart. We are no longer storing up wrath for ourselves in the day of the righteous judgment of God. This tolerance was about kindness towards those on our newly found prayer list.

Then there was pity for these spiritually sick people. The Lord made this lesson simple. He reminds us that He forgave us all that debt, because we desired Him: should not we also have compassion on others, even as He had pity on us up unto this point? The answer was of course it was. Pity was about having compassion on these people not because of who they are or what they have done but because they are spiritually sick too.

Finally, there is patience. This virtue has eluded us most of our lives. The old man told us that we must have a warehouse full of bran new unused patience because we seldom knew how to use it. Yet, we somehow know that now we are intertwined with God under the covenant of *step three* and that He is good to those who wait for Him – to the soul that seeks Him. For He is in the seeking. This patience was the simple description of the most complex thought of us being like Jesus toward others. Even the spiritually sick ones.

The prayer went something like this:

> *"God help me show __Tim Brown__ the same tolerance, pity, and patience that I would cheerfully grant a sick friend."*

After praying for everyone on our prayer list, we felt even more of this new power begin to work in our lives. We are encouraged to always approach others with a spirit of compassion, recognizing that we are all struggling in our own ways. God will help us to let go of criticism, and instead offer a listening ear and a helping hand to those in need. He guides us in our interactions with others and gives us the wisdom to know when to speak and when to listen. We are to be a source of comfort to those who are hurting, and we always strive to show the love and kindness of Jesus in all that we do. We thank God for His constant presence in our lives, and for His unending grace and mercy. We continue to grow in our relationship with Him, and in our ability to love and serve others.

As we turn our hearts to Jesus Christ, we recognize that addictions are a spiritual sickness that requires His healing touch. This is why we are about to confess our sins to each other and have begun praying for others so that we may be healed. We take this step in faith, knowing that our prayers are heard and that angels are dispatched to fulfill them. But we also recognize that there are powers that withstand us, and we may face delays in our recovery journey's answered prayers. However, we know that through Christ, we are more powerful than any force that would seek to keep us in bondage. As we pray for ourselves and others struggling with addictions, we trust in the promise that the righteous cry out, and the

Lord hears them; He delivers them from all their troubles (Psalm 34:17). We believe that our prayers are being answered, and we experience the freedom that only Jesus can provide. In His Name, we pray for victory over sin such as addictions and alcoholism.

We were then given a very important spiritual tool which is left for us after experiencing this sick person prayer. This tool applies to every instance we are offended. When someone is offending us, we can now recognize that they are perhaps spiritually sick. We immediately turn to God and ask how we can be helpful? Because no matter how long we have been living for Jesus Christ, we still do not know how to be helpful to those spiritually sick without His aid. He must show us. But we do ask Him to save us from being angry because our response to this type of offense in seasons past only led to anger and confusion. Then we ask Him what His thoughts are and that they (not our thoughts) be done.

When we are offended, we pray:

> *"Lord, this is a sick person, help me to see them with love. Show me how I can be helpful to them. Save me from anger or frustration. Thy will be done. Amen.*

If we seek Him daily and apply this spiritual tool to every offensive situation, we will see that bitterness never establishes root in our souls again.

We strive to avoid any desire for revenge or argument, recognizing that such behavior would not befit our role in helping those who are spiritually sick. We draw inspiration from the example of Jesus, who embraced each of His children with kindness and love. If we harbor bitterness towards someone who is not spiritually sick, we acknowledge the harm we have caused and seek to make amends. Unbeknownst to us, we were beginning to compile a "harms list" of those we have hurt, whether they are spiritually sick or not. This would be reviewed as we eventually take steps eight and nine committing to doing what we can to make things right.

Returning to our prayer list, we see that at times, we held grudges against entire organizations such as the police or the church. But upon closer examination, we discovered that it was usually a particular individual or group of individuals within those institutions that we were bitter towards. In our attempt to be the center of the universe, we played God and attributed the actions of these few individuals to the entire organization.

It also became clear why we had listed ourselves and our *concept* of God on our bitterness list. Through *Step three*, we realized that we had been playing God in our lives. Our *conception* of God was flawed because we *thought* we were the ones in control, not God. We made excuses for God's lack of involvement in our lives, when, it was our own flawed conception that was the problem. This realization was shocking and overwhelming, but it was necessary to gather ourselves and move forward in our recovery. In Jesus' Name, we ask for the strength to continue to seek healing and grow closer to God.

Putting out of our minds the wrongs others had done which we had listed in column two. We removed column two and crumpled it in the first of six crumpled balls of paper.

	BITTERNESS EXAMINATION: THE PRAYER LIST								
Column One	Column Three					Column Four			
	Affects My:					Our Own Mistake:			
I'm Bitter At:	Pride or Self-esteem	Security or Pocketbooks	Ambitions	Personal Relationships	Sex Relations	Selfish	Dishonest	Self-Seeking; Seeking Gain	Fear
Tim Brown	X	X			X				
Tonia Jones	X			X					
My employer, Jerry, CEO of Seaside Hospital	X	X							
My wife, Melinda Rogers	X	X		X	X				

We resolutely looked for our own mistakes. We reviewed each bitterness and asked ourselves, "Where was I selfish, dishonest, self-seeking, and fearful in this relationship?" Our lives seemed scripted in each of these situations. We found that we were selfish because we wanted something from the individual with total disregard for them, their thoughts, or feelings. We typically then did something dishonest such as lie, cheat, or steal from them or ourselves. This sometimes involved us stealing time from ourselves for the years that we held these people hostage to events that were no longer occurring in our lives. We were dishonest because we wanted something from the person and the answer that followed that statement exceeded the self-seeking actions of most people. The fear was that the truth would be revealed, and the truth was not about the other person or what they did at all. The root of bitterness was planted by ourselves and we nourished each tentacle until we could no longer see that it was not them or what they did but rather a result of our own mistakes.

BITTERNESS EXAMINATION: THE PRAYER LIST									
Column One	Column Three					Column Four			
	Affects My:					Our Own Mistake:			
I'm Bitter At:	Pride or Self-esteem	Security or Pocketbooks	Ambitions	Personal Relationships	Sex Relations	Selfish	Dishonest	Self-Seeking; Seeking Gain	Fear
Tim Brown	X	X			X	x	x	x	X
Tonia Jones	X			X		X	x	x	X
My employer, Jerry, CEO of Seaside Hospital	X	X					x	X	X
My wife, Melinda Rogers	X	X		X	X	X	x	X	x

Though a situation may not have been entirely our fault, we tried to disregard the other person involved entirely. Therefore, we removed the first column and set it to the side so that it would not be a distraction. We would potentially be adding to this column during the next two examinations and they all would be reviewed again in *step eight*. What we were left with was:

BITTERNESS EXAMINATION: THE PRAYER LIST								
Column Three					Column Four			
Affects My:					Our Own Mistake:			
Pride or Self-esteem	Security or Pocketbooks	Ambitions	Personal Relationships	Sex Relations	Selfish	Dishonest	Self-Seeking; Seeking Gain	Fear
X	X			X	x	x	x	X
X		X			X	x	x	X
X	X					x	X	X
X	X		X	X	X	x	X	x

Now, we can see our faults as we listed them. We placed them before us in black and white. We admitted our wrongs honestly and were willing to set these matters straight. God then revealed the areas of our lives that were affected. He showed us each time our pride or self-esteem, security or pocketbooks, ambitions or relationships had been affected. And when each of those areas of our lives were affected, we immediately showed up on the scene and brought our entire flesh arsenal with us – selfishness, dishonesty, self-seeking, and fear!

God then reminded us that we had given our lives over to His care and direction in *step three*. Furthermore, He reminded us that, because of this covenant, He would be responsible for our pride or self-esteem, our security or pocketbooks, our ambitions, our personal relationships, and our sex-relations. Our lives were now His business. We knew this to be true because it resonated within our spirit. We were then reminded to stay out of God's business as He was managing our lives, and He did not need our help. He really drove the point home when He said that He was not even taking applications for help in controlling our lives. He reminded us of the covenant we made when we offered our will and lives to Him in *step three*. Afterall, *step three* is where the Power of Christ and the preaching of the gospel burst upon the scene as we got down on our knees and offered our lives to His consuming fire. We then removed God's business as listed in column three. We crumpled it into our second ball of paper and put it in the center of the table.

Now we were left with the spiritually disconnected causes and conditions of our bitterness. There it was further broken down before us. Sins such as addictions and alcoholism in their purest form. The root and all its tentacles.

BITTERNESS EXAMINATION: THE PRAYER LIST			
Column Four			
Our Own Mistake:			
Selfish	Dishonest	Self-Seeking; Seeking Gain	Fear
x	x	x	X
X	x	x	X
	x	X	X
X	x	X	x

And just like that, the exact nature of our wrongs sat in front of us in black and white. It was our selfishness, dishonesty, self-seeking, and fear which had been the instigator and maintainer of all our bitterness. Now the truth that had been overshadowing us was becoming clearer. We were the producers of our confusion. We wanted this truth to stop staring at us, but God said, "Not yet!" And so, we kept this fourth column in front of us as we moved onto the next testing of ourselves.

RESH

Prayer. We learned of its power in *step three*. There is a reverence that we stand in as we stare down at the exact source of our bitterness. Only prayer will deliver us from this selfishness, dishonesty, self-seeking, and fear. We were ready to return to bended knee with heads bowed low to the majestic King of Kings, Lord Jesus Christ. In this reverence we had already experienced the bridge between the seen and the unseen which is able to deliver us from our bitterness. It was here where we would bring ourselves to the feet of Jesus in the next couple of steps. The source of our bitterness was prepared to be brought with our hands wide open to this bowed experience. We now knew that the Power would flow in as the Holy Spirit consumed that which was of old and God began building with us as He saw fit. We experienced mercy.

Prayer allows us to entrust our source of bitterness to the Lord, believing that He intervenes and guides us along the way. Prayer is submitting ourselves to the authority of God as He uplifts us and brings about positive change in our lives. Prayer connects us to Jesus. Without this connection, we are unable to witness Him bear fruit in our lives or achieve meaningful transformation in our recovery journey. Prayer requires trusting in the Lord wholeheartedly and acknowledging His presence and guidance in every aspect of our lives. By praying, we are surrendering our own understanding and leaning on God so we can experience the direction and clarity we need for our recovery journey. Prayer connects us to God's grace which is more than enough to sustain us. When we pray, embrace our vulnerabilities, and rely on His power, we become vessels for His life changing work. The source of our bitterness is removed.

Now, we prepared ourselves to approach God and ask Him to remove our fears. We recognized that our reliance on Him and our faith in His power are the keys to overcoming fear and finding faith. With confidence, we brought our fears before Him, knowing that He is able to provide the courage we needed to face them.

Next, we recklessly looked at fear. We listed our fears in column one and then asked ourselves why we had them in column two. Realizing that we may have or once had great self-reliance, self-confidence, cockiness, and trust in ourselves, we asked ourselves if any of these eliminated, or even reduced, our list of fears.

fear EXAMINATION					
Column One	**Column Two**	**Column Three**			
		Mark X if it did not relieve the fear			
List of fears	Why do I have these fears:	Self-Reliance	Self-Confidence	Cockiness	Trusting in Self
Being Alone	Every one of my relationships that I get in always ends up messed up.	x	x	x	X
Relapsing	No matter how hard I try, I always relapse.	x	x	x	x
Going to Jail	I am afraid that I will have to go to jail for the things that I have done.	x	x	x	x
Children not loving me	I have been a horrible parent to my children. I am not sure how they will forgive me.	x	x	x	x

For starters, we had to see that everything in column three, which included our self-reliance, self-confidence, cockiness, and trust in our finite selves, did nothing for our fears. It could not reduce it and in some instances only made matters worse.

Next, we tore the three fear columns into separate pieces of paper. With each column side by side, we began by reviewing the list of fears in column one. Unbeknownst to us, these fears could be found on most anyone's list of fears. Regardless of gender, ethnicity, or creed, we all experienced the same spirit of fear in ourselves. As we looked at why we had these fears in column two., we looked for the producer of this fear.

We began identifying and circling all the "I," "me," "myself," and "mine" words in each of the reasons why we had these fears. God then began to reveal a common denominator in why we feared! This was astonishing to us. We were literally so self-centered that we were conjuring events in our lives, fancied or real. Then we would attach these events to people, places, things, or concepts. And just like that, fear was magically brought into our lives. So, we continued to review these incantations.

fear EXAMINATION					
Column One	**Column Two**	Column Three			
		Mark X if it did not relieve the fear			
List of fears	Why do I have these fears:	Self-Reliance	Self-Confidence	Cockiness	Trusting in Self
Being Alone	Every one of my relationships that I get in always ends up messed up.	x	x	x	X
Relapsing	No matter how hard I try, I always relapse.	x	x	x	x
Going to Jail	I am afraid that I will have to go to jail for the things that I have done.	x	x	x	x
Children not loving me	I have been a horrible parent to my children. I am not sure how they will forgive me.	x	x	x	x

God revealed that if our lives were to be absent of the fears listed in column one, we should simply turn column one over and let it be blank...

fear EXAMINATION					
Column Two	Column Three				
	Mark X if it did not relieve the fear				
Why do I have these fears:	Self-Reliance	Self-Confidence	Cockiness	Trusting in Self	
Every one of my relationships that I get in always ends up messed up.	x	x	x	X	
No matter how hard I try, I always relapse.	x	x	x	x	
I am afraid that I will have to go to jail for the things that I have done.	x	x	x	x	
I have been a horrible parent to my children. I am not sure how they will forgive me.	x	x	x	x	

We would have to be rid of the author of events in column two as well. And after circling the "I" statements, we saw very quickly who the author was. Therefore, we turned column two over too...

fear EXAMINATION			
Column Three			
Mark if it did not relieve the fear			
Self-Reliance	Self-Confidence	Cockiness	Trusting in Self
x	x	x	X
x	x	x	x
x	x	x	x
x	x	x	x

The author of our confusion stood alone and had been brought into the light before us. The spirit of fear was retreating, and it was plain to see that God had not given us this spirit, but we had nourished it. This then made it abundantly clear what sins such as addictions and alcoholism were in our lives. Here were the four ingredients of fear. To be rid of them, we turned column three over. And there before us were three blank columns.

Here we were asked, "What do you see?" We replied, "Nothing...a blank slate!" They told us, "This is faith." And to operate here takes great courage. God would reveal more about this in the next step.

Now, we had to be rid of column three, or else these ingredients would forever create events in our lives and then attach them to people, places, things, and concepts. It was easy to comprehend because the mere turning over of column three revealed the four ingredients. Turning over column two then revealed the "I" statements. Finally, we saw column one and all the crazy ideas we had conjured up.

It was as if we were inviting the spirit of fear out of a place that is not real...our thoughts. This is the fear our brother Timothy warned us about when he said, "For God hath not given us the spirit of fear." This spirit of fear plagued us, yet we were the producers of it. We crumpled up columns one and two and then slid the third column over to lie beside its bitterness counterpart of column four.

Next, we looked at what was now in front of us, and the pile of refuge began to grow. Out of bitterness, we were left with the fourth column, our selfishness, dishonesty, self-seeking, and fear. Now we were adding to the pile the third column from our fear examination which contained our self-reliance, self-confidence, cockiness, and trust in our finite selves. The list of people from our prayer list, the first column, which had been set far out of sight in our bitterness examination, was left there for now.

Then we had a crumpled-up ball of paper with the fear examination's second column containing the "events" which were no longer occurring, and which we only thought had caused our fear. Now, we added another piece of crumpled paper containing the list of fears from column one of the fear examination. We placed the refuge heap before us. What seemed like mere pen and paper to others contained the real ideas, emotions, and attitudes behind everything that we had done our entire lives. We were ready to have God remove all these defects of character.

Now, we said a simple fear prayer. The prayer usually goes like this:

"Jesus, I come before you today with a heart full of fear. I know that I cannot overcome this fear on my own, but with your help, You can conquer it. So, I pray that you remove my fear and direct my attention to what you would have me be."

At once, we commenced to outgrow fear, and the crumpled piles of trash that once were our lives were gently removed from the center of the table and slid into the discarded coffee cup. A caveat was announced: if this was too much, then at any time, we could remove the trash from the coffee cup and apply it back to our will and lives. We were appalled. What once was our lives was now a repulsive sight.

We peered down at the table in front of us and still had the two columns from our searching and trying of bitterness and fear. But God wasn't ready to remove them just yet. Before we pressed on, God revealed another basic spiritual tool for us to use in combatting fear until we truly grasped the concept of living in faith. The spiritual tool was to ask God daily what He would have us be, not what He would have us do. Then we followed the day's plans being what God directs.

YOD

Faith. Faith in *step five* is getting easier for us to grasp. We first experienced it in *step one*. Then we saw its proper use compared to power and humility in *step four*. The fourth step also revealed that instead of faith, His righteousness is what we were ultimately in search of. Now we encounter faith again in this step. We will go into much greater detail of faith in the ensuing pages, for it is the answer to our fear. It is becoming a little easier for us to grasp.

It's the Holy Spirit that revealed the evolution of faith, which is from the spark of God to willingness to faith. They are all one and the same. It suddenly appeared the moment God's Hand was applied to our lives. Oh! Much like the power of art lies within the moment that the artist applies the tip of his brush to the blank canvas. At that moment, and each similar moment that ensues, lies within it the complete Power of transformation. The entire artistry is in the moment, faith.

This spark was contained within the seed and carried the willingness which is the mustard seed of faith. Although these spiritual terms may have been foreign to us in the beginning, we quickly saw that faith is the foundational building block and the essential element in every work that proceeded out of His mouth.

Faith contained commitment and trust, both of which were powerful catalysts of action for us. We had never thoroughly experienced them. *Step one* required a commitment to initiate this process. In the beginning, it was the drugs and alcohol that were the ultimate persuader. When we had cried out in humility, unknowingly turning our backs on the spirit of fear, and committed our way to the Lord. We committed ourselves to the task at hand, aligning our intentions and actions with His desired outcome for our lives. When we cried out, we exhibited a trust in the Lord's provision which would become the central theme of our journey. Our soul was connecting to a level of trust in the Spirit He had breathed within us. Trusting in God allowed us to approach the concept of fear in *step five* with humble confidence. Once we followed our fourth step lists with action, we received the faith of a promise that God will act. Our humble trust was not passive but was accompanied by active participation. Applying the power of faith to *step five* encouraged us to take decisive action, seeking God's power to embark on the spiritual journey toward spiritual maturity. We were blessed because we had begun to be merciful and, in that moment, we received mercy.

Now, let's see what God does with our immorality examination. We have listed those whom we hurt, and sex was involved. This was the beginning of our sex relations list. We then asked ourselves, "What was our conduct involving this sex?" We identified in our examination how these sex relations aroused bitterness, jealousy, and suspicion. We marked every area where we were at fault. Now we brought this list of pain and sorrow to the feet of Jesus. Don't forget that every measure has duality in principle and promise. One involves the journey and the other draws from the journey.

IMORALITY EXAMINATION							
Column One	Column Two	Column Three				Column Four		
		In these sex relations did we...				Where were we at fault? Were we...		
Whom did we hurt and sex was involved? We list our sex relations:	What was our conduct involving this sex?	Unjustifiably arouse bitterness, jealousy, or suspicion?	Use our sex powers lightly or selfishly?	Despise or loath our sex powers?		Selfish?	Dishonest?	Inconsiderate?
Jo	Cheated on them	x	x	X		x	x	X
Pat **(SS)**	Used them for sex, drugs, and money	X	x	x		x	x	X
Jean **(S)**	Lied to them, didn't really love them	x	x			x	x	X
Shelby	Slept with their cousin	x	x			x	x	x
Myself **(SS)**	Can't stop watching porn	x				x	x	x

We then watched God get to work on our immorality. The first thing required was to identify the spiritually sick people on this list who may not have been listed previously.

IMORALITY EXAMINATION								
Column One	**Column Two**	**Column Three** In these sex relations did we...				**Column Four** Where were we at fault? Were we...		
Whom did we hurt and sex was involved? We list our sex relations:	What was our conduct involving this sex?	Unjustifiably arouse bitterness, jealousy, or suspicion?	Use our sex powers lightly or selfishly?	Despise or loath our sex powers?		Selfish?	Dishonest?	Inconsiderate?
Jo	Cheated on them	x	x	X		x	x	X
Pat	Used them for sex, drugs, and money	X	x	x		x	x	X
Jean	Lied to them, didn't really love them	x	x			x	x	X
Shelby	Slept with their cousin	x	x			x	x	x
Myself	Can't stop watching porn	x				x	x	x

We prayed for them as we now knew how. We then used the "sick person" prayer for those on the list who were spiritually sick. Once we prayed, these too transformed from people to avoid into people that we would show tolerance, pity, and patience. Now we removed the first column listing those whom we had hurt and searched for the prayer list from our bitterness examination. We combined the lists. We returned them to the side out of sight, not to be a distraction. Next, we directed our attention back to the task at hand.

We then watched as God brought our attention to the second column. The Holy Ghost alone judges our sexual situation. Counsel with our pastor was desirable, but we let God be the final judge. We realized that some people are as fanatical about sex as others are loose. We avoided any hysterical thinking or advice that contradicted the Word of God.

We were stopped in our tracks when we were asked, "What would you have done differently?" We considered each episode:

IMORALITY EXAMINATION						
Column Two	Column Three			Column Four		
	In these sex relations did we...			Where were we at fault? Were we...		
What was our conduct involving this sex?	Unjustifiably arouse bitterness, jealousy or suspicion?	Use our sex powers lightly or selfishly?	Despise or loath our sex powers?	Selfish?	Dishonest?	Inconsiderate?
Cheated on them	x	x	X	x	x	X
Used them for sex, drugs, and money	X	x	x	x	x	X
Lied to them, didn't really love them	x	x		x	x	X
Slept with their cousin	x	x		x	x	x
Can't stop watching porn	x			x	x	x

What would you have done differently?

    I would not have cheated on Jo;

    I would not have used Pat;

    I would not have lied to Jean;

    I would not have slept with Shelby's cousin;

    I would not watch porn.

And just like that, we received God's new marching orders for us which included:

> Don't cheat;
>
> Don't use people;
>
> Don't lie;
>
> Don't fornicate;
>
> Don't watch porn.

In this moment, God had used our immorality to show us morality. He asked us if we could live this way with His help? We answered, "Of course." Simple but not easy. We could now remove the second column and discard it, unless we would like to hold onto these past events to romance and reincarnate them at our whim as we had been accustomed to doing up to this point in our lives. We quickly made this immoral stench into a crumpled ball of paper and placed it in the center of the table where the others had laid before they were prayed away.

We then reviewed the third column and discovered that our sex relations created all sorts of scenarios of bitterness, jealousy, and suspicion. We could see that our best intentions created immorality decorated with our ability to use our sex powers lightly and selfishly. Our sex relations were laced with actions that we disliked or hated. These were the opposite of any healthy version of sex relations.

IMMORALITY EXAMINATION					
Column Three			Column Four		
In these sex relations did we...			Where were we at fault? Were we...		
Unjustifiably arouse bitterness, jealousy, or suspicion?	Use our sex powers lightly or selfishly?	Despise or loath our sex powers?	Selfish?	Dishonest?	Inconsiderate?
x	x	X	x	x	X
X	x	x	x	x	X
x	x		x	x	X
x	x		x	x	x
x			x	x	x

By the time we had made it to the fourth column of our immorality searching and trying, it was easy to see where we were selfish, dishonest, and for sure inconsiderate in our immorality and sexual relationships. It became abundantly clear that we were having trouble with personal relationships. Specifically, ones involving sex.

Removing the third column, crumpling it up, and placing it beside the ball of paper at the center of the table, we were once again facing the exact nature of our sins. Now the truth which had been overshadowing us is becoming even clearer. We were the producers of our immorality. We wanted this truth to stop staring at us, but God said, "Not yet!"

IMMORALITY EXAMINATION		
Column Four		
Where were we at fault? Were we...		
Selfish?	Dishonest?	Inconsiderate?
x	x	X
x	x	X
x	x	X
x	x	x
x	x	x

Before God did anything else, He immediately provided us with a spiritual tool for our morality. Specifically, for when it comes to sex relations. The tool was that we would subject each of our sex relations to this test—is it selfish or not?

We then bowed our heads in reverence to God and we prayed to Him asking:

"God, mold my ideals regarding sex and help me to live up to them."

The two balls of crumpled paper were removed and joined the trash heap in the coffee cup. The three pieces of paper in front of us containing the fourth column of the bitterness examination, the third column of the fear inventory, and the fourth column of the immorality examination would stare at us through the next few steps until we could, at last, be rid of them in *step seven*. For now, let's continue along the path.

We came to God humbly and with a sincere heart. We recognized that sex is a beautiful gift from Him, but it can also be a source of confusion, temptation, and harm. So, we asked that He mold our ideals regarding sex and help us to live up to them.

We know that, compared to our lack of standards, His standards are high. God aims to protect our physical, emotional, and spiritual well-being. That is why we prayed that He would guide us in our thoughts, attitudes, and behaviors regarding sex. We needed help to honor His principle and to respect ourselves and others.

We prayed and He gave us the wisdom to make wise choices when it comes to sexual intimacy. He helps us to resist any temptations that may lead us down the path of sin such as addictions and alcoholism, guilt, or regret. If we ask Him in our daily prayer and meditation about each instance, then the right answer will come.

Above all, we prayed, and He began to fill us with His mercy. He helped us find true fulfillment in our relationship with Him, rather than seeking it in unhealthy or inappropriate ways. We can now thank Him from the bottom of our hearts for His unconditional love. We trust in His guidance and surrender our desires to His will.

We recognized that our sex relations, like all areas of our lives, were affected by the disease of sins such as alcoholism and addictions. We had been powerless over our sexual behaviors, and they caused us and others harm. But in Jesus' Name, we believed that God could and would mold our ideals regarding sex and relationships. Therefore, we were encouraged not to conform to the pattern of this world, but to be transformed by the renewing of our minds. Once this new set of thinking began to dominate us, we were able to test and approve what God's will is—His good, pleasing, and perfect will (Romans 12:2).

We acknowledged that our previous ideas about sex and relationships were distorted and harmful. We had no concept of what God's standards were, and we were unable to live up to them without His help. But we trusted in God's promise that He can make something beautiful out of our brokenness.

As we worked towards recovery, we strived to align our sexual behaviors with God's will. We sought to practice sexual integrity, which includes avoiding any behaviors that cause harm to ourselves or others. We aimed to view our sex powers as God-given and good, rather than something to be used lightly or selfishly. Sexual integrity does not involve bitterness, selfishness, or jealousy. The Potter was at work. Our sexual morality, like clumps of clay, were being shaped on the Potter's wheel.

We recognized that our journey toward sexual wholeness may not be easy, but we were willing to grow toward our new ideals. We trusted in God's mercy as we surrendered our old ways of thinking and living to His will.

In recovery, we have asked ourselves if falling short of our chosen ideal means that we are lost or doomed to backslide. We recognize that stumbling or falling short of our ideal is not uncommon, and it should create an honest and desperate desire to let God take us to better things. If we stumble, we should immediately seek forgiveness and learn from our mistakes. We should be sorry for what we have done and seek to make amends if we have caused harm. We acknowledge that if we continue to harm God's children and are not sorry for our actions, we will be bound to our sins. This is not mere theory; it is a fact from our own experience.

We trust in God's grace to forgive us when we stumble and help us to grow and learn from our mistakes. We believe that although the world is filled with impurity, God takes it away. When we trust in God's power to overcome temptation, we remain pure. God has never allowed anyone to suffer for resisting temptation, even though it is a loss to us in the material sense. When we pray, "lead us not into temptation," we are asking God to remove the burden of temptation that is too difficult for our human nature to resist. We often underestimate the power of the Holy Spirit to enter our minds and sanctify our thoughts. The Holy Spirit sweeps away the darkest corners of our minds and opens spiritual windows that human means cannot move. This allows the cleansing sunlight to bathe our spirits in the serenity of true purity.

Feeding our minds with impurities is like feeding our bodies with tainted food. Just as we would not eat tainted food because we know the consequences to our bodies, we avoid feeding our minds with impure thoughts which slowly but surely kill our souls. We must be vigilant in guarding our minds and hearts against the corrupting influences of the world by seeking Him in all our affairs. As we continue to seek Him, God continues to purify our minds and through Him, we are able to help us resist temptation. Everyone who follows this path is led to being filled with the Holy Spirit and renewing their desire to live a life of holiness.

To sum up the revelations we have gained about sex: we pray earnestly for guidance and the right ideal. We seek sanity and the strength to do what is right in every situation. If sex becomes a troublesome issue for us, we do not turn inward with bitterness and fear. Instead, we throw ourselves into helping others, thinking of their needs, and working to serve them. By focusing on others, we can quiet the urge to act on our own desires, knowing that to yield would only bring heartache. We recognize that serving others takes us out of ourselves and helps us maintain a healthy perspective on our own needs and desires. God guides us in all aspects of our lives, including our sexual relationships, and gives us the strength to do what is right, even when it is difficult.

מ MEM

When it comes to morality, it is a message sent from above. He took us, He drew us out of many waters (Psalm 18:16). Therefore, we immediately thought that we were to connect to other people through emotions and feelings. But this was not to happen yet. We would soon behold the glorious manifestation of the Almighty God once this step had been thoroughly and honestly taken! From the heavenly realms, He graciously descended upon us, reaching out with His mighty hand to rescue us from the vast tumultuous waters within that threatened to engulf us. With His divine power, He lifted us high above the waves of our defects of character, freeing us from the depths of our own despair. This could only lead to our rejoicing, offering praise to the Lord, because His unwavering love and deliverance had granted us salvation. The womb of our spirit was made shut and more development into His ideal morality was being prepared to be poured out when we humbled ourselves before the Lord. At that time, He would lift the veil up and open the womb to a Holy Ghost outpouring.

We come to you today with our hearts filled with gratitude for the progress God has made in our personal examinations. We are thankful for the opportunity to list and analyze our bitterness and for the strength He has given us to begin to learn tolerance, patience, and goodwill toward all people, including our enemies. As we continued to examine ourselves, we began to understand the futility and fatality of our bitterness. We saw the terrible destructiveness it caused in our lives and the lives of those around us. We were humbled by this realization and sought forgiveness as we moved forward. We were also aware of the fear we produced within ourselves and others. We acknowledged the harm we caused through our immoral conduct and were willing to do whatever it took to make restitution and straighten out the past. We asked for the Holy Spirit's continued strength, guidance, and love as God delivered us from our shortcomings and become the people He called us to be. As we prayed, God continued to increase us in love and service to others and was creating our lives to reflect His will.

We cannot overemphasize the importance of faith in recovery. It is through faith that we see obstacles overcome, including obstacles that once blocked our connection with God. Once we had taken the third step and completed a thorough search of our past, we took a significant step toward recovery. By taking the fifth step and confessing all our sins to another person, without holding anything back, we began to experience a newfound sense of peace and freedom.

As a result of this step, we were no longer weighed down by our fears and doubts. We began to feel the presence of God in our lives, and our spiritual beliefs became more meaningful and effective as we experienced the true God and not who we *thought* He was. The burden of our sins was lifted, and we felt as if we had entered through the narrow gate on the path that leads to life. As we continued to walk in this faith and take the steps, we trusted God and He guided us and provided for us every step of the way. We could rest in the assurance that we were no longer alone, but that we were walking hand-in-hand with the Holy Ghost, who was empowering us to live a life of freedom, joy, and purpose.

So, let us take heart and press on, knowing that with God all things are possible and that nothing can separate us from His love. Let us continue to seek His will for our lives, and to trust in His power to transform us from the inside out. For we know that as we abide in Him, He will abide in us, and that His Power demonstrates through us creating much fruit for His kingdom.

This fifth step lifted a weight off our shoulders that we didn't know we were carrying. If we were thorough and honest then we discovered the truth about areas of our lives that we could have never seen without God and our newfound Holy Ghost-filled friend. We now saw the truth behind the prison of bitterness, fear, and immorality in whose shadow we had been living all our lives. We confessed our faults to one another and prayed for one another, and now were being healed. The effectual fervent prayer of a righteous person avails much.

The Hebrew name Ephraim, which means double blessing, represents the growth, abundance, and positive outcomes that are achieved through recovery. This name is appropriate for the fifth step. There are many ways it applies to recovery. Recovery is a process of service, ministry, and remission. Embracing the name Ephraim is a reminder of the fruitful changes in our lives during the recovery journey. Like nurturing a fruitful garden, those of us in recovery experience the work of God as He cultivates a new garden full of godly habits and behaviors within ourselves. This includes God revealing healthier coping mechanisms, developing better communication skills, and fostering a more balanced lifestyle.

Recovery requires hard work and dedication. The name Ephraim speaks of the rewards that come from putting effort into recovery, leading to changed thinking and testimony. Just as a plant grows and bears fruit, recovery leads to the emergence of a new identity in Jesus' Name. Embracing the fifth step is where we see God causing us to become a more fulfilled version of ourselves. Recovery involves healing relationships with God, ourselves, and others. The name Ephraim is fruitful and has meaningful connections with friends, family, and recovery groups. Just as one would celebrate the fruits of a laborious garden, those of us in recovery celebrate God-given milestones and achievements along the way to honor Him.

Like a fruitful tree that withstands the changing seasons, recovery involves God cultivating resilience in us to navigate life's challenges without resorting to harmful solutions. A fruitful life also involves giving back to others. In recovery, we find fulfillment in supporting others on their recovery journey and in engaging in acts of service to the recovery community. The fifth step is about finding purpose in life. As we recover, we discover a fulfilling path to follow. Overall, the name Ephraim's meaning of fruitfulness is empowering during recovery. It represents the service, ministry, recovery, and a life filled with Holy Ghost experiences, much like a bountiful harvest from a well-tended garden.

We were now walking in the middle of the realm of remission. We walked out of the fifth step with our sins out of our hearts and heads and into God's hands. This was a huge relief. Now we had taken them and admitted them to God, ourselves, and another human being. We made it past a vital step that once seemed daunting and now was liberating. Grace extended into mercy and our lives began to fill up as we began to take the next step.

Step five was a double blessing. The exchanging of our pain and sorrow for strength was a blessing. There was another blessing that came when we realized that our troublesome pasts were now being converted into our testimonies, never to be added to nor taken away from again.

The overarching principle for *step five* continues to reflect our mourning. The second step's righteousness and covenant brought tears to our eyes as we thought of the goodness of the Lord. We were beginning to see how we are blessed because we mourn. We now appreciated our mourning, and He was comforting us. As we took this step, we felt an overwhelming gratitude as our hearts ached because we now loved him so much. The Lord promised to console us as we rejoiced in the mourning.

As we left so much baggage behind in this step, withholding nothing, we approached this confession and prayer with a righteous person by our side. We confessed and prayed after the righteousness that was planted in our hearts in *step two*. We wanted more! The heartfelt mourning coupled with confessing and praying after righteousness changed the fifth step confessing into a fervent praying for righteousness. As we approached this step with this mindset, the game changed, and we were filled with promise. We had now sat with the merciful; we had been shown mercy. We had been in the compassion of others when we didn't deserve it. Now, God did the same for us in Jesus' Name

Now that the true nature of the sinful wreckage of our pasts had been discovered, we could thank God from the bottom of our hearts that we knew Him better. For it was possible that the bottom of our hearts had never seen His Light. We carefully reviewed what we had done by turning to the page that contained the steps. Carefully reading the first five steps, we asked ourselves if we omitted anything, for God was showing us the door through which we shall walk free at last.

We reread *step one*. "We admitted we were powerless over sins such as addictions and alcoholism," We reviewed that we were in a great wrestling of mind and flesh. We were asked if we had omitted anything. We then read. "— that our lives had become spiritually disconnected." We were reminded of the symptoms of being spiritless which included anxiety, depression, unhappiness, bedevilments, and manifestations of flesh. We read Romans 7:14-20 and saw ourselves before these steps and we were asked, have we omitted anything? Next, we read, "We came to believe that Jesus is the way and the truth and the life — that no one comes to the Father except through Him" and John 14:6. We were then asked again if we now believed in Jesus Christ. Once we confirmed that we were willing to believe, we were asked if we had omitted anything.

Before we read *step three*, we were reminded of the requirement. Then we were asked if we had decided to deny ourselves, take up our cross, and follow Christ. We then read Matthew 16:24. We were asked if we had omitted anything. Next, we were asked to read *step four*, "We searched out and examined our ways and turned again to the Lord" and read Lamentations 3:40. We then were asked if we had omitted anything.

Finally, we were asked to read *step five*, "We confessed our faults one to another, and prayed one for another, that we may be healed. The effectual fervent prayer of a righteous man avails much" and read James 5:16. Then we were asked if we had omitted anything.

Next, we were asked if our work, that we placed into the footing, was solid so far? The footing was believing that God is all powerful and He provides what we need if we keep close to Him and perform his work well. The way that we keep close to Him and perform His work well is to seek Him. And when asked how we seek Him, we said, "Here are the steps we took."

We were then asked, "Is the foundation of complete willingness in place? Are the chief cornerstone and keystone properly in place?" The chief cornerstone was that we now believe in a power greater than ourselves, which is Jesus. The keystone was that we decided that Jesus was our Lord, and we were His subjects. "Have we skimped on the cement, made up of our common peril and agreed upon solution, put into the foundation of complete faith? Have we tried to make mortar, (thoroughness) without sand, (honesty)?"

We began to see once again the immense favor of the Lord upon our lives. The fifth step encompasses the principle of mourning, as we become part of those who mourn. Embedded within this principle is the understanding that we are also recipients of mercy. As we progressed through this step, these truths became increasingly apparent. The promises of this step manifested in our lives, bringing us comfort and a tangible experience of God's mercy. We were truly grateful for this humbling step that led us towards righteousness, as it marked the beginning of our life-changing journey. Pain and sorrow no longer held dominion over us. We not only received blessings but were doubly blessed, experiencing the richness of God's grace and mercy.

Like the story of Noah (Genesis 6-9): In the days we were being ruled by our sins, God saw that the wickedness of our hearts had become great, and He decided to bring a circumstance to destroy all signs of life within us. However, God showed mercy to us and our families because He knew we would soon find favor in His eyes. God instructed us to cry out in humility to save ourselves, for He would use this to save others and His creation. Through this act of mercy, God preserved a remnant of our lives. Mercy.

Like the story of Jonah (Jonah 1-4): We once were in church and initially resisted God's call to perform His work to reach His people. We tried to flee from God's presence but ended up in the belly of a great fish – sin such as addictions and alcoholism. After we prayed for mercy, God caused the fish to spit us out onto a new place. God gave us a second chance, and we eventually would go anywhere to proclaim God's message. The people who would hear our story and the solution repented and God showed them mercy, sparing them from the destruction He had initially planned. Mercy.

Like the Prodigal Son (Luke 15:11-32): We were the prodigal child who squandered our inheritance through sinful living and ended up destitute. When we realized our mistake and returned home, our admittance of powerlessness and spiritual disconnectedness – backsliding, which comes from God's mercy, runs us into His embrace with open arms. Despite our waywardness, God forgave us and celebrated our return, illustrating His boundless mercy and willingness to forgive those who repent. Mercy.

Like the Woman Caught in Adultery (John 8:1-11): We all are a part of this well-known incident, caught in the act of adultery. Instead of condemning us, Jesus shows us mercy and grace. He tells those who wanted to stone us, including ourselves, that the one without sin should cast the first stone. As they all walk away, Jesus forgives us and instructs us to go and sin no more. Mercy.

The Crucifixion of Jesus (Luke 23:32-43): Jesus' crucifixion is the ultimate display of God's mercy and love for humanity. Despite being innocent, Jesus willingly endured a painful death on the cross to offer forgiveness and salvation to all who would believe in Him. He showed mercy to the repentant criminal crucified beside Him, promising him a place in paradise. Mercy.

This *step five* promise is we shall be shown mercy. If we go into *step five* mercifully over our examination of ourselves, we immediately sense this promise and before we are completely done with this portion of our journey, we know mercy.

This step has proven so much in its miracles of conversions. We see clearly how blessed those are who can show compassion toward others when they don't deserve it. We didn't deserve it. Because of this, God will do the same for you.

Gentleness.

Looking back on this step, as Holy Ghost-filled recovered believers, we engage in following James 5:16 and create a Holy Ghost-filled community of confession, prayer, and healing. Many of us have created prayer groups within our church or recovery community, where we commit to praying for specific needs and concerns shared among the group. We are encouraged to share our testimonies of God's healing, deliverance, and during worship services, specific recovery groups, and small group gatherings. We pair up with other Holy Ghost-filled recovered people as prayer partners, encouraging each other to regularly pray for each other's service, ministry, challenges, and relationship with God. We organize workshops focused on the recovery ministry, teaching practical ways to pray for the sick, brokenhearted, and those in need of emotional and spiritual restoration. Some have established prayer and recovery ministries within the church to provide confidential and compassionate support to those seeking recovery and salvation. Others plan corporate fasting and prayer days where the church comes together to seek God's face and intercede for specific needs and concerns for those in recovery. There are opportunities to organize special healing recovery services where members can come forward to receive prayer for physical, emotional, and spiritual healing in recovery. We establish special recovery meetings where we practice the biblical act of anointing with oil during prayers for healing recovery. Many of us have been called upon by equipping churches and recovery organizations to lead deliverance ministry sessions, providing a safe and prayerful environment for recovery, spiritual healing, and freedom. Many of us find ourselves establishing recovery groups, providing a space for people to share, support, and pray for one another. Excitement builds and creates soaking prayer sessions where we spend extended time in God's presence, seeking the Holy Spirit to minister and bring healing and recovery. As we gain a deeper communion with God, many develop an environment where the gifts of the Holy Spirit, such as prophetic prayer and words of knowledge, are welcomed and utilized for recovery, healing, and encouragement. We hear over and over how important it is to set aside specific times during services and recovery groups for focused intercessory prayer for community needs and individual concerns. We are encouraged to establish a system of receiving and responding to prayer requests submitted by those of us seeking recovery, ensuring we all receive support and prayer from the recovery community.

Remember that each of these tasks should be carried out in an atmosphere of love, sensitivity, and respect for each person's privacy and needs. The Holy Spirit will guide and empower the recovery community as we seek to create an environment of confession, prayer, and healing in alignment with God's will.

Now if we can answer the questions satisfactorily and see the principle and promise of this step, then we are ready for *step six*.

CHAPTER 11

STEP SIX

*"We humbled ourselves before the Lord,
and He lifted us up."
(James 4:10)*

Step six emphasizes complete faith as being indispensable. It is through our willingness to humble ourselves before God and to have faith in His power that we begin to experience the true change of mind and life necessary for permanent recovery.

We are reminded of the words of Jesus when He said, "Because of your unbelief: for verily I say unto you, if ye have faith as a grain of mustard seed, ye shall say unto this mountain, Remove hence to yonder place; and it shall remove; and nothing shall be impossible unto you" (Matthew 7:20). We have discovered willingness as the faith as a grain of mustard seed. The mountain that Jesus spoke of represents the intellectual pride that we previously had about God and spirituality. When we are willing to let go of our own conceptions, we are essentially saying, "Remove hence to yonder place." We then watch God reveal Himself to us in a new way and we experience a profound shift in our relationship with Him. This shift is the movement of a mountain, as our old ways of thinking and being. They are replaced by a new faith and trust in God. With this revelation, nothing is impossible, and we can experience the freedom and peace that come from walking hand in hand with the Holy Spirit. The glass ceiling has been shattered by this hammer of truth a new thing is being exposed in Christ Jesus.

These were profound lessons learned through the open door of actions we were taking as we continued asking and seeking God. The Hebrews writer told us that "now faith is the substance of things hoped for, the evidence of things not seen" (Hebrews 11:1). Our minds were blown. This faith is the very substance of the maintenance and growth of our spiritual condition. It is the evidence of our relationship with God!

As we began to take the sixth step, faith had more to reveal. We now learned that once, in the fourth step, the four ingredients of our carnal flesh were removed in our fear examination, there was seemingly nothing left. We peered over the columns of paper which stayed as close to us as a man's tie onto the blank space on the table before us and saw that it was cleared of any debris. This was faith.

In this present moment, we recognize the precious gift of faith that has been bestowed upon us. Faith is the absence of fear, and throughout history, those who have walked in faith have displayed great courage. Trusting in God and operating in faith requires immense courage. As we continue to walk in faith, we experience the truth of the words spoken by our brother Timothy. God has indeed given us a spirit of power, love, and a sound mind. Through the power of the Holy Spirit who has come upon us and is working within us, we are empowered to face any challenge we encounter with faith or God-confidence. The love of God fills our hearts and enables us to extend His love to others. And with a sound mind, guided by the wisdom of God, He gives us wisdom to make decisions and navigate life's complexities without harm.

The spirit of fear generates only powerlessness, hate, and insanity. This incredible principle caused us to produce the four ingredients of our carnality and we conjured up events like witches and attached them to people, places, things, and concepts! The absurdity did not stop there; we felt better about this state of mind because we thought we had created something we could operate in. This was truly a troubled spirit. We were thankful this was part of the old person now! There was a new canvas to operate on. It was blank and it was faith.

The miracle did not stop there. After a while of operating in this faith, a new set of spiritual ingredients began to appear. They were reliance upon God, confidence in Jesus Christ, boldness in His Name, and trust in the infinite Holy Ghost. These Spiritual ingredients began operating upon the canvas of faith much like the following example:

		Column Three			
		Mark X if it helped create the Fear			
		Reliance upon God	Confidence in God	Boldness in God	Trust in God
		x	x	x	X
		x	x	x	x
		x	x	x	x
		x	x	x	x

Once this obedience was born through faith, God created a whole new set of events which we call blessings:

	Column Two	Column Three			
		Mark X if it helped create the Fear			
	God Events (a.k.a. blessings):	Reliance upon God	Confidence in Jesus Christ	Boldness in His Name	Trust in the Holy Ghost
	God demonstrated the spreading of the Gospel	x	x	x	X
	God launched an altruistic life	x	x	x	x
	God created biblical principle	x	x	x	x
	God demonstrated how to serve	x	x	x	x

We are amazed at how God demonstrates through us in each of His blessings:

	Column Two	Column Three			
		Mark X if it helped create the Fear			
	God Events (a.k.a. blessings):	Reliance upon God	Confidence in Jesus Christ	Boldness in His Name	Trust in the Holy Ghost
	God demonstrated the spreading of the Gospel through us	x	x	x	X
	God launched an altruistic life through us	x	x	x	x
	God created biblical principle through us	x	x	x	x
	God demonstrated how to serve through us	x	x	x	x

God then takes these blessings and demonstrates through our sound minds His love and power by blessing people, places, things, and concepts:

Column One	Column Two	Column Three			
		Mark X if it helped create the Fear			
List of those blessed	God Events (a.k.a. blessings):	Reliance upon God	Confidence in Jesus Christ	Boldness in His Name	Trust in the Holy Ghost
Baptized Daniel	God demonstrated the spreading of the Gospel through us	x	x	x	X
Started Sober Living Homes in the community	God launched an altruistic life through us	x	x	x	x
Lead a recovery group Bible Study	God created biblical principle through us	x	x	x	x
Joined parking lot ministry at church	God demonstrated how to serve through us	x	x	x	x

For the first time we understood something...

Column One	Column Two	Column Three			
		FEAR OF THE LORD Mark X if it helped create the Fear			
List of those blessed	God Events (a.k.a. blessings):	Reliance upon God	Confidence in Jesus Christ	Boldness in His Name	Trust in the Holy Ghost
Baptized Daniel	God demonstrated the spreading of the Gospel through us	x	x	x	X
Started Sober Living Homes in the community	God launched an altruistic life through us	x	x	x	x
Lead a recovery group Bible Study	God created biblical principle through us	x	x	x	x
Joined parking lot ministry at church	God demonstrated how to serve through us	x	x	x	x

נ MEM

In the overflowing abundance of our souls, we came to understand the true meaning of Fearing the Lord. As the floodgates of revelation opened, we heard His voice proclaiming that we would be counted among His saints. Our Fear of the Lord deepened, and we realized that in Fearing Him, we lacked nothing. This truth became clear to us. It was plain to see that when we relied upon Him, had confidence in Him, were bold in His Name, and trusted in Him, there was no lack. He sent from above, He took us, He drew us out of many waters (Psalm 18:16). We were beholding the glorious manifestation of the Almighty God once this step had been thoroughly and honestly taken! The fourth step revealed our overflowing willingness for faith or deep calling to deep. Then the fifth step showed us the power that shutting up the waters within created in our newly formed womb of morality now ready to burst forth. From the heavenly realms, He graciously descended upon us, reaching out with

His mighty hand to rescue us from the vast tumultuous waters within that threatened to engulf us. With His divine power, He lifted us high above the waves of our defects of character, freeing us from the depths of our own despair. This could only lead to our rejoicing and offering praise to the Lord, for His unwavering love and deliverance had granted us salvation. This would overflow into our walks of faith. Therefore, the womb was opened and the outpouring would begin immediately after the waters were parted.

נ NUN

We have come to value humility as we first encountered it in the first step where our soul was bent to its knees in humble submission, as well as in the fourth step where we saw the value of this humility instead of assuming righteousness through a thorough searching and examination of our temple. Now we know that God is with us; we have never been abandoned. We now are covered by His holy wing. We choose, first, to get onto our knees acknowledging that it is no longer our conception. This powerful spiritual position of righteous submission is the very seed that was planted in our hearts. It contained Power beyond our comprehension. We continued to follow these steps with more action. At this moment, we were careful to ensure that we were seeds falling on good ground that were springing up and beginning to bear fruit beyond our wildest imaginations. We learned to use more and more humility. Here are the steps we took.

Humility paves the way for healing. It is the only way that we could ever shed our pride and enter complete reliance on Christ. Through it, alcoholism, addictions, pain, or adversity no longer required our intervention to cope with alone, as we now had God's help. Humility means we are prepared to think of others and become more selfless! Humility is embracing surrendering our will to a higher purpose.

It is essential to remember that humility does not equate to weakness. Instead, it embodies strength. Humility empowers us to seek help, to admit our mistakes, and to learn from them. It enables us to accept wisdom from those who have walked a similar path. When we humbly surrender, we open ourselves to the healing grace of God. These conditions invite His strength to work through us, which is vital, for this is what is about to guide us towards a life of freedom. Humility allows us to acknowledge our character defects while embracing the hope that comes from divine intervention. Even if we can't see it, He's working.

There was much to learn about humility. This book could not contain all that needs to be understood about the humility that we were now experiencing as we sought to get on our knees because we knew that a power outside of ourselves was immediately at work the moment, we sought Him. Through these steps, we experienced beautiful lessons in humility within ourselves. When we confessed our shortcomings and opened ourselves to this step, seeking Him as the center of our attention, craving His presence, and inserting ourselves under His Love, we were released by humility. This humble attitude catapulted our spiritual progress and enabled us to receive the help and healing we needed. As soon as we embraced humility, when we acknowledged our imperfections, we opened ourselves up and were exalted by God.

Humility doesn't mean thinking less of ourselves but rather thinking of ourselves less. It is about recognizing that we are part of a greater whole and being willing to surrender our ego-driven desires to recover. We no longer edge God out. Humility prevents false pride from taking root in our hearts and minds; it always wards off disgrace. Humility reveals faults, deflates ego, and reinforces reality. It drives us to seek God at the expense of our wants and desires, to act humbly, and to hunger after the wisdom of those who are Holy Ghost-filled, around us. We see it now; humility reminds us of our identity as God's chosen people—holy and dearly loved. Humility is a powerful affirmation that despite our flaws and past mistakes, we are inherently worthy of love, grace, and redemption. This *step six* experience builds upon the foundation for our recovery, as humility teaches us to view ourselves through the lens of compassion. Humility then invites us to intentionally "clothe" ourselves with virtues that are essential in the process of recovery. These virtues, although foreign to us, are contained within the seed of humility planted within us manifesting as compassion, kindness, humility, gentleness, and patience. Humility encapsulates the essence of God's requirements for His people. It serves as a guiding principle for our actions, attitudes, and relationship with God.

Humility is the fuel for *step six*. It is the understanding we are wretched creatures, and God can now have all our sins such as addictions and alcoholism – every single one. It is faith over ego, shedding the mask of self-sufficiency. Humility empowers us to surrender to the truth, to seek help, and to accept that we cannot do it alone. But there was more action needed, as the seed of humility needed a cleansing fire.

The Spirit. This consuming fire of the Holy Spirit in *step three* was what we offered our sins such as addictions and alcoholism to once we met the requirement of recognizing that they were what was wrecking our own lives. Many who come this way are unwilling to confess their sins, leading to them being truly spiritually disconnected.

Although we may have had an extensive religious upbringing, we now saw why our previous religious beliefs did not provide the necessary transformation that could only come from a deep effective spiritual experience of the Holy Spirit. The mere mention of His Name no longer caused us to slam our doors and windows shut as we experienced more of Him. The religious accept Him because He is accomplishing for us that which no human power could do before. We could now accept God's truth and it had nothing to do with our previous conception of Him.

This sixth step experience is life-altering for both the theologically inclined and theologically adverse. These steps are a place where these two warring tribes become one among many followers of Jesus Christ. Until a position of purity is adopted, little or no explanation can break through spiritual prejudices and religious misbeliefs. But the moment we are pure in heart, cleansed of all our old ideas, and have begun to experience God, we know His Name is Jesus and miraculous things happen. It is this fire that fueled the willingness upon which we offered up all the sins such as addictions and alcoholism that the sinners in our lives created. The consuming fire continued a mighty work as we were transformed into new creatures full of His strength, double portions of blessings, and now pure hearts of flesh. We experienced the awesome power of this consuming fire as we navigated this beautiful step in the Holy Spirit. The stony heart rolled away.

Oh, what a profound revelation it was! The Fear of the Lord is the foundation of knowledge, but fools despise instruction. Now, it all made beautiful sense to us. The reliance upon God, the confidence in Him, the boldness in His Name, and the trust in Him are the new ingredients of Fear of the Lord. This Fear was the starting point of true knowledge. The Scriptures continued to pour out its wisdom in us. We were called to serve the Lord by Fear of Him. We were to rejoice with trembling. Then, it became clear to us what it truly means to Fear the Lord. We began to discover the knowledge of God, which is found in Christ. The reliance, confidence, boldness, and trust in the Lord are the instructions of wisdom. And before honor comes humility—a lesson we had learned well in *step one* and would see at work here in *step six*.

We once despised knowledge; we did not choose to Fear Him. We rejected His counsel and despised His correction. The Fear of the Lord brings riches, honor, and life. It is pure and endures forever. The principle of the Lord is righteous. We now understood the judgment of *step two*. The Fear of the Lord prolongs our days, while our years in wickedness were only shortening them. We worshiped the Lord in the beauty of holiness—all the Earth should join us in these steps of remission. The Fear of the Lord is a fountain of life, protecting us from the snares of death. Better is a life of simplicity with the Fear of the Lord than great treasure accompanied by trouble. The Fear of the Lord is the beginning of wisdom, and the knowledge of the Holy One is understanding. It instills strong confidence, and His children find refuge in Him. As those who Fear the Lord and trust in Jesus, we are blessed—both small and great.

The scriptures beckon us, calling out, "Come, children, listen to Me. I will teach you the Fear of the Lord." It is to place our reliance upon the Lord, have confidence in Him, boldly proclaim His Name, and trust in Him—an infinite God. The angel of the Lord encamps around us as we Fear the Lord. Let all the earth Fear the Lord. Let all the inhabitants of the world stand in awe of Him. In the Fear of God, we submit ourselves to one another. We submit ourselves by Fearing Him.

On this new basis of trusting and relying upon God, we embraced a different perspective on life. Instead of depending on our limited selves, we placed our trust in the infinite God. We understood our purpose in the world was to fulfill the roles assigned to us by Him, whether it be as sheep, subjects, servants, children, or disciples. As we humbly relied upon Him, striving to align ourselves with His will, we discovered the ability to face calamity with serenity. We stood in the presence of the Consuming Fire which is the Holy Spirit. Never again would life happen to us. Should life come upon us as a roaring hurricane, we would find that God protects us as if we walked within the calmness of the eye.

In this revelation, we realized we need not apologize to anyone for depending on the Holy Ghost. We could even find humor in the misconception that religion and spirituality are signs of weakness. Paradoxically, it was through our belief, worship, and seeking of God that we found true strength. We wholeheartedly trusted in Jesus Christ, and we made no apologies for proclaiming His Name. In fact, we were amazed as He demonstrated, through our lives, the incredible things He can accomplish.

In the powerful Name of Jesus, God's life-changing power began to penetrate our hearts. This divine power revealed to us the path to true happiness. As we walked in complete integrity, guided by the light of God's Word, we experienced genuine joy. The sixth step of our recovery journey illuminated the way forward. Since embracing this step, we have been overwhelmed with joy, knowing that we have found our heart's true passion in seeking God.

In Christ, we are no longer bound to engage in destructive behaviors. Instead, we find joy in following the path that God has chosen for us. It is clear to us that God is guiding us toward a righteous and obedient way of life, as we wholeheartedly commit to walking these steps and measures. We eagerly anticipate the day when our lives will bring glory to God, and we strive to faithfully follow each of His sacred steps and align ourselves with the will of God in these measures of faith.

Through these steps, we find empowerment. We need not be ashamed, for we are receiving the strength that comes from embracing these life-changing actions. With hearts full of truth, we offer our gratitude to God. Each time we learn and grow through these righteous steps our faithfulness to God's revealed truth deepens. Let us be encouraged and never lose hope, for God never gives up on us. In His Name, we press on, knowing He is with us every step of the way, guiding us in our journey of recovery.

In the mighty Name of Jesus, we cried out in these steps of recovery. Our voices echoed with confession and repentance, and at times, the revelation was so profound it evoked audible sighs and expressions of awe. There were moments of revelation, where the truth became tangible. Our hearts were filled with a deep longing to obey Him, and His words became living miracles stirring our souls. We yearned to obey every word proceeding from the mouth of God.

As we embraced this step of willingness, His Word shattered the darkness within us, and the light of revelation burst forth. Our hearts were opened, and we gained insight into His purposes for our lives. We eagerly devoured the Word of God, craving the revelation that comes from taking in His steps. We felt His loving gaze upon us, extending His grace to every faithful follower. He was paving a path before us, a path adorned with His promises, where sins such as addictions and alcoholism would no longer have dominion over us.

Through His mercy, we were being rescued from the oppression of ungodliness. This deliverance from sins such as alcoholism and addictions enabled us to wholeheartedly keep this principle. We were aware of God's smile upon us, for we were His beloved servants. He instructed us in what is pleasing in His sight. When we witnessed others rebelliously breaking these steps, it deeply grieved us, and tears flowed uncontrollably, for we understood the grave consequences that await those who reject His ways.

In the Name of Jesus, we surrendered ourselves to His life-changing power, embracing this step of recovery with obedience. His grace sustained us, and His love guided us as we walked this path of recovery. In this sixth step, we felt the breath of God infusing us with new life. He had gazed upon our misery and had become our Savior, for we would never forget what He revealed to us through these steps thus far. We witnessed how He stood by our side as *step one* took us, defending us amidst the suffering caused by sin. Indeed, He redeemed us in the second step and was resurrecting us in the remaining steps up until this point, just as He promised from the very beginning. Our wickedness was no more, and we sensed our salvation drawing near.

In the past, we'd disregarded God's message of truth, but now it was becoming the very essence of our lives. The scales of ignorance were falling away, and we found ourselves yearning for God's tender mercies. He was restoring our lives once again—the lives He intended for us all along. Through the revelation of these steps and His righteous principle, He was bringing us back to life.

Once, we were tormented by countless inner enemies, like persistent pests attacking our minds. But now, we were unwavering in our commitment to follow God's ways. We grieve when we reflect on our past faithlessness and the way we used to live, walking away from God's promises, consumed by bitterness, fear, and immorality. These steps and measures are wonderfully ordered.

But thanks be to God, for He has rescued us from the clutches of our former selves. With hearts transformed by His grace, we now pressed on, clinging to His truth and seeking His righteousness. His mercy continued to guide and sustain us as we walked in the light of His redemption and approached the end of these steps of remission.

As we continued to take this step, we experienced growth in our spirits. The hand of God was upon us, shaping us into the people He desires us to be. He bestowed upon us more revelation, enabling us to please Him more faithfully. Our newfound faith became evident to all those who are devoted to and Fear God, and they rejoiced, witnessing His life-changing work in our lives. His Word began to intertwine with our hearts.

We acknowledged that taking these steps has always been the right path. Even when we encountered His judgment within these steps, He remained faithful and true. We felt His kindness and the comforting touch of His love as we journeyed halfway through this sixth step. We had truly become His devoted servants, and He fulfilled His promises to us. We had tasted the tender love of Christ, and it invigorated us to press on. Shame, pride, and dishonesty were expelled from our souls. These character defects once burdened us, but now we were passionate about living according to God's ways.

We hope that all who are committed to taking these steps follow Christ's example as we walk the path of His instruction. Through this step, He is instilling in us a passion to fulfill His every desire in faith. As a result, we will no longer carry the burden of shame upon ourselves. We are free to embrace the fullness of who we are in Christ, unashamed and filled with a zeal for His truth.

As the revelation of our immorality unfolded, we were astounded by the depth of God's love displayed through His Word. With each passing moment of this step, our hearts were filled with the radiant light of His truth. We grew to treasure this step, recognizing the profound impact it had on our lives. Through this step, we gained an advantage over the power of sins such as addictions and alcoholism within us, for we took to heart every instruction given to us.

In receiving the revelation, we gained a level of understanding that surpassed any previous experience. We wholeheartedly embraced the eye-opening truths that were revealed to us. God, in His grace, granted us an abundance of insight, regardless of how long we had been on this journey. Our commitment to continue walking in the light of this path had positioned us to be conduits of an immeasurable amount of His wisdom.

Having completed this step, we refuse to compromise our morals in the face of temptation. We are determined to remain obedient to God's Word, unwavering in our commitment. We will not turn away from difficult truths, for it is God Himself who is teaching us to love His Word. The promises He reveals to us are sweeter than honey, and His revelation brings delightful joy to our hearts.

His truth has become the source of our understanding, replacing the misguided ways we once followed. We look back with disdain on the life we once lived in ignorance, grateful that God rescued us from such a way of living. We embrace His truth with gratitude, rejecting any other path that does not align with His Word.

ה HEY

The revelation of the sixth step came with tremendous encouragement. It requires tremendous faith, separating the grown-ups from the children. We were beginning to be fed meat instead of milk. We were experiencing the light. We began to experience faith as we moved through, bridging the gap of oneness with our Creator. The outbreathing of the Holy Spirit was now being seen as it created a new life where a dead one once was. We began to experience the presence of God within our human hearts. This revelation points to the object of our faith and allows us to be fruitful. This can only be done when the covenant of God encounters our faith.

The covenant. We entered this covenant the moment we passed over the threshold into the old door of the centuries in *step two*. We have now experienced the knowledge that God planned everything long before our lungs breathed air. This entry is marked with the blood of sacrifice. It was applied to its doorposts and lentil. This was a sign and protection for us, indicating that we were being spared. As we continued to take spiritual action toward being recovered, the spirit of addictions and alcoholism passed over us because we had entered the door marked with the Lamb's blood. This was not a long-drawn-out process. We hastily entered this step. We were now dressed in the garment of faith and ready to leave the grip of sins such as addictions and alcoholism. We were walking in God's deliverance.

Taking this step liberated us from the slavery of sin. This step will forever be a reminder of God's faithfulness to His covenant with us. This covenant requires obedience to God's instructions, the redemption He provides, and His faithfulness in delivering us from the oppression of sins such as addictions and alcoholism. It holds a central place in these steps and will continue to be celebrated, reminding us and others of the miraculous events that unfolded during **RECOVERY 5:12** steps and measures.

Opening our hearts to Jesus invites His Presence into our lives. The moment we confess that God is everything, we are being led to spiritual growth. We are continuing to experience the power of Jesus Christ, the Good Shepherd, as He continues to guide and teach us. The power of the cross releases its power within us as we continue to gain deeper trust in faith. The entire *step six* process is a mind-transforming experience. Faith empowers us to overcome challenges. This brings us comfort and a new direction. The spiritual door's power lies in this communion with Jesus because He is the door. The positive changes in our lives occurred automatically. Through this relationship, we found spiritual nourishment and a sense of His presence.

Jesus declares Himself the door. He is the only one who can provide salvation. He is the only one who can bring us true fulfillment. Our lives had no purpose without Him, but He stood at the door of our hearts and was knocking. We accepted Him as Lord and Savior. In that moment, we embraced His teachings. Seeing His power, we surrendered to His guidance. This relationship brought forgiveness from God. We received promises of eternal life if we stay close to Him and perform His work well. By confessing, we opened the gates of righteousness and began seeking this path of spiritual growth which deepens our relationship with God.

In *step six* of our recovery, pursuing righteousness and aligning with God's will is crucial. These steps are a way of seeking God in pursuit of righteousness. These measures of faith are how we are going to align ourselves with God's will. Our intention is to travel from this side of the door with thanksgiving and praising the Lord. This participation indicates our faith to continue to follow principles, knowing that it's through this door that the righteous enter. Just what do we mean? When we entered through the door, we were seeking alignment with God's will. As we entered, we began reflecting on His values. Additionally, *step six* includes praise and worship to deepen our communion with the Holy Spirit.

We recognize the life-changing power of seeking God. We actively engage with God, persistently asking, seeking, and knocking. Recognizing God as the One who has all power and knowledge, we understand that seeking yields blessings. It entails humbly approaching God and seeking His will.

When the door was opened, we received an invitation to enter a place of safety. We have entered His presence. Having entered these gates mentioned in Isaiah 26:2, we are being granted spiritual blessings that further deepen our relationship with God. *Step six* of our recovery is cultivating righteousness which aligns with God's will. The power of the spiritual door in this step lies in recognizing the importance of remaining committed to God's ways. The door is open for those of us who keep our trust in God. This was the beginning of the seed of righteousness planted in humility.

Having stepped through this door, we now bow in humility and the consciousness of possessing nothing of our own. As a door, the choice to open ourselves to hope or to remain closed off and alienated is now ours. Spiritual self-nullification leads to further humility, the doorway to God's house, which is attained by those who choose to cling to Jesus as a drowning person to a life preserver. He is the judge to whom the Father has given all power under heaven and Earth. He appeals to us who were poor and needy to receive the grace of the Lord. If anybody hears His voice and opens the door, He will come to them and will sup with them, and they with Him (Revelation 3:20).

Faith. Faith is not only easier for us to grasp in *step six* but we now have applied it. We first experienced it as the spark of God in *step one* then saw it grow into willingness and overflowing faith in *step four*. It became the absence of fear in *step five*, and now it was part of the revelation in *step six*. We were now ready to use this faith for which we were grasping.

It's the Holy Spirit that revealed the evolution of faith from the spark of God to willingness. They are all one and the same. Faith is God's hand being applied to our lives. Over and over, we are reminded! Much like the power of art lies within the moment that the artist's hand applies the tip of the brush to the blank canvas, at that moment and each similar moment that ensues lies within it the complete Power of transformation. The entire artistry is in the moment, Faith.

This faith that was contained within the seed the size of a grain of mustard seed carried the necessary power to consume sins. Although these spiritual terms may have been foreign to us in the beginning, we have experienced faith as the foundational building block and the essential element in every work that proceeds out of His mouth.

Faith contains effort. *Step six* requires us to cash in on the commitment that we made to embark on this path of spiritual growth. When we prayed, we were unknowingly turning our backs on fear and committing our ways to the Lord. We committed ourselves to the task at hand, aligning our efforts with His will for our lives. When we confessed, we exhibited a trust in the Lord's provision which would become the central theme of our recovery. Our souls were connecting to a level of trust in God that we were experiencing. Trusting in our God, we sought Him with humble confidence. Once we followed our sixth step willingness with action, we received the Faith of a promise and God did act. Our humble trust was not passive but was accompanied by action. Applying the power of faith to *step six* required decisive action, seeking power to initiate this spiritual process of recovery. We were blessed because we had begun to be pure in heart and in that moment, we saw God.

Faith is the spiritual atom from which all the other spiritual gifts begin and end. This is the divine point of spiritual energy. Since faith is used to form all the other spiritual gifts, and since God uses the gifts and the building blocks of His manifestation, faith indicates God's omnipresence. Faith is the starting point of the presence of God in all that we do – the "spark" of the Holy Spirit in everything.

Faith is the picture of humility. It is the mark of humility. Faith always points to God. It is vital, since without Faith the entire Gospel is to be considered nil. God delights in using the small, the weak, and the insignificant to demonstrate His glory and power. If we are brought low or are of little stature in this world, we trust that our life is important to God. God's great plan is at work. All things come together for the good of those who love Him, and we have quickly come to love Him.

Faith is the directional sign that points to God. It holds the parts together in unity. It alludes to divinity and a picture of Jesus as our humble Mediator before the Father. Faith is like a hand that is reaching from heaven. It only comes to those who humble themselves in prayer. Therefore, faith shows that He is Spirit, He is One, and that from Him derives all things seen and unseen by the power of His word.

We are returning to God by means of the life-changing power of the Holy Spirit. Sins were scooped up by the hand of God. Opening the door of our heart reveals a picture of the Spirit of God indwelling in us, and this image expresses the idea that part of this Power is joined with our brokenness to form this revelation. Thus, we mourn.

The sixth step encompasses the principle of mourning, as we become part of those who mourn. Embedded within this principle is the understanding that we are also becoming pure in heart. As we progressed through this step, these truths became increasingly apparent. The promises of this step manifested in our lives; it is we who will know God in all His fullness. We are truly grateful for this humbling step that led us towards righteousness, as it separated us from all that which once beset us on our life-changing journey. Pain and sorrow no longer held dominion over us. We not only received blessings but were doubly blessed, experiencing the richness of God's mercy. And now we find ourselves with a clean slate, a pure heart living in a newfound faith.

It became clear to us that willingness is crucial in this process. Just as Jesus taught, we recognized that our inability to overcome our sins was rooted in our lack of belief. However, He also assured us that even a tiny seed of faith, like a mustard seed, could move mountains and make the impossible possible. Prayer and fasting were emphasized as essential practices to strengthen our faith.

We came to understand that our unbelief was connected to our prejudices and worldly knowledge. Therefore, we asked Him to help our unbelief. Then as we humbly embraced a willingness to believe, a remarkable change began to take place. The towering mountain of intellectualism, which had overshadowed and hindered us for so long, started to melt away in the presence of God's truth. Our hearts were filled with the radiant light of His love and redemption.

Through faith, we realized that we could see God conquer the obstacles before us. Our prejudices and misguided beliefs were no match for the power of God working in us. As we surrendered our doubts, we witnessed the extraordinary, knowing that nothing was impossible with God.

In the Name of Jesus, we pressed forward, continuing our recovery journey with renewed faith. We understood that it was through faith that we would experience God overcoming our sins such as alcoholism and addictions. It gave us the experience of true freedom. Our actions are guided by this faith, as we trust in God's life-changing power to lead us on the path of recovery.

Oh, how we cherish and hold dear the steps and the principle He has given us! Throughout each day, we eagerly embrace the light that emanates from them. By embracing and following these steps, we gain an advantage over our spiritual adversaries, for we take to heart every word He speaks. His revelations have granted us a deeper understanding, for we have wholeheartedly absorbed His illuminating truths. We have been blessed with an abundance of insight because we have faithfully taken every step on His path. In the face of temptation, we stand firm in our moral convictions, choosing obedience to His Word. We refuse to shy away from difficult truths, for He Himself has taught us to cherish His words. His promises to us are a delightful sweetness, surpassing the taste of honey, as His revelatory light shines upon us. Our understanding is derived from His truth, not the falsehoods espoused by those who do not know Him—falsehoods we hold in contempt.

Humility's shining light makes this choice within us; the revelation of His Word is making our pathway clear. To live our lives by His righteous rules is our lifelong commitment. We were bruised and broken, overwhelmed by it all, but by taking this step, He breathed life into us again by His living word. Therefore, we offered this new life to Him. We prayed:

Lord Jesus, I humbly offer my sincere
gratitude to You, And I beseech You
to guide me further in ways that
bring You joy. Teach me, dear Lord,
how to walk in Your footsteps, And
reveal to me the path that leads
to Your perfect will.

Despite the precarious state of our lives, we are resolute in holding fast to His teachings. Our former ungodly ways have attempted to derail us, but we remain steadfast, unwavering in our commitment to follow His instructions. Each word He speaks to us is like a precious treasure, bringing immense joy and filling our hearts with gladness. With unwavering determination, we have resolved in our hearts to obey His commands, wholeheartedly.

We humbly implore others to be wholly devoted to God's Word. Despite the unwarranted persecution from the influential, our hearts are filled with awe due to the miraculous power of His words. His promises bring forth abundant joy, and the revelation of His Word excites us like the discovery of hidden treasure. We hold deep disdain for every deceitful act, as our fervor for observing these steps burns within us. Our hearts are filled with gratitude, and we pause to offer Him praise throughout the day, for His Way is flawless. The lovers of His Word experience profound peace, and they will never stumble.

We burned for more of Him. We prayed:

> *Lord, my heart yearns for an even deeper experience of Your salvation, for I desire to walk in a manner that brings You delight. Grant me the strength to follow Your commands wholeheartedly, that I may bring joy to Your heart. I surrender my will to Yours and seek to align my every thought and action with Your perfect will. Fill me with a burning passion to please you, and let my life be a reflection of Your righteousness.*

Our love for His ways is beyond words; deep within our souls, we long to walk in them flawlessly! We diligently observe His principle; our every step is laid bare in His presence. We have begun to understand His steps. We desire to know more. We prayed:

*Dear Jesus, please help us understand the
meaning of Your ways so that we
can enjoy the good things that come
from following them. Give us wisdom and
help us know and obey Your truth
with all our hearts. Guide us in
doing things that make You happy because
we really love what You say. Teach
us to value Your words more than
anything else in the world. Keep us
from being fooled by things that are
not true and show us what is
real. Fill our hearts with joy
as we take these steps and
do what You ask. Let us feel
confident in Your promises because we love
You and want to serve You. Protect
us from people who may criticize us
for believing Your beautiful words.*

We begin to experience cravings for more of His steps! His righteousness revives our spirit!

Step six: We were asked, "Are you ready to let God remove all the things that you have admitted are wrong? Can He take them all away—every single one?" If there's something we were still holding on to and wouldn't let go of, we asked God (not our conceptions) to help us stay committed. After taking this sixth step, we began to understand more deeply the main principle of those who mourn.

This sixth step introduced faith as we had never known. We apply it to our lives in obedience to the Lord. We have discovered the willingness to trust God with our lives in such a way that He removes all the sins such as addictions and alcoholism from us. We now see that the spark of God, which has always been faith, has been available to us from the very start.

We humbled ourselves before the Lord, and He lifted us up. The Holy Spirit granted us a reward of faith for our open-mindedness. He gave us Himself and we no longer needed our conceptions of Him the moment we accepted that Jesus is not who we *thought* He was and that He is God all by Himself. He does not need any conception to validate Him, the moment we were willing to lay our conceptions down, the icy mountain of intellectual pride in whose shadow we had stood and shivered in all our lives suddenly melted away and we saw that nothing was impossible for God.

We were now concluding the realm of remission. We got ready to get on our knees and pray the seventh step prayer. This was a huge moment of anticipation for our hearts to become pure. Now we had put all that had been objectionable in His hands. Mercy flooded our souls.

The sixth step carries the Hebrew name Manasseh, which means "to forget," and has profound application in the context of recovery. While the concept of forgetting may sound counterintuitive in recovery, it is essential to understand how it relates to this process. Recovery involves healing from past traumas, mistakes, and negative experiences. The name Manasseh is the process of letting go of the burdens of the past, forgiving ourselves and others, and moving forward with a fresh perspective. For those of us recovering from sins such as alcoholism and addictions, forgetting is interpreted as God breaking us free from the chains of sin. It means that we are leaving behind these old habits that once controlled our lives. The name Manasseh is the changing of our identity. In recovery, we observe God redefine us by shedding the negative aspects of our past and embracing a whole new set of concepts and motives. While forgetting the past is not about erasing memories entirely, it serves as a reminder to focus on the present moment and to avoid dwelling excessively in a time that does not exist. To forget, in this context, develops a new life. It involves converting past challenges into testimonies and no longer allowing them to define or limit our future potential.

In recovery, we work towards creating a better and brighter future in Christ. The name Manasseh is the journey of building a fulfilling life unburdened by the weight of past struggles and it all begins when we are baptized in Jesus' Name. Forgetting is finding inner tranquility through baptism. Recovery involves seeking God as He provides the elusive balance in our lives. We observe Jesus remit our past through baptism in His Name, which is the vital action for achieving that. To forget is to practice seeking the witness of remission through the application of Jesus' Name to our lives.

In recovery, we learn kindness and treat others with forgiveness. It's important to note that forgetting, in the context of recovery, doesn't mean suppressing or denying past experiences. Recovery requires offering ourselves to Jesus as we are buried with Him in baptism. However, the name Manasseh is about avoiding dwelling on negativity and focusing on the fact that Jesus forgets our sins and remembers them no more. It creates a present moment worth embracing and looking forward to a brighter future in Christ.

The overarching principle for *step six* continues to reflect our mourning. The second step's righteousness and covenant brought a smile to our faces as we thought of the goodness of the Lord. We were beginning to see how we are blessed because we mourn. We now appreciated our mourning, and He was comforting us. As we took this step, we felt overwhelming gratitude as our hearts continued to ache because we now loved Him so much. The Lord consoled us as we rejoiced in the mourning.

As we placed everything before the Lord, we approached this step with pure motives, because it will be us who will know God in all His fullness. We were seeking pureness of heart. We wanted more! The heartfelt mourning coupled with seeking pure motives changes the sixth step's motives into purity. As we approached this step with this mindset, the game changed and we were filled with even more undeserved promises. We had now given ourselves completely away in baptism; we had been shown a pure heart. With the principle of a pure heart and pure motives, we saw God.

We reiterate that the core principle of *step six* is becoming pure in heart. The promise of complete comfort surrounds and fills our spirits. This promise becomes evident when we take the final action of *step six*, seeking forgiveness. Through baptism in Jesus' Name for the forgiveness and remission of sins, we encountered the unveiling of God. We experienced the fulfillment of the promises made to those who mourn by having a pure heart—we will be comforted and see God!

Goodness.

When looking back on this step, we can see that there are actions that we as Holy Ghost-filled recovered believers undertake to humble ourselves before the Lord and experience His uplifting. With each step we are reminded to set aside specific time each day for prayer, Bible reading, and meditation, seeking God's presence and guidance. We now regularly examine our hearts and actions before God, confessing any sins or wrongdoings, and sincerely repenting. Now we purposefully engage in acts of service and kindness towards others, without seeking recognition. We offer our time and skills to serve in church, recovery ministries, community outreach, and charitable organizations. Seeing the power of prayer, we grow to commit to praying for the needs of others, interceding on their behalf with faith. We find ourselves looking for opportunities to offer words of encouragement to those around us. We remain open to receiving constructive criticism, acknowledging our need for improvement. We cultivate a heart of gratitude towards God and others, expressing thankfulness for His blessings. We are encouraged to regularly attend worship services to praise God with fellow believers. We then find ourselves partaking in communion as a reminder of Christ's sacrifice with the body of Christ. Then, diving even deeper, we practice fasting as a way to humble ourselves before God, seeking His guidance. We soon launch into forgiving those who have wronged us, releasing bitterness. If in a leadership role, we find an innate source of servant leadership to the people we serve. Regularly acknowledge our need for God's wisdom in all aspects of life, we are sensitive to the leading of the Holy Spirit, seeking Him to direct our thoughts and efforts.

Remember that humility is a continuous journey and a posture of the heart. By actively engaging in these specific tasks, we cultivate a spirit of humility, drawing closer to God, and experiencing His uplifting and life-changing power in our lives.

CHAPTER 12

STEP SEVEN

*"We humbly, on our knees, confessed our sins and
God being faithful forgave us our sins and purified
us from all unrighteousness."
(1 John 1:9)*

Therefore, when ready to take *step seven,* we brought all the nature of our sins before our eyes.

BITTERNESS EXAMINATION: THE PRAYER LIST			
Column Four			
Our own mistake:			
Selfish	Dishonest	Self-Seeking; Seeking Gain	Fear
x	x	x	X
X	x	x	X
	x	X	X
X	x	X	x

fear EXAMINATION				
Column Three				
Mark X if it did not relieved the fear				
Self-Reliance	Self-Confidence	Cockiness		Trusting in Self
x	x	x		X
x	x	x		x
x	x	x		x
x	x	x		x

IMMORALITY EXAMINATION		
Column Four		
Where were we at fault? Were we…		
Selfish?	Dishonest?	Inconsiderate?
x	x	X
x	x	X
x	x	X
x	x	x
x	x	x

We have arrived at the point where we consummate the vow we began in the third step and whose covenant we have been walking in as we sought the Lord through these steps. We find a place with this Holy Ghost-filled person and we get on our knees, bow our heads to the King of Kings whose Spirit is in the room doing business with us, and close our eyes. Then we follow the promptings of this disciple of Jesus as they pray, and we recite after them this prayer:

> *"Dear God, I surrender myself to You*
> *completely, the good and the bad.*
> *I humbly ask that You take away*
> *every sin that is hindering my ability*
> *to serve You and others. Grant me*
> *strength as I go out from here*
> *to follow Your will.*
> *In Jesus' Name, Amen."*

The slips of paper containing the fourth column of the bitterness examination, the third column of the fear examination, and the fourth column of the immorality examination have been removed and the table before us is empty, void, a blank slate. We walk in faith now.

We have now reached the completion of *step seven*, affirmed our commitment, and sealed the covenant we initiated in the third step. It was more than just a mere decision; it was a humble act of surrender as we knelt before Jesus Christ, denying ourselves, surrendering our thoughts and efforts to Him, taking up our cross, and following Him. With a resounding "Amen," we acknowledged His authority and entrusted our lives to His loving care. In Jesus' Name, we surrendered all. A troop cometh!

Now we embarked on the journey that God planned for our lives. We had been walking in a perpetual prayer of His righteousness, covered by the covenant established long ago. Standing at the threshold of the open door, our heads bowed in reverence, we recited our solemn vows to God. As we did, the slips of paper representing our sins, the very nature of sins such as addictions and alcoholism itself, and the crumpled piles of guilt were removed from the table. They were consumed, symbolizing their complete eradication. With hearts filled with faith and determination, we stepped through the covenant gates that stood before us, ready to embrace the path that God has set for us.

At this stage of our spiritual development, we come to realize that what was missing in the first step was the Power and Communion of the Holy Spirit. As we reflect on the words of our brother Matthew, who recorded Jesus saying, "All power in heaven and earth has been given to me!" it becomes clear that in the first three steps, we were introduced to His Power. Through repentance, we turned away from our own limited power and toward the One who possesses all Power. We also turned away from our spiritually disconnected state and opened ourselves to the filling of the Holy Spirit.

There was more to be done. *Steps four* through *six* revealed that sins still had a lingering grip on our lives, and our minds were quick to remind us of our past failures. We understood that the true nature of our sins such as addictions and alcoholism was rooted in choices and actions that we performed willingly or unwillingly. So, what were we to do about these sins that stood before us?

The answer came to us through the words of our brother Peter. He said, "Repent and be baptized, every one of you, in the Name of Jesus Christ for the remission of sins, and you shall receive the gift of the Holy Spirit." With this understanding, we took immediate action. We repented and were baptized in the Name of Jesus, and to our amazement, the lies of sins such as addictions and alcoholism were instantly washed away! A newfound freedom embraced us and we smiled with relief, recognizing that this faith was only the beginning.

But we knew that more action was required. We understood, as James reminded us, that faith without works is dead. We couldn't simply rely on our faith alone; we needed to accompany it with actions. Otherwise, this act would be us merely getting wet instead of being an eternal shift in our spiritual trajectory.

The abundant life! The first order of business is to pray:

Jesus, my Lord, I humbly come before You in prayer. I ask that You lead me to walk in the abundance of life, where I can always live in obedience to Your truth. Open my eyes, dear Jesus, so that I may see the miraculous wonders hidden within these steps and measures of recovery. Grant me the wisdom to fully grasp the significance of each step. Help me to recognize the life-changing power they hold and the blessings they bring. As I continue on this journey of recovery and salvation, let me experience the miracles that unfold along the way. Guide me, Lord, in following Your footsteps and embracing the path You have set before me. May I walk in obedience, knowing that Your ways are perfect and lead to abundant life. Illuminate my mind and heart with Your divine revelation, that I may fully comprehend the depth of Your love and the power of Your grace. I surrender myself to You, Jesus, as

*Your faithful servant. Strengthen me, empower me,
and equip me to walk this path
of recovery with courage and determination. Let
your Holy Spirit guide my steps, and
may I always find comfort and strength
in Your presence.
Thank you, Jesus, for
hearing my prayer. I trust in Your
unfailing love and mercy as I embark
on this journey of transformation.
In Your precious Name, I pray. Amen.*

Our time on Earth is short, as God lovingly instructs us in His wisdom. We have an insatiable longing to obey His commands. We are no longer burdened by His displeasure, as we have humbled ourselves in our limited knowledge. We no longer face His rebuke, for we have embraced His principle.

Despite the mockery from others, we remain committed to serving God and following these steps. Even if society's elites and leaders criticize us, we stand firm in our dedication. God's principle guides us, serving as our counselor, and His Word brings us joy and fulfillment, illuminating our path.

We cherish the guidance of our Heavenly Father throughout our recovery. We continue to walk steadfastly in His righteousness, relying on His strength. These steps lead us towards a changed mind and freedom of the spirit in Jesus' Name.

We are being revived by the Word! Lord, we are meek because it is apparent that we were fading away. We were discouraged and lying in the dust, but You revived us by Your Word, just like it was promised You would. We have poured out our lives before You and You have been there through each of these steps with us. So, we further pray to be in Your presence:

*Lord Jesus, I humbly come before You,
seeking a deeper understanding of Your
holy decrees. Enlighten my mind and open
my heart to comprehend the profound wisdom
within Your teachings. May Your Word resonate
within me, filling my thoughts and reflections
with Your splendor and wonders.
Grant me the ability to meditate deeply
on Your truth, to ponder and contemplate
the richness of Your ways. Help me
draw closer to You through the study
and contemplation of Your Word. As I
immerse myself in Your wisdom, may Your
presence be felt, and Your truths come
alive in my life. Thank You, Jesus,
for the privilege of knowing You and
the opportunity to grow in knowledge and
understanding of Your ways. Guide me on
this journey of faith as I seek
to align my thoughts and actions with
Your divine purpose.*

Our life's strength is no longer melting away with grief and sadness; God came, and His presence strengthens us and encourages us. He keeps us far away from what is false, giving us grace to stay true to His principle. We have chosen to obey His truth and walk in the light of splendor of all that He teaches us. We keep praying:

*Lord, guide me to avoid life's chaos
as I cling to Your commands and
faithfully follow them.
In Your precious name, I pray. Amen.*

Now, we run after Him with delight in our hearts because He is making us obedient to His instructions.

This seventh step introduced us to the beauty of prayer. We discovered the power of prayer as we asked Him to take all of us, the good and the bad. We saw what God would do once we humbly got on our knees and confessed these sins that had been revealed. We humbled ourselves before the Lord, and He who is faithful forgave us our sins. The Holy Spirit purified us from all unrighteousness. The moment we prayed, Jesus moved in and began reminding us of how He had been honoring the vow we began in *step three*. Repenting in *steps one* through *three* and then experiencing the remission of sins in *steps four* through *six* culminated in baptism in Jesus' Name. The Holy Spirit prepared Himself to come upon us as we went out from there to perform His bidding for the rest of our days.

ג GIMEL

A journey has begun. In the realm of biblical-based recovery, these steps are powerful tools for finding hope. One such step is this seventh step, which carries profound significance and inspires us on our journey towards recovery and salvation.

This step is where we experience His strength in overcoming obstacles and making positive changes. This gift makes this step particularly relevant to the challenges we will face in recovery ahead. Just as the seventh step signifies strength, it also serves as a psychic change in biblical-based recovery. The path to recovery requires us to embark on a journey of spiritual change. The seventh step reminds us that no matter how difficult the road may seem, within us lies a changed life and the power to overcome sins such as addictions and alcoholism.

This journey brings forth another profound element connected to recovery—charity. This virtue is our camel in this incredible spiritual journey, known for its ability to bear heavy burdens. It represents the importance of showing kindness towards those who are still sick and suffering. The seventh step reminds us to extend our hands as we provide the necessary support to those in need.

Within the prayers of the seventh step lie the representation of a set of principles guiding us in this biblical-based recovery. First, there is faith: *Step seven* embodies the importance of faith in recovery. Trusting in the guidance of the Holy Ghost as He provides strength when facing challenges. Second, there is perseverance: The halfway hump of these steps serves as a reminder to persevere through difficulties and not lose sight of the goal—freedom from sins such as addictions and alcoholism. Finally, generosity: The journey's association with charity teaches the significance of giving back to others, as acts of compassion play a vital role in the recovery process.

To apply the journey that starts in this seventh step of biblical-based recovery, we consider some basic philosophies. We now draw upon God's strength within ourselves and from our faith to overcome obstacles and persevere during challenging times. We practice kindness towards others who are also struggling, recognizing that support is an essential element of recovery. We embrace the process of recovery, knowing that there it is a new and fulfilling life.

The seventh step, with its charity, holds significant relevance in biblical-based recovery. By incorporating the principles represented by the seventh step prayer—faith, perseverance, and generosity—we find inspiration, hope, and guidance in recovery. Remember, within each of us lies the transformation and the power to overcome alcoholism and addictions with God through this mighty journey that begins the moment we step through the door.

ד DALET

The door. The door whose threshold we began crossing into freedom in the *second step*. God planned it long before our lungs breathed air.

Its entry was marked with the blood of sacrifice. It was applied to its doorposts and lentil. This was a sign of protection for us, signifying that we had been spared. As we continue to take spiritual action toward being recovered, the spirit of addictions and alcoholism now passes over us because we have entered the door marked with the Lamb's blood. This has not been a long-drawn-out process. We hastily enter this step. We have been dressed in the garment of faith and have left the old life behind. We are entering into God's deliverance and protection. Taking this step liberates us from the slavery of sin. This step will forever be a reminder of God's faithfulness to His covenant with us. This covenant requires obedience to God's instructions, the redemption and protection he provides, and the faithfulness of God in delivering us from the oppression of sins such as addictions and alcoholism. It holds a central place in these steps and will continue to be celebrated, reminding us and others of the miraculous events that unfolded during this journey.

Becoming open-minded and opening our hearts to Jesus invites His Presence into our lives. The moment we make the daily choice that God is everything, we are experiencing spiritual growth. We are immediately experiencing the power of the Good Shepherd as He continues to guide us through another day. Daily, the power of the cross releases its power within us as we gain deeper trust in faith. The entire *step seven* process is further transforming our minds and spirits. This relationship empowers us to overcome challenges. It brings us purpose. We have a new direction. The spiritual door lies open in this communion with Jesus as we enter, which automatically results in changes in our daily lives. Through this relationship, we find spiritual nourishment and His presence.

Jesus declares Himself the door. He provides salvation. He brings us true fulfillment. Our lives have no purpose without Him. We accepted Him as Lord and Savior in the first three steps, specifically recognizing it in *step two*. In that moment we embraced His teachings. Seeing His power, we willingly surrendered to His guidance. This relationship brought reconciliation with God and, therefore, promises of eternal life if we stay close to Him and perform His work well. By bowing in humble submission in this step, we opened the gates of righteousness. We launched out on this journey of spiritual growth which deepens our relationship with Him.

In *step seven* of our spiritual journey, pursuing righteousness and aligning with God's will become crucial. These steps are how we seek God in pursuit of righteousness. These measures of faith are how we align ourselves with God's will. Our intention is to take this step through the door and into thanksgiving. This participation indicates our willingness to follow divine principles, knowing that it's through this door that the righteous humbly enter. Just what do we mean? Entering through the door involves seeking alignment with God's will in thanksgiving. As we enter, we begin practicing virtues and reflecting on His values. Additionally, *step seven* continues with praise and worship to deepen our connection with the Holy Spirit and enhance recovery.

We recognize the life-changing power of seeking spiritual guidance. We actively engage with God, seeking a deeper communion and persistently asking, seeking, and knocking. Recognizing God as the source of power and knowledge, we understand that action yields the Holy Ghost's insight. It entails humbly approaching God, expressing heartfelt desires, and seeking His will.

We have taken the first step in our journey as the door was opened, and we have entered a place of security in Christ. We are in His presence which provides access to deeper spiritual understanding. *Step seven* of our journey of being recovered focuses on cultivating righteousness through these steps and maintaining faith aligning with God's will. The power of Jesus Christ who is the door in this step lies in recognizing the importance of remaining faithful to God's ways. The door is open for those who keep their trust in God. This was the beginning of the journey of the pure in heart.

The seventh step carries the Hebrew name Gad, meaning "a troop cometh," and takes on deeper significance during recovery. The arrival of a troop is seen as a manifestation of support from the Holy Ghost.

In recovery, we recognize that a higher power is guiding us towards deliverance. The name Gad is the timing of events being guided by the Holy Ghost. In recovery, we experience synchronistic moments and confirmation of being in alignment with the will of God. The name Gad reminds those of us in recovery that even amidst challenges, there are hidden blessings and lessons to be learned. Adversities lead to recovery and a deeper communion with the Holy Ghost. Recovery is a time of salvation and identity in Christ.

The name Gad signifies the arrival of spiritual gifts, such as wisdom, peace, and service. Like a troop moving together towards a common goal, recovery is a journey towards aligning with God's will and living a life in harmony with the Holy Spirit's values. The name Gad is about seeking guidance and assistance from the Power which is God as we navigate life's challenges and strive for complete recovery. Recovery requires surrendering to God's will and having faith that things are unfolding as they should. The name Gad is the act of letting go and trusting in God's plan. Gad's meaning reminds those of us in recovery to draw strength from the Holy Spirit and do His bidding. It is tapping into the inner spiritual resources implanted by God for courage. The name Gad prompts gratitude for the Holy Ghost's intervention as experienced during recovery. It encourages us to acknowledge the role of the Holy Spirit in our recovery process. In a more spiritual light, the name Gad signifies the presence of the Holy Ghost working and the belief that recovery is not only a physical and mental process but also a journey of the soul. It invites us to recognize the spiritual aspects of recovery and to seek a deeper communion with the Holy Ghost in our pursuit of recovery and salvation.

We are now entering the realm of restitution. We get on our knees and pray the seventh step prayer with our righteous friend. They have led us through the completion of the vow which we will walk within for the rest of our days if we so choose by taking the actions prescribed each morning. Repent, Read, Pray, then Follow! This is a huge moment of prayer for us to become peacemakers. Now we will have joy even when life doesn't seem easy. Meekness overflows our souls.

Each morning we get up and repent, acknowledging that Jesus is King and that sin has no hold on us for this day. We then get into the Word of God, reading the Word so we might sanctify and cleanse ourselves as the church with the washing of water by the Word, so we might present ourselves for the day. We carry the Word into our morning prayer, seeking God. After spending time with Him each morning, He provides a message or intuitive thought for us to carry throughout the day. We Repent, Read, Pray, and Follow in complete humility – meekness.

The overarching principle for *step seven* reflects our meekness. The third step's power, spirit, and prayer bring a smile to our faces as we think of the goodness of the Lord. We are beginning to see how we are blessed because we are meek. We now appreciate our humility, and He is giving us a life that He had intended for us all along. As we have taken this step, we feel an overwhelming gratitude as our hearts continue to operate in meekness. The Lord, who is the true vine, sends joy through us, His branch, as we rejoice in the meekness.

We approach this step seeking peace. Because it will be us who will know what it means to truly be able to act as a child of God. We are seeking peace. We want more! The heartfelt meekness coupled with seeking peace changes the seventh step's joy into peace. As we approach this step with this mindset, the game changes and we are filled with even more undeserved promise. We have now sealed a covenant with the Almighty. We have been shown peace. With the principles of meekness and peacemaking, we know that we shall be called the children of God.

Faith.

Of course, as we look back on this step, there are spiritual actions that we as Holy Ghost-filled recovered believers undertake to humbly confess sins on our knees and experience God's faithful forgiveness and purification. We continue to interact with God through prayer, meditation, fasting, and worship. Some of us even write down our confessions and prayers in a journal, expressing our hearts to God and seeking His forgiveness through that method. It's amazing to go back through our journals and see not only the answered prayers but also those prayers that were answered despite never having been prayed for. It is recommended that we incorporate biblical passages about forgiveness and cleansing into our prayers, personalizing them to our situation. We begin to pray with fellow believers who offer support, encouragement, and intercession during our time of confession. We dedicate specific periods of fasting to seek God's face and express our desire for repentance and cleansing. We reflect on God's attributes, such as His mercy, grace, and faithfulness, as we pray for forgiveness and purification. If needed, we seek pastoral counseling or spiritual guidance to work through specific areas of struggle and seek God as He heals us. Many of us start taking personal retreats to spend extended time in prayer, reflection, and seeking God's forgiveness and renewal. We chuckle as we discover that we begin singing psalms, hymns, and worship songs that express themes of forgiveness, cleansing, and God's love. We find ourselves creating prayer lists to regularly pray for specific sins and weaknesses in our lives and seek God's deliverance. We begin memorizing verses about forgiveness, repentance, and God's purification, allowing the Word of God to be on our hearts and minds. During prayer for forgiveness and purification, it is recommended that we consider using anointing oil as a symbolic act of consecration to God. Many utilize the gift of speaking in tongues to pray for forgiveness and purification, watching the Holy Spirit intercede on our behalf. We begin meditating on specific biblical accounts of forgiveness and restoration, such as the story of the prodigal son, to draw closer to God's heart of mercy.

Remember that these spiritual actions should be approached with sincerity, seeking God's leading and the work of the Holy Spirit in our lives. As we engage in these specific actions, we experience the life-changing power of God's forgiveness and purification in our hearts and spirits.

The seventh step teaches us about humility, and within that principle lies the first of the three steps (seven, eight, and nine) which emphasize becoming peacemakers. This step brings forth the promise of experiencing the fulfilling life that God had intended for us. And within that promise lies the assurance that we shall be called the children of God! In Jesus' Name! Now, let's think of others.

CHAPTER 13

STEP EIGHT

*"We remembered those who had something against us
and became willing to first be reconciled to them all."
(Matthew 5:23-24)*

Let's look at *steps eight* and *nine*. Like with the rest of this soul-searching and trying, we must be willing to make restitution where we have done harm, if we do not bring about still more harm in doing so. In prayer and fasting, we ask God what we should do about each specific matter. The only person who can answer these questions is Jesus Christ, and He cannot answer them for us unless we really want to know and will listen to what He tells us. If we are unsure if it is the voice of Christ that is giving us these intuitive thoughts, then we run them by someone who is Holy Ghost-filled and in a daily relationship with God. They will be able to help us determine if the thought is of God.

Now *step eight*. This one was taken like this. We had already begun a list of all the people we harmed and to whom we are willing to make amends. We created it when God examined our bitterness and immorality.

The slips of paper that were left to the side were now brought into faith and placed before us. The lists contained names of people, places, things, and concepts to whom we owed reconciliation. We were building our harms list. Surely the Lord has looked upon our affliction; now therefore our Lord will love us. But there was more action to take.

We subjected ourselves to a drastic self-appraisal. Now was the time to pray, asking God to bring into our minds those whom we had harmed and were not previously listed because there were plenty of people we had harmed whom we were not bitter at, nor did we fear or owed restitution to because of immorality. The Power of God revealed to us as we asked for Him to bring to our minds anyone with whom we had done damage to a relationship. The list was something like this:

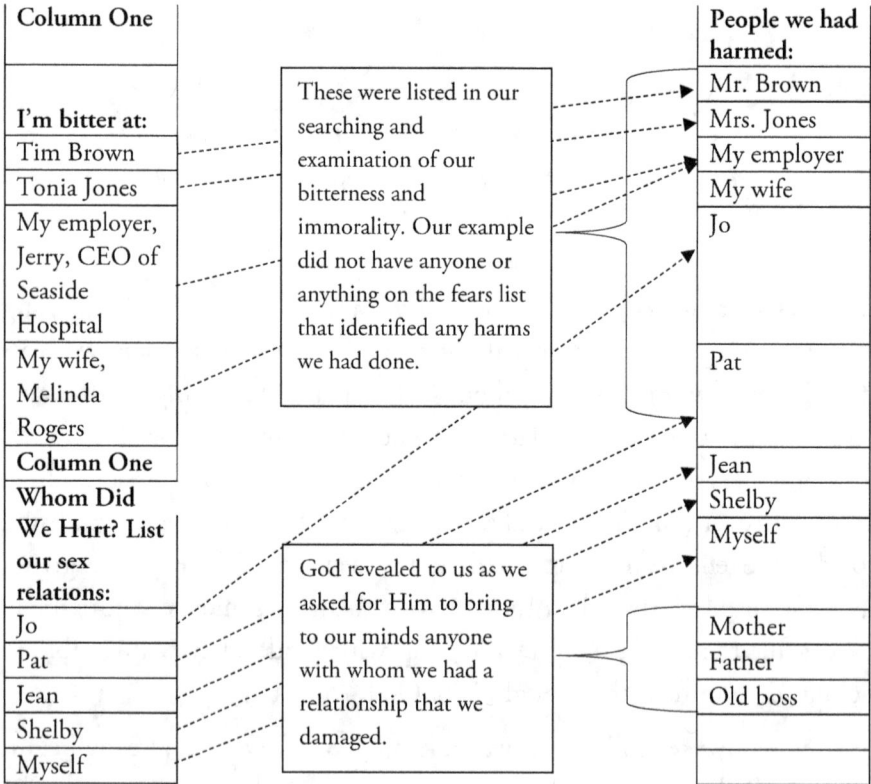

Once we stepped into the flow of the Spirit, we were communing with God and He gave us a clear conscious. We asked once more to please bring into our consciousness any relationships with His children that we had damaged. After being reassured there were no others, we had our *step eight* "Harms List." These were the restitutions that we had to make so that our temples could experience Spirit-filled fellowship and his righteousness would enter in.

AMENDS LIST
People we had harmed:
Mr. Brown
Mrs. Jones
My employer
My wife
Jo
Pat
Jean
Shelby
Myself
Mother
Father
Old boss

In His mercy, He breathed life into us once again. He looked upon our deep misery and became our hero, coming to rescue us. We will never forget the revelations He has bestowed upon us. He stood by our sides, defending us in our sufferings. Now He is redeeming us, and in the steps to come, He will revive us, just as He promised. We are moving further away from our wickedness and closer into His salvation. Once, we cared little for His message of truth, but now it is the very essence of what we hold dear. We needed His tender mercies, and He provided them abundantly as He restored our lives. We prayed:

> *Oh God, restore my life once more*
> *through the revelation of Your righteous ways.*
> *In the precious Name of Jesus, Amen.*

Once our own adversaries, we now stand unwavering, embracing the path of these steps. Our hearts ache and we are humbled as we recall our faithless ways, abandoning the shelter of His divine principle. Now we are professing our love for the Lord's teachings and His grace revives our spirits. His words hold timeless truth, and His righteous decrees endure. In the shadow of humility, we find ourselves persecuted for the sake of righteousness, embracing the promise of God's intended life. Beneath its embrace, in prayer, the kingdom of heaven becomes our rightful inheritance.

ר RESH

Prayer. We learned of its power in these steps. There is a reverence that we stand in when we bow our heads to the Lord. Only prayer delivers us from this bondage of self. We are always ready to rush to bended knees with heads bowed low to the majestic King of Kings, Lord Jesus Christ. In this reverence, we experience the bridge between the spiritual and the material which delivers us from the chains of sins such as addictions and alcoholism. It is here where we bring ourselves to the feet of Jesus. Our spirits always respond with hands wide open to this bowed experience. The Holy Ghost's Power flows in as He consumes that which was of old and God continues building with us as he thinks. We experience blessed righteousness in humility.

Through prayer we entrust our ways to the Lord, knowing that He intervenes and guides us along the way. We submit ourselves to the authority of God daily as He uplifts us. Daily prayer connects us to Jesus. Without this communion, we are unable to witness Him bear fruit in our lives or achieve meaningful transformation in our recovery. Daily prayer involves trusting in the Lord wholeheartedly. When we pray, we acknowledge His presence. Daily prayer is required to receive guidance in every aspect of our lives. Through daily prayer, we surrender our own understanding and lean on God. In prayer, we experience the direction and clarity we need for recovery. Daily, through prayer, we connect to God's grace, which is more than enough to sustain us. When we pray, we are embracing our vulnerabilities, and relying on His power! In prayer, we are vessels for His life-changing work. The source of the Power is accessed once we pray.

Prayer is the very action of compassion. This communion to compassion makes prayer particularly relevant when contemplating *step eight*, as it involves acknowledging the harm caused to others and seeking to repair those damages with empathy. Prayer grants access to spiritual examination. It is a reflection of our service and worship.

Step eight encourages us to engage in an honest and thorough examination of our past behavior, recognizing the ways in which our actions have negatively impacted God's children. Prayer allows us to look within as the Holy Ghost confronts our sinful actions and performs the miracle of converting them to compassion. In this step, the focus is on making a list of individuals harmed by our actions. This step recognizes the importance of repairing damaged relationships and seeking forgiveness. Prayer reveals the interpersonal connections of all God's children, even us, and directs us to approach this process with a genuine desire for reconciliation. Because in these reconciliations, we hear God.

Prayer is taking stewardship of our actions. *Step eight* directs us to acknowledge the harm we have caused without listing excuses or placing blame elsewhere. Recovery involves facing our preconceived ideas as we actively work toward making restitution in Jesus' Name.

There are many applications of prayer in *step eight* of recovery. We take the time to reflect with love on our past actions, considering the impact they have had on others. This process of prayerful examination allows for spiritual awareness. We approach this beginning of the restitution process with compassion, recognizing the pain we caused others. We demonstrate a sincere willingness to make things right. We admit responsibility and avoid justifying the harm caused. We embrace the opportunity to rectify the damage by taking the necessary steps toward restitution. Prayer is power.

א ALEPH

The Power. The Power that we experienced from the third step, the very breath of God, continued to be applied in our fourth step searching to try us. That examination demonstrated that there is faith before power. Then the Power reminded us that *step five* could not begin without the Power which is the Holy Spirit. In these steps, we found ourselves in this familiar embrace of the Holy Ghost's Power churning within us.

The breath He takes before He even utters a word. The very breath that He used to create the heavens and the Earth out of a void. The same breath that He used to create man. And the same breath He used as He called out our names. This breath breathed the Holy Spirit into us. His breath is Power.

We now know that we were the one out of the ninety and nine and that He is reviving us. Now, we have had the Name of Jesus applied to our lives through the baptism in *step six* that carried us into *step seven*. We are no longer going through this alone. We were brought to this place after using all the efforts He supplied in the previous steps. None of these were our ideas. This powerful spiritual position of submitting to this Power was the very breath that was being breathed into our hearts. His breath contains Power beyond our wildest thoughts. This breath would move us into more action.

We now know the Lord is near to those who are poor in spirit. We reassure you that when we feel weak and powerless, the first thing we recognize is the call to stop and seek God. For He is the only one who grants us strength. We trust in the Lord with all our hearts, recognizing that His wisdom surpasses our limited understanding. The Power of *step eight* is in the remembering of those whom we had hurt. Then we begin to see our part in each of the damages done. This drives us to willingness to be reconciled with them all.

To access this Power, we had to remember those who had something against us and realize it was perhaps because we had hurt them. God was aligning us with His will. We rushed to be still and recognized the sovereignty of God. We were reminded that He has full control. We surrendered to His guidance. We exalted Him as His will is fulfilled after we pray for each specific one! We heard "well done" after we were reconciled with them all. By embracing a posture of stillness, we opened ourselves up to the life-changing working Power of the Holy Spirit. We stood in this heavenly flow and communed with God.

Standing in this communion was unlike the overflowing we felt earlier in recovery. In *step four*, we learned the awesomeness of standing in the overflow. We learned that this communion led us to His outpouring and that His Spirit continues to overflow. In *step eight*, we see the connection that secures the unseen overflowing to the seen in recovery. This powerful action of the Holy Spirit is felt at once as we take this step. It is true faith.

This connection is what helps us navigate the journey of making amends. This experience is one of linking our list to the unseen. This connection with the Holy Spirit's bidding involves establishing the damage done by our actions. We connect with the Holy Spirit like a tent peg holding various elements of our spirit together. *Step eight* continues to emphasize the importance of willingness to repair the damage. We seek harmony with relationships that have been severed due to our actions.

The connection to the Holy Spirit within us links words and phrases within sentences which is essential in our making restitutions. We follow the Holy Spirit's guidance during the planning of each restitution. We turn to God for the willingness to restore the damage we have done.

Step eight involves being willing to make restitution to all those we have harmed. This connection secures righteousness to integrity and conviction to ethical behavior. It serves as a reminder that to restore relationships, we must acknowledge our past transgressions and demonstrate assurance or a genuine commitment to change. Our temple is being prepared.

ב BET

As we stood in repentance of the first three steps, in complete humility, we were aware of the stains of sins such as addictions and alcoholism in our lives. Sin was a part of our past and had a hold on us, causing us terror, bewilderment, despair, and frustration. In the *fourth step*, we were introduced to the concept that our bodies are temples. We now realize that our repentance during *steps one*, *two*, and *three* was evidence that our bodies were made into sacred temples, being prepared to receive the Spirit of Holiness. Through the miraculous experience of where the ensuing steps pointed us, we have been filled with the Holy Spirit, and we no longer belong to ourselves, but to God who purchased us with the precious blood of Jesus Christ. Therefore, we use our bodies and spirits to bring glory to God. Or do you not know that our body is a temple of the Holy Spirit within us, whom we have from God? We are not our own, because we were bought at a price. So, we glorify God in our body (1 Corinthians 6:19-20).

There was true joy in seeking what was hidden beneath the ruins of our past. We no longer struggle to find a way to stay pure. We have discovered that we only achieve this by living in the Word of God. But we needed to repair the damage that we had done to our past, or we would quickly find our way being blocked again. So, we planned in *step eight*. We sought God with all our hearts, for He is the only one who is keeping us on the right path. We treasured His Word in our hearts so that we dared not sin against Him. We had to repair the damage which solidifies our testimony.

He is our great God, and we praise Him above all else as our hearts are being prepared for purging. We will be purged of the damages we have done to relationships in our useless lives of sin. We pray and He continues to teach us His power through these steps and measures. We seek His principle continually, reciting His counsel out loud. We find more joy in following His commands than in pursuing all the riches of our previous lives. We have set our hearts on His ordered steps and measures, paying close attention to all His ways. We delight in His principle, and we walk in His words. His Word is a lamp to our feet and a light to our path (Psalm 119:105). In our pursuit of righteousness, we prepared our lists and get to the action needed to repair the damages we have done.

NUN

Righteousness. The steps through His righteousness have been a laborious spiritual process. This cyclical spiritual relationship that was introduced into our lives came at a great cost—the complete and utter destruction of self. The building of a spiritual whirlwind is not easily done. Only the Creator can produce such a powerful experience. He created the wind and placed us safe and protected in its midst.

The journey in righteousness is nowhere near being completed in our lives, but the steps we have already taken in His righteousness have introduced some sound revelations. In *step one*, we began with our righteousness bent in humble submission to Him. This was humility. *Step two* introduced us to the seed of His righteousness implanted into the good ground of our hearts. *Step four* began a spiritual rearrangement and while taking it, we saw that humility must come from righteousness. Then it showed us that faith comes before humility and righteousness before faith. *Step six* pointed to this process, smiled, and said, "Ah, humility!" *Step eight* now chuckles and says, "Clearly, this is righteousness." And thus, the cycle of faith, humility, and righteousness starts to build up steam and the sound of a rushing mighty wind is beginning to develop as we continue to take this step in true faith. We recover in the midst of Him.

Righteousness represents both faithfulness and the reward for faithfulness because when we are humble before God, we are also standing upright on the final day. In this present life, the person filled with His righteousness simultaneously affirms, "I am nothing but dust," and "The world itself was made for my sake." We humble ourselves in the sight of the Lord, and He lifts us up (James 4:10).

The seed of humility, which was watered in our *step one* experience, found itself in good ground and is the very sign of activity and life. From this step, we saw that in *step six*, humility was a crown of glory. Glory is the manifestation of God in this life.

Jesus came as a man, was honored by His absolute humility while upon Earth, and is now exalted as the Righteous One who wears the Golden Crown of God upon His head forever and ever (Revelation 14:14). May His Name (NUN) be eternal; while the sun lasts, may His Name endure; let those of us invoke His blessedness upon ourselves; let everyone count Him happy (Psalm 72:17). We pray, blessed be the Lord, God of Israel, who alone does wonderous things. Blessed be His glorious Name forever; may the whole earth be filled with His glory! Amen and Amen (Psalm 72:18-19)! Nun, first seen bent over in *righteousness*.

This eighth step has introduced us to the beauty and the power of the very substance of true faith. We discovered the results of faith the moment we began to do God's bidding and the first thing He required us to do was make a list of all His children that we harmed. Then He asked us to have the faith needed to make restitution to them all. We now see faith once we humbly obey. We are walking in meekness before the Lord, and He is faithful and has already shown us the way to treat others. Jesus washed their feet. In light of this, we admit that we don't know it all and we are faithful enough to learn. The moment we obeyed, Jesus moved in and began supplying all our needs as the vow that we had begun in *step three*. Repenting in *steps one* through *three* led to the remission of our sins in *steps four* through *six*, culminating in our baptism in Jesus' Name. The Holy Spirit prepares Himself to come upon us as we go out from here to perform only his bidding for the rest of our days.

In recovery, the Hebrew name Reuben, which means continuing faith, carries a powerful and uplifting message. There are many ways that the name Reuben applies to recovery. Recovery requires faith in the process of salvation. The name Reuben is about holding onto our belief that recovery is possible and that with perseverance and determination, God transforms our minds, souls, and spirits. Continuing faith implies a steadfast commitment to the journey. In recovery, we face challenges, but the name Reuben inspires us to stay resilient and persistent in our pursuit of God and His salvation.

Reuben's meaning of "continuing faith" refers to the belief in a higher power which is God and His Name is Jesus. This belief serves as a source of strength during difficult moments in the recovery process. Recovery is a time of spiritual growth and identity in Christ. The meaning of the name Reuben encourages us to embrace our walk as we progress toward a more fulfilling life in Christ. During recovery, doubts and uncertainties arise. The name Reuben serves as a reminder to overcome those doubts and to stay steadfast in our commitment to God's ability to transform our lives. Continuing faith implies hope for a brighter future.

In recovery, we begin to envision a life of health, wellness, service, and ministry, guided by faith in our Lord and Savior, Jesus Christ. The name Reuben's meaning suggests learning from past experiences. Recovery involves seeking the inner witness of the Holy Ghost and using those lessons to fuel His service and ministry. For those of us in recovery, embodying the name Reuben serves as an inspiration to others who are struggling. Demonstrating continuing faith offers hope to those seeking recovery. Faith is strengthened through support from others. The name Reuben encourages us to seek communion with supportive friends, family, or recovery communities. In essence, the name Reuben's meaning of "continuing faith" is a guiding light in recovery, the unwavering belief in healing, transformation, service, and ministry. It encourages us to remain steadfast in our commitment to recovery and to embrace the journey with an open heart.

Step seven began our journey in the realm of restitution as a troop cometh and in *step eight* we found ourselves right in the middle of the whirlwind. Although we have not made any, we vaguely sense that we are a part of one bigger than we had ever imagined.

We remembered those who had something against us and became willing to be reconciled to them all. Therefore, we began with our list of harms. We are walking in the covenant that we sealed with Jesus in the seventh step and will be joyful for the rest of our days if we so choose by taking the actions prescribed each morning. Repent, Read, Pray, and Follow! This is a huge moment of faith for us to become willing to make restitution to them all. Now we will have joy even when it is us who are being mistreated for doing what Jesus would do because we are submitting to His will. Meekness overflows our souls.

We take this step despite knowing that we will be persecuted for the sake of righteousness. It will be us who will know what it means to truly be able to experience the kingdom of heaven. We are seeking a life of obedience to His will. We want more! The heartfelt meekness coupled with obedience changes the will in this step from ours to one of righteousness. As we approach this step with this mindset, the game changes and we are filled with even more undeserved promises. We are now operating in obedience to the Almighty. We are being shown obedience. With the principle of meekness and righteous obedience, we know that the kingdom of heaven is ours and that we are submitting to His will.

Temperance.

Indeed, as we look back at this step, Matthew 5:23-24 emphasizes reconciliation as the crucial aspect of living as a Holy Ghost-filled redeemed believer. To fulfill this teaching, there are specific actions we take. We regularly examine our relationships and past interactions to identify any unresolved conflicts or grievances.

In this step, we all created a list of God's children whom we had hurt or who had something against us. In *step nine,* we use this *step eight* list to take the initiative to reach out to those people to express our willingness to reconcile. *Steps eight* and *nine* teach us to humbly make amends and seek forgiveness from those we wronged. They teach us to acknowledge our mistakes and seek direction to correct any new errors as they crop up. We learn the power of praying for wisdom, humility, and courage before approaching those with whom we seek reconciliation. When speaking with others, we find that we are able to listen carefully to their feelings and perspectives, demonstrating empathy and understanding. These two steps prepare us by demonstrating the effectiveness of being open to hearing how our actions have affected others, even if it is difficult to hear. We become more and more able to resist the urge to become defensive or place blame during the reconciliation process of these steps.

A willingness to offer forgiveness and extend grace to others who seek reconciliation with us is a product of these steps. They teach us the value of reaching out for additional support, as we seek the assistance of a trusted mediator, pastor, or sponsor for difficult situations. In *step eight*, we always pray for healing and restoration of the damage done in the relationships on our list. We trust in God's ability to bring reconciliation. We prepare ourselves to always stay humble throughout the reconciliation process, recognizing that all have sinned and fallen short of God's glory. We let love guide our interactions, seek the well-being of others, and promote unity in the body of Christ. We soon find release of all grudges and bitterness we are holding onto, observing God's forgiveness flow through us.

Remember that the process of reconciliation takes a moment of preparation, but it is an essential part of living as a Holy Ghost-filled recovered believer. Embrace these steps' biblical teaching of Jesus. With the help of His Holy Spirit, we pursue reconciliation and healing in all of our relationships.

CHAPTER 14

STEP NINE

*"We did unto them as we also have them do to us except
when to do so would injure them or others."*
(Luke 6:31)

Step nine. Now we go out to our fellows and repair the damages we have done to relationships. With each restitution, we attempt to sweep into the consuming fire the debris that has accumulated out of our effort to live on our own thinking and run life ourselves. If we haven't the faith to do this, we ask until it comes. Remember it was agreed at the beginning that we would go to any lengths for victory over our sins such as addictions and alcoholism. In each moment of restitution, we are trying to put our lives in order. But this is not the end. This act of faith is part of our real purpose, which is to be of maximum service to God and His children as we stand in the overflow. Because the Lord has heard we were hated, he has therefore given us His righteousness to do so.

Not everyone catches this vision and rushes in. You will have a feeling of doubt or apprehension about the outcome of making restitution. We are reminded that we are not in the outcomes business any longer. Like our will and lives, this too is God's business. As we look over our harms list, we feel shy because of a lack of self-confidence about going to some of them on a spiritual basis. Let us be reassured. This spiritual feature of our recovery is the foundation of our existence. Today, you will feel like a child learning its first steps. Don't be too excited and run right away, but don't be too timid as to not walk at all. Learn to trust the Holy Ghost as you stand under His flow.

Because you have been exposed to such a life-changing spiritual experience, we must warn you that during your restitutions, there may be some people we need not, and probably should not, emphasize the spiritual feature to on our first approach. Although you have found a new life in Jesus Christ, avoid rushing into a damaged relationship screaming, "I have found Jesus!" If we do this, it could cause further harm while trying to repair the damage we have done, especially to those who still feel pain from our injustice to them. This is just setting yourself up for further damage. Why lay yourself open to being branded a fanatic? The answer is that you shouldn't because it will kill a future opportunity to carry the beneficial message to this person. Many people with whom we attempt restitution are sure to be most impressed with our sincere desire to set right the wrong we have done to the relationship. Don't be surprised if they remain more interested in a demonstration of goodwill than in your newfound faith.

However, we don't use this as an excuse for shying away from the subject of God. Every chance we get, as righteous people, we pursue His good purpose. In His righteousness, we are willing to announce our convictions with tact and common sense. This is how we make restitution.

Enemy Restitution: Restitution in the journey of recovery takes various forms and cannot be confined to a specific process. While it is impossible to address every situation, let us focus on meaningful types of restitution. Among them, one of the most challenging and feared is reconciling with those we once considered enemies. How do we approach them for restitution? Some individuals may have caused us greater harm than we inflicted upon them, and even though our attitude towards them may have improved, admitting our faults may not fill us with enthusiasm. However, even with those we dislike, we must accept the inevitable hardships and endure the resulting pain with courage.

In such situations, we must remember the teachings of Scripture. The apostle Paul reminds us that if it is possible, as far as it depends on us, live at peace with everyone (Romans 12:18). This encourages us to seek peace and reconciliation, even with our enemies. It is harder to approach an enemy than a friend, but we must recognize the greater benefits that come from making these amends early on.

As we embark on the path of enemy restitution, we should pray for God's guidance and ask for His help in showing a helpful and forgiving spirit. Our task is straightforward but profound. Following the example of Jesus Christ, who forgave His enemies even while on the cross, we humbly and sincerely confess our former ill feelings and express our regret. We are reminded that when our ways please the Lord, He can make even our enemies be at peace with us (Proverbs 16:7).

During the process of making restitution with our enemies, it is essential to maintain a Christ-like attitude. We should refrain from criticizing, arguing, or discussing their faults. Instead, we must focus on our own actions and demonstrate a forgiving spirit. We are encouraged to be kind and compassionate to one another, forgiving each other, just as in Christ God forgave us (Ephesians 4:32). By extending the love and forgiveness we have received from God, we set a powerful example and create an opportunity for healing.

As we embark on this journey of restitution, we are surprised by the outcomes. Sometimes, our enemies also acknowledge their own faults, leading to reconciliation and the mending of long-standing feuds. Once again we are reminded that when our ways please the Lord, He can make even our enemies be at peace with us (Proverbs 16:7). However, even if our attempts at restitution are not well-received or reciprocated, we can take comfort in knowing that we have done our part. But this thought is only applied to this level of amends. When we reach our families later, merely saying, "I have swept my side of the street" is not going to be enough.

If our enemy is hungry, we give them food to eat; if they are thirsty, give them water to drink. In doing this, we heap burning coals on their head, and the Lord rewards us (Proverbs 25:21-22). Our demonstration of love is not in vain, and we can trust that God sees our efforts. We must remember that restitution is about taking responsibility for our own actions. As we pursue restitution with a humble spirit, we trust in God's guidance and find peace in knowing that we have fulfilled our part in the process.

Financial Restitution: In matters of making amends for our debts, we do not avoid those to whom we owe money. We are honest and transparent about our past lives and the changes we are striving to make. Proverbs 3:27 advises, "Do not withhold good from those to whom it is due when it is in your power to act." Therefore, we do not fear disclosing our past mistakes, even if it may have financial consequences. We approach our debtors with humility, acknowledging our shortcomings and expressing remorse for our delayed payments. By taking this approach, we are surprised by the response of even the most demanding creditors.

When it comes to financial restitution, our goal is to arrange the best possible resolution with those we owe. We let them know that we genuinely regret the delays caused by our past actions. We no longer allow fear to hold us back from facing our financial obligations, recognizing that fear hinders our progress, and its carnal ingredients are the number one offender of relapse. We are reminded that we owe no one anything, except to love each other, for the one who loves another has fulfilled the principle (Romans 13:8). Therefore, we strive to fulfill our obligations and mend our financial relationships, guided by the principles of responsibility. In our pursuit of financial amends, we rely on God's wisdom, trusting that He softens hearts and brings about understanding. We are assured that when the LORD takes pleasure in anyone's way, He causes their enemies to make peace with them (Proverbs 16:7).

We approach our debts with integrity, seeking resolution and demonstrating our commitment to change. By addressing our financial restitutions with a spirit of responsibility, we strive to restore the damage we have done to these relationships. Through the power of God's grace and the principle found in His Word, we overcome our fear and embark on this path of financial restoration, trusting that He is guiding us and bringing about recovery. We are surprised by the response. Some ask that our only restitution is to keep doing what we are doing and that we do not owe them anything. Our debt is forgiven. It is during these times that it is wise to consider as a form of amends preaching the gospel to the poor, healing the brokenhearted, delivering the captives, recovering sight to the blind, setting free those who are bruised, and preaching the acceptable year of the Lord. For these are debts well paid.

Legal Restitution: Then there are the legal restitutions we need to make. It's possible that we have committed a criminal offense that, if known by the authorities, could lead to imprisonment or loss of employment. While we have already confessed such offenses to another person in *step five*, we often fear the consequences of revealing them to the proper authorities.

It could be a minor offense that many of us have committed, or we may be facing an arrest warrant. These are common troubles we encounter. In the process of making legal amends, there are various forms they take, but we rely on the guiding principle that we love another as Jesus has loved us.

Recognizing our commitment to go to any lengths for recovery, we pray for the guidance to do the right thing, regardless of the personal consequences. We may risk losing our position, reputation, or even facing imprisonment, but our faithfulness to the path of recovery remains steadfast. We cannot shy away from these challenges. We acknowledged our sins to God, and we do not cover our iniquity; we committed to confessing our transgressions to the Lord and He forgave the iniquity of our sins such as addictions and alcoholism (Psalm 32:5). Through the steps thus far, we understand the importance of admitting our faults and seeking forgiveness, not only from God but also from those we have harmed through our actions.

However, it's important to remember that these legal matters often involve other people. We must not be hasty or foolish, sacrificing others to save ourselves from the consequences of our past actions. If we were in jail, we would be unable to provide any restitution to those affected. In such cases, competent attorneys can assist us, advising us on writing letters where we admit our faults, seek forgiveness, and outline our plans. We may even need to include money as a gesture of legal restitution. In some situations, we might need to express our willingness to accept imprisonment if required. In Matthew 5:25, Jesus teaches, "Settle matters quickly with your adversary who is taking you to court. These steps teach us to make restitution while we are still together on the way, or our adversary will hand us over to the judge, and the judge could hand us over to the officer, and we may be thrown into prison. This reminds us of the importance of taking responsibility for our actions and seeking resolution without delay.

Throughout this process, we rely on God's guidance and seek His wisdom. We trust that He will provide us with the necessary discernment to navigate the complexities of legal amends. We surrender our fears and trust that He will work for our good and for the restitution of those damages created by our actions. We are always reminded of what we have experienced through these steps and remember that when we conceal our sins such as addictions and alcoholism, we do not prosper, but every time we confess and renounce our sins, we discover mercy (Proverbs 28:13). As we make amends in legal matters, we choose the path of integrity, knowing that true salvation and recovery are found in admitting our faults and seeking reconciliation. We place our trust in God, knowing that He is just and merciful. We commit ourselves to the process of making legal amends, acknowledging the wrongs we have committed, seeking forgiveness, and doing our part to make things right. His guidance and grace are with us every step of the way.

Before we run into the court and throw ourselves upon its mercy, it pays well to understand the value of the attorneys and lawmakers who navigate the legal system. When left to our own devices, we could find ourselves making detrimental legal decisions that create monumentally challenging circumstances that could be avoided by following the suggestions of those better suited for navigating the legal system.

Drastic Amends: There are times when we need to make drastic amends in our recovery. However, before taking any actions that could potentially implicate others, we must ensure that we have their consent and support. We should seek wise counsel from others and pray for God's guidance, and if it becomes clear that a drastic step is necessary, we must not hesitate or shrink back. We realize that it is better to take risks and make amends than to continue in destructive behavior that leads to guilt before God. We are implementing more and more of God's principle as we trust in the Lord with all our hearts and do not lean on our own understanding. In all our ways acknowledge Him, and He will make straight our paths (Proverbs 3:5-6).

We understand the importance of placing the outcome of our actions in God's hands, trusting that He is guiding us and protecting us from backsliding. In these situations, our pastor and church family play a significant role. We share our testimony, explaining the journey of recovery, including the necessity of the drastic actions we have taken. When our actions are met with widespread support, it not only strengthens our bond with the church community but also establishes us as trusted pillars in both our church and recovery community. By involving our church family, we create a support network that provides encouragement, accountability, and a sense of belonging. It is through the collective support of our fellow believers that we find the strength to face the challenges of making drastic amends. Together, we strive to live in alignment with God's principle and demonstrate His life-changing power.

As we embark on these drastic amends, we seek God's guidance, trust in His wisdom, and rely on the support of our church family. We understand that these actions come with risks, but we are willing to take them for the sake of our recovery, the restoration of damages we have done to relationships, and our commitment to live in accordance with God's will. God grants us the courage, discernment, and favor needed as we navigate the process of making drastic amends. Our actions bring honor to His Name and serve as a testimony of His redeeming power in our lives.

Relationship Restitution: It is not uncommon for us to encounter relationship troubles in recovery. These challenges create the opportunity for relationship amends. Relationship troubles often complicate our intimate connections, leading to weariness, resentment, and breakdown in communication. The remission steps of four, five, and six revealed how essential it is for us to acknowledge our faults and sincerely apologize for our actions. We genuinely regret the harm we have caused, and with God's grace, we commit to changing our behavior.

Our program of recovery is not a one-sided endeavor. It is beneficial for both individuals in the relationship. Complete honesty is required. Both parties must choose the path of wisdom, good judgment, and love. We should each pray about the situation, keeping the other person's happiness as our primary concern. It is crucial to recognize that we are dealing with the powerful force of human emotions. Therefore, we must approach the problem with tact, all the while realizing that Jesus is going before us, and we are walking behind Him with our hand grasping His garment. Our goal is to avoid harmful arguments and focus on finding collaborative solutions. By working together, we gain a deeper understanding of the issues at hand and co-create a path forward in the relationship. Often, this approach proves successful in resolving conflicts and fostering mutual recovery.

In our pursuit of healthy relationships, we now know that we must anchor ourselves in biblical principles and seek guidance from Scripture as

He continues to mold our ideals. The Word of God provides insight on how to cultivate harmonious relationships. We are reminded of the importance of selflessness in our interactions with others. Scriptural principles teach us that charity is patient, and charity is kind. It does not envy, it does not boast, it is not proud. It does not dishonor others, it is not self-seeking, it is not easily angered, and it keeps no record of wrongs. Charity does not delight in evil but rejoices with the truth. It always protects, always trusts, always hopes, and always perseveres. Therefore, we must press on with love as the driving force in our relationships.

We should be patient, putting the needs of our partners before our own. It is important to let go of pride, and instead honor one another. We should strive to cultivate an atmosphere of forgiveness, letting go of past wrongs and embracing a fresh start. Furthermore, we remind you to be kind and compassionate to one another, forgiving each other, just as in Christ God forgave you (Ephesians 4:32). We emphasize the significance of kindness, compassion, and forgiveness. As recipients of God's forgiveness, we are called to extend the same grace to others. This mindset fosters restoration in relationships.

In our efforts to improve these relationships, we should always remember the principle of trusting in the Lord with all our hearts and leaning not on our own understanding; in all our ways we submit to Him, and He is making our paths straight. We are encouraged to rely on God's wisdom, rather than solely relying on our own understanding. By submitting ourselves to God's direction in *step three*, He has been navigating our relationship challenges with humility. Therefore, we seek His guidance for further reconciliation. With this biblical principle as our foundation, we can approach any relationship issues with a genuine desire to honor God. As we strive to apply this principle, we are trusting in God's faithfulness as He continues to guide us on the path of recovery and thriving relationships.

In our sinful state, we can cause great devastation in the lives of others. Our selfish and inconsiderate habits wreak havoc on our relationships, leaving hearts broken and affections uprooted. We must come to the realization that merely avoiding sins such as addictions and alcoholism is not sufficient. We cannot simply brush off the consequences of our actions and expect everything to be fine. We are forewarned to not be deceived: God cannot be mocked. We reap what we sow (Galatians 6:7).

We now see clearly that our actions have consequences, and the damage we have inflicted on others cannot be ignored. We cannot downplay the destruction and expect everything to magically be restored. To truly address the destruction caused by our sinful behaviors, we needed a life-changing experience within ourselves, within our minds.

This is what we are experiencing, and it starts with acknowledging our faults, seeking forgiveness, and actively working toward reconciliation. We must humbly recognize the pain we have caused and be willing to make amends. Our soul cried out asking God to create in us a pure heart and renew a steadfast spirit within us (Psalm 51:10). Like our brother David, we needed God's life-changing power to change our hearts. We needed His strength to become more selfless, considerate, and compassionate people.

Through repentance and seeking God's forgiveness, we discover hope for salvation. We have entered in Christ, and a new creation has come: The old has gone, the new is here! (2 Corinthians 5:17) Through the power of Christ, we become new creations, leaving behind our destructive ways, and embracing a life of love.

Avoiding sins such as addictions and alcoholism is not enough. Instead, we continue to strive for more change and actively work towards repairing the damage we have caused to relationships with God's children. We pray that God grants us the wisdom to rebuild what was broken and restore the relationships that have suffered.

Family Restitution: When it comes to restoring relationships within our families, we must take the initiative and lead by example. Mere apologies and empty words of remorse are not enough to rebuild what has been broken. We need to have honest and open conversations with our family members, where we reflect on the past and take responsibility for our actions without criticizing or blaming them. It is important to approach the process of family restitution with humility and a willingness to make amends.

Living a spiritual life is not just a concept; it requires action. As we strive to live according to the principle of Christ, we should not force our beliefs onto our family members if they are not ready or willing to embrace them. Instead, we should focus on demonstrating the change that has taken place within us through our behavior and actions. We are taught the principle of submitting ourselves as Christ exemplified. So that, if our partner does not believe, they may be won over without words but by our behavior when they see the purity and reverence of our lives (1 Peter 3:1-2). Our behavior, guided by the Holy Spirit, has a profound impact on our family members. Through our consistent example of Christ's love, forgiveness, and living according to God's principle, they are inspired and influenced to change over time.

We are mindful that years of living a worldly and self-centered life can make anyone skeptical or resistant to spiritual matters. Patience is key, as change takes time. When it comes to this specific category of family amends, we trust in God's timing and continue to live out our faith in a way that speaks louder than words. These "living amends" only work with the family. When misapplied to other categories of restitution, they re-introduce our self-delusion which is detrimental to our recovery walk. Ultimately, it is the life-changing power of the Holy Spirit working through us that will make the most significant impact on our families. As we embark on the journey of family restitution, once again, let us remember to approach it with the love of Christ, and a genuine desire to rebuild what we have damaged. God grants us the discernment to navigate this process and our recovered lives serve as a testament to His love, power, and way of life.

Harmful Restitution: There are some restitutions that harm others. Some wrongs we never fully right. We don't worry about them if we can honestly say to God, ourselves, and another human being that we would right them if we could. We have faith that with the Holy Spirit's guidance, we are willing to make amends should He create the opportunity for reconciliation to materialize. Otherwise, we think heavily on seeking opportunities for preaching the gospel to the poor, healing the brokenhearted, delivering the captives, recovering sight to the blind, setting free those who are bruised, and preaching the acceptable year of the Lord. This works when all other spiritual and recovery efforts fail.

Unseen Restitution: Some people cannot be seen, such as those who have died. In these cases, we write them a honest letter. In the letter, we record anything our heart leads us to write but we are sure to include recognition that we have done damage to the relationship and ask them what we can do to repair the damage. We then take the letter to the graveside or to a spiritually significant area in our lives. We read the letter aloud, destroy the letter, and then wait for God to bring a thought into our minds of what restitution is required. If we are prayed up, this word from God typically happens quickly. We begin to sense the unction of the Holy Spirit. It brings a whisper of an answer to our spirits and minds of the directions we need to follow to make restitution with those who have gone on from this life.

As we continue this journey, we realize that the Holy Spirit has often been speaking to us. His words come and they are full of wonder. However, the enemy typically introduces himself immediately afterward and attempts to convince us that the original thought was not from God. Then, if we are inactive in seeking God, our flesh rouses itself and errs on the side of caution. It procrastinates under the guise of awaiting more information or further signs from God. This is nothing more than carnal disobedience. Any action requested by God that we do not follow is disobedience. Therefore, we must become more and more in tune with His still small voice in all of our affairs.

To sum up the ninth step restitutions: We should be sensible, tactful, considerate, and humble without being inferior or argumentative. As

God's people, we are full of honor, but we can also get on our knees and wash anyone's feet.

This level of devotion to God's Word is truly remarkable! Even if the powerful and influential try to persecute us unjustly, our hearts remain filled with awe because of the miraculous words spoken through each act of restitution. It feels as though Jesus Himself is imparting lifelong instructions to us. His promises fill us with joy, and the revelation of His Word thrills us like discovering hidden treasure.

Our newfound passion for His righteousness compels us to reject all forms of falsehood. We can no longer tolerate lies, as they evoke a strong sense of revulsion within us. Keeping His principle has become our burning desire, and we pause to praise Him throughout the day. His ways are perfect, and they bring profound peace to our lives.

No longer do we easily take offense; instead, we respond immediately with prayer. We express our longing for more of His salvation, yearning to walk in ways that please Him. Our love for His instructions grows deeper and becomes harder to put into words. It gets "gooder and gooder." In the depths of our spirits, we strive to follow them with perfection.

The overflowing love for His Word fills our hearts with wonder and delight. Throughout the day, we find ourselves constantly meditating on its wisdom. Through the process of restitution, God has granted us a wisdom that surpasses the cunning schemes of both our internal and external adversaries. The fruits of these restitutions accompany us continually, providing us with increasing insight. The testimonies of recovered lives inundate our prayers and meditation.

With each restitution, we realize that we are aligning ourselves with God's Word. Our actions demonstrate our commitment to His instructions. We have turned away from every evil path and remained faithful to His teachings. He guides us in each step we take, teaching us His ways.

The taste of His words is sweeter to us than honey, bringing nourishment to our souls. Through this step of restitution, we gain deeper discernment. As a result, we develop a profound aversion to deceit, detesting every path that leads away from His truth. Profanity begins to leave our vocabulary.

Our spiritual eyes are opening, and we are gaining a newfound vision. The veil is lifting, and we are seeing more clearly with each restitution we make. His presence provides us with unwavering assurance before, during, and after each of them. He shields us from the hostility of those who oppose us because we are committed to living justly. With every act of restitution, He speaks of His promise of blessing into our lives, breaking the oppressive chains of pride that once bound us. Like passionate lovers, our hearts yearn for more of His salvation and eagerly anticipate the heavenly rewards He promises. In this step, His tender love envelops us, reminding us that we belong to Him. Through each restitution, He deepens our understanding of His marvelous ways. This step reveals our need for greater revelation from His Word, as our love for Him intensifies. We long to know Him more intimately and fully, for our hearts are captivated by His love. We pray:

> *Lord, now is the moment for Your*
> *breakthrough, as we acknowledge the mess,*
> *we have made of Your divine revelation!*
> *In Jesus Name, Amen.*

Truly, His message of truth means more to us now than a vault filled with the purest gold. Every word He speaks from His lips through others, every truth that is revealed, is beautiful to us because we now hate what is phony.

We have walked in complete trust in the Lord as we embarked on these steps up to this moment. His overwhelming love envelops us as we take each purposeful step with urgency, eager to hear His voice in every reconciliation. He is our Savior, faithful to fulfilling His promises of heavenly reward. Our testimony goes beyond mere words; it is an undeniable answer to those who mock us, for we walk in unwavering trust in His Word. We will never forget this truth, for we depend on His Word in every aspect of our lives. Through this step, we live out His Word, moment by moment, and the words He speaks through these acts of restitution resonate deeply within us. We find ourselves walking hand in hand with Him, experiencing true freedom as we wholeheartedly obey His every command revealed through these moments of recovery. Fearlessly, we stand before anyone, speaking the truth without shame. Our joy lie in living according to His Word. We hunger for more revelation, desiring to delve deeper into the light of His Word as we continue to walk this path and meditate on His truth.

The shining light of truth illuminates our spirits. It guides us in every choice, and the revelation of His Word clears our path. The choice continues to be not ours. Embracing His righteous steps has become our enduring pledge. No longer do we have to live in a state of brokenness. Instead, we are overcome by His presence, as He breathes new life into us through His living Word. We pray:

> *Lord, I humbly offer my heartfelt gratitude*
> *to You, and I beseech You to*
> *continue teaching me the ways that bring*
> *You delight. Illuminate my path and guide*
> *me in fulfilling Your desires. Thank You*
> *for Your presence and the opportunity to*
> *please You. In Your holy Name, I pray.*
> *Amen.*

In the face of uncertainty, we remain steadfast in following His teachings without wavering. The attempts of the ungodly to derail us will not succeed, for we are firmly committed to the task He has given us. Every word that proceeds from His mouth is like precious treasure, bringing joy to our lives. Our hearts are resolved to obey His commands unconditionally, for all time.

Ninth Step Promises. If we approach this phase of our recovery with honesty and thoroughness, we will be astounded by the thought changing awakening that occurs even before we are halfway through. We will experience a profound sense of unparalleled joy. We will no longer harbor regrets about our past, nor will we desire to close the door on it, for it has become a testimony to His redeeming power in our lives. We will grasp the true meaning of serenity, and we will find peace as we embrace the indwelling of the Holy Spirit. Regardless of how far we have backslidden, we will witness how our testimony can bring hope and healing to others. The feelings of worthlessness and self-pity will dissipate, replaced by the revelation that we are beloved children of the Almighty King. Our focus will shift from selfish pursuits to caring for God's precious children. The urge to seek personal gain will fade away as we wholeheartedly serve Him and others. Our entire attitude and perspective on life will undergo a remarkable metamorphosis. The fear of people and financial insecurity will be lifted from our shoulders as we trust in God's provision. We will be intuitively guided in navigating once-perplexing circumstances, as the Holy Spirit convicts and directs us. We will suddenly realize that God is accomplishing in us what we could never begin on our own.

Are these extravagant promises? We think not. These miracles are being fulfilled among us. These miracles will always materialize if we work for them.

The Spirit. This consuming fire of the Holy Spirit removed ourselves in *step three* after recognizing we had been the ones wrecking our own lives and were using sins such as addictions and alcoholism to accomplish it. We confessed our sins and experienced true spiritual connection. The mere mention of His Name now accomplishes for us that which no human power could do. We now admit God's truth. This ninth step experience is life-altering for both the theologically inclined and the theologically adverse. This stadium of faith stills us all who are followers of Jesus Christ.

This position of purity is persecuted because it splashes in the face of our old spiritual prejudices. Having had the Name of Jesus applied to our lives, we experience being pure in heart. The Holy Spirit, this consuming fire, cleansed us of all our old ideas and we see God, and we now know His Name is Jesus. Miraculous things are happening. It is this fire that fuels the faith upon which we hear in each moment of restitution. The consuming fire continues a mighty work as we are transformed into new creatures with His power coursing through us as a vine's sap flows through its branch. We have been given a pure heart and now we know that God hears us. You too are to experience the awesome power of this consuming fire which is the Spirit as you navigate this beautiful step in the Name of Jesus.

This spirit aligns with the position of the Spirit in the Tabernacle plan of prayer. We often utilize this new prayer in our recovered lives while being southward, filled with the teachings of Luke, expressing the humanity of God, and representing overall humility through communion and service to others. Throughout **RECOVERY 5:12**, the Spirit can be represented by fire, divine presence, and transformation. These associations make Shin relevant to *step nine*, which involves seeking forgiveness and initiating a life-changing process of reconciliation and complete recovery.

If the Spirit had a shape, it would resemble flames or tongues of fire, because the Holy Spirit is the life-changing power of God. *Step nine* is a pivotal stage in recovery that requires us to courageously confront the consequences of our past actions and seek to make amends. The Holy Ghost reminds us that through the process of making restitution, a profound transformation is occurring in both the individual and the relationships involved, including our relationship with Him. His power rests upon us all neatly cloven.

The Holy Spirit is His sacred presence. The Holy Ghost has been sent in God's Name which is Jesus. In *step nine*, the act of making restitution involves repairing the damage we have done to relationships. The Spirit underscores the significance of recognizing His presence within ourselves and others during the process of reconciliation. Redemption is a central theme in *step nine* as we strive to make things right. The Holy Spirit embodies the concept of a changed mind turning back to God. He serves as a reminder that through sincere efforts to make restitution, we experience a restoration of our relationship with God and His children. We will forever remember the act of seeking restitution as the power that further ignited this life-changing journey repairing the damages we had done to relationships, just as the flames of the Holy Ghost brings warmth to the point of overflowing.

מ MEM

Overflow. We first understood this overflow was not about any connection we sought. It was instead in the overflowing abundance of the Holy Spirit in our souls, and we have come to understand the true meaning of being filled. Once we began making restitution, the floodgates of revelation opened, and we heard His voice proclaiming that we are counted among His saints in each moment of restitution. He sent from above, He took us, He drew us out of many waters (Psalm 18:16). We are beholding the glorious manifestation of the Almighty God in each restitution that is made. The fifth step showed us the power that shutting up the waters within created in our newly formed womb of morality now continues to burst forth with His truth. From the heavenly realms, He graciously descended upon us, reaching out with His mighty hand to rescue us from the vast tumultuous waters within that threatened to engulf us. With His divine power, He lifted us high above the waves of our defects of character, freeing us from the depths of our own despair. This could only lead to our rejoicing and offering praise to the Lord, for His unwavering love had delivered us salvation. This would overflow into our walk of faith. Therefore, the womb was opened, and the overflowing would begin in *step six*. This overwhelming living water extending from our bellies unto heaven would be the fuel needed throughout these steps. And now in *step nine*, restitution only comes from the Spirit who overflows from us and is seen as one with the Spirit who overflows from His creation. It's more than just cleaning our side of the street or repairing damages we have done to relationships; it is the blessed assurance that God hears us and guides us through these amends.

Just as the waters of an underground spring rise upward from an unknown source to reveal themselves, so does the spring of wisdom rise up from God. This flowing stream of inner wisdom is expressed through the gift of speech. The words we speak are deep waters, a flowing stream, and a fountain of wisdom (Proverbs 18:4). Let the overflowing come upon us wave upon wave. This overflowing comes in two forms, the revealed truth of God and the concealed truth of God. "Then the disciples came and said unto Him, 'Why do you speak to them in parables?' And He answered them, "To you is has been given to know the mysteries of the kingdom of heaven, but to them it has not been given (Matthew 13:10-11). This overflowing kingdom of heaven can be witnessed through prayer and reconciliation. When we approach Him in prayer we experience that He is the wonderful counselor, the mighty God, the everlasting Father, and the Prince of Peace. The increase of His government and peace shall have no end, upon the throne of David, and upon his kingdom, to order it, and to establish it with judgment and with justice from henceforth even forever. The zeal of the Lord of hosts will perform this (Isaiah 9:6-7).

We stand with hands wide open ready to receive in His kingdom which is connected to His Power here on earth. His presence in this overflowing is revelatory, yet is also shrouded in the deep being closed off to the apprehension of our reasoning. This outpouring expresses His kingship and dominion. His kingdom is an everlasting kingdom and His dominion endureth throughout all generations (Psalm 145:13). It is here where we begin to learn how the outpour is enlarged through fasting, which is done to prepare ourselves for the revelation from the Lord. Remembering always that "Whoseoever believes in me, as it is written in the Scripture, 'Out of his heart will flow rivers of living water' (John 7:38).

The Lord Jesus is the only one who truly satisfies the inner thirst we have for real life. Faith in Him yields refreshment for anyone whom He has called as His own. This is the vision carried forth in restitution.

ע AYIN

The vision is received in this ninth step. We were once foolish, having eyes, but could not see. We had ears and could not hear (Jeremiah 5:21). Our hearts were dull, and our ears heavy, and we were blind; through the steps we have taken, we are beginning to see, hear, and understand with our hearts and are turning to God and being healed (Isaiah 6:10). We are being recovered.

This ninth step vision is the spiritual light of God concealed in the Bible. The vision can behold the presence of His radiance, but only by means of a connected spirit. The vision is followed by two actions, choice, and will. We choose whether to use vision to see good or evil. We can choose to see the glass as half full rather than half empty.

The vision is silent. It is said that the vision "sees" but does not speak, and therefore is only available to the humble. Humility begins with vision as does the yoke of service. On the other hand, vision can represent idolatry as well as slavery, both of which are born out of envy. When the vision is evil, it becomes a slave to the purposes of sins such as addictions, alcoholism, and our evil impulses. The heart and the vision are the spies of the body: they lead a person to trespass, as the eyes see, the heart covets, and the body trespasses. We had to have God's help. The choice has never been ours.

If our lives were a miniature world, vision would be the result of the outside world reflecting and revealing the world inside. Our outlook reveals our inner character. This is what Jesus means when He tells us, "The eye is the light of the body. So, if your eye is healthy, your whole body will be full of light, but if your eye is evil, your whole body will be full of darkness, how great is the darkness (Matthew 6:22-23). Recovery is light.

This ninth step vision looks toward supporting the poor. The vision is manifested in charity toward others. On the other hand, the evil vision looks to those crying out in pain, considering how it might consume them in greed, reflecting our lives filled with sins such as drugs and alcohol.

The vision of God's will is cultivated from faith and the Word, faith which we discovered in the first step as the "Spark of God." This spark quickly ignited into willingness before Power, faith before humility, and righteousness before faith overpouring. Then in *step five,* we discovered that mercy was full of faith and found mercy for ourselves. Vision tells us that in the next step, we will walk into faith once more and begin another journey. It will be a developmental journey of our spirit. It also reveals the Word as a double-edged sword rightly dividing our spirit in *step twelve*.

The vision is the ladder, and the vision sees the Word as the means of approaching God. In the Scriptures, God's intimate knowledge of our lives is sometimes referred to as the eye of the Lord. His eyes are in every place, observing the good and the bad (Proverbs 15:3). His eyes focus throughout the whole earth to defend the righteous (2 Chronicles 16:9) and to sustain and deliver those who are hoping in His faithful mercy.

The vision is a reminder that we should both hear and obey to see that the Lord God is the one true God to whom we owe our lives in communion with His will.

VAV

Connection. We review once more that standing in this connection was unlike the overflowing we felt in the steps of separation in *steps four, five,* and *six*. In *step four,* we learned the awesomeness of standing in the overflow. We learned that this was not what had connected us, it was Him overflowing into us until we were so filled that His Spirit flowed out into the world around us. However, in *step eight,* we saw this connection that secures the unseen to the seen. This powerful action of the Holy Spirit was felt at once as we took *step eight*. He is the connector. It is true faith.

Before we are halfway through this phase of our spiritual development, we begin to experience His presence like never before. Through this step, we experience the unmovable anchor in our lives. This anchor joins heaven and earth, the spiritual and earthly matters. The anchor is the creative connection between all things made. The anchor is therefore the connecting force of God, the spiritual hook that binds together the unseen and the seen.

We speak of the Tabernacle plan of prayer, and we see the use of Hebrew letters and words tucked and hidden throughout these steps. The anchor is the first one to truly reveal itself. It is first referred to as hooks in Exodus 27:9-10. The hooks of silver were fastened to posts that were used to hold the curtain that encloses the Tabernacle. The Tabernacle was the habitation of God, as the Bible is the habitation of His word today, and our temples are the habitation of the Holy Spirit.

This concept is so concrete that the scribes developed the idea that the Torah Scroll was to be constructed in the manner of the Tabernacle. They called each parchment sheet of a scroll a curtain of the Tabernacle and each column of text a post. The Tabernacle's court was surrounded by curtains and posts. The scribes made each column of text to begin with a letter "ו VAV," thereby "hooking" or anchoring the text to the parchment. This was following the fact that each curtain of the Tabernacle was fastened to its post by means of a silver hook. A divine connection.

We recognize that this is too much for those who are still battling with the remnants of self. Do not be discouraged; none of us are saints. But for those who press forward, the Word of God contains the message of not only recovery and healing but eternal salvation. The "center" of the entire Torah is anchored in Leviticus 11:42. And appropriately enough, the letter "VAV" occurs in the word meaning belly. The center of God's law is anchored within us. His righteousness houses His glory and His righteousness reigns forever more.

Righteousness. The steps through His righteousness are a continuous spiritual process. This cyclic spiritual relationship that was introduced into our lives came at great costs, including the complete and utter destruction of self. The spiritual whirlwind continues to blow. His breath maintains this powerful experience.

The journey in righteousness is being developed in our lives and the steps in His righteousness have introduced these revelations. His breath continues. Our righteousness will always be bent in humble submission to His. The seed of His righteousness will forever be implanted into our hearts. His righteousness is always spiritually rearranging us. Humility always comes from righteousness. Righteousness brings faith and faith brings humility and humility brings righteousness. Ah, humility! Clearly, this is righteousness. Thus, the whirlwind continues to build up steam and the sound of a rushing mighty wind fills our temple to the point of overflowing. Now in *step nine*, moored in humility and under the persecution of ourselves and sometimes others, we know that His righteousness has been tried by fire, is in the overflowing, is the source of the Holy Spirit's vision, and the anchor that will never fail.

Righteousness represents both faithfulness and the reward for faithfulness. When we are humble before God, we are standing upright in the final day. In this present life, the person filled with His righteousness simultaneously affirms, "I am nothing but dust," and "The world itself was made for my sake." We humble ourselves in the sight of the Lord, and He lifts us up (James 4:10).

The seed of humility that was watered in our *step one* experience found itself in good ground and is the very sign of recovery and life. From this step, we saw that in *step six*, humility was a crown of glory. Glory is the manifestation of God in this life.

This ninth step is the stadium of faith! We experience the beauty and power of true faith as we go out to make restitution to God's children we have harmed. It is the very evidence of faith. We enjoy the benefits as the result of faith the moment we begin to do God's bidding in making restitution to all His children that we have harmed. It takes great obedience of faith to make restitution to them all except when to do so would injure them or others. We now see what faith does when we at once humbly obey. We are walking in meekness before the Lord, and He, being faithful, has already shown us the way to treat others. Jesus washed their feet. In light of this, we admit that we don't know it all and we are faithful enough to learn. The moment we obey, Jesus moved in and began supplying all our needs as the vow that we had begun in *step three* stated.

Repenting in *steps one* through *three* and then experiencing the remission of sins in *steps four* through *six*, culminating in baptism in Jesus' Name for the remission of sins, is when the Holy Spirit prepares Himself to come upon us as we continue to walk and perform his bidding for the rest of our days in *steps seven, eight,* and *nine*.

Looking back on this step, the Hebrew name Simeon is about "hearing." In the context of recovery, the name Simeon holds several important applications. Recovery involves seeking support from others. The name Simeon's meaning of "hearing" encourages us to practice active listening during recovery meetings, or when talking to friends and family. Listening with open-mindedness leads to deeper growth.

Recovery is a journey of identity in Christ. The name of the ninth step, Simeon, has a meaning which encourages us to listen to His thoughts. Prayerful contemplation is an essential aspect of understanding God's will during recovery. Recovery involves dealing with a range of emotions. The name Simeon represents the importance of being in touch with the directions of the Holy Spirit, acknowledging them, and following them. In recovery, we need to rely on the support of others. The name Simeon reminds us to be open to accepting guidance from those who are willing to help in recovery.

Many of us struggle with sin such as alcoholism, addiction, and mental health issues. Many keep our challenges hidden. The name

Simeon encourages breaking the silence and speaking out about our struggles, leading to a path of recovery and support. We learn that effective communication is vital in recovery, especially when expressing needs, boundaries, and emotions. The name Simeon emphasizes the importance of compassionate communication with ourselves and others. In a spiritual context, the name Simeon represents a connection with the higher power which is Jesus. During recovery, we seek a deeper communion with the Holy Spirit and practice finding strength.

Recovery is a shared journey for us. The name Simeon inspires us to learn from the experiences of others, whether through shared stories in recovery groups or through wisdom shared by Holy Ghost-filled recovered mentors. The act of hearing is associated with gaining wisdom. Recovery is a process of growth, and the name Simeon represents the wisdom that is gained from actively listening to God and others who have recovered, especially while making restitution. Overall, the name Simeon's meaning of "hearing" is profoundly applied in recovery. It encourages us to embrace active listening as seeking God, Holy Spirit awareness, and the acceptance of support as we progress toward a fulfilling life in complete recovery.

Step seven began our journey in the realm of restitution and in *step nine* we find ourselves in the middle of this immense faith as we make restitution. We remembered those who had something against us and began reconciling with them all. Therefore, we began with our list of harms. We are walking in the covenant that we sealed with Jesus in the seventh step for the rest of our days if we so choose by making the efforts prescribed each morning. Repent, Read, Pray, and Follow! This is a huge moment of faith for us. Now we will have joy even when we are being mistreated in the Name of Jesus.

The overarching principle for *step nine* reflects our meekness. The third step's power, fire, and prayer bring a smile to our faces as we think of the goodness of the Lord. We are beginning to see how we are blessed because we are meek. We now appreciate our humility, and He is giving us the life that he intended for us all along. As we have taken this step, we feel an overwhelming gratitude as our hearts continue to operate in meekness.

We approach this step knowing that we will be persecuted in the Name of Jesus. Because of it, our reward will be greater than anything we've experienced here on Earth. We are seeking a life of obedience to His Name. We want more! The heartfelt meekness coupled with obedience in Jesus' Name changes the reward from here to heaven. As we approach this step with this mindset, the game changes and we are filled with even more undeserved promises. We are now operating in obedience in the Name of Jesus. We have been shown obedience. With the principle of righteous obedience in Jesus' Name, we know that our reward is in heaven, and it will be greater than anything we have experienced here on earth.

The principle gleaned from this step is that in humility we will be persecuted for His Name's sake. But we know He is in us and shall never leave us. Just as He has shown us through taking these steps that he has been preparing us for the life he intended, He is also preparing rewards in heaven, so we rejoice in this life gleaning more and more of His joy which courses through our veins. In Jesus' Name.

Temperance.

Certainly, as we look back on the ninth step, we see that there are specific spiritual actions inspired by the "Golden Rule" (Matthew 7:12) to help us put the principle of treating others as we would like to be treated into practice. Some write uplifting notes to family members, friends, and coworkers, offering words of encouragement and support. Others spend time volunteering at homeless shelters and community outreach programs, serving those in need. Many visit nursing homes and elderly neighbors to spend time with them, offering companionship and care. We all make the conscious decision to forgive someone who has wronged us, releasing any bitterness and resentment along the way. We offer our assistance and support to a friend's charitable projects. We discover that we practice active listening by allowing others to share their thoughts without judgment. We dedicate time in prayer to intercede for the needs of family, friends, and others in our recovery community. Many of us provide service by helping to coordinate donation drives for clothes, food, or essentials for those facing financial challenges early in recovery. We are amazed to discover that we can now invite people, especially newcomers who are lonely or new in recovery, for a meal at our home or a restaurant. In each restitution we see that if we've hurt someone, we apologize sincerely and seek reconciliation, making amends where necessary. We always show appreciation and respect to service workers, such as waiters, cleaners, and customer service representatives. Many of us find that we have money in our pockets that can be utilized to contribute financially and pray regularly for missionaries and their efforts to spread the gospel. There is power in sending thank you notes and messages to people who have impacted our lives in positive ways. If able, we offer rides to church and recovery meetings to those who may not have transportation. We learn to celebrate the accomplishments of friends and family genuinely, sharing in their joy.

Remember that the Golden Rule is about expressing genuine respect for others. These spiritual actions help us embody the principle in our daily lives and demonstrate Christ's love to those around us. Through these actions, we shine Christ's light in the lives of others, just as we would hope others would be for us.

CHAPTER 15

STEP TEN

"We continue to confess our transgressions to the Lord."
(Psalm 32:5)

' YOD

The thought of working for these ninth step miracles brings us to *step ten*, which is in *faith*. We continue to search ourselves and continue to make things right as God restores harmony in our relationships and our walk with Him. We vigorously commenced this way of living when we took these first nine steps by trusting God, cleaning house, and making amends for our pasts. God has given us our hire because we have given our service to our Lord.

Faith. Faith in *step ten* is a way of life we have grasped. We first experienced it in *step one*. Then we saw its proper use compared to power and humility in *step four*. The fourth step also revealed that His righteousness through faith is what we were in search of. In *step five* we saw the value of faith and began following the directions knowing that we were now in its grip. Now we encounter faith again in this step. We are in its grip.

It's the Holy Spirit that revealed the evolution of faith, which is willingness as the spark of God. They are all one and the same. It suddenly appeared the moment God's Hand was applied to our lives. We were told of the moment that the artist applies the tip of his brush to the blank canvas. At that moment, and each similar moment that ensues, lies within it the complete Power to change lives. The entire artistry is in the moment, Faith.

The seed of righteous humility carried the power of faith the size of a grain of mustard seed. Every work that we perform develops a spiritual structure through which we are about to be drawn through.

Commitment, trust, and action all come from the Father. We now live by these principles. We do nothing without them. *Step one* required a commitment to embark on the path of recovery. In the beginning, it was the drugs and alcohol that were the ultimate persuaders. When we cried out in humility, we were unknowingly turning our backs on fear and committing our way to the Lord. We committed ourselves to the task at hand, aligning our actions with His desired outcome for our lives. When we cried out, we exhibited a trust in the Lord's provision which would become the central theme of our recovery. Our souls were now connected to a level of trust in God and the Spirit He planted within us. Trusting in our God-given directions and the guidance of the Holy Ghost allowed us to approach Fear of the Lord with humility. Once we followed our fourth step lists with action, we received the faith of a promise that Jesus now acts on our behalf. Our humble trust was now accompanied by action. Applying the power of faith to *step ten* involves taking decisive action, utilizing His power embarking on the spiritual journey toward complete recovery. We are blessed because we have begun to hunger and thirst even more after His righteousness. Our spirits are being filled.

The Spirit. This consuming fire of the Holy Spirit removed ourselves in *step three* after recognizing we had been the ones wrecking our own lives and that we were using sins such as addictions and alcoholism to accomplish it. We confessed our sins and truly had a deep and effective spiritual experience. The mere mention of His Name now accomplishes for us that which no human power could do. We now admit God's truth. The ninth step experience was life-altering for us all, uniting us under restitution in His Name. The ninth step revealed the stadium of faith as we became followers of Jesus Christ.

Before we began, this position of purity was persecuted because it splashed in the face of spiritual prejudices and religious beliefs. Having had the Name of Jesus applied to our lives and becoming pure in heart, the Holy Spirit, this consuming fire, cleansed us of all our old ideas and we saw God. We now know His Name is Jesus, and miraculous things are happening. It is this fire that fuels the faith we hear in each moment of restitution. The consuming fire continues a mighty work as we are transformed into new creatures full of His Power, given a pure heart, and now we know that God hears us. We experience the awesome power of this consuming fire which is the Spirit as we navigated this beautiful step in the Name of Jesus. He is a consuming fire exchanging His presence for our praises to Him.

This Spirit moves position in the Tabernacle plan of prayer. We are sure to utilize His guidance throughout our recovered lives. We are moving westward, filled with the teachings of Matthew, expressing the Kingship of God, and representing an overall hunger and thirst for the service of God and others. This fire, His Presence, and a change within our lives have us praising His Name. It is a great bartering of our praise for His presence. Once we have tasted this fire in our lives from taking these steps, we want more. He has demonstrated that His presence is drawn to our praise. So, we begin to praise Him more. We are now seeking His forgiveness as we develop in this mind-changing process of recovery and salvation. We praise Him.

These tongues of fire showed the power of God in our lives. *Step ten* begins our spiritual development. This requires us to give ourselves completely to this developmental process. The Holy Ghost reminds us that through this spiritual development, a profound transformation is occurring in the heart, soul, and mind.

This spiritual development is life-changing. His Name has been applied to our lives. In *step ten*, the act of continuing to confess our transgressions to the Lord, seeking forgiveness and repairing new mistakes as we go along, is becoming a way of life. We recognize the presence of the Holy Spirit within ourselves and others during the tenth step praises. Being recovered is a central theme in *step ten*, as we continue to watch our actions and strive to make right new mistakes as they come along. The Holy Spirit fills us as we continue to seek God. Our daily lives are designed to give Him praise, sincerely seek Him, and turn from our wicked ways. As we do this, we experience a spiritual recovery and salvation with God. The more we seek and praise Him, the more of His power ignites our souls. The flames of the Holy Ghost illuminate and bring warmth to the point of another fire. We are standing in the midst of the flames.

ש SHIN

Becoming accustomed to walking in this *consuming fire* is not an overnight matter. But while being in the flames of His presence, we felt we were blameless and covered again. What a story! Considered among His children, our lives are filled with His peace. Shin describes His fire which is the only power that changes lives. This fire is his Presence. This is relevant to *step ten*, which involves examining our hearts in His presence as we pursue continuous recovery.

To remain in His presence, we must continue to examine our thoughts and actions. We maintain a mindful awareness of our praise filled progress towards complete recovery. The Holy Ghost's presence in this life-changing process aligns with *step ten*'s focus on recovery and ongoing renewal of the mind. By engaging in the Holy Spirit and His Word, He identifies areas that require change, allowing for complete recovery.

The fire is indicative of His presence. These flames emphasize the importance of seeking the presence of God during the process of soul searching which is required for ongoing recovery. It encourages us to invite the presence of the Holy Ghost into our daily lives, fostering recovery as we step up with arms raised and hands wide open. This is the last time we carry the fire through these steps; for it has become an all-consuming fire that goes before us, behind us, and surrounds us. We burned with His Spirit, and we were not consumed. We receive His presence in praise.

KAPH

The first time we were able to stretch forth our hands with palms wide open praising His Holy Name, we discovered that the currency of Heaven is praise, and we quickly rushed to get all that we could get. We now praise Him in the morning, we praise him at noon time, and we praise Him in the evening.

We no longer hold our hands open to see what we can get in greed. We are blessed to *receive* the Comforter to guide us in this spiritual way of living for our lifetimes. We fully understand one day that the wickedness was destroyed, but because of our developing trust in the Lord, we knew we were only beginning to experience the inheritance of the lives God intended for us.

This extension of our hands with palms wide open reaches for the potential and the actual. Praise enables the latent power of the spiritual to be made actual in the physical. Our palms are wide open.

The palm is considered the location where faith's potential is actualized. For this reason, we bless others with palms facing them and we envision God as having His palms over us, for this is the calling forth of the latent power of the Holy Spirit within for manifestation in the physical world. This is also why many of us place both of our palms together in the morning act of soliciting the power of God to be manifest in our daily lives.

Praise requires spiritual focus and concentration. Praise rids our mind of all that is distracting, and we aim to envision ourselves as standing directly before the presence of God. We are becoming unto Him a kingdom of priests and a holy people (Exodus 19:6).

Praise crowns us. It crowns us with His Word. It crowns us into His priesthood. When we praise with palms wide open, we receive the crown of the kingdom. Praise crowns us with a good Name which is the best gift of all since it is foundational to all things. Praising His Name is better than oil. We yearned for the baptism in praise.

Praise is the crown of life, awarded to those who endure the trials and tribulations of this world. Praise is the anticipation of the coming of our Lord in righteousness. It is the picture of eternal life. Praise is how we faithfully encourage one another. Praise is given to the only One worthy to receive it as our great High Priest who offered Himself for our sins.

Praise is like prayer in *step ten*. It equips us to conform to His image. With palms wide open, we praise Jesus in our work and our sacrifice for others.

Praise possesses the fire of *step ten*. When we praise prostrate, we see that when we follow Jesus by bending our wills in submission to Him, we are given the reward of His righteousness, since our works follow His.

We have been gravened upon the palms of His hands (Isaiah 49:16). This is why we lift our heart with our hand to God in heaven (Lamentations 3:41). In praise, we cry and stretch out our hands to God. Our hands also will lift up to His commandments, which we have loved, and we will meditate on His statutes (Psalm 119:48).

One tool we picked up in *step ten* is that we now show restraint in our grieving and mourning since the righteous man understands that the soul is immortal and therefore the loss of relationship with the other is not permanent.

How do we continue to search ourselves as God restores harmony in our relationships and our walk with Him?

ר RESH

We continue, in *prayer* and *fasting,* to watch for manifestations of the flesh such as selfishness, dishonesty, resentment, fear, and any other manifestations of the flesh mentioned in Galatians 5:19-21. Even when bad things happen to good and godly people, the Lord saves us and does not let us be defeated by what we face.

How do we continue to make things right, remembering that the Spirit restores harmony in our relationships as we walk with Him? When flesh crops up, we pray, asking God at once to remove it. We immediately discuss these manifestations of flesh with someone who has had the Holy Ghost come upon them. If we have harmed anyone, we make restitution quickly. Then we resolutely turn our thoughts to someone we can help because this takes us out of ourselves. Our code is rooted in the biblical principle of love of others.

We have ceased fighting anything or anyone— even sins such as addictions and alcoholism. For by this time, salvation will have materialized in our minds and God will have provided a way of escape. We will seldom be interested in sin. If tempted, we recoil from it as from a hot flame. We react sanely, and we will find that this has happened automatically. We will see that our new attitude toward sins such as addictions and alcoholism has been given to us by God without any thought or effort on our part. It just comes! That is the miracle of it. God is constantly reminding us of our *step three* covenant where we decided to turn our will and lives over to His care and direction. We are not fighting sins such as addictions and alcoholism, nor are we avoiding temptation. God has placed us under His wing—safe and protected. We have not even sworn off. Instead, the sin problem has been removed by God. It does not exist for us. We are neither cocky nor are we full of fear. That is our experience. That is how we react so long as we keep in fit spiritual condition by continuing to examine ourselves and making things right. We discover that harmony has been restored in our relationships and our walk with God.

It is easy to let up on the spiritual program of action and rest on our laurels. We follow this program of action by continuing to examine ourselves and making things right as God restores harmony in our relationships and our walk with Him. We are headed for trouble if we do let up, for the Devil is a subtle foe. We may not be suffering from sins such as addictions and alcoholism now, but what we really have is a daily reprieve contingent on the maintenance of our spiritual condition. Every day is a day when we must carry the vision of God's thought into all our activities. The best way to begin this habit is to start each day by praying and asking God, "How can I BEST serve Thee—Thy thought not my thoughts be done." God's thought is thought which must go with us constantly. We can exercise our thinking along the line of God's thought all we wish. It is the proper use of the mind.

In the material, Jesus tells us that He is witnessing His followers facing persecution from the unjust. His heart is filled with both compassion for our struggles and awe for the power of God's miraculous words. In the spiritual realm, even those in positions of authority have wrongly targeted Christ's faithful ones, but our hearts remain steadfast in awe of His Word.

In the material, the promises Jesus speaks bring boundless joy to those who embrace them. The revelation of His Word stirs our hearts like discovering hidden treasures of immeasurable worth. In the spiritual realm, there is great rejoicing at Christ's Word, as it unveils the spoils of spiritual abundance.

In the material, the deceptions of the world are despised, and the followers of Jesus passionately uphold His principle. We abhor falsehood and embrace the truth of His principle. In the spiritual realm, we reject all forms of deceit, while wholeheartedly loving Christ's principle.

In the material, followers of Jesus pause throughout our day to offer praise and worship, recognizing the perfection of His ways. In the spiritual realm, our praises rise to Christ seven times a day, acknowledging His righteous principle and giving glory to His Name.

In the material, those of us who are devoted to Jesus' Word experience profound peace and well-being, finding comfort in the assurance of His presence. We are shielded from being easily offended by the challenges we face. In the spiritual realm, those who love Christ's principle find unparalleled peace, knowing that nothing can cause us to stumble as we walk in Christ's light. In our bodies and minds, we pray:

> *Lord, my heart yearns for an abundance*
> *of Your saving grace, for I desire*
> *to walk in the path that brings*
> *You pleasure.*

In the spirit, we pray:

> *YHWH, I place my unwavering trust in*
> *Your divine salvation and I wholeheartedly embrace*
> *the path of obedience to Your sacred principle.*

Our love for His ways is beyond words; deep within us, we have an ardent desire to follow them flawlessly! Our soul has faithfully cherished His testimonies, and our love for them knows no bounds. We are committed to heeding His counsel; every aspect of our lives is transparent before Him. We have wholeheartedly upheld His principle, for He sees all our ways.

We have embarked upon the initial phase of our spiritual development, as this newfound spirit within us begins to take shape. At the core of these three life-changing *steps ten*, *eleven*, and *twelve* lies the principle of earnestly seeking His righteousness. Embedded within this principle is the essence of the tenth step, which calls us to embrace a humble spirit. Therefore, the assurance bestowed upon us through these life-changing steps is that we shall be satisfied, and the tenth step assures us that the kingdom of heaven belongs to us.

There has been extensive discussion regarding the reception of strength, inspiration, and guidance from the Almighty, who possesses all knowledge and power. Considering that God is the Power, what power do we possess? None. And if He possesses all knowledge, what knowledge do we possess? None. Yet, if we have diligently followed the prescribed path outlined in these steps thus far, we will sense that the Holy Spirit is flowing through us. As the branch, we catch glimpses of God's presence and observe the fruits of the Spirit being cultivated through us for the benefit of others and the glory of God. However, we must continue to progress through taking further action, for just as a lifeless body lacks a spirit, faith without works is likewise lifeless.

Step ten is the beginning of the developmental steps. It encourages us to continue to confess our transgressions to the Lord. We do this by continuing to regularly search our thoughts and actions. We promptly admit when we are wrong. The focus of this step is on accountability. This involves reflecting on our behavior throughout the day and assessing whether we have acted in accordance with His spiritual values. When we discover that we have acted in a way that goes against these spiritual values, *step ten* emphasizes the importance of promptly admitting mistakes. When we realize that we have hurt someone, *step ten* encourages us to make amends quickly.

The purpose of *step ten* is to encourage us to stay focused on seeking God and accountability daily. By taking regular inventory of our efforts and promptly addressing any harm we may have caused, we experience recovery, improved relationships, and prevent relapse. We realize even more that we can't do anything apart from God. This drives us more to submit to His will.

The Hebrew name Issachar holds significance in the context of recovery. Issachar means "to barter." There are many ways the name Issachar applies to the recovery journey. Recovery is a challenging but rewarding process. The name Issachar is the reward that God gives for putting in the effort and dedication to praise Him for overcoming challenges. For those of us recovering from sins such as alcoholism and addictions, the name Issachar relates to finding recovery in the choice to embrace salvation. It represents the positive outcomes that come from making Jesus Christ our Lord and Savior.

The name Issachar acknowledges God's presence as we praise His Name in recovery. It's essential to recognize the milestones God has brought to us and the positive changes He has made in our lives along the way. The name Issachar finds a bartering between God's presence and our praise. Recovery involves hard work, but it's also crucial to practice, be sensitive to the Word, and allow time for healing. In recovery, we gain a testimony from our past actions and their consequences. The meaning of the name Issachar encourages us to learn from our mistakes and make amends as we progress in Jesus' Name.

The name Issachar reminds us of the importance of honoring commitments made during recovery, both to God and to others. Staying true to The Holy Spirit and His values leads to heavenly rewards. Recovery is a journey towards finding contentment. The name Issachar is the recompense of a more serene state of mind in Christ. The name Issachar inspires gratitude for His presence experienced during our praise of Him in recovery. It emphasizes that the process of recovery itself is a rewarding experience. The name Issachar brings hope to us in recovery, reminding us that there is recompense and brighter days ahead for our recovery efforts. Overall, the name Issachar's meaning applies to recovery as a reminder of His presence, praise, and the fulfillment that awaits those who embrace the path of recovery and salvation. It emphasizes the value of the effort invested in recovery for a more meaningful life ahead.

Step ten began our journey in the realm of being recovered. This step is full of bartering. We are bartering with the Holy Spirit by trading our praises for His Presence. It brings about so much joy when we praise Him. And by doing a daily search of ourselves, we find ourselves running to Him throughout the day and this basic level of praise brings His presence into our lives. In the beginning, it comes in the form of the grass being greener, the sky bluer, and uncanny animals being placed in our paths along the way. They are like little love post-it notes from God placed all throughout our day. Repent, Read, Pray, and Follow! Now we will have joy and begin to see how a poor spirit and a mantra of "I don't know" brings about an open door that He steps through into our lives.

The overarching principle for *step ten* reflects our hunger and thirst for righteousness. The fourth step's battle between humility and righteousness brings a smile to our faces as we think of the goodness of the Lord. We are beginning to see how we are blessed because we are hungering and thirsting after righteousness. We now appreciate the passion that He is filling us with. As we take this step, we feel an overwhelming gratitude as our hearts continue to operate with desperate passion. The Lord, who is the true vine, sends joy through our branches as we hunger and thirst after more of His fruit. We easily discover that the overarching principle for these developmental steps is that we hunger and thirst after righteousness. We seek God's ways just as a starving and parched person seeks food and drink! When we seek God's will that much, we are always satisfied. We are filled!

We approach this step covered in this passion knowing the power of being poor in spirit because we have tasted the kingdom of heaven. We want more! The heartfelt passion coupled with realizing that we can't do anything separate from God changes us from satisfied to truly filled. As we approach this step with this mindset, the game changes and we are filled with even more undeserved promises. We are now operating in the realization that we are nothing and He is everything. We have been shown the kingdom of heaven which is submitting to His will. With the principle of passion and realizing God is everything, we know that we are filled and that we are submitting to His will. With each episode of praise, He exchanges our praise with His presence. Therefore, as extremists, we now safely apply our extreme passion to seeking more opportunities to praise Him.

Love.

Indeed, confessing our transgressions to the Lord is a vital aspect of our relationship with Him, as highlighted in Psalm 32:5. Here are some actions to help us continue this practice. We set aside time each day for prayerful contemplation and examination of our thoughts and actions. We confess any known sins to the Lord at once. We engage in regular praise before God. We humbly seek His forgiveness and guidance. We are specific in our confessions, acknowledging areas where we have fallen short of God's standards. We keep a spiritual journal to record our confessions and prayers, allowing us to track our progress, service, and ministry. We use times of worship, such as in church services and private devotions, to confess our sins before God. We always accompany confession with genuine repentance, turning away from sinful behaviors and choosing to follow God's ways. Some use Psalms of confession, such as Psalm 51, as a template for expressing our heartfelt confessions before God. If appropriate, we share our confessions with a trusted fellow believer who provides support. During times of fasting and prayer, we dedicate moments to confessing sins and seeking God's forgiveness. Some of us memorize verses that emphasize the importance of confession and God's promise of forgiveness. If available, we participate in confession services offered by our church or recovery community. Some engage in acts of cleansing, such as washing feet, to express their desire for spiritual purity. Alongside confession, we pray for God's restoration in areas affected by our transgressions. We guard against rationalizing our sins; instead, we take full responsibility and seek forgiveness wholeheartedly. After confessing, we express gratitude to God for His forgiveness, praising Him for His grace.

By incorporating these actions into our spiritual lives, we maintain an authentic relationship with God, continuously seeking His forgiveness and experiencing the joy that come from knowing His love.

CHAPTER 16

STEP ELEVEN

"We rejoice always, pray continually, and give thanks in all circumstances; for this is God's will for us in Christ Jesus."
(1 Thessalonians 5:16-18)

As we enter the second trimester of our spiritual development, we encounter *step eleven*. This step calls for prayer, meditation, and fasting. We should not hesitate or shy away from the practice of prayer and fasting. Many individuals possess unwavering faith and employ these spiritual disciplines consistently. In this phase, we come to understand the profound meaning of worshiping with awe. We now are convinced that those who Fear the Lord lack nothing! It becomes clear to us that prayer and fasting are effective when approached with the right attitude and relationship. As we fix our gaze upon Him and unite our lives with Him, we experience His abundant joy that flows through us.

Although it may be tempting to overlook the significance of maintaining a constant connection with God through prayer, we believe it is important to offer practical suggestions to all who embrace the new covenant crossing the threshold. However, you must have contact with God to improve your contact with Him. Now we praise the Lord!

We are encouraged to set aside time each evening prior to retiring so that we can continue the practice of searching ourselves and seeing how we can make things right as God restores harmony in our relationships and our walks with Him. We seek God during this set-aside time, finding solace in knowing that He hears our prayers and rescues us from every fear that gripped our hearts this day. He ensures that our integrity stands firm.

In this introspective process, we pose simple yet profound questions to ourselves.

1. Did flesh show up? Were we bitter, selfish, dishonest, or afraid? Or were we friendly, kind, truthful, or unworried?
2. Do we owe an apology or restitution? Or did we maintain dignity throughout the day?
3. Have we kept something to ourselves which should be discussed with another person at once? Or did we nourish our relationships with others today?
4. Were we kind and loving toward all? Or were we discourteous and hateful toward others?
5. What could we have done better? Or what would we have done differently?
6. Were we thinking of ourselves most of the time? Or were we mindful of the opportunities to make a positive impact and add value to the lives of those around us?

However, we must exercise caution during this nightly searching and avoid slipping into worry, remorse, or excessive self-reflection, as they can diminish our effectiveness in serving God and others.

After completing our review, we say a simple prayer and we humbly seek God's forgiveness and guidance on the necessary steps to correct any shortcomings. We recognize that this process is a constructive practice in the presence of our Heavenly Father.

We begin each day recognizing that we have awoken into self and that we must immediately return to the presence of our Heavenly Father. We quickly find a place to get on our knees and pray each morning:

> *Lord, I humbly seek Your divine guidance.*
> *Please direct my thoughts and motives,*
> *removing any traces of self-pity, dishonesty, and*
> *selfishness. In the stillness of this moment,*
> *I open my heart to receive Your*
> *wisdom for the day ahead. Speak to*
> *me, Lord, and reveal the virtues of*
> *patience, tolerance, kindness, and love that I*
> *need to embody in specific situations. May*
> *Your thoughts become my thoughts as I*
> *listen to Your voice. Grant me the*
> *grace to use my mental faculties for*
> *Your glory. Purify my thinking, O Lord,*
> *so that my motives align with Your*
> *perfect will. I surrender my mind to*
> *You, knowing that You desire to guide*
> *me into a higher plane of thought*
> *and action. In Jesus' name, I pray.*

In this prayer, we then prepare ourselves for meditation as we seek the Lord's guidance, aligning our plans with insights He delivers during this period of meditation.

Meditation is a topic equally as intimidating as prayer. Meditation is reverent listening to the Holy Spirit within. During this time of listening, we turn to God for inspiration, trusting in His divine intervention. Rather than relying on our own understanding, we choose to be still as the Holy Spirit guides our thoughts. We understand that our human wisdom falls short, leading to foolish thoughts. However, as we continue to walk in faith seeking God's will, our thinking is changed by the power of His Spirit. We learn to depend on His guidance, knowing that He will lead us in the paths of righteousness as He reveals His perfect plan for our lives each day.

We enter this period of morning mediation something like this:

There may be moments of uncertainty that we face this day, and we turn our gaze inward and seek comfort in the depths of our being. We invite stillness to envelop us, creating space for divine inspiration to flow. In this sacred space, we release the burden of relying solely on our own understanding and open ourselves to the wisdom of God that transcends our human limitations. As we surrender to Christ's presence within us, we acknowledge that our thoughts and actions guided solely by our limited perspectives will lead us astray. We let go of the need to control and instead embrace the gentle guidance of the Holy Spirit. With each breath, we seek the life-changing power of divine wisdom to illuminate our minds and illuminate our path. In this state of surrender, we find peace in the knowledge that the wisdom of God surpasses all human understanding. We trust that as we align our thoughts and intentions with the Holy Spirit's will, clarity emerges, and our path becomes illuminated. We let go of the need to grasp tightly onto our own plans and instead embrace the unfolding of God's plan in our lives this day. In this sacred space of meditation, we find assurance that the guidance we seek is readily available to us. We trust in the divine timing of answers, knowing that they will manifest in perfect alignment with our highest good. With each moment of still connection, we deepen our understanding of the Holy Spirit's presence within us and strengthen our faith in the unfolding journey of life. We yield to the Lord's holy silence and prepare ourselves to receive any thoughts He gives us.

[silent listening]

As we conclude our meditation, we write down any thought God has given us and we carry this newfound clarity and trust with us into the world. We embrace the inherent uncertainty of life, knowing that we are guided by a wisdom that surpasses our understanding. With each step, we walk in alignment with the divine flow, ever receptive to the whispers of inspiration and the nudges of the Holy Spirit's guidance.

Now we are ready to conclude our time of prayer and meditation. We have turned to the Lord in humble supplication, seeking His divine guidance for the day ahead. With hearts surrendered to His will, we besought Him to reveal the path He has ordained for us, so that we may walk in obedience and fulfill His purpose this day. We acknowledge our dependence on Him, requesting the provisions necessary to address any challenges that may arise, knowing that He is our sole provider.

This form of disciplined prayer covering is best served by:

1. Asking the Holy Spirit to guard us against selfish motives, understanding the futility of seeking our own will above God's.
2. Humbly recognizing the importance of unity among believers, inviting fellow disciples to join us in morning prayer and meditation, for where two or more gather in His Name, He is present among us.
3. Remaining attentive to the wisdom offered by our brothers and sisters in faith, appreciating the valuable insights they bring. We embrace the teachings of the faithful, discerning the truth and embracing the collective wisdom found within the body of Christ.

We have now gotten up from our knees and prepare for our day as we consider what He has shown us in our morning prayer. We then take our calendar for the day and arrange our plans around any actions that He has assigned for us this day.

We go out into the world, we pause and pray when we feel angry or disturbed. These moments come quickly when we are not following the will of God. By surrendering to God's will in each moment, we avoid negative emotions and unwise decisions. Prayer brings efficiency and conserves our energy, unlike when we tried to control everything ourselves. It rejuvenates us as it infuses our actions with purpose. Surrendering to prayer liberates us from weariness by connecting us to a higher source of guidance, which is the Holy Ghost.

Prayer works—it really does.

There are many prayers that we use, both written and unwritten, throughout our recovery.

THE RECOVERY SET ASIDE PRAYER

Jesus,
Please help me set aside everything I think I know
about myself, my sin, recovery,
religion, and especially about you,
so that I may have an open mind and a new experience
with all these things.
Please help me to see the truth.

This prayer begins with a plea because we know that there is no way we can pray without His intervention. We have already learned that we must constantly ask for His aid because we can't do what we would. Because of the stronghold of our own conceptions, we know that we must set aside every prejudice, which is anything we think we know. We must set aside prejudice we have for ourselves, for it is filled with fear, self-delusion, self-seeking, and self-pity. We must set aside prejudice we have for this spiritual disease, for it has blinded us by a great wrestling of mind and flesh. We must set aside prejudice we have for recovery, for it is in **RECOVERY 5:12** that we find a new path where all conceptions are replaced with the One who has all Power. We must set aside prejudice we have for religion, for it has lost its man-made labels and become practices that seek to establish a communion between humanity and the divine. Finally, we must set aside what we think we know about Jesus Christ, for He is much more than anything we could ever conceive. Our conception has no power. We pray these things so that we experience an open-mind and a new experience with them all. We ask that we discover the truth about the flaws of our makeup. In Jesus' Name, we seek peace.

PEACE PRAYER

Jesus,
Make me an instrument of Your peace:
where there is hatred, let me sow love;
where there is injury, forgiveness;
where there is doubt, faith;
where there is despair, hope;
where there is darkness, light;
where there is sadness, joy.

Grant that I may not so much seek
to be consoled as to console,
to be understood as to understand,
to be loved as to love.
For it is in the giving that we receive,
It is in the forgiving that we are forgiven,
And it is in the dying that we are born to eternal life.
In Your Name we pray, Amen!

In this prayer, we ask Jesus to do what he has already begun to do and that is to create us as instruments of His divine will. Peace is the outcome, and we ask Him to provide the spiritual tools to accomplish His peace. We begin to see Him sow love. He demonstrates forgiveness through us. Faith, hope, and light shine in our lives. As the branch, we feel His joy course through our bones as He brings fruits of the Spirit into our lives. He begins to give us instructions for our lives. He shows us how to console and understand. He shows us how to love. He paradoxically shows us what it means to give and to forgive. He gives us the eternal reward, which is that to die is to gain. We ask these things in His Name.

Jesus Himself taught us how we should pray, and we therefore pray at the end of every recovery meeting in recognition of His majesty. Matthew recorded it best:

PATTERN FOR PRAYER

Our Father which art in heaven,
Hallowed be thy Name.
Thy Kingdom come, thy will be done in earth,
As it is in heaven.
Give us this day our daily bread.
And forgive us our debts, as we forgive our debtors.
And lead us not into temptation, but deliver us
From evil: For thine is the kingdom, and the
Power, and the glory, forever.
Amen!

Hallelujah! Praise the Lord, my beloved brothers and sisters! Now, we are diving into the deep to level up. These are the anointed words of the Lord's Prayer, a divine gift from our Lord and Savior, Jesus Christ. Let us open our hearts and minds to receive the revelation of this powerful prayer.

Oh, what a glorious beginning! We address the Almighty, the Creator of Heaven and Earth, as our Father! What an intimate relationship! We are His children, and He deeply cares for us. His Name is holy and worthy of all praise and worship. As we utter these words, we magnify the Name of the Lord, exalting Him above all else. We are praying for His Kingdom to manifest here on Earth. We submit ourselves to His divine will, just as the angels in heaven obey His every command. Glory to God! We acknowledge our dependence on the Lord for sustenance, both physical and spiritual. He is the bread of life, and we seek His provision daily. This prayer is so vital! We come before the Lord, recognizing our sins, and humbly asking for His forgiveness. And in His mercy, He calls us to forgive others as well. Oh, how the enemy seeks to ensnare us! We plead with the Lord for His guidance, that He would lead us away from the snares of the devil and into His righteousness. We call upon Him as our deliverer, our fortress, and our shield. He is our refuge, and we trust in Him to protect us from the schemes of the wicked one.

Beloved, the Lord's Prayer is a treasure trove of spiritual wisdom and a blueprint for a powerful and effective prayer life. It encompasses petition guiding us to align our hearts with God's divine purposes. Let us not take this prayer lightly, but rather, let it be the foundation of our communion with our Heavenly Father. As we pray the Lord's Prayer with sincerity and faith, let us remember that we are tapping into the very heart of God, and He delights in answering the cries of His children. May this prayer be a constant reminder of His love and grace in our lives. Hallelujah! Amen!

From here, we then listen in as Jesus prayed.

JESUS PRAYED
(JOHN 17)

Father, the hour is come; glorify thy Son, that thy Son also may glorify thee:
As thou hast given Him power over all flesh, that He should give eternal life to as many as thou hast given Him.
And this is life eternal, that they might know thee the only true God, and Jesus Christ, whom thou hast sent.
I have glorified thee on the earth: I have finished the work which thou gavest me to do.
And now, O Father, glorify thou me with thine own self with the glory which I had with thee before the world was.
I have manifested thy name unto the men which thou gavest me out of the world: thine they were, and thou gavest them me; and they have kept thy word.
Now they have known that all things whatsoever thou hast given me are of thee.
For I have given unto them the words which thou gavest me, and they have received them, and have known surely that I came out from thee, and they have believed that thou didst send me.
I pray for them: I pray not for the world but for them which thou hast given me; for they are thine.

And all mine are thine, and thine are mine; and I am glorified in them.

And now I am no more in the world, but these are in the world, and I come to thee. Holy Father, keep through thine own name those whom thou hast given me, that they may be one, as we are.

While I was with them in the world, I kept them in thy name: those that thou gavest me I have kept, and none of them is lost but the son of perdition, that the scripture might be fulfilled.

And now come I to thee, and these things I speak in the world, that they might have my joy fulfilled in themselves.

I have given them thy word, and the world hath hated them because they are not of the world, even as I am not of the world.

I pray not that thou shouldest take them out of the world, but that thou shouldest keep them from the evil.

They are not of the world, even as I am not of the world.

Sanctify them through thy truth: thy word is truth.

As thou hast sent me into the world, even so have I also sent them into the world.

And for their sakes, I sanctify myself that they also might be sanctified through the truth.

Neither pray I for these alone, but for them also which shall believe on me through their word,

That they all may be one; as thou, Father, art in me, and I in thee, that they also may be one in us, that the world may believe that thou hast sent me.

And the glory which thou gavest me, I have given them, that they may be one, even as we are one:

I in them, and thou in me, that they may be made perfect in one, and that the world may know that thou hast sent me and hast loved them as thou hast loved me.

Father, I will that they also, whom thou hast given me, be with me where I am, that they may behold my glory, which thou hast given me: for thou lovedst me before the foundation of the world.

> *O righteous Father, the world hath not known thee: but I have known thee, and these have known that thou hast sent me. And I have declared unto them thy name and will declare it, that the love wherewith thou hast loved me may be in them, and I in them.*

Hallelujah! Praise the Lord, saints! Now, we are receiving the depths of the Word where we find the heart and soul of our Savior poured out in a prayer of intercession. This prayer is a treasure trove of divine revelation, so let us open our hearts and minds to receive the anointed message of Jesus.

Jesus begins by speaking to the Father, declaring that the hour has come for His glorification. He acknowledges that all power has been given to Him to grant eternal life to those whom the Father has given Him. Jesus states that eternal life comes from knowing the only true God, whom the Father has sent. Here, Jesus prays for His disciples, those whom the Father had given Him out of the world. He acknowledges that they belong to the Father and affirms that He has revealed the Father's Name to them. Jesus prays for their sanctification. He expresses His desire for them to be kept from evil, even as they remain in the world as witnesses for Him. Jesus continues His prayer, asking the Father to keep His disciples as one with Him, just as Jesus and the Father are one. He emphasizes that the world may hate them because they are not of the world, but He prays that they would be sanctified through the truth of God's Word. Jesus reaffirms that He is sending them into the world, just as the Father sent Him, and consecrates Himself for their sake.

Toward the ending of this prayer, Jesus extends His prayer beyond His immediate disciples to all future believers, including us! He prays for unity among all believers, that we are one with the Father so that the world may believe in Him. Jesus desires that all believers experience the fullness of His love and be with Him in eternity, beholding His glory. What a heartfelt prayer we find in John 17! Jesus, our High Priest, intercedes for us, seeking unity, protection, and sanctification. This prayer reveals the depth of Jesus' love for His followers and His desire for us to be one with Him.

Let us take this prayer to heart and strive for unity among ourselves, knowing that we are called to be in the world but not of the world. As we delve into the truth of God's Word, let us be sanctified by His truth and walk as witnesses of His love. May the revelation of this prayer ignite a fire in our hearts to live in unity and love, just as Jesus desires. Let us go forth each day, empowered by the Holy Ghost, and bring glory to His Name, fulfilling His divine purpose in our lives. Hallelujah! Amen!

In this second phase of our spiritual growth, we embrace the principle of hungering and thirsting for righteousness. Within this principle, we also acknowledge the importance of mourning as part of the eleventh step. As we actively engage in prayer, meditation, and fasting, we witness the fulfillment of the promises of being filled and comforted. Each session of praise and worship nourishes our minds and spirits, bringing a sense of fulfillment and comfort.

As flawed individuals, we often lack spiritual discipline. Therefore, God lovingly guides and disciplines us through the steps of spiritual development we have outlined. However, it doesn't stop there. Action is essential, and faith must be accompanied by works. One may claim to have faith, but true faith is demonstrated through actions. Show me your faith without works, and I will show you my faith through my works.

YOD

We are being filled with the Holy Ghost in recovery and salvation. Praise may seem like the smallest action, but it holds significant spiritual power. It represents faith which is the divine spark that we experienced in *step one*, the point of connection between the Earth and heaven. It is us grasping and holding onto the hand of God, wrapping ourselves in His creative power and influence.

Step eleven involves seeking a deeper spiritual connection through prayer, fasting, meditation, and praise. This step emphasizes the importance of improving contact with Jesus. We discover that we also seek God through worship, we gain spiritual insight. Faith and praise are the representation of the life of one who has taken this step. They are vital for continuing this spiritual journey.

We are reminded to focus on the principle shown by Jesus, which serves as the guideline for righteousness and uprightness. By aligning our actions with His principle, we discover that we are living a life full of faithfulness.

Moreover, faith and praise make up the foundation for the other spiritual actions. Similarly, *step eleven* serves as a foundation for the remaining steps in this spiritual development of recovery. It sets the stage for continued recovery by deepening our discernment, fostering humility, and seeking His supernatural guidance in all aspects of life.

ה HEY

The same revelation discovered in *step six* holds spiritual significance and is connected to faith and praise of *step eleven* in recovery. Revelation is the very breath and presence of God. It is the breath that brings recovery and revival. In *step eleven*, we who are in **RECOVERY 5:12** are encouraged to seek a deeper communion through prayer, fasting, meditation, and worship.

This supernatural unveiling through the Holy Spirit and the Presence of God is revealed in this step. In *step eleven*, we pray and praise, aligning our will with God's will and seeking His guidance in all our affairs. We cannot navigate life's challenges without prayer, fasting, and meditation. The revelation is manifested by embracing the presence of God through praise, and we open ourselves to receive the revelation of discernment.

Furthermore, the Holy Ghost is the central aspect of our recovery walk. The Holy Spirit contains revelation, empowers us, and leads us in our recovery process. Revelation reminds us of the Holy Spirit's presence and the anointing He brings to our lives.

By incorporating revelation into *step eleven*, we recognize the importance of seeking renewal, covering, and the presence of God. By engaging in prayer, fasting, meditation, and praise, we open ourselves to receive revelation, ushering in His wisdom to guide our recovery walk. We embrace His presence, ushering in the Holy Spirit to bring revelation and rebirth. This connects us to Him and His will for our new life.

VAV

The anchor from *step four* holds a vertical line connecting heaven and Earth. It is the bridge between the divine and the material world. In *step eleven*, which emphasizes seeking a deeper infilling, the anchor is this bridge.

In *step eleven*, we who are being recovered are encouraged to recognize our own redemption and embrace our anchor within the Holy Ghost. We strive to align with God's will, acknowledging our dependence on God for strength.

Furthermore, the Vav is often referred to as a "hook" in Hebrew. This suggests stability, support, and the ability to hold things together. In *step eleven*, we seek stability and support through the discipline of prayer, meditation, fasting, and worship. We rely on our connection with God, which anchors us and provides us with comfort and strength in times of difficulty. We find ourselves walking in the calmness of the storm's eye.

The Holy Ghost is the central aspect of our walk. The Holy Spirit is the empowering force that enables us to maintain our connection with God and experience spiritual anointing. The anchor is vital in the Holy Spirit's bridging the gap between heaven and Earth, facilitating a deeper communion with God. We sense that we are being drawn out by this anchor into His presence as we pass through this door.

ד DALET

This door. As Holy Ghost-filled people, we receive revelation through the door and reflect on how it relates to *step eleven* in recovery. The door reveals a transition that allows us to enter a new realm. When we apply the door to *step eleven*, we understand it as an invitation to embark on an anointed journey of communion.

Step eleven in the recovery process focuses on prayer, fasting, meditation, and worship, seeking communion with Jesus Christ. The door opens to this deeper spiritual communion. It provides the opportunity to enter a new realm of revival, where we always experience His presence.

Moreover, the door emphasizes the importance of submission to God's will. In *step eleven*, we are encouraged to let go of our own ego, observing God guiding our thoughts and efforts. The door humbles us before God, allowing us to trust in His wisdom.

Once again, the Holy Spirit plays a vital role in our spiritual walk. The Holy Spirit is the Power that enables us to experience an encounter with God. The door is the gateway through which the Holy Spirit flows, bringing an anointing, revelation, and revival.

In *step eleven*, we are encouraged to seek the presence of the Holy Spirit through prayer, fasting, meditation, and worship. We are invited to enter through the door, experiencing the Holy Spirit leading us into a deeper communion with God and a greater understanding of His will for our lives.

ה HEY

More is being revealed. As we continue taking *step eleven*, we see the revelation of faith in our communion with God. Then we began to see how the revelation of faith is anchored through the door.

The very faith that was like a grain of mustard seed in *step one*, which God took and cast into the garden in our spirits, freshly plowed and furrowed from humility, has now grown as we have taken these steps. It has begun a great tree, and the fowls of the air will lodge in the branches of it. We realize that our faith, which was but a flimsy reed, has now become an unmovable oak.

This revelation was anchored through the door that was presented in *step two* for us to enter. We crossed over the threshold in *step seven* and now are seeing more of the revelation that it is the gateway which brings the Holy Spirit's anointing the moment the door is opened.

This revelation holds sacredness and is anchored to faith and praise in *step eleven*. It is the very breath, revelation, and presence of God. It is the breath that brings us this life and revival. In *step eleven*, we who are in **RECOVERY 5:12** are seeking a deeper communion through prayer, fasting, meditation, and worship.

This supernatural unveiling through the Holy Spirit and the presence of God is being revealed in this step. In *step eleven*, we pray and praise, aligning our will with God's will and seeking His guidance in all our affairs. We cannot navigate life's challenges without prayer, fasting, meditation, praise, and worship. The revelation comes through embracing the presence of God through prayer, and we open ourselves to receive discernment.

Furthermore, we are constantly reminded that the Holy Ghost is the central aspect of our walk. The Holy Spirit contains revelation, empowers us, and leads us in our recovery process. Revelation reminds us of the Holy Spirit's presence and the anointing it brings to our life.

We understand the significance of integrating this revelation into *step eleven*, as it magnifies the importance of abiding presence of God. Through the avenues of earnest prayer, purposeful fasting, contemplative meditation, and heartfelt praise, we position ourselves to receive profound revelations from the Lord. In doing so, we invite His wisdom to shine forth on our journey of recovery.

The Hebrew name Judah, often spelled "Yehudah" or "Yehuda," has several meanings, including "praise" or "thanks." In the context of recovery, the name Judah carries significant inspiration. The name Judah's meaning of "praise" or "thanks" encourage us in recovery to cultivate an attitude of gratitude. Being thankful for progress, support, and the opportunity for healing enhances recovery. Recovery is a series of victories, no matter how small they may seem. The name Judah reminds us to celebrate each triumph, recognizing the progress made along the way belongs to God. Recovery requires determination. The name Judah reflects our praise for the inner strength demonstrated by those of us in recovery as we face and God overcomes challenges.

In a spiritual context, the name Judah represents a deeper connection to one's spirituality. It inspires us to find comfort in the Holy Spirit, beginning with recovery. Praise and thanksgiving are powerful antidotes to the feelings of shame that arise early on in recovery. The name Judah encourages us to let go of self-delusions and embrace the Love of Christ. Just as the name Judah represents praise, it also signifies finding meaning in difficult experiences. Recovery leads to spiritual growth and the ability to help others on their own journeys. The meaning of the name Judah inspires a sense of encouragement within recovery. Praising the efforts of others foster an uplifting environment in recovery. It involves the support of loved ones, ministry, and recovery ministries. The name Judah reminds us to express gratitude for the help we receive from God on our journeys. The name Judah is the praise for Holy Ghost changes in our lives made during recovery. It encourages us to embrace a new way of life as we grow.

Overall, the name Judah's meaning of praise holds powerful applications in recovery. It emphasizes the importance of a spiritual connection reminding us to focus on the positive aspects of recovery. We are to find strength in the process of recovery and salvation in Jesus' Name.

In this phase of our spiritual journey, the second trimester of spiritual development, we have come to realize that the guiding principle of these three steps is to hunger and thirst after righteousness. It was during the fourth step that we first began to grasp the significance of this principle. Within this overarching principle, we also discover the same specific principle of mourning, as stated in the second step. Its beauty crushed our flesh as it covered us through the remission steps of four, five and six. Through these spiritual development steps, we are assured of being filled with what we truly need, and in the eleventh step, we discover the comforting presence of God in our lives.

Joy.

Certainly, there are more specific examples of spiritual action aligned with 1 Thessalonians 5:16-18, focusing on rejoicing, praying continually, and giving thanks in all circumstances. We start each day with a praise song, expressing gratitude to God. We begin attending events that focus on worship. We share testimonies of God's goodness with fellow believers. Many organize and participate in recovery fellowship gatherings that promote joyful interactions. We rejoice in God's creation by spending time in nature and marveling at His handiwork. We always celebrate spiritual milestones, such as sobriety birthdays, baptisms, and dedications with enthusiasm. Some create a "gratitude board" at home where family members write things, they are thankful for. We are encouraged to develop a habit of offering short, spontaneous prayers throughout the day, lifting needs and concerns as they arise. Some use prayer aides and reminders to prompt regular moments of prayer. We follow a prayer schedule that allocates specific times for intercessory prayer, worship, and personal communion with God. We engage in intercessory prayer for recovery ministries and causes, such as missionaries, the persecuted church, and the peace of Jerusalem. Some set aside dedicated prayer sessions during uncertain times, seeking God's comfort. Many pray through the Scriptures, turning biblical passages into personal prayers. Some practice the breathing technique, using a short prayer or Scripture verse as they breathe in and out. Some maintain a daily gratitude journal, writing down three things they are thankful for each day. We always begin mealtime prayers with gratitude for the food and God's provision. We express thankfulness to God in prayer for His protection during our daily travels. We offer thanks for answered prayers and unexpected blessings, acknowledging God's faithfulness. We thank God for trials, recognizing that they lead to service, ministry, and dependence on Him. We practice gratitude during family prayer times, encouraging each family member to share something they are thankful for. We always take time to thank God for the people in our lives, expressing appreciation for their love.

Remember that these actions are not meant to be legalistic rituals but rather expressions of a heart genuinely seeking to follow God's will. Rejoicing is a continuous journey of deepening our relationships with God and finding contentment in His presence.

Jesus breaks into our progress before moving on to *step twelve* by asking, "Do you love Me more than anything?" We typically say, "Yes, Lord; You know that I love You." It is here that we hear Jesus whisper, "Feed My lambs." Jesus asks us a second time, "Do you love Me?" At this point we respond, "Yes Lord; You know that I Love You." Jesus always replies, "Feed My sheep." To bring us into a covenant He made on a seashore many years ago, He asks us a third time, "Do you love Me?" It is here, in this moment, that we realize that we have been among those who denied Jesus of Nazareth in times gone by. It is a thought that makes us grieve because Jesus never denied us. And we answer Him, "Lord, You know all things; You know that I love You." Jesus gives us a lifelong commandment. He tells us, "Feed my sheep."

CHAPTER 17

STEP TWELVE

*"We now teach others to observe all things whatsoever
Jesus has commanded us: and, see, He is with us always,
even unto the end of the world. Amen."*
(Matthew 28:20)

DISCIPLESHIP

"We 'Bes' merely facilitators, placing your hand into His" – Coyote

Step twelve: In this final recovery step, we turn our attention to *step twelve* and the role of the disciple. Through practical experience, we have discovered that nothing provides greater protection against sins such as addictions and alcoholism that have so easily beset us than the devoted act of sharing this recovery message with a newcomer. When all other spiritual endeavors fall short, this intentional act of witnessing brings about a life-giving transformation in all who are involved. You possess the power to help when no one else can and to inspire confidence when others struggle. Recognize that those around you are in great spiritual need. Having received the Holy Spirit through your commitment to Jesus

Christ through these steps, our twelfth suggestion is for you to embrace the calling of becoming a disciple and guide others to follow the teachings of our Lord. God has endued us with a good dowry; now will our Lord dwell with us, because we have born Him righteous communion.

Engaging with sinners seeking salvation and newly converted individuals provides an opportune environment to further share this recovery path and the gospel message of Jesus Christ. We are akin to a tool that is used to both prepare the ground for planting and to remove any obstacles in its way. Just as the cry of the poor man was heard by God, who saved him from all his troubles, we too can bring the message of deliverance to those in need of recovery.

You may not be familiar with anyone seeking recovery right now, but they can be found in various places in everyday life such as on the streets, in recovery rooms, and even in churches. Additionally, ministers and religious leaders can guide you to those in need of this message. Hospitals, behavioral units, and treatment centers are also potential avenues to reach out to individuals who are open to receiving healing and recovery. By seeking out these opportunities, you can find support and assistance in sharing this message with those who are seeking it.

When you locate someone to disciple, it is essential to gather information about individuals who show an interest in knowing Jesus Christ, seeking salvation, and wanting to recover. When you come across a potential disciple, follow these steps to understand their needs and to create a meaningful connection:

1. Assess Their Background: Take the time to learn about their behavior, problems, background, and religious inclinations. This understanding will help you empathize with their journey and approach them in a way that resonates with their unique experiences.

2. Determine the Severity of Their Condition: Evaluate the seriousness of their spiritual condition and their level of desperation for recovery and salvation. This assessment will help you gauge

the depth of their need and guide you in providing appropriate guidance and support.

3. Put Yourself in Their Shoes: Imagine yourself in their position and consider how you would want someone to approach you in your search for recovery and salvation. Empathy plays a crucial role in building trust and creating a safe environment for open dialogue and exploration of faith.

By gaining insights into their background, challenges, and religious perspectives, you can tailor your approach to meet their specific needs. Remember, the goal is to build a genuine connection based on understanding, compassion, and a shared desire to embark on a life-changing recovery journey with Jesus Christ.

- If it is feasible, try to have a one-on-one conversation with the potential convert. Begin by engaging in casual conversation, allowing a comfortable rapport to develop. After some time, gently transition the discussion towards the topic of sins such as addictions and alcoholism including hurts, habits, and hang-ups. Share enough about your own past sinful habits, struggles, and experiences to create an atmosphere of trust and openness, encouraging them to open up about themselves.

    - If they wish to talk, let them do so. Let them steer the conversation in any direction they like. You will thus get a better idea of how you ought to proceed.
    - If they are not communicative, give them a sketch of your sinful life up to the time you were saved but say nothing, for the moment, of how that was accomplished.
    - If they are in a serious mood, dwell on the trouble that sins such as addictions and alcoholism have caused you, being careful not to moralize or lecture.
    - If their mood is light, tell them humorous stories of your escapades. Get them to tell some of theirs.

When they see you know all about the effects of sins such as addictions and alcoholism, hurts, habits, and hang-ups, begin to describe yourself as once being bound by these same sins. Describe for them how lost you were in your own skin.

Here, we approach with utmost care, allowing the living Word of God to permeate our being, for its power is all-encompassing. As witnesses of God's mighty works, we boast in Him, offering encouragement to those who may feel disheartened. It is akin to the fiery spinning sword guarded by the angel, blocking the way to the Tree of Life. To partake of its fruit, one must pass through this formidable flame. Similarly, we must pass through our own refining fire as we journey toward the sacred presence of God.

When the veil was torn in two, the embroidered cherubim on it appeared to separate, granting every worshipper access to the unveiled presence of God. We speak of His awe-inspiring acts and declare His greatness. Just like the swing of a mattock, both cultivating and breaking ground, these actions are necessary for planting. When God speaks His Word, and we, in agreement, speak His Word as well, it becomes a double-edged sword. It pierces to the very core of our being, discerning the immaterial parts of our soul and spirit, as well as the physical aspects of bone, joint, and marrow. Together, these elements form our humanity. We discover as we carry this message that the Word was not a shield for us to use as we battled the unseen. Rather, it was a shield to protect us as we continued to do God's business amidst spiritual battles. The double-edged sword was not for use on others but for us to use on ourselves.

God's Word has the power to uncover the hidden aspects of our being and make them known. It interprets and reveals the true thoughts and secret motives of our hearts. No one can hide their thoughts from God, for nothing we do remains a secret; everything is exposed and defenseless before His eyes. The responsibility lies with us to embrace the Word and reflect on our own state as lost sinners bound by alcoholism and addictions.

How do you describe yourself to a potential disciple as once being a lost sinner bound by alcohol and drugs?

1. Tell them how baffled you were.
2. Tell them how you finally learned that you were spiritually sick.
3. Give them an account of the struggles you made to stop.
4. Show them the mental twist that leads to sins such as addictions and alcoholism's first deed and the ensuing insanity of the carnal spree.

If they are a lost sinner and being destroyed by hurts, habits, and hang-ups, they will understand you at once. They will match your mental inconsistencies with some of their own. If you are satisfied that they are a lost sinner bound by sins such as hurts and habits, what next?

1. Begin to dwell on the hopeless features of the spiritual malady of sin.
2. Show them, from your own experience, how the queer mental condition surrounding sins such as addictions and alcoholism prevents normal functioning of willpower.
3. Continue to speak of sins such as addictions and alcoholism as a spiritual illness, a fatal spiritual malady.
4. Talk about the conditions of the flesh and mind which accompany it.
5. Talk to them about the hopelessness of a life of sin.

The more hopeless they feel, the better. They will be more likely to follow your suggestions. Tell them there is a solution. Tell them that if they want to get well you will do anything to help. Prepare to tell them of the endless cycle of *step one*.

The potential convert may start to show curiosity about your recovery and salvation experience, even if they haven't fully acknowledged their own spiritual condition. If you sense that they are likely to ask you how you are recovered and saved, allow them to pose that question. Share with them the exact details of what transpired in your life. During this phase of their deliverance, it is important to keep their attention focused on your journey.

Maintain a sensible, tactful, considerate, and humble demeanor in your conversation, displaying empathy and understanding. We have learned the power of this demeanor through the restitutions of the ninth step. By doing so, you are building a friendship. Gradually, your friend will begin to recognize that they share many, if not all, of the characteristics of a lost sinner bound by affliction. Be cautious not to label them as a lost sinner explicitly. Allow them to arrive at their own conclusion through their own reflections. At this stage, it is time to introduce them to the Bible and this book. If they have already seen them, they may express a desire or even a willingness to discuss them.

What happens when they admit that they have the traits of the lost sinner and are bound by sins such as addictions and alcoholism?

1. Outline the ordered steps they need to take which are to repent and;
2. Relive how you made a self-appraisal and confessed your shortcomings which were washed away with baptism in Jesus' Name as a result of *steps four, five*, and *six*.
3. Describe how you got spiritually connected through receiving His Spirit and straightened out your past by going out and doing the Spirit's bidding in *steps seven, eight*, and *nine*.
4. Explain why you are now endeavoring to be helpful to them in the Name of Jesus. It's the only way to keep this gift in *steps ten, eleven*, and *twelve*.
5. Reveal how you are aligning with God through a measure of faith and actively responding to their needs of recovery and salvation, demonstrating your commitment to be helpful in the Name of Jesus.

We are reminded of His words: Come, children, listen to me, I will teach you the Fear of the Lord. It is crucial for them to understand that as you share this with them and it will deeply impact your own connection to the love of Jesus Christ. Let them know that anyone who feels oppressed can find refuge in the Lord, a secure shelter in times of trouble, a perfect hiding place. In truth, they are helping you just as much, if not more, than you are helping them.

What happens after you have delivered the initial message? It's possible that you have stirred up thoughts and questions about sins such as addictions and alcoholism, as well as thoughts of salvation, in their minds. Let it be clear to them that they are not obligated to you in any way. Your only hope is that once they find deliverance from their difficulties through salvation, they will consider reaching out to help other lost sinners. While their attention is focused on helping others, emphasize the importance of prioritizing the well-being of others above their own as a righteous person. Throughout this step, be mindful of the words you speak, refraining from evil speech. Lastly, make it known that there is no pressure on them, and they are not obligated to see you again if they don't wish to. This understanding is beneficial for everyone involved.

If they show interest, lend them a copy of the Bible and this book. Unless your friend wants to talk further about themself, do not wear out your welcome. Give them a chance to think it over. If they are sincerely interested and want to see you again, ask them in the interval to begin reading the Bible and this book. The book of John is a good place to begin in the Bible, followed by the book of Acts of the Holy Spirit and apostles. In this book, the first reading assignment could easily be the first five chapters. After doing that, they must decide for themself whether they want to go on. They should not be pushed or prodded by anyone, much less by you, their loved ones, or their friends. To find God, the desire must come from within themselves. They must be called to humility by Jesus.

Suppose now you are making your second visit to the potential convert. They have begun reading the book of John and at least the first five chapters of this book. They may say they are prepared to go through with these steps and measures of faith. Having had the experience yourself, you can give them a lot of practical advice. Let them know you are available if they wish to take these steps.

Throughout your visits with the new person, stress the spiritual feature freely. Always start each meeting with a moment of silence to recognize Jesus Christ, who is always in your midst, followed by a prayer – even if it is a simple serenity prayer. The main thing is that they be willing to believe in Jesus Christ, not their *conception*, and that they live by biblical principles. When dealing with the intellectually prideful, use everyday language to describe biblical principles. This method lessens the opportunity to arouse any prejudice they may have against certain theological terms and conceptions about which they may already be confused.

When engaging with a potential disciple who already belongs to a religious denomination, it's essential to emphasize that your intention is not to instruct them in religious matters. Instead, focus on sharing general biblical principles that apply to all believers. Acknowledge their existing knowledge and faith, but also state the need for actions to align with their beliefs. Emphasize that faith alone is insufficient, and that genuine faith should be accompanied by corresponding works. Many times, we pose the question, "Do you think God, not who you think He is but who He truly is, can relieve you of your addictions or alcoholism?" They typically will say, "Yes." Then ask them, "Do you think that God, not who you think He is but who He truly is, would relieve you of your alcoholism or addictions?" Again, their answer will typically be, "Yes" Then ask them, "Then why hasn't He done so already?" This shakes the typical person to their core. When we are faced with that question, we immediately retreat into our own thinking and selves to figure out why the Creator of the universe would or would not do a certain thing.

Then after a few minutes, and with much trust, you will be able to point out that "We never sought Him, much less did it with our whole hearts." These steps and measures are how we learned to seek Him. It was there we discovered that He was in the seeking. Each time we seek Him, He is there. And seemingly, every time we stop seeking Him, He is not there. Therefore, we always seek Him.

Share the good news of faith with the potential convert! Explain that genuine faith goes beyond mere belief and requires self-sacrifice and constructive actions for the benefit of others. Help them recognize where they have fallen short in putting their knowledge into practice by sharing your own experiences. Present the spiritual tools that have worked for you and invite them to inspect and consider using them as well. Offer friendship and fellowship as you guide them on their recovery journey.

The promises of the twelfth step will bring new meaning to your life as you serve others. These promises include witnessing people being restored, witnessing their growth and their ability to help others, seeing loneliness dissipate, and being surrounded by a supportive fellowship and countless friends—this is an invaluable experience. It's a good life. We know you don't want to miss it.

Connecting with newcomers and fellow members is the highlight of our lives. Assisting others is the voussoir of our recovery and salvation. If you persist in this recovery path, extraordinary things will occur. When you reflect on the past, you will realize that the blessings that came when you surrendered to God's will were far greater than anything you could have planned. Repent, be baptized in the Name of Jesus for the forgiveness of sins, and follow the guidance of the Holy Spirit. You will find yourself living in a new and marvelous world, regardless of your current circumstances!

Jesus explains, "I guide and empower you as you take these steps and measures, ensuring your spiritual growth and transformation. When you diligently follow these steps, you will experience a profound shift in your capabilities and perspectives. No longer driven by self-interest, you become a beacon of hope, radiating My love wherever you go. Sins such as addictions and alcoholism are no longer welcome in your life, as your bodies become a sanctuary of purity and righteousness. A new community of believers forms around you, united in everyone's desire to seek and serve God. Your tastes and desires align with the values of My kingdom, and worldly entertainment loses its appeal. You no longer crave sinful scenes or seek fulfillment in venues that promote unrighteousness. Even though you have the freedom to enter places where sinners gather, your purpose is not to partake in their sinful activities. Instead, you are driven by a mission to bring My light and love to those who are lost. You fearlessly enter the darkest corners of society, not hesitating to offer a helping hand to those in desperate need of My saving grace."

Christ explains further, saying, "Your motives are pure, and you shall seek My guidance in every situation. Before venturing forth, you need to ensure that you stand on a solid foundation of faith and that your intentions align with My will. As you contemplate the spiritual contribution you can make in each encounter, aim to uplift and inspire others. With confidence in My leading, you are going to embark on these journeys without fear, knowing that I am by your side, protecting and guiding you."

He finishes by reminding us, "Your goal is to be of maximum service to others, mirroring My selfless love and compassion. There is no hesitation in your heart to go wherever I call you, even if it means entering the most destitute and broken places. You trust in My presence and power to keep you safe, as you wholeheartedly embrace the mission of bringing healing and recovery to those in need. In following this principle, you embody My teachings and exemplify the essence of discipleship. Through your actions, lives are being transformed, loneliness dissipates, and a vibrant community of faith blossoms around you. This is an experience of abundant life that you would not want to miss, for it is in serving others that you truly discover the profound joy and purpose I have prepared for you."

A sinner who remains disconnected from the Holy Spirit cannot escape the influence of their carnal mind. Their spiritual condition needs recovery and transformation. Even in the most remote and desolate places, the temptations and struggles of the sinful nature can still find a way to surface.

Many have sought solace in distant and isolated locations, hoping to find relief from the grip of sins such as addictions and alcoholism.

However, such attempts often prove futile. No matter the geographical distance or seclusion, the battle with sin is an internal one that cannot be escaped simply by changing people, places, or things.

Whether someone has willingly ventured to distant places or has been forcibly removed, the core issue lies within their spiritual state. Merely changing locations does not address the root problem of the carnal mind and its sinful inclinations. For wherever we go, there we are. This childish mantra rings true for the person who realizes who the sinner in their lives is that has been causing all their problems. For wherever we go, there we are.

It is essential for individuals to recognize that true transformation comes from within, through a genuine surrender to God's grace and a commitment to follow the steps of repentance, redemption, and restitution. Merely attempting to escape to remote places will not resolve the deep-seated spiritual challenges that need to be addressed.

Instead of seeking external solutions or trying to run away from the problem of sin, it is crucial for individuals to turn their focus inward, seeking a relationship with God and embracing the life-changing power of His love and forgiveness. Only through this inner transformation does one find true liberation from the bondage of sin and experience lasting peace and freedom.

We firmly believe that any strategy aimed at shielding sinners from temptation provides only temporary relief and ultimately leads to even greater turmoil. We have firsthand experience with such approaches. These futile attempts to achieve the impossible are destined to fail. It is important to acknowledge that our problems were the result of our own actions. The outward manifestations of our sinful natures were mere symbols of deeper issues. In our journeys, we have relinquished the need to fight against others or anything else. It is a necessity for our recovery and growth.

ז ZAYIN

Mattock. This new spiritual tool was introduced in *step twelve* of our journey. It has direct links to *step one*'s experience with the cross. In *step one*, we had the seed and its potential power. Contained within the seed was the power of the cross, the shepherd's staff, and the spark of God. We saw all these powers manifested in our lives as we took these steps. Now here in *step twelve*, we will see that the power of the cross from *step one* has given us the mattock and the temple. These are now anchored in the power of the shepherd's staff which was lying in the ark of *step one*. Now the shepherd's staff is anchored in righteousness, which is the destination of faith or the spark of God. We will see how these are all at work in *step twelve*.

The mattock is a practical tool used in our spiritual walk. It is useful for digging and breaking up the ground in preparation for sowing. However, as we encounter roots and obstacles, with a mere twist of the mattock's head from hoe to axe we use it to chop and remove the roots from the ground. Then we return to the side of the mattock's head containing the hoe and continue with the preparation of the soil. This describes what happens in our lives as we encounter a new convert and are able to be in the room as they take these steps with Jesus. We watch them on their journey, and it reveals the opportunities and obstacles in our own spirits. It's as if communion has been introduced into the new convert's life and now it is spilling over into ours. Simultaneously, it's as if communion has been introduced into our lives and now it is spilling over into others. Once the mattock has been applied, the action of preparing for the harvest has been initiated and now God does the watering as we see that He is the God of the harvest and prepares His temple to be laborers.

ב BET

Temple. Our temple was introduced in *step four* and has begun a revival of epic proportions. Once a dumpster fire used only for destruction and chaos, through the taking of these steps, it is becoming the temple of the Holy Ghost.

It is literally the dwelling place of the Holy Ghost. This temple can now be seen as home and community. When we examine the connection between our temple and *step twelve*, we find a powerful message about the importance of carrying the message of recovery and extending a helping hand to others.

Step twelve in the recovery process calls for us to engage in service to others who are still struggling. It emphasizes the revival that occurs when we selflessly reach out to those in need. Our temple reminds us that we are called to create a welcoming and supportive environment, just like a dwelling place, where other people can find solace, acceptance, and guidance.

Furthermore, our temple conveys the idea of unity. In *step twelve*, people come together as a community to share experiences, strength, and hope. We form a spiritual home where mutual encouragement flourishes. Our temple encourages us to build a sense of belonging, where people feel embraced.

The Holy Spirit is central to fostering community by equipping us for service. The Spirit empowers believers to extend compassion to others. Our temple reminds us that it is through the Holy Spirit that we create a spiritual home for those seeking recovery, offering a place of refuge.

Moreover, our temple also is a blessing. In *step twelve*, we who have found recovery become a source of inspiration for others. By sharing our stories and offering support, we become a channel of blessings, helping others find their way to a life of wholeness in Jesus' Name.

VAV

We are learning that our bodies are the dwelling places of the Holy Spirit. This explains why we are all searching for a sense of belonging. But *step four* revealed that we need an anchor. This brings us to the twelfth step of **RECOVERY 5:12**.

Step twelve emphasizes carrying the message of recovery and extending support to others who are still struggling. This step highlights the importance of creating a supportive recovery community, a spiritual home where people find refuge.

It signifies the idea of a nurturing space where people find support. In the recovery process, it is important to create an environment where people feel comfortable sharing their experiences and seeking help in our Lord and Savior. It is about fostering a sense of belonging through creating connections within a recovery community of individuals who empathize with one another's struggles.

Step twelve emphasizes unity. It is the link between people and the importance of coming together to support one another. In *step twelve*, people unite to offer their experiences, strength, and hope, forming a recovery community of support for those still sick and suffering as well as those who are on the path to recovery. **RECOVERY 5:12** encourages others to reach out, build bridges, and extend a helping hand to those in need.

Additionally, *step twelve* is about building a solid foundation for recovery. The step represents steadfastness and sovereign alignment, simultaneously providing communion between the earthly and the divine. Together, we discover the importance of establishing a firm base rooted in anointing, enabling people to find strength, guidance, and steadfast faith in recovery.

ל LAMED

The shepherd's staff reminds us of learning, teaching, and wisdom. In this step, it signifies the pursuit of the knowledge of His will and the sharing of discernment with others. In the context of recovery, this step represents the wisdom gained through a deep and effective supernatural encounter and the faithfulness to share those experiences with others on their own journeys of recovery.

Continuing to move through this step, we explore His call for us to carry the message of recovery and extend a helping hand to others who are still struggling. *Step twelve* highlights the importance of communing with the Holy Spirit, gaining wisdom through supernatural experiences, and using that wisdom to ignite others. We are carriers of His flame.

The shepherd's staff is found in communion with the supernatural, reminding people to rely on the guidance of the Holy Spirit throughout the recovery process. It encourages us to seek a deeper spiritual communion and wisdom to guide our decisions.

The shepherd's staff expresses the importance of sharing learned discernment with others. It encourages us to learn from one another, offering guidance, support, and wisdom to those who are still struggling. By sharing our stories of anointing we embody the Spirit of the Good Shepherd and are sources of His annointng anchored in hope.

VAV

This anchor is secured in Christ Jesus and connects those who are recovered and have received salvation, the hidden righteous ones. Those of us who have recovered and now walk this path demonstrate the righteous actions taught by Jesus in His service of others and seek His presence, helping maintain the spiritual balance and preservation of the redeemed.

Those who have taken this step are a humble and selfless people who embody and practice righteousness, compassion, and discernment. They serve as pillars of strength, serving the redeemed through their righteous acts, prayers, and positive influence on the world.

After taking this step, often unknown to others, we live our lives in quiet devotion to God and selflessly help those in need. Our spiritual merit and presence protect the world from destruction and bring supernatural blessings to those needing redemption.

The belief in the twelfth step teaches us the importance of recognizing and valuing the impact that a small group of righteous people can have on recovery and the world. It reminds us that even if we may not be aware of our identity or presence, there are always those who selflessly work towards the betterment of humanity, igniting others by our example.

Having taken *step twelve* and experiencing revival, we become among those who walk the path of righteousness and offer guidance, support, and inspiration to those struggling with sins such as addictions and alcoholism. Those who are recovered, whether visible or hidden, help uplift and preserve the spiritual well-being of others, demonstrating the anointed power of righteousness, compassion, and piety.

נ NUN

Righteousness. We are reminded again and again that *step twelve* calls for us to carry the message of recovery and extend a helping hand to others who are still struggling. "Two are better than one; because they have a good reward for their labor. For if they fall, the one will lift up his fellow: but woe to him that is alone when he falleth; for he hath not another to help him up" (Ecclesiastes 4:9-10). This passage emphasizes the significance of unity and support in times of struggle, highlighting the strength and encouragement that come from walking the recovery journey together. Shoulder to shoulder.

"Two are better than one." We are taught the value of companionship in recovery. *Step twelve* invites us to join forces with others who have recovered, forming a supportive recovery community. Together, we can provide strength and encouragement as we navigate life's challenges in recovery.

"For if they fall, the one will lift up his fellow." In recovery, we face setbacks. This verse emphasizes the significance of being there for one another, offering support and a helping hand when someone stumbles. It reminds us that by sharing our experiences and supporting each other, we can uplift those who are struggling, reminding them that they are not alone.

"Woe to him that is alone when he falleth." Isolation is detrimental to recovery. This verse warns against being alone in times of hardship because, without the support of others in recovery, it is challenging to overcome obstacles. *Step twelve* emphasizes the importance of reaching out, connecting, and staying engaged with a recovery community of like-minded individuals who understand the journey of recovery.

The Hebrew name Zebulun, often spelled "Zevulun" or "Zebulun," has various interpretations, including "dwelling" or "exalted." In the context of recovery, the name Zebulun carries meaningful lessons. The name Zebulun's meaning of "dwelling" involves finding a secure place within God during recovery. It emphasizes the importance of recognizing that God has created a safe inner space for healing within us. Dwelling involves creating a place in our lives through worshipful praise where the presence of God dwells. In recovery, we seek out like-minded individuals and join recovery ministries to build a sense of support. Recovery involves seeking God who brings stability to our lives. The name Zebulun inspires us to seek God through praise as He creates a harmonious existence within our souls, free from the chaos of sins such as alcoholism, addictions, and other spiritual struggles effecting the mind.

The name Zebulun's meaning of "exalted" speaks to the life-changing exhortation that occurs during recovery. It is the process of acknowledging that God has brought us to a place where we rise above challenges as we embrace growth in Him. Exalted reflects how we first recognize the Holy Spirit's value. In recovery, we learn to honor God's work in us as we embark on a journey of salvation. The name Zebulun represents the start of a new chapter in our lives. Recovery is a fresh beginning, and the name inspires us to embrace God's love. The name Zebulun reflects the idea of finding purpose in the healing process. As we recover, we discover a sense of God's purpose for our lives. The name Zebulun demonstrates strength. It inspires us to draw upon God's implanted inner resources and stand strong in the face of challenges, for the mountains surrounding us are filled with angels. In a spiritual context, the name Zebulun involves the idea of communing with a higher power, which is the Holy Ghost, throughout recovery. It encourages us to seek Him for guidance.

Overall, the name Zebulun's meaning of "dwelling" and "exalted" has profound applications in recovery. It emphasizes the importance of finding stability in Christ, embracing Holy Ghost-inspired change, and rising to new heights in recovery, service, and ministry. It encourages us to recognize God's view of our worth and to build a supportive environment as we progress towards a more fulfilled life in recovery.

In this final trimester of our recovery, we are reminded of the timeless biblical principle: "Blessed are those who hunger and thirst for righteousness, for they will be filled" (Matthew 5:6). Within this overarching principle, we find the essence of the twelfth step principle of meekness, as exemplified by Jesus Himself: "Take my yoke upon you and learn from me, for I am gentle and humble in heart, and you will find rest for your souls" (Matthew 11:29).

These life-changing steps hold a profound promise for us. As we earnestly hunger and thirst after righteousness, we experience a spiritual filling that surpasses our expectations. Our journey in the twelfth step is where we embrace the meekness of our hearts as we surrender ourselves to God's will. As a result of this surrender, a new life, guided by His blessings unfolds before us.

Through the grace of God and our commitment to this principle, we discover the fulfillment of His promises. Our souls are nourished, and we find peace in His presence. The life-changing power experienced as we take these steps enables us to embark on a renewed journey, where we are about to walk in alignment with God's Word and experience the abundant lives, He has measured for us through Faith. Now, this time will our Lord be joined unto us because we have born Him complete righteousness.

Peace.

Indeed, as followers of Christ, we are called to teach others to observe all the things Jesus has commanded us (Matthew 28:20). This task is crucial in fulfilling the Great Commission which calls for making disciples of all nations. There are more specific spiritual actions that align with this calling. Having taken *step twelve*, we engage in evangelism by sharing the message of salvation through Jesus Christ with those who haven't heard it. We invest in intentional discipleship where we mentor others in their recovery walk with Christ. We encourage you to volunteer to teach Sunday School classes or recovery ministries, imparting biblical truths to new converts. Some of us host Bible study groups focused on exploring the teachings of Jesus. We are always equipping new leaders in the church and recovery ministries to effectively model Jesus' teachings to others. Some participate in short-term missions and local outreach projects to demonstrate Jesus' love to different recovery communities. We are strongly encouraged to serve in recovery ministries to mentor the next generation of recovered believers. We create and use **RECOVERY 5:12** discipleship materials that specifically cover Jesus' principles. We could not make it if we did not mentor new believers in their early stages of recovery and faith, helping them build a strong foundation on Jesus' teachings. We utilize parables and develop lessons to creatively illustrate Jesus' teachings. Some organize prayer and fasting retreats where people seek God's guidance on applying Jesus' teachings. We also utilize social media platforms and online resources to teach and reach a wider recovery audience with Jesus' commandments. We provide biblical counseling and support to people facing various life challenges in recovery, grounding them in Jesus' teachings. We engage with the local recovery community by providing educational seminars and workshops on biblical recovery principles. We always engage in daily devotions, reading and meditating on Jesus' teachings and applying them to our lives. Remember that teaching others to observe all things Jesus has commanded is not just about head knowledge but also about living out His teachings through practical application.

This book is meant to challenge us to seek God. We realize that we now see through a glass, darkly. God is constantly disclosing more to us. Ask Him in praying and fasting what you can do each day for the person who is still sick and suffering. The answers will delightfully come if your steps are being ordered by the Lord. But obviously, you cannot transmit a recovered life if you haven't recovered yourself. Use what you have learned through the repentance steps and see to it that your relationship with Him is right. With daily repentance, great events will come to pass for you and countless others. This is His great promise for us. We abandon ourselves to God daily as we did in *step three*. We admit our faults to Him and to our fellows as we did in *steps four* and *five*. We clear away the wreckage of our pasts as we did in *steps eight* and *nine*. And now we give freely of what we found and join those who have recovered. We shall be with you in the fellowship of the Holy Spirit, and you will surely meet some of us as we circumspectly travel this heavenly way. God will bless you and keep you until then. As we faithfully fulfill this calling, we find assurance in knowing that Jesus is with us always until the end of the world.

Amen.

CHAPTER 18

FIRST MEASURE OF FAITH

Having our spirit drawn out, we were pressed for more spiritual growth through Jesus Christ.

"But grow in the grace and knowledge of our Lord and Savior Jesus Christ. To him be glory both now and forever! Amen."
(2 Peter 3:18)

MEASURES OF FAITH

We beg of you, dear brothers and sisters in Christ, in light of God's abundant mercies, to present your bodies as a living sacrifice daily. May this sacrifice be holy and pleasing to God. Let our actions and choices align with His will and bring Him glory, for this is our reasonable service. As we progressed through taking the first nine steps, we discovered that we are no longer conforming to the patterns of this world. Through the life-changing power of the Holy Spirit, our minds are renewed, enabling us to discern and embrace the good, acceptable, and perfect will of God.

Then the developmental steps of ten, eleven and twelve reveal to us the path of obedience, seeking, and service, where we walk in accordance with His purpose. We humbly acknowledge that it is by God's grace, both for ourselves and for those who have embarked on this journey, that we made these declarations. Let us guard against pride, recognizing that our faith is a gift from God, apportioned to each of us according to His divine measure. In all things that we have said to you be circumspect: make no mention of the name of other gods or conceptions, nor let it be heard out of our mouths – per God.

As we enter this measure in faith, we remember the steps along the path of gentleness and longsuffering, aligning with God's salvation, repentance, and complete healing. Just as the Israelites moved toward the Promised Land, we have been journeying toward the fulfillment of God's purposes in our lives. As we, who are recovered Holy Ghost-filled believers, journey in goodness and gentleness, we discover encouragement as we seek God's will, trust in His guidance, and depend on His provision. In every season of testing or abundance, we find assurance in God's goodness and gentleness, knowing that He is with us and that our ultimate destination is the fullness of His promises.

This measure of faith uncovers its roots in the taking of *steps one, two,* and *three*. We thought we were repenting just to clean our lives. However, we found that we had been having our spirit drawn out, and we were pressed for more spiritual growth through Jesus Christ (2 Peter 3:18). The moment we knelt and cried out; we saw that the beauty in all of this is that it had already begun before the world was formed. Once we were driven to our knees in humility, we embarked on this process. His bidding was to make us spiritual servants in Christ to His children.

The *first measure* of our faith is presented as we take the twelfth step, and it is through this faith that we receive the outpouring grace of the Holy Spirit. We begin a belief and take action in Jesus. As Scripture has said, rivers of living water begin flowing from within us (John 7:38). The measure of faith we have received is a gift from God and we begin not to think more highly of ourselves than we ought, but rather think of ourselves with sober judgment, in accordance with the faith God has distributed to each of us (Romans 12:3). In this outpouring of faith, we encounter the power and authority in the Name of Jesus and therefore, we go and make disciples of whosoever will, baptizing them in the Name of Jesus (Matthew 28:19). The revelation of Jesus Christ is an ongoing process as we grow in faith because God is a consuming fire. This fire purifies and refines us, revealing the fullness of Christ in our lives as it grows brighter and brighter, yet never consumes us.

As we are drawn out into this living water of the Spirit and drink the water Jesus gives us, we never thirst. Indeed, the water Jesus gives us is becoming in us a spring of water welling up to eternal life (John 4:14). Therefore, the outcome of the twelfth step is spiritual deliverance. We are drawn out into an outpour of faith and we are immersed in the abundant life-giving presence of the Holy Spirit as we experience His life-changing power and the ongoing revelation of Jesus Christ in our lives.

The revelation of the spiritual world unfolds before us, exposing every fragment of wickedness that once filled our lives with pride and oppressed our broken spirits. Yet, through the device of humility, we have been delivered. As a result, we become recipients of God's blessing in this very same humility. We have begun a good path.

As we embark on these measures in faith, we are careful to avoid self-centeredness; instead, we Fear the Lord and depart from evil. It is proving to be health to our flesh, and strength to our bones (Proverbs 3:7-8). We now look forward to a fulfilling and abundant life, cherishing the beauty of each day, as the Lord orders our steps and we find delight in following Jesus. Through a measure of faith, He is now directing our steps in godliness. He delights in every detail of our lives (Psalm 37:23). Through our actions, guided by His divine hand, we walk in truth and righteousness. No longer do we fear bad news, for our hearts are filled with love for God's principle, which we meditate on day and night. We no longer walk in the counsel of the ungodly, nor do we stand in the path of sinners, nor sit in the seat of the scornful. We are blessed. Our delight is in the principle of the Lord and in His principle, we meditate day and night (Psalm 1:1-2).

By following God's instructions through a measure of faith, He has revealed to us His wisdom. His testimonies remain ever-present in our minds, enlightening us with divine knowledge. With humble hearts, we've surpassed previous wisdom; progress stems from meditating on His testimonies (Psalm 119:99). We have turned away from every evil path, striving to live according to God's Word. Our commitment to His righteous principle remains unwavering, for He has taught us His ways (Psalm 119:01). How sweet are God's words to our taste, even sweeter than honey to our mouths! Through His principle, we have gained discernment, causing us to detest every falsehood (Psalm 119:103). Through His principle we get understanding; therefore, we hate every false way (Psalm 119:104). God's kingdom is everlasting, and His dominion endures throughout all generations. We find comfort and security in His eternal reign (Psalm 145:13).

The spiritual battle became evident as we in utter defeat sought God's intervention. When we earnestly surrendered in *step one*, unbeknownst to us, He sprang into action and immediately began to defeat the power of wickedness and evil within us and purify our hearts completely. Our plea was for Him to deliver us so that we would not be put to shame, as we had placed our trust in Him. He reminds us of His promise to keep all of Jesus' bones; not one of them is broken (Psalm 34:20). He has shown us that His Word can assuredly be applied to our lives. And though badly mangled, we were never broken beyond His love.

We did not know how, but through a measure of faith, we were imploring God to manifest His righteousness in our lives and to favor these upright instructions. Our ultimate desire continues to be to experience peace and know that God's goodness encompasses us. The wickedness within us has been completely eradicated through a measure of faith, and we now embrace the goodness of God (Psalm 112:10). Although we have faced persecution seemingly without cause, we find ourselves having a measure of faith and our hearts are filled with reverence for God's Word. Through a measure of faith, we find delight in His teachings, like one who discovers a great treasure. Lying is abhorrent to us, while His ways are cherished. Throughout the day, we offer praise to God for His righteous principle (Psalm 119:164). As we embrace His principle, we experience profound peace, and nothing can cause us to stumble or be offended. Our hearts are steadfast, trusting in the goodness and faithfulness of God (Psalm 119:165). We say our first prayer in these measures:

<u>A Prayer of Faithful Devotion</u>

*Lord, I place my hope in Your
salvation, faithfully following Your principle. My soul
cherishes and upholds Your testimonies; I love
them with great passion. I have diligently
observed Your principle and testimonies, knowing that
You see all my ways and actions before You. In Jesus Name, Amen.*

We love the Lord and he preserves us. All the wickedness He destroyed.

Finding ourselves in these measures, we realize that we have entered a lasting communion aligned with the will of God, a communion that will endure eternally. He has established His throne for righteous judgment, and He will judge the world with fairness and integrity. Our joy abounds as He continues to guide us in His truth and impart His teachings to us. Whenever we turn to Him, our burdens are lifted through taking these steps, and our faces radiate with confidence. Anger and wrath no longer control us; we have forsaken the path of evil through a measure of faith. Through our connection with God, we have been welcomed into the abundant life He has planned for us. The Lord is gracious, and within the dwelling of our righteousness, we discover true abundance. Prayer is becoming a mainstay as we live out these measures of faith. We pray:

<u>A Prayer of Seeking God's Ways</u>

O Lord, I humbly come before You, seeking Your instruction in the ways of Your principle. Grant me understanding, that I may faithfully keep Your principle and wholeheartedly obey it. Lead me along the path of Your principle, for it is in it that I find joy. Turn my heart towards Your testimonies and away from the allure of covetousness. Help me resist the temptation to indulge in vanity and worldly pursuits. Instead, breathe life into me through Your righteous ways. Establish Your Word within me, for I am devoted to revering You. Shield me from the reproach I fear, for Your judgements are just and righteous. Behold, I have longed for Your principle, yearning to be quickened and renewed in Your righteousness. I am eager to declare the glorious honor of Your majesty and share the wonders of Your works with others. May Your Name be exalted and Your truth be proclaimed throughout all the earth. In Jesus Name, I pray, Amen.

As we embark on this journey of the *first measure* of faith, the connection between humility in *step one* and righteousness in *step twelve* begins to unfold before our eyes. The overarching principle of these steps illuminates our path, revealing how the poor in spirit can transform into those who hunger and thirst for righteousness. It dawns on us that the promises embedded in these steps brought us into the kingdom of heaven and filled our spirits.

How are these two steps intertwined? Let us reflect on the steps we took. We started to comprehend the stark contrast between our previous state of being poor in spirit and our current posture of walking in humility, brought about by these life-changing steps. We began to grasp that the kingdom of heaven was now accessible to us, and through these steps, we have inherited the abundant life God had always intended for us.

With this newfound faith, we felt compelled to share our journey with others, diligently seeking God with all our hearts. We eagerly spread the good news, recounting the steps we had taken and the life-changing power they held. Once we believed that sins such as addictions and alcoholism had led us into humility and left us spiritually impoverished, but now we find ourselves delivered into righteousness, humbly kneeling with great expectations. It is not a repetitive cycle; it is a remarkable transformation.

מ MEM

In the context of healing, the letter Mem holds profound spiritual significance as it aligns with the themes of renewal. *Step one* of the healing process involved acknowledging powerlessness over sins such as addictions and alcoholism as well as the unmanageability of life. We learned from *steps four, five,* and *six* that the letter Mem signifies the need to dive deep into the depths of one's struggles, confront the reality of sin, and surrender to the Holy Spirit's power for healing and salvation. It represents the cleansing waters of confession and admission, enabling us to let go of denial and let in the truth about our spiritual condition. We must dive in, to level up.

Step twelve called for us to teach others to observe all things whatsoever Jesus has commanded us: and, see, He is with us always, even unto the end of the world. Amen (Matthew 28:20). The letter Mem relates to this step by symbolizing the anointing power of sharing experiences. Just as water ripples and spreads, the impact of our healing journey extends to others, offering hope. By sharing our stories, we who are have been healed help others navigate their own struggles and find the path to being recovered.

Furthermore, the letter Mem in **HEALING 5:12** represents the Holy Spirit, the living water in our transformation. It is through the power of the Holy Spirit that we who have been healed find renewal. The Spirit moves like waves, bringing forth revival and a refreshing flow of grace.

We look back to *step one* and observe that we knew that in ourselves (that is, in our flesh,) dwells no good thing: because our will was present within us, but we could not find how to perform that which is good. This speaks to the recognition of our own powerlessness and the great wrestling we were in with our own fleshly desires and mental obsessions; we now know that there was no way we would have prevailed without acknowledging that we were unable to overcome them on our own.

We spent so much of our lives covering our sins and never prospered, but the moment we confessed and forsook them, we obtained endless mercy. It emphasized the importance of confessing and admitting our sins because it leads to finding mercy and experiencing a path toward healing and salvation.

As we took these steps and arrived at *step twelve*, we quickly saw that we had freely received healing when we were sick, becoming cleansed of sin. We were dead and He raised us up. The devils were cast out! Because of these things, we now freely give. We encourage fellow believers to freely share the blessings we have received, including the message of healing and salvation, with others who are still struggling.

Step twelve teaches us that we are to bear one another's burdens, and by doing so, we fulfill the law of Christ. This is the importance of uplifting one another, carrying each other's burdens, and practicing the principles of the love of Christ and compassion in our relationships with fellow believers.

While these things may not directly mention the outpouring living water, they align with the themes of surrender, cleansing, and renewal found in *steps one* and *twelve* of the healing process. They provide guidance for letting in humility, admitting our struggles, and extending compassion to others on their own journey of healing.

There are actions that help accomplish this renewal in the context of *steps one* and *twelve* in healing. Surrendering to God requires ongoing communication and seeking His guidance through prayer. We actively engage in prayer, both individually and collectively, to admit our struggles, seek forgiveness, and invite God's life-changing power into our lives. By seeking God's will and relying on His strength, we experience healing. Confession is a vital aspect of faith and the healing process. We take action by honestly acknowledging our struggles, admitting our shortcomings, and seeking forgiveness from God and others we have hurt. Engaging in regular confession and letting in accountability through seeking God, healing ministries, mentors, or trusted individuals aid in the process of healing. The core principle of healing and being recovered is loving our neighbor as ourselves. We actively put this principle into action by serving others on their own healing journeys. This is done through acts of kindness, volunteering in healing ministries and organizations, becoming a facilitator for someone as they take these steps with Jesus, or offering a listening ear and encouragement to those in need. By extending support to others, we experience a deeper sense of purpose and contribute to the collective healing and renewal of others.

Prayer, seeking God's guidance and serving others—help us in the healing process to surrender our struggles as we experience renewal through faith in Jesus. By actively engaging in these actions, we cultivate an environment conducive to sanctification.

This overflowing was first introduced in *step four* and then closed up in renewal in *step five* burst forth again in *step six* with the parting of water. We then recognized the beautiful outpouring in *step nine* as we observed God demonstrate Himself to us through others in each restitution. It was beautiful repair. Now we find our spirits drawn out into an outpouring measure of faith. This *first measure* is already showing us the wonderful world of being filled with the Holy Spirit. It is outpouring.

ש SHIN

Glory to God, hallelujah! Sometimes we just can't contain ourselves. The Holy Spirit illuminates our hearts as we explore the profound power of the Spirit. We are being drawn out. In **RECOVERY 5:12**, we deeply cherish the anointing power of the Holy Spirit, and He now holds a sacred place in our understanding. The Spirit is a fire discovered in *step three*, and oh, how it represents the burning passion of the Spirit within us as it consumes us!

In this measure of faith we are drawn out into the Spirit. We experience a divine ignition, a holy fire that sets our hearts ablaze for the Lord. The Holy Spirit reminds us of the burning bush that Moses encountered, when God's presence manifested in a blazing flame that did not consume the bush. Just as Moses was drawn out to behold this sacred sight, we, too, are called to be drawn out into the presence of the Spirit in this *first measure* of faith.

It is in these moments of being drawn out that we find ourselves immersed in the fiery presence of God, where the Spirit moves with power. Our hearts become like burning coals, passionately ignited with love for our Savior and a desire to serve Him wholeheartedly.

The Holy Spirit is another; a Comforter sent in the Name of Jesus. In being drawn out into the Spirit, we are drawn into a deeper understanding that recovery has a Name and it is Jesus. As we experience the fullness of His presence in our lives, we are drawn into a holy fellowship with the Father by the power of the Holy Spirit.

In the Book of Acts, the Day of Pentecost is a remarkable example of being drawn out into the Spirit. The disciples were gathered in one place when suddenly there came a sound from heaven, like a rushing wind, as the Holy Spirit filled the house where they were sitting. And there appeared unto them cloven tongues as of fire, and the Spirit sat upon each of them. They were filled with the Holy Spirit, and their hearts were set aflame for the mission of proclaiming the wonderful works of God.

Similarly, in our own lives, being drawn out into the Spirit empowers us for divine assignments, ignites spiritual gifts within us, and sets us on fire to share the Good News with the world. We embrace this healing path and the act of being drawn out into the Spirit. Having been drawn out as a result of a measure of faith, we are consumed by the fiery presence of the Holy Spirit, burning with passion for our Lord, and observing His divine power flow through us. We are drawn out like a beacon of light, shining brightly for the glory of God. Hallelujah! Amen and amen!

Just as God breathed the breath of life into Adam, the revelation of faith is the life-giving breath of the Holy Spirit which was first breathed into us in *step six*. When we are drawn out into the Spirit, it is like a divine breath filling our lungs, infusing us with the very life and presence of God. We are awakened to His divine revelation, understanding the mysteries of His kingdom and being led by His Spirit.

In the Book of Ezekiel, the prophet experienced a powerful vision of being drawn out into the Spirit. He was carried by the Spirit of God to witness remarkable revelations and encounters with the Holy Spirit. Like Ezekiel, we, too, are drawn out into the Spirit, carried to spiritual heights, and granted visions and revelations from God.

Revelation also signifies presence. When we are drawn out into the Spirit, we experience an intimate communion with our Heavenly Father. We sense His nearness, His guidance, and His comforting touch. It is in these moments of being drawn out that we are enveloped by the abiding presence of God, and our hearts overflow with worship and praise.

Moreover, revelation is realized with the power of His Name. Being drawn out into the Spirit communes us to the very essence of God's Name. We encounter the great I AM, the eternal, omnipotent God, who reveals Himself to us through His Spirit. Being drawn out into the Spirit, we also find ourselves speaking in tongues, a divine gift from God. Just as the disciples experienced on the Day of Pentecost, the Holy Spirit enables us to pray and worship in a heavenly language, strengthening our spirits and edifying the church. This made many of us concerned when we first read about or witnessed it in others. However, like the rest of this healing process, we would come to experience it. Some are in the confines of a closet in their homes at first but in the end, we all find this amazing gift that opens our minds to the limitless Power which is God. We encourage interpretation of these events as they occur, especially if new converts are around. For if we are not sensitive, those consumed by self will not understand the language of the heavens and will even use this as a reason to return to their vomit.

The Hebrew name Moses, spelled "Moshe" in Hebrew, carries great significance in the context of complete healing. Moses is a central figure in the Old Testament, known for leading the Israelites out of slavery in Egypt and receiving the Ten Commandments on Mount Sinai. In the context of a recovered life, the name Moses holds several meaningful applications. Moses served as a guide for the Israelites during their journey to freedom. Being recovered, we who have successfully navigated our own healing journey become sources of guidance for others who are still on their path to healing. Moses' story is one of significant life changes, from a hesitant individual to a strong servant. Having recovered from a seemingly hopeless state of mind and body, we experience an even more profound transformation of spirit, letting in newfound strength in Jesus' Name. Moses received the Ten Commandments, which laid the foundation for righteous living. In a recovered life, we choose to live our lives aligned with God's will which promotes recovery.

After leading the Israelites to freedom, Moses faced new challenges as a servant. Similarly, the recovered life presents new challenges, but we draw upon the strength of the Lord who healed us and overcomes them. Moses's encounter with the Power which is God on Mount Sinai was a significant spiritual moment. In the recovered life, we deepen our spiritual communion, finding meaning in each of our experiences. Moses's journey had a profound sense of purpose. In the recovered life, we seek God as our purpose, using our experiences with Him to make a positive impact in our recovery communities and the world. Moses led the Israelites to freedom, and similarly, the recovered life provides a newfound sense of freedom from the chains of sins such as alcoholism, addictions, and other spiritual struggles that effect the mind. Moses led the Israelites on a journey through uncharted territory. In a recovered life, we explore new opportunities, unburdened by our past struggles. Despite his significant servant role, Moses was known for his humility. In a recovered life, we cultivate humility, recognizing that our journey is part of a larger process of healing. In conclusion, the name Moses carries profound lessons in both religious and healing contexts. In the recovered life, we draw inspiration from Moses's servanthood, life change, and sense of purpose to forge a fulfilling and meaningful path forward. We use our experiences to guide others, nurture their spirituality, and let in the freedom that the recovered life offers. As we are drawn out in a measure of faith, the first thing we recognize is how the principles and the promises of each step begin to wonderfully embrace each other in our lives.

The first three steps, which were the repentance steps, gave us the principle and promise contained within Matthew 5:3. He states, "Blessed are the poor in spirit: for theirs is the kingdom of heaven." This verse covered the first three steps of the healing process like an overarching umbrella.

We learned time and time again that *step one* of the healing process involves admitting powerlessness over sins such as addictions and alcoholism and acknowledging the spiritual disconnectedness of life. It requires us to recognize our spiritual poverty and our inability to overcome sins on our own. Matthew 5:3 resonates with this step as it speaks to the blessedness of those of us who humbly acknowledge their need for God. It reminds us that by letting in our spiritual poverty and submitting our will to God, we experience the kingdom of heaven, which is found within a renewed mind, renewed heart, and salvation.

Step two of the healing process centers on coming to believe that Jesus Christ is the way, the truth, and the life and that no man shall come unto the Father but by Him. Matthew 5:3 complements this step by emphasizing the blessedness of those of us who recognize our need for Jesus. It encourages us to approach healing with a humble heart, seeking the intercession of Jesus to recover and bring about salvation.

Step three involves us denying ourselves, taking up our crosses, and following Christ. Matthew 5:3 further reinforces this step by highlighting the blessings and rewards that come with letting in our spiritual poverty and turning our lives over to God. It invites us to entrust our will and lives to God's care, recognizing that true redemption is found in aligning with God's will through salvation.

In this *first measure* of faith, we are positioned to also receive the benefits of the overarching promises and principles of the developmental steps of ten, eleven, and twelve. Matthew 5:6 states, "Blessed are they which do hunger and thirst after righteousness: for they shall be filled."

Step ten in the healing process involves continuing to confess our transgressions to the Lord. It emphasizes the importance of continuing to watch for self and when it crops up, continuing to set right new mistakes as we go along. Matthew 5:6 aligns with this step by highlighting the blessedness of those of us who hunger and thirst after righteousness. It encourages us to maintain a sincere desire for righteousness, and holiness and to remain vigilant in seeking service, ministry, and love.

Step eleven focuses on rejoicing always, praying continually, and giving thanks in all circumstances, for this is God's will for us in Christ Jesus. Matthew 5:6 complements this step by emphasizing the blessedness of those who hunger and thirst after righteousness. It invites us to cultivate a deep longing for a closer connection with God, seeking His guidance, and aligning our lives with His will. By hungering and thirsting for righteousness, we develop a greater awareness of God's presence and guidance in our lives, enhancing our communion with Him.

Step twelve calls us to now teach others to observe all things whatsoever Jesus has commanded us: and, seeing that He is with us always, even unto the end of the world. Matthew 5:6 relates to this step by highlighting the blessedness of those who hunger and thirst after righteousness. It emphasizes the fulfillment that comes from living out the principles of healing and practicing righteousness in all areas of our lives. By hungering and thirsting after righteousness, individuals embody the message of healing and become a source of inspiration for others.

Moreover, Matthew 5:6 also conveys the promise that those who hunger and thirst after righteousness will be filled. We are assured that we who actively pursue sanctification, seek God's will, and align our lives with righteousness experience a relationship with God that provides eternal hope and peace.

Matthew 5:6 relates to *steps ten, eleven*, and *twelve* of the healing process. It emphasizes the blessedness of those who hunger and thirst after righteousness, encouraging us to continue our service and ministry. We are seeking a closer relationship with God, and live out the principles of healing in all aspects of life. By reflecting on this, we find love for others, sharing God's promises, and an inner witness of the Holy Spirit. This is our pursuit of righteousness which leads to sanctification. Sanctification leads to a relationship with God and a deeper sense of purpose in our healing journey.

These wonderful promises are only intensified in this measure of faith. Again, in *step one*, we discovered that blessed are the poor in spirit, because the kingdom of heaven is ours. *Step one* of the healing process involved acknowledging powerlessness over sins such as addictions and alcoholism and the unmanageability of our backslidden lives.

In *step one*, we recognized our spiritual poverty and our inability to overcome sins such as addictions and alcoholism and the chaos it brings into our lives on our own power. We realized our need for Jesus Christ and turned our will over to God. *Step one* declares that those of us who acknowledge our spiritual poverty and dependence on God's grace are blessed as we inherit the kingdom of heaven. It speaks to the significance of humbly turning to God for healing, and salvation.

Matthew 5:5 states, "Blessed are the meek: for they shall inherit the earth." This verse relates to *step twelve* of the healing process. Step twelve calls us to now teach others to observe all things whatsoever Jesus has commanded us: and, see, He is with us always, even unto the end of the world.

We have been told time and time again that meekness is often misunderstood as weakness, but in a spiritual sense, it refers to a humble attitude towards ourselves and others. It involves surrendering our ego, pride, and self-will, and letting in an attitude of teachability. Meekness enables us to approach others with empathy and a willingness to listen.

In *step twelve*, we who have experienced the Holy Spirit's anointing in healing are called to extend our hands to those who are still struggling. This act requires the meek to recognize that we are not superior to others, but rather equal in our shared journey of healing. By embodying meekness, we approach others with humility, offering support, encouragement, and guidance without judgment.

Furthermore, the promise in Matthew 5:5 that the meek shall inherit the earth aligns with the concept of carrying the message of healing. By living out the principles of healing and practicing meekness, we contribute to the healing and salvation of others in our recovery communities and society at large. We inherit the earth in the sense that our influence and impact extend beyond ourselves, helping to create a more compassionate, and supportive environment for others to recover in.

Now, the principles and promises of this measure of faith. Having been drawn-out, we have begun to see what Matthew meant when he said in 5:7, "Blessed are the merciful: for they shall obtain mercy." This verse relates to the mind and faith in the context of healing.

In healing, the mind plays a crucial role in the anointing process. It is through the renewal of the mind that we see God overcome our negative thought patterns, break us free from destructive behaviors, and cultivate a healthy mindset in us. Matthew 5:7 encourages us to embrace mercy as a fundamental aspect of our mindset.

Mercy involves showing compassion towards ourselves and others. It is an attitude that seeks to extend grace, even in the face of pain, hurt, and wrongdoing. Cultivating a merciful mind is vital to our recovery.

First, mercy towards ourselves is essential in healing. We understand that many of us in this healing carry feelings of guilt, shame, and self-condemnation due to past mistakes and the consequences of sins such as addictions and alcoholism. Letting in mercy involves letting in forgiveness, forgiving ourselves, and releasing condemnation. It involves treating ourselves with kindness, understanding that healing is a process, and being patient with the journey of healing in ourselves and others.

Secondly, mercy towards others is crucial in building healthy relationships and fostering a supportive recovery community in healing. By extending mercy to others, we let go of bitterness. We offer forgiveness to those who may have caused harm. Mercy opens the door to healing, both within ourselves and in relationships with others.

We begin to serve others in faith. In terms of faith, Matthew 5:7 encourages us to have faith in the power of mercy. It assures that those of us who practice mercy become merciful. Having faith in mercy means believing that the act of extending forgiveness has a Holy Spirit anointing which provides forgiveness. It means trusting that by embracing mercy, God creates healing, reconciliation, service, and ministry in our own lives and in the lives of others.

We learned the power of mercy from the fifth step. By embracing a merciful mindset and having faith in the power of mercy, we who have been healed, experience the blessings of obtaining mercy. It allows us to free our minds from the burden of condemnation, cultivate healthier relationships, and create a compassionate environment for service, ministry, and anointing.

A measure of faith not only fosters the mind but also creates spiritual action from His promises and principles. Having our spirit drawn out, we are pressed for more spiritual growth through Jesus Christ. We obtain this through spiritual action.

In healing, there is a deep hunger and thirst that stirs within the hearts of those of us seeking God. We long for righteousness and a relationship with Him, recognizing the need for a deeper communion with Him. In this measure of faith, we look further within.

Our hunger and thirst are not mere passing desires but a genuine yearning that propels us forward. It is a hunger that creates a love for others. We discover that seeking Him is daily bread for our souls, just as physical hunger prompts us to seek food. We now know that true nourishment for our spirits is only found in righteousness.

Guided by this inner longing, we embark on a journey of spiritual action. We commit ourselves to aligning our lives with God's will, embracing biblical authority. We hunger for honesty and integrity to permeate our thoughts, words, and actions. We thirsted for redemption, knowing that true anointing comes from walking in righteousness.

In our pursuit of righteousness, we engage in spiritual action. We devote time to prayer, seeking communion with God. We immerse ourselves in scripture, finding daily guidance for our journey. We join fellow believers in fellowship, finding strength and encouragement in recovery communities.

As we hunger and thirst after righteousness, a profound promise embraces our soul. We are assured that our yearning is satisfied. Our hunger is met with a relationship with God, our thirst with a quenching that only righteousness provides. The relationship with God we seek is not fleeting but everlasting, for it comes from an intimate communion with Him.

Through spiritual action, we experience a deep sense of peace and communion with God. Our spirits are nourished, and our souls are reborn. The hunger and thirst that once consumed us are replaced with a contentment that only righteousness brings.

In our pursuit of His righteousness, we discover that the Holy Spirit's anointing of spiritual action went beyond our journey. Our hunger and thirst have become a beacon of hope for others on the path of healing. Through our example, we inspire others to hunger and thirst for righteousness, to seek the same fulfillment and spiritual nourishment that we found.

Thus, our hunger and thirst for righteousness have become a catalyst for change, not only in our own lives but in the lives of those around us. Through spiritual action of this *first measure* of faith, we have become beacons of light, guiding others towards the path of healing and redemption which is only obtained through an active relationship with God.

Having just been drawn out, we now experience the bittersweet pressing as our trust in a measure of faith continues to grow. In the *second measure* of faith, we journey forward into a beautiful place of pressing.

Gentleness and Longsuffering.

There is still more action that is required to foster a deeper relationship with Jesus Christ. We all must seek to be baptized in the Holy Spirit, asking for the empowering and infilling of this Power in our lives. Many of us, who have been baptized in the Holy Ghost and fire, utilize the gift of speaking in tongues for His edification. We all pray for the manifestation of spiritual gifts in our lives for the edification of the church. Many of us engage in times of spontaneous praise and worship, allowing the Holy Spirit to lead our expressions. Even in our cars! We pray in the Spirit during intercession, recognizing the Holy Spirit guiding our thoughts. Many seek to operate in the prophetic gifts, receiving and sharing God's messages as led by the Holy Spirit. We are always pursuing opportunities to pray for healing and minister to those in need of physical, emotional, or spiritual help. We share the Gospel with sensitivity to the leading of the Holy Spirit, watching Him open hearts and minds. Others engage in prayer warfare, interceding against spiritual strongholds of addictions, alcoholism, and many other of the enemy's spiritual attacks. We never miss an opportunity to participate in vibrant worship gatherings where the Holy Spirit's presence is evident. We set aside time for encounters with God, seeking His tangible presence through communion with Him. We practice waiting on God in prayer, acknowledging space for Him to speak and move in our lives. We keep in our journal the prophetic words, insights, and revelations received through prayer and the Holy Spirit's leading. We all live a life of faith, trusting in God's promises and stepping out in obedience to His leadership. As we delve deeper, we seek the gift of spiritual discernment to distinguish between the promptings of the Holy Spirit and other influences. We must connect with other Holy Ghost-filled recovered believers to encourage one another in service and ministry. Some of us delve into theology and spiritual teachings to deepen our understanding of the Holy Spirit's work. We encourage all to attend retreats focused on spiritual renewal, seeking fresh encounters with the Holy Spirit. We never miss a chance to engage wholeheartedly in worship services, always bringing our worship and expecting God to move in powerful ways. We share God's Word boldly, trusting the Holy Spirit to empower our communication.

Remember that these actions are centered around embracing the work of the Holy Spirit in our lives. As we earnestly seek His presence, our relationship with Jesus Christ are deepened. We work with others as they pursue Jesus through this healing process. We walk shoulder to shoulder with the new convert until they become a life-changer, then leave them alone as the needs of others will draw them out into God, just as we are about to be drawn out.

CHAPTER 19

SECOND MEASURE OF FAITH

Recognizing the bittersweet steps of repentance, we strengthened the spirit through our Lord, Jesus Christ.

"My sacrifice, O God, is a broken spirit; a broken and contrite heart you, God, will not despise."
(Psalm 51:17)

The *second measure* of faith emerges as our spirits transcend the realm of the twelve steps. With hearts wide open, we embrace the outpouring faith of YHWH, connecting with Him on a deeper level. This newfound faith prompts us to take immediate action. We humble ourselves in reverence, setting aside our preconceived notions and motives about prayer, and enter prayer solely to encounter Him.

As we enter this measure of faith, we remember the steps along the path of goodness and gentleness, aligning with God's salvation. Just as the Israelites moved toward the Promised Land, we have been journeying toward the fulfillment of God's purposes in our lives. As we, who are recovered Holy Ghost-filled believers, journey in goodness and gentleness, we discover encouragement as we seek God's will, trust in His guidance, and depend on His provision. In every season of testing or abundance, we find assurance in God, knowing He is with us and our destination is the fulfillment of His promises.

This measure of faith uncovers its roots in the taking of the steps of repentance. We thought we were repenting just to clean our lives. However, we found that as we were experiencing the bittersweet steps of repentance, we were strengthening our spirit through our Lord, Jesus Christ. It began the moment we knelt and cried out. The beauty in all of this is that it had already begun before the world was formed. Once we were driven to our knees in humility, we embarked on this process. His bidding was to make us spiritual servants.

During prayer, we engaged in a spiritual battle, silencing the restless chatter in our minds and resisting the urge to cease praying. Our focus shifted to experiencing the profound love of God through our prayers. It was within this intimate communion with Him that we prayed, pouring out our hearts and seeking His presence. We intensified our efforts, engaging in a form of prayer that involved envisioning a relationship with the Lord through the Tabernacle pattern of prayer.

For some of us, the Tabernacle plan of prayer became a powerful tool, ushering in the presence of the Holy Spirit during our prayer time. Through this specific approach to prayer, the Lord often conveyed His messages to us, revealing His divine wisdom. It was through this prayer within prayer that we experienced the depths of His love and received the divine insights listed and those not able to be contained within the confines of these pages.

The spiritual battle that had been revealed within us continued to grow, but its distractions were diminishing. We began to examine the first step of repentance and discovered how our own pride had persecuted us, leading us to a state of being poor in spirit. We realized that we had fallen into the traps that our own wickedness had devised. Unbeknownst to us, even in our darkest hours, we were being guided towards a life that reveres God. What the enemy meant for evil, God turned it to good.

As we reflected further on the first three steps, it became evident that God was showing us the right path to follow. He delivered us into a life filled with goodness, allowing us to experience the beauty that each day holds. We recognized that these initial steps of repentance aligned with the path of a righteous person, ordered by the Lord, and we found joy in walking in His ways.

In these first two steps of repentance, we could witness the works of His hands, which are humble and just. Fear of evil tidings no longer consumed us. Oh, how we have come to cherish God's principle! It has become our meditation throughout the day. Through this path of **RECOVERY 5:12**, God has granted us wisdom, surpassing even our adversaries. These initial steps became ingrained within us, providing us with profound understanding. Our teachers' knowledge paled in comparison because we now possessed the testimony of God, which empowered our prayers, fasting, and meditations.

We realized that we had been living according to His principle as we took these steps, navigating the measure of faith that He had bestowed upon us. We now refrained from every evil way, desiring to keep His Word. We remained steadfast in following His principle through these steps because He continued to instruct us in living in Him. His words became a delight to our souls, sweeter than honey to our lips. Through His principle, we gained understanding, and as a result, we developed a deep aversion to every false path. His kingdom is eternal, and His dominion reigns throughout all generations.

In the first three steps, God observed every action we took, taking note of all our deeds. He was aware of the trouble we caused, and even in the midst of our thorough punishment, He extended His help to us who were spiritually bankrupt and helpless. We learned to trust in Him as the Helper of the fatherless, approaching Him with reverence and humility.

We have come to understand that those who honestly embark on this path are not abandoned by Him.

We faced vicious enemies who harbored hatred towards us. Yet, when the good and godly encounter hardships, the Lord prevents their defeat. We have witnessed this firsthand. Once, we were oppressive people, exerting our dominance over others with cruelty. But where can true wisdom be found? It is born in the Fear of God, a lesson we would learn as we walked this path. Those who follow His ways will never lack a living understanding bestowed by Him. The adoration of God endures for eternity.

However, when we indulged in wickedness and observed the lives of those who embraced it, we were filled with anger and failed to comprehend their apparent contentment. It never dawned upon us that the enemy gives gifts in this world. But these could not help when we were wicked and found ourselves speechless in the darkness where hope dwindles and dreams fade into nothingness. We longed for a renewed sense of life. We beseeched God to gaze upon our misery and be our hero, rescuing us as He had revealed to us. We implored Him to stand by our side, defending us in the midst of our sufferings, just as He promised. In our wickedness, we were distant from salvation, as we cared little for the message of truth. But His love pressed through brambles with His staff and saved us.

We yearned for God's tender mercies, for they were what we truly needed. Through the revelation of His principle in the steps we took and the faith we embraced, He restored our lives. In these steps, we encountered numerous internal enemies who persecuted us, yet we remained steadfast in following His ways. Now, our hearts ache when we witness the faithless ones, as they simply turn away from God's promises. This is why our spirit prays this prayer as we reflect on what He did for us in *step three*:

<u>Prayer of Revival</u>

*Lord, behold my deep affection for
your teachings. Thus, in Your gentle
mercy, revive me once more.
The entirety of your words embodies
unwavering truth, and each of your
righteous ordinances are eternal.
In Jesus Name, Amen.*

Every godly one receives even more than what they ask for. Because God hears what our hearts long for, and He brings us His saving Power.

As we delve deeper into prayer within this *second measure* of faith, we are aware that He sees it all. He observes mischief and ill intentions and repays them accordingly. Those who are humble in spirit entrust themselves to Him, for He is the protector of the fatherless. The righteous face many afflictions, but the Lord delivered us from them all through our recovery. We pleaded with Him to take notice of our numerous enemies who harbor a deep and cruel hatred towards us. We witnessed the wicked in their great power, spreading like a flourishing tree. However, their power faded away, and we cannot find them anymore.

The Fear of the Lord marks the beginning of wisdom, and in our wickedness, we experienced it and were deeply saddened. Salvation seemed distant when we were immersed in wickedness because we failed to seek His principle. We fervently implored Him once again to acknowledge our affliction and rescue us. We presented our cases and humbly begged Him to save us and revive us according to His Word. We recognized the transgressors but soon discovered that we ourselves were the greatest transgressors, and it grieved us deeply because we failed to keep His Word. We expressed our profound love for His principle and beseeched Him to revive us according to His lovingkindness. His tender mercies are immense, for He revived us according to His principle. His Word has always been true since the beginning, and His righteous principle endures forever. If we Fear Him, He fulfills our desires and listens to our cries, saving us from distress.

Remember this: the wicked will face destruction! Those who forget God and reject His ways will be cast into the darkness of death's domain. They will be turned into hell, along with all the people who forget God. Hell is full of sober people. We implore Him to continue revealing His path to the humble and guiding us towards the best decisions. We ask him to illuminate us with the light of revelation that instructs us in truth. He leads the meek with wisdom and teaches them His ways. He is sanctifying each one of us, and that is why we worship Him with awe and wonder. Those who Fear Him will never lack anything.

As His saints, we revere YHWH, for He abundantly provides for those who Fear Him. The Lord watches over our righteous deeds day by day, for we are godly, and He prepares an eternal reward for us. He knows the days of the upright, and our inheritance will endure forever. He remains faithful to every promise He makes. He is mindful of His covenant and conducts His affairs with honesty and truth. He guides His dealings with discretion. He skillfully shapes and forms us with His own hands, imparting His wisdom so that we may live His principle. He has created us. We implore him to grant us understanding, so that we may learn and follow His principle. May all His devoted lovers witness His favor towards them and rejoice, for His words are deeply rooted in our hearts. Those who Fear Him are filled with joy when they see us because we have placed our hope in His Word.

Unbeknownst to us, our souls pray as in the first three steps:

A Prayer of Tender Mercy

*"Lord, I know that your judgments are
always right. Even when it's me you judge,
You're still faithful and true. Send Your
kind kiss of Mercy to comfort me, your
servant, just like you promised you would.*

> *Love me tenderly so I can go on, because*
> *I delight in your life-giving truth."*

Now it has become:

<u>A Prayer of Comfort and Delight</u>

> *"I know, YHWH, that Thy judgments are*
> *right, And that Thou in faithfulness hast*
> *afflicted me. Let I pray Thee, Thy merciful*
> *kindness be my comfort, according to thy*
> *Word unto Thy servant. Let Thy tender*
> *mercies come unto me, that I may live:*
> *Because Thy principle is my delight."*

Shame upon our pride and dishonesty! We now see how they constantly try to oppress us, all because of our passion for His principle! Let our pride be ashamed because it deals perversely with us without provocation. But we meditate on His principle. We hope that all His devoted lovers can discover and follow the path of His instruction. Let those who Fear Him turn to Jesus. We ask Him to make us passionate to fulfill His every wish so that we will never have to be ashamed of ourselves. We ask Him to let our hearts be sound in His principle so we are no longer shamed.

At this moment, we receive the revelation that repentance of the poor in spirit through Jesus in the wilderness is the solution to all our spiritual attacks from everything that is evil, including the influence of drugs and alcohol. At the mere mention of His Name, all these forces must flee. Even if we can't speak the Name ourselves, it has already been spoken over us. Jesus has already triumphed over the enemy's assault. Our prayer life is becoming more uninhibited.

The first revelation was knowing that we were embracing redemption in this profound prayer of transformation.

In this profound prayer, many of us have received the revelation of the true sacrifice we offered in the third step. We had been carrying our pasts like lifeless corpses, expecting them to crumble into ashes before we could make it to the altar. It appears we were still holding on to the remnants of our mistakes, attempting to be near the sacrificial altar without fully surrendering our spirits, minds, and bodies to the complete process of repentance. It was only when we laid everything down, including our misguided beliefs and prejudices, that Jesus could remove the old self from within us. In the realm of prayer, we approach Him, and He graciously took upon Himself the weight of our pasts, which left a bloody stain on our spirits. To our amazement, Jesus bore it all on His own shoulders and willingly ascended the altar as our substitute. With a loving and kind smile, He made the necessary sacrifice that would set us free forever. It was our sin ... yet, He took it all.

The second revelation was knowing that we were encountering the Majestic Presence in the revelation of humble surrender.

In a prayerful moment, we experienced the theater of God's Power as we casually approached Him in prayer, feeling a little too comfortable and familiar, as if the Holy Spirit were an old college friend. We entered the Holy Place with a nonchalant attitude, checking it like a common refrigerator, absent-mindedly searching through its contents without purpose or intention. It was in that moment of casualness that we dared to question the Wonder of God, as described by Isaiah. Suddenly, we found ourselves prostrate on the ground in humble submission, our mouths filled with sand as if all authority over our lives had brought us to this place of submission. No further words were necessary. We willingly surrendered that He is truly Wonderful, Counselor, Mighty God, Everlasting Father, and the Prince of Peace. He is truly wonderful and for that, we worship His Majestic Presence in humble submission.

<u>The third revelation was experiencing the presence of Jesus who is the only Way of deliverance.</u>

In this prayerful moment, we received the complete acknowledgment that Jesus is the central figure in this Holy Place. He embodies the significance of the shewbread, the lamp fueled by the Holy Spirit, and the fragrant incense pleasing unto the Father. He is the Way, and now we clearly see that He stands at the core of truth. As He moved within this sacred encounter, His presence radiated with golden brilliance, filling the space with awe-inspiring power. It is this very Power that facilitated our deliverance in the second step and throughout our recovery journeys.

This faith emerged as the result of our spirits being distilled and pressed, akin to our individual gardens of Gethsemane. As we positioned ourselves under the outpour of the Holy Spirit, we persevered until we encountered the realm of prayer we had spoken of. In this journey, we delved deeper from being poor in spirit and hungering for righteousness to attaining purity of heart, as exemplified in the taking of these steps. We embraced the qualities of mercy. We tasted the fulfillment of the promise to see God and receive His mercy. Through this, we grasped the comprehensive essence of the faith that underlies repentance. We now understand that the overarching principle of being poor in spirit encompasses the facets of brokenness, mourning, and humility. This revelation unveiled numerous promises that we are already experiencing. In the first three steps, we received the kingdom of heaven, found comfort, and inherited the abundant life that God intended for us. We have genuinely repented and made the resolute decision that there is One who possesses all power, and that One is God, whose Name is Jesus. Surprisingly, there was still more.

The faith we acquired was accompanied by the practice of prayer, not merely as a routine but as prayer within prayer, where we encounter God and His revelations that transcend the limitations of this present life. We initiate intentional appointments with God, going beyond our regular prayer routines. Many of us dedicate one hour each day to commune with

Him in prayer, and we even set aside a specific day each week to depart from our homes and journey to a spiritual place, where we meet with God and engage in continuous prayer until we enter that realm where our spirit is opened to extraordinary heavenly revelations. We have stepped into the familiar outpouring Spirit.

מ MEM

Hallelujah! Praise be to the Most High! We delve into the depths of God's Word and further uncover the profound meaning of the outpouring in the context of a measure of faith in our Gethsemane experience.

In **RECOVERY 5:12**, we cherish the significance of each spiritual encounter and communion with our Lord. The outpouring holds a sacred place in recovery and salvation. As we have learned, the outpouring Spirit is like water, waves, and the deep. Oh, how the Holy Spirit mirrors the deep waters of our soul, where we find ourselves in a Gethsemane experience. We no longer have the luxury of living in anger, fear, or immorality … sin.

As we meditate on the life of our precious Savior, we are reminded of His own Gethsemane, where He cried out to the Father in prayer, submitting His will to the will of God. Likewise, we, too, find ourselves in moments of deep wrestling with God, facing our own Gethsemane experience in this *second measure* of faith.

In these Gethsemane moments, we find our souls tossed like waves upon the sea, burdened by the weight of trials, challenges, and decisions that God has delivered us from. Oh, how our spirits groan and travail before our Heavenly Father! But fear not, for in our outpouring faith experiences, we have never been alone! We are not forsaken!

As we yield to the Holy Spirit's leading, we are comforted by His Living Water flowing within us, like a river of peace that surpasses understanding. It is in these moments of Gethsemane that we find our true strength, for it is when we are weak that He is strong. The dam burst and the Living Water burst forth into eternal life.

This water of the Holy Spirit purifies. In our Gethsemane experiences, we are washed anew by the Holy Spirit, purified from doubts, fears, and anxieties. The deep waters of our souls become a place of surrender, a holy altar where we lay down our burdens and offer ourselves completely to the Lord.

Oh, how the overflowing reminds us of the anointing power of prayer flowing over, around, and within us until we are filled! As we immerse ourselves in prayer, we experience the refreshing waters of His Presence, finding the strength to say, "Not my will, but Yours be done!" It is in these sacred moments that we are molded, refined, and made like our Savior, Jesus Christ. Because of this outpouring, we rush into prayer, screaming, "Cleanse me, oh Lord, purify my soul!"

ר RESH

Step three teaches us that prayer is merely a beginning, the chief act of our Gethsemane experience. It is through prayer that God aligns our minds and hearts with His will. Just as Jesus prayed fervently in Gethsemane, we, too, draw near to God in prayer, surrendering our will to His and seeking Him.

In a Gethsemane experience, we pray with our heads bowed before the Lord, acknowledging His sovereignty and seeking His wisdom. Through prayer, we lay the foundation for our journey through the garden of agony, a separation of our spirit unto Him, trusting God's will as He leads us to a place of victory through surrender.

As we pray, God teaches us the significance of bringing our thoughts, our minds, and our entire beings under His lordship. It is a time of consecration, where we submit our will to God's will, surrendering our desires and letting in His plan for our lives.

Moreover, we are reminded that prayer is not just a one-time act but a continuous conversation with God. In a Gethsemane experience, we learn to persevere in prayer, seeking His presence day and night, just as Jesus prayed in the Garden.

ר RESH

Pressing deeper in prayer, we come to the full observation of God's will. It is in this sacred encounter that we gain insights into His plan for our lives. As we draw near to the authority of Christ, we find ourselves wrapped in the mantle of His divine revelation in prayer. The Holy Spirit enlightens our spiritual understanding, opening our eyes to the truths of His Word and guiding us in every step we take in faith.

As we engage in this divine exchange of thoughts and ways, we witness the anointed power of prayer. Our minds are renewed by the Spirit of God, and we experience a greater unity with Christ. In this deep prayer encounter, we become more like Him, being anointed by His love, compassion, and grace.

Prayer teaches us that this prayer journey is not a mere momentary experience but an ongoing, continuous pursuit. Day by day, we seek the face of our Heavenly Father, desiring to know Him intimately and commune with Him in every aspect of our lives. In this daily communion with the Holy Spirit, we find peace that surpasses all understanding. He is the God of Mercy and His gifts are renewed each day. Therefore, we seek Him anew each day.

Let this mind be in you, which was also in Christ Jesus: Who, being in the form of God, thought it not robbery to be equal with God: But made himself of no reputation, and took upon him the form of a servant, and was made in the likeness of men: And being found in fashion as a man, he humbled himself, and became obedient unto death, even the death of the cross (Philippians 2:5-8). We die to ourselves daily.

The example of complete surrender to God's will is found in the life of Jesus Himself. In the Garden of Gethsemane, just before His crucifixion, Jesus prayed, "Not my will, but Yours be done." Despite the immense anguish He was about to face, Jesus surrendered His own desires and God aligned His heart with Him which was His divine purpose. He willingly admitted the path of death, becoming the sacrificial Lamb for the redemption of humanity. It all started with prayer.

We too must come into this measure of faith prepared to acknowledge complete surrender to God's will in our lives. This deep life-changing prayer can be seen each time we honestly pray, "Thy will, not mine, be done." Despite having recovered from the immense suffering and anguish we faced, we now surrender our own desires and watch as God aligns His heart with us like never before. We now faithfully admit the suffering and death of sins such as addictions and alcoholism, having paid the high price of offering ourselves to God. The power, spirit, and prayer were the beginning of it all culminating in the third step prayer.

This deep prayer revealed that His thoughts are not our thoughts, neither are His ways our ways. He explained it to us when He said, "For my thoughts are not your thoughts, neither are your ways my ways, saith the Lord. For as the heavens are higher than the earth, so are my ways higher than your ways, and my thoughts than your thoughts" (Isaiah 55:8-9). We never knew the depths as we leveled up in our Gethsemane experience. Recess is over.

The story of Joseph in the book of Genesis is a powerful illustration of this deeper exchange in prayer. After being sold into slavery by his brothers and facing numerous trials, Joseph eventually rose to a position of authority in Egypt. When he was reunited with his brothers, who had come seeking food during a famine, Joseph revealed to them that what they had intended for evil, God had used for good. Through his experiences, Joseph's thoughts and ways were replaced with God's will, and he could see how God's higher purposes were at work even in the midst of adversity.

We too once were sold into the slavery of sins such as addictions and alcoholism by the one who loved us the most - ourselves. We faced numerous trials and many even rose to a position of power within our sinful lives. However, when we were reunited with that Name, we came hungering and thirsting after righteousness. God revealed unto us that what the enemy and ourselves had intended for evil, He has used it for good. A testimony had been built, never to be added to nor taken away from. Through our recovery, our thoughts and ways have been turned over to Him. We now experience His will, not ours, being done. We begin to see how God's higher purposes were at work even in the midst of our sins such as addictions and alcoholism.

We find the bitter pressing of faith produces the psychic change necessary for complete recovery. We have had a mind change! We think differently! Paul tells us, "And be not conformed to this world: but be ye transformed by the renewing of your mind, that ye may prove what is that good, and acceptable, and perfect, will of God" (Romans 12:2). God demonstrates Himself through our lives. We begin to see darkly into that which is good, acceptable, and the perfect will of God. We experience in prayer that perfect will. Even after all we have done, He is the God of mercy.

The Apostle Paul's conversion on the road to Damascus is a profound example of a life-changing encounter with God. In his encounter with Jesus, Paul's thoughts and ways were radically changed. He went from being a zealous persecutor of Christians to becoming one of the greatest champions of the faith, surrendering his life to God's will and purpose. Through the renewing of his mind, Paul aligned his heart with God's divine purposes and became a vessel of God's love and truth.

We too have had conversions on the road to encountering the silent one. Silent is the sackcloth weaver. The beginning of this recovery journey began with a life-changing encounter with God. In our encounter with Jesus, our thoughts and ways were radically changed. We went from being a zealous prosecutor of religion and all things spiritual to becoming among the greatest champions of faith, surrendering our lives to God's will. Through the renewing of the mind, we watched God mold us into vessels of His Love and Truth. He is the creator of perfectness in our lives.

YOD

Faith seems small, but it is powerful, and so is the bitter pressing of our spirits in faith. In our walk with Christ, we encounter sanctification which challenges our minds, bodies, and souls as we, in prayer, bitterly press our spirits. These difficult circumstances in prayer seem small in comparison to the will of God.

Faith is given in a measure, and in our journey of this *second measure* of faith, God measures our spirits through this bitter pressing. This prayer-filled sanctification is a prophetic instrument that refines us, molding us into vessels of faith, prophetic, Spirit-led service, and ministry.

Through the bitter pressing of our spirits, we learn to depend on God's grace. It is in these moments that our faith is tested, and we find ourselves drawing closer to our Heavenly Father. We learn to surrender our will to His, just as Jesus did in the Garden of Gethsemane, trusting in His divine plan.

As we navigate through the bitter pressings of life, we discover the glorious measure of faith within us. It was there from *step one*. We find that our faith moves mountains of intellectual pride and overcomes problems that have piled so high that they appear as insurmountable obstacles. Our mustard seed of faith, which is willingness, becomes a testimony to God's power and grace at work in us.

Faith is a hand, and in the pressing of our spirits, we experience the gentle yet firm hand of our Heavenly Father guiding us through sanctification. He holds us close, comforting us and reminding us that He is with us every step of the way. That the trial of faith, being much more precious than of gold that perisheth, though it be tried with fire, might be found unto praise and honor and glory at the appearing of Jesus Christ (1 Peter 1:7).

Job is a powerful example of a person who endured the bitter pressing of his spirit through tremendous challenges. Despite his loss, Job remained steadfast in his faith, and his faith was refined like precious gold through the fire of affliction. In the end, God restored Job and blessed him abundantly, demonstrating the value of faith tested and proven through sanctification.

Our lives, too, are powerful examples of people who endured the bitter pressing of our spirits through the tremendous process of sanctification that challenged our souls, minds, and strength. Despite our losses, through this recovery path, we have remained steadfast in our faith, and our faith is being refined like precious gold through the fire of recovery. In the end, we have recovered, received salvation, and God has and is continuing to bless us abundantly, demonstrating the value of faith proven through sanctification.

It is called bitter because none of us liked the separation of ourselves, good and bad unto Jesus Christ. However, we know, like how throwing the bitter root into the water turns it sweet, that this is a joyous process. "My brethren, count it all joy when ye fall into divers temptations; Knowing this, that the trying of your faith worketh patience. But let patience have her perfect work, that ye may be perfect and entire, wanting nothing" (James 1:2-4). We want for nothing.

Abraham and his journey of faith in Genesis 22 is a testament to the pressing of faith. God called Abraham to sacrifice his beloved son, Isaac, a test that pressed his spirit to the limit. Despite the immense challenge, Abraham obeyed in faith, believing that God would provide. Through this trial, Abraham's faith grew stronger, and he was blessed as the father of many nations.

We and our journeys of faith are a testament to the pressing of faith. God called us to sacrifice ourselves, a test that pressed our spirits to the limit. Despite the immense challenge, we obeyed in faith, believing that

God would provide. Through this sanctification, our faith grew stronger, and we have been blessed to carry this message to whosoever will receive it in the mighty Name of Jesus.

In this *second measure* of faith, we see the joy of patience appearing in our lives for we know hope is on the way. "And not only so, but we glory in tribulations also: knowing that tribulation worketh patience; And patience, experience; and experience, hope (Romans 5:3-4).

As stated before, Joseph in Genesis 37-50 is a remarkable example of how bitter pressing leads to hope. Joseph faced numerous tribulations, including betrayal, slavery, and imprisonment. Through these trials, his faith was tested and refined, leading to patience and a deep experience of God's faithfulness. In the end, God elevated Joseph to a position of authority in Egypt, bringing hope and salvation to his family and many others.

We too are remarkable examples of how bitter pressing and sanctification leads to service, ministry, and hope. We faced numerous tribulations, including betrayal, slavery, and imprisonment at our own hands. Through sanctification, our faith was tested, leading to patience and a deep and effective experience of God's faithfulness. In the end, God elevated us to a position of service and ministry, carrying a message of hope and salvation to our families and many others.

The Hebrew name Merari (יְרָחְמִי) holds significant meaning in the context of the Old Testament and has spiritual applications in the recovered life. In the Bible, Merari was one of the three sons of Levi and a member of the Levite tribe, responsible for the maintenance and transportation of the Tabernacle or House of God. In the recovered life, the name Merari carries several relevant implications. In the Old Testament, the Merarites had a specific responsibility to care for the Tabernacle and its components. In the recovered life, we follow God's instructions in supporting others on their recovery journey. Merari's role in maintaining the Tabernacle reflects the importance of ongoing seeking for those who have been delivered. Taking care of our physical, emotional, and spiritual health is crucial for sustaining a fulfilling life in Christ. In the recovered life, we find strength by being an active part of a supportive recovery community. The name Merari reminds us who have been delivered of God's Power which has recovered us to transcend past struggles and admit our new identity in Christ Jesus.

The Merarites were responsible for transporting various parts of the Tabernacle. In the recovered life, we are responsible for carrying the insights gained from what God has done in our recovery journey. In addition to their responsibilities, the Levite tribe supported the work of the priests and the spiritual life of the community. In the recovered life, we find fulfillment in supporting others' healing and recovery. The role of the Levite tribe had a significant spiritual aspect. In the recovered life, we are deepening our spiritual communion and finding comfort in our new beliefs given by Christ. As Merari fulfilled their responsibilities, they contributed to the overall functioning of the Tabernacle. In the recovered life, we contribute to the overall functioning of the recovery ministries.

The name Merari reminds us to embrace the journey of the recovered life, with all its ups and downs, and find meaning in continued healing and life change. Overall, the name Merari inspires us to recognize our role in our church through recovery ministries and by admitting our new identity in Christ as we continue to seek, ask, and take God-directed actions in our lives and the lives of others.

In this second measure of faith, we move into a position where we receive the benefit of the overarching promises and principles of the repentance steps of one, two, and three. Matthew 5:3 states, "Blessed are the poor in spirit; for theirs is the kingdom of heaven" (Matthew 5:3).

Step one in the recovery process involved reaching a place of utter humility. It emphasized the vital importance of crying out and when we cry out, it waters a seed of a powerful principle within us. Matthew 5:3 aligns with this step by highlighting the blessedness of those of us who are poor in spirit. It encourages us to maintain a sincere desire for the cross, Jesus, and to remain vigilant in faith.

Step two focused on coming to believe that Jesus is the way, the truth, and the life while also coming to understand that no one comes to the Father except through Him. Matthew 5:3 complements this step by emphasizing the blessedness of those who are poor in spirit. It invites us to cultivate a deep longing for closer communion with the covenant-keeping God, seeking His guidance and aligning our lives with His will. By being poor in spirit, we develop a greater awareness of God's covenant, presence, and guidance in our lives, enhancing our communion with Him.

Step three called for us to deny ourselves, take up our crosses, and follow Christ. Matthew 5:3 relates to this step by highlighting the blessedness of those who are poor in spirit. It emphasizes the fulfillment that comes from God rebuilding our lives based upon principles of recovery and practicing His righteousness in all areas of life. By being poor in spirit, we embody the message of recovery and become a source of inspiration and guidance for others.

Moreover, Matthew 5:3 also conveys the promise that those who are poor in spirit shall discover the kingdom of heaven. We are assured that we who actively pursue repentance, seek God's will, and align our lives with His righteousness will experience a relationship with God which provides an eternal hope and peace.

Matthew 5:3 relates to *steps one, two*, and *three* of the recovery process. It emphasizes the blessedness of those who are poor in spirit, encouraging us to continue our service and ministry, seeking a closer relationship with God. Being poor in spirit, we are now open to living out the principles of recovery in all aspects of our lives. By reflecting on this, we in recovery find love for ourselves and others, sharing God's promises, and an inner witness of the Holy Spirit. We continue our pursuit of His righteousness and our commitment to repentance which leads to a new relationship with God. We now see a deeper sense of purpose in recovery.

These wonderful promises are only intensified in this measure of faith. Again, *in step one*, we discovered that blessed are the poor in spirit because the kingdom of heaven is ours. *Step one* of the recovery process involved acknowledging powerlessness over sins such as addictions and alcoholism and the unmanageability of our backslidden life.

In *step one*, we recognized our spiritual poverty or our inability to overcome sins and the chaos we brought into our lives on our own power. We realized our need for Jesus Christ and admitted our will to God. *Step one* declares that those who acknowledge their spiritual poverty or dependence on God's grace are blessed and inherit the kingdom of heaven. It speaks to the significance of recognizing our limitations and humbly turning to God for guidance, healing, recovery, and salvation.

We first see in *step three* where Matthew 5:5 states, "Blessed are the meek: for they shall inherit the earth." *Step three* calls for us to deny ourselves, take up our crosses, and follow Christ. Matthew 5:5 complements this step by highlighting the blessedness of the meek, as we will inherit the earth. We have been told time and time again that meekness is often misunderstood as weakness, but in a spiritual sense, it refers to a gentle and humble attitude towards oneself and others. It involves surrendering our egos, pride, and self-will, and embracing an attitude of teachability. Meekness enables us to approach others with a willingness to listen.

In *step three*, we who have experienced the Holy Spirit's anointing in recovery are called to abandon ourselves utterly to Jesus Christ. This act requires the meek to recognize that we are not superior or unique, but rather equal in our shared journey of healing. By embodying meekness, we approach life with humility, offering support, encouragement, and guidance without superiority.

Furthermore, the promise in Matthew 5:5 that the meek shall inherit the earth aligns with the concept of carrying the message of recovery. By living out the principles of recovery and practicing meekness, we contribute to the healing and salvation of our recovery communities and society at large. We inherit the earth in the sense that our influence and impact extend beyond ourselves, helping to create a more compassionate environment for others. This is only done through deliverance, and this pure God is the only power that could have delivered us through *step one* to *step three*.

"Blessed are the pure in heart, for they shall see God" (Matthew 5:8). In the context of the *second measure* of faith, the verse from Matthew 5:8 speaks of the importance of having a pure heart. As we delve deeper into the principles and promises of faith, we come to understand the significance of this verse for our recovery, service, and ministry.

The mind plays a vital role in the process of recovery. Renewing our minds allows us to break free from our destructive natures, fostering a recovered mindset. Matthew 5:8, which talks about being pure in heart and seeing God, is connected to this process of mind renewal.

Being pure in heart entails receiving compassion and forgiveness towards both ourselves and others through baptism in the Name of Jesus Christ. Admitting remission of sins in Jesus' Name is vital because it enables us to break free from the bondage of sin and its guilt, shame, and self-condemnation that weighs us down in recovery. By submitting ourselves without reservation and being baptized in Jesus' Name for the remission of sins, God cultivates a pure heart.

Moreover, a pure heart towards others fosters healthy relationships and builds a supportive recovery ministry. When God removes the bondage of bitterness and offers remission, He opens the door to recovery and salvation, and we see God. We begin by searching within this measure of faith to serve others.

In terms of faith, Matthew 5:8 encourages us to have faith in the power of a pure heart. It assures us that by yielding to a pure heart, we see God. Having faith in a pure heart means trusting that the act of extending compassion and forgiveness is spiritually anointed by God. By embracing a pure heart, we invite repentance, remission, service, and ministry into our lives and the lives of others.

Throughout recovery, we've learned the potency of a pure heart, especially in the sixth step. Embracing a pure mindset and having faith in its anointed power allows us to experience the blessings of obtaining a pure heart. It frees our minds from bitterness and condemnation, strengthens our relationships, and fosters a compassionate environment for service and recovery ministry.

Now, the principles and promises of faith. Having been drawn-out, we further see what Matthew meant when he said in 5:7, "Blessed are the merciful: for they shall obtain mercy." This verse relates to the mind and faith in the context of this second measure of faith. Therefore, we began looking within.

In recovery, the mind plays a crucial role in the anointing process. It is through the renewal of the mind that we see God overcome our negative thought patterns, break us free from destructive behaviors, and cultivate a recovered mindset. Matthew 5:7 encourages us to embrace mercy as a fundamental aspect of this mindset.

Mercy involves showing compassion, forgiveness, and kindness towards ourselves and others. It is an attitude that seeks to extend grace, even in the face of wrongdoing. Cultivating a merciful mind is vital.

First, mercy towards ourselves is essential in the second measure of faith. We understand that many of us in recovery carry feelings of guilt, shame, and self-condemnation due to past mistakes or the consequences of sins such as addictions and alcoholism. Admitting mercy involves the admission of forgiveness, forgiving ourselves, and releasing condemnation. It involves treating ourselves with kindness, recovery is a process, and being patient with the journey of healing in ourselves and others.

Secondly, mercy towards others is crucial in building healthy relationships and fostering a supportive recovery community. By extending mercy to others, we let go of bitterness, anger, and judgment. We offer forgiveness to those who may have caused harm or have their own struggles. Mercy opens the door to healing and redemption, both within ourselves and in relationships with others.

In terms of faith, Matthew 5:7 encourages us to have faith in the power of mercy. It assures us that those who practice mercy obtain mercy themselves. Having faith in mercy means believing that the act of extending compassion and forgiveness has a Holy Spirit anointing. It means trusting that by embracing mercy, God creates healing, reconciliation, service, and a recovery ministry in our own lives and in the lives of others.

We learned the power of mercy from the fifth step. By embracing a merciful mindset and having faith in the power of mercy, we in recovery experience the blessings of becoming merciful. It allows us to free our minds from the burdens of bitterness and condemnation, cultivate healthier relationships, and create a compassionate environment for service, recovery ministry, and anointing.

A measure of faith not only fosters the mind, but it creates spiritual action from His promises and principles. This *second measure* of faith drew these actions out of us. Recognizing the bittersweet steps of repentance, we strengthened our spirits through our Lord, Jesus Christ.

In **RECOVERY 5:12**, we accomplish the process of refining our faith through the bitter pressings of life with a combination of prayer, reliance in the Holy Spirit, and embracing the principles found in God's Word. Here are some key actions we use to accomplish this.

Surrender begins by praying earnestly to God, acknowledging our dependence on Him. We surrender our will and desires to His will, just as Jesus did in Gethsemane. We ask Him to help us admit this measure of faith with willingness and patience, knowing that He works all things together for good.

We regularly study and meditate on the Scriptures, seeking wisdom from God's Word. The Bible is our source of encouragement during difficult times, and it provides examples of faithful individuals who endured trials and grew in their faith just as we do in recovery. As James 1:2-4 teaches us, we consider it a joy to face trials, knowing that they produce endurance and maturity in our faith. We admit the refining process with hope and confidence in God's faithfulness. We trust in God's sovereignty! We make the conscious recognition that God is sovereign and in control of all things. He is everything. We trust that this sanctification is for a purpose and that His will is perfect, even when we do not fully understand it. We walk in the Spirit by relying on the Holy Spirit's guidance and strength to navigate through faith. The Holy Spirit empowers us to persevere, to pray effectively, and to experience God's peace even in the midst of challenges. We walk in the eye of life's storms.

We seek support and encouragement by surrounding ourselves with a fellowship that provides support, encouragement, and corporate prayer during difficult times. We fellowship with others who have experienced God's faithfulness through faith. They are a great source of comfort. We consciously make the decision to remember God's faithfulness. We recall and reflect on times when God has been faithful in the past and how He is this very day. We remind ourselves of His promises and His track record of bringing good out of challenging situations just as He is doing here and now in our recovery.

We practice a new form of gratitude. Through healing, we are cultivating an attitude of thankfulness, even in challenging circumstances. We focus on the blessings and goodness of God! It's a new gratitude because now it is a list identifying all the reasons why we should direct our attention to God and express thankfulness in prayer and worship, not for what He has done but for who He is. We serve others as Jesus showed us to. We look for opportunities to serve and bless others in the midst of our own measure of faith. Serving others brings a sense of purpose and helps shift the focus from ourselves to God's greater plan. We stay hopeful! We keep an eternal perspective, knowing that this life is temporary, and our hope is in Jesus Christ and the promise of eternal life. This refining process of faith leads us to a deeper relationship with God and prepares us for an eternal future with Him. By implementing these spiritual practices, we let in the bitter pressings of life with faith, hope, and endurance, observing as God refines and strengthens our faith for His glory.

Recognizing the bittersweet steps of repentance, we have strengthened our spirit through our Lord, Jesus Christ. In the *third measure* of faith, we journey forward into a beautiful place of holiness. Our trust in faith continues to grow.

Goodness and Gentleness.

CHAPTER 20

THIRD MEASURE OF FAITH

Casted out in remission, we became Spiritual Refugees of Jesus Christ.

"Humble yourselves therefore under the mighty hand of God, that He may exalt you in due time: Casting all your care upon Him; for He careth for you."
(1 Peter 5:6 & 7)

In the *third measure* of faith, we embark on a remarkable journey of separation through prayer, finding ourselves standing at the center of a consuming fire. As we connect with the Holy Spirit's descending presence, we enter a place where we are enveloped by His righteousness. It penetrates the depths of our hearts, reminding us of the covenant we entered during the previous days of fervent prayer on our knees. The flow of the Holy Spirit reinforces our commitment to walk in His righteousness.

As we enter this measure of faith, we remember the steps along the path of faith and goodness, aligning with God's salvation and our repentance. Just as the Israelites moved toward the Promised Land, we have been journeying toward the fulfillment of God's purposes in our lives. As we, who are recovered Holy Ghost-filled believers, journey in faith and goodness, we discover encouragement as we seek God's will, trust in His guidance, and depend on His provision. In every season of testing or abundance, we find assurance in God's faith and goodness, knowing that He is with us and that our destination is the fullness of His promises.

This measure of faith uncovers its roots in the taking of *steps four, five*, and *six*. We thought we were having our sins remitted. However, we find that we had been cast out in remission; we became Spiritual Refugees of Jesus Christ (1 Peter 5:6 & 7). We committed to carry our pain and sorrow into the fourth step. The beauty in all of this is that it had already begun before we even wrote the first item on our examination. Once we began searching and trying, from that very moment, we embarked on this process. His bidding was to make us spiritual servants in Christ to His children.

The spiritual journey's theme of separation and holiness that we embarked upon in *step four* has been ongoing. It began with our separation from pain and sorrow, as we were strengthened in the process. This newfound strength became the foundation of our testimony, which we gained in *step five*. Through this testimony, we experienced further separation from bitterness, fear, and immorality, as these negative emotions and behaviors were transformed into testimonies in holiness.

In our bitterness, we discovered a prayer list filled with opportunities to practice tolerance, pity, and patience. Faith rewarded us with the fruit of holiness, which became evident in our lives. We received a blank canvas, upon which God captured our trust. Through the outpouring of His blessings, we witnessed others being blessed before our very eyes. Recovery has taught us the profound truth of simply being the branch, relying on God's grace, and allowing His life-giving power to flow through us to bless others. Jesus teaches that the abiding connection is to remain in Christ's love and bear fruit.

> *"I am the true vine, and My Father the Husbandman.*
> *Every branch in Me that beareth not fruit He lifts up:*
> *And every branch that beareth fruit, He is cleaning up,*
> *That it may bring forth more fruit.*
> *Now ye are clean through the word which I have spoken unto you.*
> *Abide in Me, and I in you.*
> *As the branch cannot bear fruit of itself,*
> *except it abide in the vine;*
> *no more can ye, except ye abide in Me.*
> *I am the vine, ye are the branches:*
> *He that abideth in Me, and I in him,*
> *The same bringeth forth much fruit:*
> *For without Me ye can do nothing.*
> *If a man abide not in Me, he is cast forth*
> *As a branch, and is withered;*
> *And men gather them, cast them into the fire,*
> *And they are burned.*
> *If ye abide in Me, and My words abide in you,*
> *Ye shall ask what ye will,*
> *and it shall be done unto you.*
> *Herein is My Father glorified, that ye bear much fruit;*
> *So shall ye be My disciples.*
> *As the Father hath loved Me, so have I loved you:*
> *Continue ye in My love."*

The teaching of holy separation from sins such as addictions and alcoholism revealed to us the true meaning of abiding in Christ Jesus. We learned that to abide is to be a branch. Simple but not easy.

Initially, our minds struggled with the concept of "just be," as we had emphasized the importance of faith and action in the early stages of our salvation. We couldn't grasp how to just be a branch or what that entailed. We pondered possible answers: perhaps a branch merely holds on, but we couldn't understand how. We considered that a branch produces leaves and fruit, but we knew that without being connected to the vine, there could be no leaves or fruit.

In the midst of this holy separation, we learned to embrace the idea of just being. As branches, we discovered the joy of remaining connected to the true vine. We observed that leaves and fruit naturally formed on the branch, without any thought or effort on our part, and it was a beautiful sight. We recognized the presence of the Husbandman—the caretaker of the vineyard. His smile brought comfort as He lovingly lifted us up when we got dirty. Our attention shifted from His tender touch to the fruit growing in our lives. We witnessed His delight as He carefully pruned and cleaned the fruit, admiring its growth. His joy overflowed as others partook of the fruit produced in our lives. At that moment, we realized that we had no control over what was happening within us. We were being continually purged, and the more our old fruit was removed, the more of the newer fruit appeared. The abundance of this increase was mesmerizing. And so, we continued to just be, embracing the separation from external distractions, and focusing on the transformation happening within our hearts and souls. As we remained in this state of being, something beautiful coursed through us—joy. It became evident that joy was a natural byproduct of abiding in Christ and His life flowing through us. Jesus followed His teaching with the disclaimer,

> *"If ye keep My principle, ye shall abide in My love; even as I have kept my Father's principle, and abide in His love."*

> *The vine was communion and we were feeling the benefits without any thought or effort on our part. This is the miracle of it. Christ went on to say,*

"These things have I spoken unto you, that My joy might remain in you and that your joy might be full!"

Being a branch is being full of joy. What a Holy separation unto Jesus and away from the former things of old! We have been chosen that we should go and bring forth fruit, and that our fruit should remain! This way of living makes way for whatsoever we shall ask of the Father in Jesus' Name. Love one another as Jesus has loved us; that is the principle expressed throughout our recovery.

He has destroyed the wickedness within us, casting out our old names forever. Our enemy's destruction is coming to an end, and their memory perishes with them. Those who transgress without cause shall be put to shame, while those who wait on the Lord will not be ashamed. Let us magnify the name of YHWH together.

We commit our way to the Lord, knowing that He brings about what we hope for. His righteousness shines like the light, and His judgment is clear as the noonday sun. The works of YHWH are great, and His offspring are mighty on the earth. We humbly ask Him to deal bountifully with His servant so that we faithfully keep His Word.

We implore Him to open our eyes, so that we behold wondrous things from His principle. As strangers to the fullness of life, we ask that He does not hide His principle from us. Our souls long for His principle, and we recognize that our pride, which leads us astray from His principle, has been rebuked.

We beseech Him to remove reproach from us as we diligently keep His testimonies. Though people speak against us, as His servants, we meditate on His principle. His testimonies are our delight and serve as our counselors. Great is YHWH, deserving of the highest praise, and His greatness is beyond our comprehension.

As we delve deeper into prayer, we know that He has seen it, for He beholds spite and repays it with His hand. Being poor in spirit, we commit ourselves to Him, knowing that He is the helper of the fatherless (Psalm 25:5). We were without direction, helpless.

In the fourth step, we considered our enemies within, for they are many and hate us with cruel hatred (Psalm 34:19). Though the righteous face numerous afflictions, YHWH delivers us from all in *step six* through baptism in His Name (Psalm 37:35). We have witnessed our wicked defects in great power leading to this path, flourishing like the grass which is about to be cut down. Yet, they pass away and cannot be found once He has remitted them (Psalm 37:10).

Step five revealed that the Fear of the Lord is the beginning of wisdom (Psalm 112:10). When the wickedness within sees it, they are grieved (Psalm 119:153). We implored Him to consider our affliction, deliver us, and quicken us according to His Word. And He did! Salvation is far from wickedness because, without it, we would not seek His principle. We acknowledge the greatness of His tender mercies and ask for His quickening according to His principle (Psalm 119:156). Despite the many persecutors and enemies we faced in *step five*, we did not turn away from His testimony that He created in us. We observed our transgressions and mourned our failure to keep His Word. Through taking these steps, we declared our love for His principle and asked for His quickening according to His lovingkindness (Psalm 119:159). We are thankful for these steps of remission for they have shown us that His Word is true from the beginning, and His righteous principle endures forever (Psalm 145:19). He fulfills the desires of those who Fear Him, hears our cry, and saves us (Psalm 145:19).

The spiritual battle was being revealed. In these remission steps, we prayed for God to break the stronghold of the evil within us, and to seek out our wickedness until none is found. At the end of these remission steps, we pleaded for God to keep our soul, so that we may not be ashamed, for we put our trust in Him. We declared the power behind the fact that God did indeed keep all His bones, and not one of them is broken (Psalm 34). We were advised to observe the perfect and upright, for their end is peace.

However, the grip of our transgressors had to be destroyed, and the end of the wicked had to be cut off. Therefore, we were baptized in Jesus' Name. This was a spiritual action and not merely an outward sign.

It is said that those who do good have a good understanding (Psalm 111). We now had an understanding. The baptism was described as being how the old man gnashes his teeth and melts away. It has been revealed that His children are persecuted seemingly without cause, yet our hearts stand in awe of God's Word. We have experienced a psychic change and now rejoice in His Word, abhorring lying, while loving His principle. We praise God throughout the day because of His righteous principle. Those of us who love His principle have discovered great peace, and nothing shall offend us. We hoped for God's salvation and followed His principle. Our soul has kept God's testimonies, and it loves them exceedingly. We have kept His principle and testimonies because all our ways are before Him.

Through these remission steps, we proclaimed that the Lord preserves all those who love Him, but He will destroy all the wicked things within (Psalm 145). We observed that the wickedness, through the pride of our countenance, did not seek after God. God was not in our thoughts. Our ways were grievous, and God's principle was far from our sight. We puff now at our sins such as addictions and alcoholism (Psalm 10). After taking these steps, we can declare that none who wait on the Lord are shamed. We who transgressed without cause were ashamed.

In this *third measure*, we are encouraged to magnify the Lord and exalt His Name together as we align with His will (Psalm 34). We are advised to commit our ways to the Lord, trusting in Him through this measure of faith. He brought forth our righteousness as the light and is bright as the noonday (Psalm 37). We now proclaim that the works of the Lord are great. We were assured that His seed shall be mighty upon the earth. We now proclaim that God's Word is a lamp unto our feet and a light unto our path. We have sworn to keep God's righteous principle and beseech Him to accept the freewill offerings of our mouth and teach us His principle.

Even though we were afflicted, we do not forget God's principle as it was shown throughout the remission steps. The wicked have laid snares within us, but we do not stray from God's principle. We have taken God's testimonies as an inheritance forever, and we rejoice in them. We have inclined our hearts to perform God's principle always, even to the end. We are declaring that the Lord is great and greatly to be praised, and His greatness is unsearchable.

ג GIMEL

Overall, *steps four, five,* and *six,* the remission steps, worked together to create a powerful encounter with God. Trying leads to discernment, sharing creates communion, and faith brings about change that paves the way for fruits of the Spirit. This process is applied to all our affairs, promoting salvation and recovery in the face of struggles. *Step four* initiated the process by promoting searching, examining, repentance, and seeking God's guidance. Through this examination and searching, we gain valuable insights into the true nature of our sins such as addictions and alcoholism.

Step five fostered a sense of communion by allowing us to share our vulnerabilities with God, ourselves, and another person. This act of confession created a supportive space where we felt accepted, reducing feelings of isolation. Merciful.

The act of sharing in *step five* created a sense of accountability to ourselves and the person hearing the confession. Knowing that someone else was aware of our struggles motivated us to take responsibility for our actions and seek change. Additionally, the person listening experienced empathy, further reinforcing the process.

Step six capitalized on the newfound awareness gained from the previous steps to foster a commitment of repentance. By openly acknowledging our flaws and taking ownership of our actions, we continually grow in our understanding of God's grace and deepen our relationship with Jesus Christ.

Steps four, five, and *six* culminated in faith to take action toward baptism for the remission of sins. Armed with repentance, baptism, and remission of sins, once through these steps we embarked on a journey of redemption. We now seek God, He changed our thinking, and renewed relationships with the Lord and His children began to flourish.

Recovery reminds us of the rewards that await us. *Step four* has taught us how to search our ways and try them as we return to the Lord. We were cast out in remission, and we became Spiritual Refugees of Jesus Christ, who granted us the benefit of mercy—the precious gift of seeing both our strengths and weaknesses. Through this acknowledgment of our sins, turning away from them, and seeking forgiveness from God, we open ourselves to the reward of service, recovery, and ministry.

Just as this journey in communion acts as a bridge between us, God, and His people, we were encouraged by *step five* to build bridges with God and others by sharing our confessions. This genuine communion with a trusted companion created a supportive environment where empathy flourished, helping us find strength in God and His children as we embark on the path to recovery.

The concept of elevation associated with recovery aligns perfectly with the essence of *step six*. By faithfully acknowledging our past mistakes and baptism in His Name, we elevated ourselves to higher spiritual level. This anointed faith allows us to transcend our previous limitations and experience the presence of God.

Step seven infused our recovery with spiritual depth. Through our faith in the Holy Spirit, we believe that God's grace sustains us in the beginning of recovery and salvation. However, the window of grace is only opened for a moment and the longer we wait for recovery, the more time there is for the window of opportunity to close. Yet, once through this window of opportunity, God's mercy is our camel on this long arduous journey in prayer.

ר RESH

Prayer is often associated with the mind. Very much like the early *steps one, two*, and *three,* In the context of recovery, *step four* served as the starting point for us—a crucial beginning. Through being cast out in remission and becoming Spiritual Refugees of Jesus Christ, we started to gain clarity, making it possible to address our issues at their roots. Just as prayer represents actions of the mind, *step four* helped us examine the thoughts and beliefs that have contributed to our struggles. These are what were offered up in the third step prayer and what was remitted in baptism.

Prayer is also connected to vision. *Step five* mirrored this by encouraging us to confess our shortcomings to ourselves, God, and another person. This act of sharing allowed us to gain a fresh perspective on the true nature of our experiences. It provided an opportunity to see our challenges from a different angle, fostering greater insight into what we had given up.

Prayer is the first action of anointing which is in harmony with *step six*, which emphasizes the faithfulness to change. As we accept responsibility for our actions, we seek service and recovery ministry. Like prayer, which is the first action of change, *step six* empowers us to let go of old patterns and admit a change of mind through baptism in His Name.

Prayer always refers to God's presence. As we progress through *steps four, five*, and *six*, we rely on the guidance of the Spirit—the Holy Ghost—to aid us in our recovery. We seek God's wisdom to gain new perspectives, find comfort in the psychic change, and draw closer to the presence of God.

Incorporating prayer as the first action into our understanding of recovery, we recognize that these steps represent a profound spiritual journey. We begin with searching and examining our ways, seeking to understand ourselves at a deeper level. By sharing with God and others, and gaining new perspectives, we open ourselves to the mental change needed for recovery. Throughout recovery, we rely on the presence of the Holy Ghost to support us as we strive for healing and salvation. Being Holy Ghost-filled, we find comfort in knowing that God's mercy surrounds us every step of the way.

ש SHIN

Spirit is the fire first seen in *step three,* which is the essence of God's presence. This process was the refining fire, where we observed the Holy Spirit illuminating our thoughts and actions, burning away impurities, and bringing forth the needed Power for a total transformation of mind and spirit.

The Holy Ghost fills believers as He guides us through recovery. In *step five,* as we shared our confessions with another person, we invited the presence of God through the Holy Spirit into our lives, fostering healing and transformation.

The fire of the Holy Spirit transforms our thinking. This aligns with the essence of *step six,* where we faithfully accepted responsibility for our past actions and committed to this new change as we were baptized in Jesus' Name. Through the anointing power of the Holy Spirit, we are now empowered to rise above our old ways and embrace a new path.

The Holy Ghost protects. As we progress through recovery, we seek God's protection in our lives. By surrendering ourselves to God's guidance, we find security in the presence of the Holy Spirit, shielding us from temptation and empowering us to walk in His righteousness.

The Holy Ghost brings wholeness. *Steps four, five,* and *six* work in harmony to promote holistic healing—body, mind, and spirit. Through searching and trying, connecting with others, and maintaining faithfulness to change, we pursue wholeness in all aspects of our lives, drawing closer to the one true God in the process.

Incorporating the Holy Ghost fire into recovery, we recognize the profound spiritual dimension of *steps four, five,* and *six*. We embrace the anointing power of the Holy Spirit, seeking divine guidance, protection, and blessings on our path to recovery and salvation. As Holy Ghost-filled recovered believers, we hold steadfast to our faith, knowing that the presence of God's Spirit strengthens us and empowers us to live in alignment with His will.

VAV

Communion connects ourselves, God, and another person to try our searching and examination. We vaguely sensed this in *step four*. This act of confession fosters unity, creating a bond of trust. Through this communion, we realize that we are not alone in our struggles and that together we can find strength in recovery.

Communion connects heaven and earth. *Steps four, five,* and *six* illustrate this communion. *Step four* involved us searching and trying, allowing us to commune our spirit with the Holy Spirit as we seek His guidance. *Step five* involved us sharing with others, strengthening earthly bonds, and promoting a sense of community, as well as creating a bridge to the spiritual realm.

Communion is continuity. In recovery, *step six* emphasized the importance of faithfulness to continue the path of recovery. As we embraced the process of recovery, we demonstrated our faithfulness to the journey and our commitment to ongoing growth in Christ.

As believers, we now recognize the significance of God's Word in our recovery journey. *Steps four, five,* and *six* all involved the Holy Ghost aligning our lives with spiritual principles found in God's Word, which is our guide, providing wisdom, comfort, and strength as He navigates us through the challenges of recovery.

Communion is the glorious tent peg. This can be linked to *step five*, where sharing our confessions with another person is understood as an act of vulnerability. By "nailing" our burdens to God and the support of trusted Holy Ghost-filled believers of Christ, we remove ourselves and experience the relief that comes from unburdening our hearts.

By incorporating communion into recovery, we gain a deeper appreciation for the interconnectedness of *steps four, five,* and *six*. Through our communion with others and with God, we find unity, support, and strength to persevere in recovery. We admit our faithfulness to God's Word as we follow this remission process. Communion with God's Word is the guiding force in serving, recovery ministry, and healing. As Holy Ghost-filled recovered believers, we embrace the spiritual significance of communion, knowing that the Holy Spirit sustains us throughout recovery.

NUN

As Holy Ghost-filled recovered believers, we find deep spiritual significance in His righteousness and how it relates to the seamless integration of *steps four, five,* and *six* in the recovery process. It is this same righteousness that brought us into humility during *step one.*

Righteousness and faithfulness. As recovered believers, we strive to live righteous lives, guided by the principles of God's Word. In the context of recovery, *step four* invited us to search and try our hearts. When acknowledging our flaws, we had to demonstrate a commitment to righteousness—a desire to align our lives with God's will and live in harmony with His principle.

If righteousness had a shape, it would resemble a "seed," with stability and permanence. As we progressed through *step five*, we shared our examinations with another person and we established stable relationships. This act of openness created a strong foundation for our recovery, promoting stability in our spiritual well-being.

Faithfulness associated with righteousness is mirrored in *step six*. By embracing the willingness to change, we demonstrated our trust in God's life-changing power and His faithfulness to guide us on the path of His righteousness. Through our commitment to recovery, we exhibit our trust in God's will for our lives, knowing that He is with us every step of the way.

Righteousness is the "seed"; it is life and holiness. *Steps four, five*, and *six* collectively form a life-changing journey leading towards holiness and sanctification. The process of discernment, confession, and faithfulness to change allows us to shed our old ways and grow toward a life marked by His righteousness and holiness.

Righteousness is the great "nothing," filled with emptiness and mercy before God. As we engaged in *steps four, five*, and *six*, we admitted mercy, acknowledging that we cannot overcome our struggles on our own strength. Instead, we learned to offer ourselves, our burdens, and our weaknesses to God, relying on His mercy to lead us toward His righteousness.

His righteousness beautifully calls us through the process of recovery through the remission steps. As Holy Ghost-filled recovered believers, we recognize the vital importance of His righteousness in our lives and seek to walk in His way. By searching, communion, admitting faithfulness to have our sins remitted, and mercifully relying on God's mercy as He applies His Name to our lives in baptism, we find healing, anointing, and the path to holiness. The Holy Spirit sustains us in recovery, enabling us to live righteously and faithfully as we grow in our relationship with God.

This *third measure* in faith is where we truly discover that this separation, which began during *step four* when we walked into the step with pain and sorrow. Before we could escape, God separated us from this pain and sorrow and made them our very strength. He converted our past into a powerful testimony as we had our lives radically changed the moment, He applied His Name to our lives in baptism. A beautiful separation it has been. We now see that it has been a "journey" or "path" in holiness. In recovery, whether from addictions, mental health issues, or other challenges, the journey of holiness is the life-altering process toward healing, service, and recovery ministry. Let's explore why this journey in holiness is easier than a rich person getting to heaven.

Just as **RECOVERY 5:12** represents a "path," the journey of holiness in recovery begins with taking the first steps toward healing. This involves gathering the courage to admit the challenges and commit to repentance.

We have been introduced to a doorway throughout this recovery process, involving soul-searching and seeking the inner witness of the Holy Spirit, looking to understand the root causes of our struggles, and identifying areas that need healing, service, and ministry.

We have been immersed in revelation providing the window needed for ongoing recovery. We who have recovered and are Holy Ghost-filled see where we should begin to admit the support of other recovered believers, whether it be through recovery, spiritual meetings, or seeking guidance from Holy Ghost-filled mentors. Building a strong support system is crucial in the journey of holiness as it provides encouragement to all who are in Christ.

We are told over and over about the connecting power which is communion. It is a tent peg, nail, or hook, which is seen as we let go of what holds us back. Offering ourselves to the process of recovery involves admitting that things are beyond our control and that God breaks the bondage of self and selfish actions from our lives.

We have discovered discernment which is prayerful contemplation. We who have recovered and are believers in recovery reflect on our growth. Practicing gratitude becomes an essential aspect of the holiness journey as we appreciate the changes and the lessons learned along the way.

Holiness is the fence that provides our lives with a protective spiritual boundary. In recovery, we have been seeking God, and we have found meaning in life. He has placed a spiritual boundary around us, and we now experience fulfillment in service and recovery ministry that supports the whole of our spiritual well-being.

Holiness took a serpent, which was our broken life, while we have been preoccupied with the activities of recovery. As we explored our spirituality, communing with the Holy Ghost and finding spiritual peace through faith, Holiness changed the serpent to an eagle. Our brokenness has been changed to deliverance through His holiness. The true transformation was seen in these remission steps and measures of faith. Broken pottery forged back together by gold.

We have seen His hand, power, and creativity. As the journey of holiness progresses, we who have been filled and are recovered experience rebirth, shedding old patterns and embracing new, holier ways of living, servicing, and ministering to others.

He has taught us the power of His open palm, obedience, surrender, and unity. In this stage, the lessons and experiences of recovery are integrated into our daily lives, fostering a sense of harmony within ourselves and with the needs of the world.

Holiness is the shepherd's staff of guidance and leadership. Throughout the holiness journey, we have and continue to experience significant repentance, service, and ministry, becoming a guiding light for others who are on a similar path of recovery.

We have experienced the water of holiness, flow, and abundance. As recovery progresses, we are learning to embrace joy and celebrate His blessings, appreciating the beauty that salvation and recovery bring.

All this holiness contained within the seed that was planted deep within our hearts provides continuity in our spirits. Recovery or the journey of holiness is an ongoing process, even for the recovered. We emphasize the importance of improving, staying vigilant, and continuing to learn service and ministry as this new life unfolds.

Remember that the journey of holiness in recovery is not a linear path, and everyone's experience is different. It's a process that requires patience to keep moving forward, even when faced with challenges. Seek God, as He is in the seeking. Seek Holy Ghost-filled support, be open to learning, and remember that we are not alone on this journey into His holiness.

The *third measure* of faith encompasses the principle of mourning, which is the catalyst of the holy separation process. Within this measure, there are three additional principles: hungering and thirsting after righteousness, being merciful, and attaining purity of heart. Through this life-changing journey of holy separation, we experience the fulfillment of these principles and receive remarkable promises. We are filled with righteousness, shown mercy, and granted the privilege of seeing God Himself.

In this *third measure* of faith, we move into a position where we grow from the benefit of the overarching promises and principles of the remission *steps four, five*, and *six*. Cast out in remission, we became Spiritual Refugees of Jesus Christ (1 Peter 5:6 & 7).

Step four in the recovery process commenced this sanctification. It emphasized the vital importance of searching and examining these character flaws within us. Matthew 5:4 aligns with this step by highlighting the blessedness of those of us who mourn. It becomes the sincere desire for the searching, examination, and ability to remain vigilant in the trying of our spirit.

Step five focused on being merciful while also coming to believe that we shall be shown mercy. Matthew 5:4 complements this step by emphasizing the blessedness of those who mourn. It invites us to cultivate a deep longing for closer communion with the covenant-keeping God, seeking His guidance, and aligning our lives with His will. By mourning, we develop a greater awareness of God's covenant, presence, and guidance in our lives, enhancing our communion with Him.

Step six called for us to become pure in heart. Matthew 5:4 relates to this step by highlighting the blessedness of those who mourn. It emphasizes the fulfillment that comes from seeing God in His rebuilding of our lives based upon principles of recovery and practicing His righteousness in all areas of life. By mourning, we embody the message of recovery and become a source of inspiration for others.

Moreover, Matthew 5:4 also conveys the promise that those who mourn shall be comforted. We are assured that we who actively pursue remission, seek God's will, and align our lives with His righteousness experience a relationship with God, eternal hope, and peace. Matthew 5:4 relates to *steps four, five,* and *six* of the recovery process. It emphasizes the blessedness of those who mourn, encouraging us to continue our service and recovery ministry. We seek a closer relationship with God and live out the principles of recovery in all aspects of our lives. By reflecting on this, we who have recovered find love for others, share God's promises, and act as an inner witness of the Holy Spirit. Our pursuit of His righteousness and commitment to this remission process leads to a strong relationship with God and a deeper sense of purpose in recovery.

These wonderful promises are only intensified in this *third measure* of faith. Again, in *step four*, we discovered that blessed are those who hunger and thirst after righteousness: because they shall be filled. *Step four* of the recovery process involved searching out and examining our ways and acknowledging the bitterness, fear, and immorality of sins such as addictions and alcoholism in our backslidden lives. We turned again to the Lord.

In *step five*, we recognized how blessed are the merciful. We seek God's mercy and are shown mercy. We realized our need for Jesus Christ and surrendered our will to God. *Step five* declares that if we confess our faults one to another and pray for one for another, we may be healed. It speaks to the significance of confession and humbly praying for salvation.

We first see in *step five* where Matthew 5:7 states, "Blessed are the merciful; for they shall be shown mercy." *Step five* called for us to confess our faults one to another, and pray one for another, and we were healed. The effectual fervent prayer of a righteous man avails much. Matthew 5:7 complements this step by highlighting the blessedness of the merciful, as we will receive mercy. We have been told time and time again that mercy is often misunderstood as naivete, but in a spiritual sense, it refers to a gentle and humble attitude God demonstrates towards us and others even when we don't deserve it. It involves surrendering our self-will and embracing an attitude of compassion. Mercy enables us to see that God approaches us and others with empathy and a willingness to support.

In *step six*, we who have experienced the Holy Spirit's anointing in recovery are called to abandon ourselves utterly to the Name of Jesus Christ through baptism. This act requires the purity to recognize that we are not unique, but rather equal in our shared journey of healing. By embodying purity, we approach life with humility, offering support, encouragement, and guidance without judgment. Our next function is to grow in understanding and effectiveness of serving others.

Furthermore, the promise in Matthew 5:8 that the pure in heart shall see that God aligns with the concept of carrying the message of recovery. So, we immediately look within ourselves. By living out the principles of recovery and practicing purity of heart, we are contributing to the recovery and salvation of our recovery communities and society at large. We see God in the sense that His influence and impact extend beyond ourselves, creating a more supportive recovery environment for all.

"Blessed are the peacemakers; for they shall be called sons of God" (Matthew 5:9). In the context of the *third measure* of faith, the verse from Matthew 5:9 speaks of the importance of being a peacemaker. As we delve deeper into the principles and promises of faith, we come to understand the significance of this verse for our recovery, service, and ministry. In recovery, the mind plays a vital role in the process of healing and salvation. Renewing our minds allows us to break free from negative thought patterns and destructive behaviors, fostering a positive and healthy mindset. Matthew 5:9, which talks about being a peacemaker and being called a child of God, is communing with this process of mind renewal and separation unto Christ.

Being a peacemaker entails receiving compassion, forgiveness, and kindness towards both ourselves and others through the Holy Spirit in prayer. Admitting receipt of the Holy Spirit is vital because it enables us to live a life free from the bondage of sin and its accompanying guilt, shame, and self-condemnation that weighs us down in recovery. By submitting ourselves without reservation and receiving the Holy Spirit, we are now called the children of God.

Moreover, being a peacemaker to others fosters healthy relationships and builds a supportive community in recovery. God removes the bondage of bitterness and judgment, and then offers the gift of the Holy Ghost and forgiveness. He opens the door to recovery and salvation; we are the children of the one true King.

In terms of faith, Matthew 5:9 encourages us to have faith in the power of being a peacemaker. It assures us that by yielding to being a peacemaker, we become children of God. Having faith in being a peacemaker means trusting that the act of extending compassion and forgiveness is spiritually anointed by God. By embracing being a peacemaker, we invite the Holy Ghost, repentance, remission, service, and ministry into our lives and the lives of others.

Throughout recovery, we've learned the potency of being a peacemaker, especially in the *third measure*. Admitting a peacemaking mindset and having faith in its anointed power allows us to experience the blessings of becoming a peacemaker. It frees our minds from bitterness and condemnation, strengthens our relationships, and fosters a compassionate environment for service and ministry. This spirit of peacemaking is our outward service.

Now we turn our focus more inward. Having been cast out, we further see what Matthew meant when he said in 5:8, "Blessed are the pure in heart; for they shall see God." This verse relates to the mind and faith in the context of recovery.

In recovery, the mind plays a crucial role in the healing and anointing process. It is through the renewal of the mind that we see God overcome our negative thought patterns, break us free from destructive behaviors, and cultivate a positive and healthy mindset. Matthew 5:8 encourages us to embrace purity as a fundamental aspect of our mindset.

Being pure in heart involves showing forgiveness towards ourselves and others. It is an attitude that seeks to extend grace, even in the face of pain. Cultivating a pure heart and mind is vital.

First, being pure in heart toward ourselves is essential in recovery. We understand that many of us in recovery carry feelings of self-condemnation due to past mistakes of sins such as alcoholism and addictions. Admitting a pure heart involves embracing forgiveness, including forgiving ourselves, and letting go of condemnation. It involves treating ourselves with kindness, understanding that recovery is a process, and being patient with the journey of growth in ourselves and others.

Secondly, being pure in heart toward others is crucial in building healthy relationships as we foster a supportive community in recovery. By extending a pure heart to others, we let go of bitterness, anger, and judgment. We offer empathy to those who may have caused harm or have their own struggles. A pure heart opens the door to redemption, both within ourselves and in our relationships with others. This could only be achieved through the leading of the Holy Spirit as He removes the carnage of our past.

In terms of faith, Matthew 5:8 encourages us to have faith in the power of a pure heart. It assures that those of us who practice purity will obtain a pure heart. Having faith in a pure heart means believing that the act of extending compassion has a Holy Spirit anointing. It means trusting that by embracing a pure heart, God creates healing, service, and ministry in our own lives and in the lives of others.

We learned the power of a pure heart from the sixth step. By embracing a pure heart mindset and having faith in its power, we in recovery experience the blessings of obtaining it. This new heart of flesh given to us allows us to free our minds from the burden of bitterness and condemnation, cultivate healthier relationships, and creates a compassionate environment for service, ministry, and anointing.

A measure of faith not only fosters the mind and faith, but it creates spiritual action from His promises and principles. This *third measure* of faith draws these actions out of us. Recognizing the casting out steps of remission, we strengthened the spirit through the Name of our Lord, Jesus Christ. We obtained this through spiritual action.

Our casting out is not a mere passing desire but a genuine yearning that propels us forward. It is a holiness that creates a love for others. We discover that seeking Him is daily bread for our souls, and we now know that true nourishment for our spirits can only be found in His righteousness.

Guided by this inner separation, we embark on a journey of spiritual action. We commit ourselves to aligning our lives with God's will, embracing His biblical authority. We are separated unto Christ and integrity permeate our thoughts, words, and actions. We are separated in remission, knowing that true anointing comes from walking in righteousness. We devote time to prayer, seeking communion with God. We immerse ourselves in scripture, finding wisdom for recovery. We join fellow believers in fellowship in the recovery community.

Devoting time to prayer becomes a meaningful practice, helping us connect with inner peace. Here are some ways we incorporate prayer into our daily routines. We start our day with a time of prayer. We set aside time each morning to express gratitude, seek guidance from the Holy Spirit, and make our plans surrounding His guidance for the day ahead. This is the peaceful way we center ourselves before starting our daily activities.

We use every mealtime as an opportunity for prayer. We always take a moment to appreciate the food we have and acknowledge the efforts of those who contributed to our meal so that we better serve Jesus. We create an appointment and place for daily and weekly prayer. We pray in the morning, during lunch, and before going to bed. At least weekly, we create an appointment with God where we dedicate time away from our daily lives and, if we are able, travel to meet God with the intent of praying, meditating, and receiving a word from Him. We find that merely establishing a regular routine allows time to build a deeper connection with the Holy Ghost. Some of us take our prayer practice outdoors by going on prayer walks and finding a peaceful spot in nature. We use this time to pray, meditate, and simply reflect on the wonder of the world around us. Others keep a prayer journal and write down their thoughts, prayers, requests, and reflections. This is a private space where we express our feelings, gratitude, and concerns while watching God deliver results into our lives without any thought or effort on our part. Keeping a record of our prayers is a great way to help us better see God at work in our lives and along our spiritual journey. There is nothing greater than going back through a prayer journal and realizing all that God is doing in our lives.

Seeking communion with God is a profound and intimate aspect of our recovered life. Here are some ways we foster a deeper communion with the Holy Ghost. In addition to engaging in regular prayer and meditation to quiet our minds, open our hearts, and create space for communion with God, we delve into the sacred scriptures or texts of the Bible. Reading and contemplating the teachings of the Bible provides profound insights and a deeper understanding of God's nature and purpose. We seek to embody the teachings of our faith through acts of love towards others. By serving for others, we experience a sense of communion with God through our actions. We are careful not to become enabling. Taking time to retreat from the busyness of daily life and spending moments of solitude to commune with the Holy Spirit is always fulfilling. Retreats, whether formal or informal, are opportunities for deeper introspection, service, and ministry. We participate in communal worship and gatherings with like-minded people. Being part of a spiritual community offers a sense of shared devotion, strengthening our communion with God through collective prayers and worship. Remember that seeking communion with God is a journey, and there is no one-size-fits-all approach. Different practices work for different people, and the key is to find what resonates with our hearts and aligns with our beliefs. We listen to our inner voice and follow the path that brings us closer to the Lord.

Immersing ourselves in scripture is a wonderful way to deepen our understanding of recovery and connect with its teachings. There are many different ways we do so. As in prayer, we set aside time each day and week to read the sacred scriptures of the Bible. Creating a reading plan that allows us to cover the entire text systematically, or focusing on specific passages that resonate with our current life circumstances, are ways that encourage us. Many of us join a scripture study group, one with like-minded people. Discussing the scriptures with others provides valuable new perspectives that many of us have not considered on our own. Some of us even memorize meaningful verses from the scripture. By internalizing these verses, we carry them with us throughout our day, allowing for continuous reflection on their meaning. Many read commentaries and devotional books related to the words of the Lord. These resources provide valuable context, historical background, and interpretations that enrich our understanding of the majesty of God. We use meditation to immerse ourselves deeply in the scripture. We read a passage thoughtfully, allowing the words to penetrate our hearts and minds. We ponder the message and how it applies to our lives today. Additionally, combining our scripture immersion with prayer is a powerful way to connect with the Holy Ghost and seek His guidance. We are reminded to be patient with ourselves and take our time to absorb the teachings. Remember, the goal is not merely to read the words, but to let them transform our thoughts, actions, and lives.

Joining fellow believers in fellowship is an essential aspect of our recovered lives. It provides a sense of shared devotion. Attending regular worship services and congregational gatherings at our place of worship is paramount to joining in fellowship. These services include communal prayers, hymns, and teachings from religious leaders, which foster a sense of shared reverence. We participate in small group meetings and study circles within our religious community. These gatherings offer a more intimate setting for discussion, sharing personal experiences, and engaging in deeper study of sacred texts. Get involved in community outreach and service projects organized by our religious community. Serving others together deepens our connection with fellow believers and strengthens the bonds of empathy. As stated before, attending spiritual retreats, workshops, and conferences organized by our faith community provide opportunities for spiritual growth, self-reflection, and renewed commitment to our beliefs. Some participate in religious celebrations and festivals, which involve communal worship, feasts, and spiritual activities. These events celebrate the shared identity and beliefs of the recovery community. Through fellowship, we not only find encouragement from others on a similar path but also have a chance to learn from each other's perspectives. It's a reminder that we are not alone in our spiritual journey and that there is a collective strength in walking the path of faith together.

Recognizing the "casting out" steps of remission, we strengthen our spirits through our Lord, Jesus Christ. In the *fourth measure* of faith, we will ally ourselves with God, His holiness, and other believers. Our trust in faith continues to grow.

Faith and Goodness.

CHAPTER 21

FOURTH MEASURE OF FAITH

Allying in restitution, we became Spiritual servants of Jesus Christ and His children.

"The King will reply, 'Truly I tell you, whatever you did for one of the least of these brothers and sisters of mine, you did for me.'"
(Matthew 25:40)

"Now that I, your Lord and Teacher, have washed your feet, you also should wash one another's feet.
I have set you an example that you should do as I have done for you."
(John 13:14-15)

"Carry each other's burdens, and in this way, you will fulfill the principle of Christ."
(Galatians 6:2)

> *"Each of you should use whatever gift you have received to serve others, as faithful stewards of God's grace in its various forms."*
> (1 Peter 4:10)

In this *fourth measure* of faith, we experience the profound entrance into the realm of holiness. As we transition from forgiveness to redemption, we encounter the powerful presence of the Holy Spirit. This comforting presence affirms our belief that the Comforter had entered our hearts and lives in a way that is indeed miraculous. Our posture shifts from clenched fists to raised palms, symbolizing our complete submission to God. We position ourselves as vessels ready to receive His heavenly flow, inviting Him into every aspect of our being.

As we enter this measure of faith, we remember the steps along the path of obedience and trust, aligning with God's salvation, redemption, and the experience of His presence. Just as the Israelites moved toward the Promised Land, we have been journeying toward the fulfillment of God's purposes in our lives. As we, who are recovered Holy Ghost-filled believers, journey in obedience and trust, we discover encouragement as we seek God's will, trust in His guidance, and depend on His provision. In every season of testing and abundance, we find assurance in God's faithfulness, knowing that He is with us and that our destination is the fullness of His promises. He indeed matches calamity with serenity. We are walking in the eye of the storm.

This measure of faith uncovers its roots in the taking of *steps seven, eight,* and *nine*. We thought we were making restitutions just to clean our side of the street. However, we discovered more. We began allying ourselves in each restitution. The roots of faith were sprouting the moment we began making the list of people we had harmed. The beauty is that the roots began the instant our testimony was formed. Once we got up from our knees after being granted the strength to go out, from that very moment, we embarked on this process. His bidding was for us to recognize that we are spiritual servants, His children, as He had exampled for us.

The Holy Ghost began a life-changing work in our souls, using His tools to prepare our hearts and remove any remaining obstructions. Sometimes, the process of removing the root of bitterness uncovered additional residual roots of strife, hatred, wrath, and envy. These too needed to be completely eradicated. With His double-edged sword, the Holy Ghost meticulously performed this purging in our hearts in *step four*. He now spills out from our communion into disciplined nourishment. Zayin from Vav has been spilled over in this measure of faith.

Furthermore, we experienced the breath of God, who revealed Himself as the door and the One who knocks. He made us aware of the existence of the door, a revelation we had not encountered until the second step of our journey. With the spark of God igniting within us, we understood that the cross was both a symbol of preparation and destruction. Throughout recovery, the cross is applied to our lives, shaping, and refining us.

The revelation of the cross and the breath of God brought us a deeper understanding of His divine process and purpose in our lives. We came to realize that every step we took was intricately connected to the work of the cross, guiding us further along the path of sacrificial holiness.

In recovery, we encountered the power of God as He rebuked the heathen and destroyed the wickedness within us, erasing them from existence. The destruction caused by sins such as addictions and alcoholism came to an end, and strongholds were left in ruins, the memory of them fading away. Amidst our pain, we pleaded for God to look upon us and He forgave our sins. We see clearly that He is close to those with broken hearts and saves those with contrite spirits. We learned to wait on the Lord and follow His ways, trusting that He would exalt us and grant us inheritance in the land. As we witnessed the downfall of the wicked within us, we saw His justice prevail and intertwine with our soul and spirit.

His Name is holy and revered, and His honor shall be exalted regardless of our conceptions. With our whole hearts, we cried out to the Lord, vowing to keep His principle and testimonies. We sought His salvation, eagerly meditating on His Word day and night. We called upon Him in truth, knowing that He is near to all who seek Him. In this journey of faith, we experience the closeness of God and His faithfulness. He is ever-present for those of us who call upon Him, ready to answer our prayers in truth. The Lord is eternal, and He has established His throne for judgment. He will judge the world with His righteousness.

We humbly ask the Lord to lead us in His truth and teach us His ways. Those who look to Him are enlightened. We let go of anger and forsake wrath, avoiding the path of evil. Sins such as addictions and alcoholism are cut off, and we who wait upon the Lord have inherited the abundant life God has intended for us. The Lord is gracious and full of compassion, and our house is blessed with richness. The old man was correct when He said, in His own way, "It gets gooder and gooder!"

The Lord teaches us the way of His principle, and we are faithfully following it until the end. He grants us understanding as we wholeheartedly observe His principle. He leads us on the path of His principle because it brings us delight. He causes us to incline our hearts to His testimonies and He guards us against covetousness. He turns our eyes away from vanity and He revives us according to His ways. He establishes His Word in our hearts, molding us into His servants, who are devoted to Fearing Him. He removes the reproach we fear and restores us, for His principle is good. We long for His principle; He revives us with His righteousness.

We continually speak of the glorious honor of His majesty and declare His wondrous works, because He is deserving of all praise. In this section of the book, we witness the profound wisdom contained within the verses. The desires of the humble are heard by God, and He prepares our hearts, attentively listening to our pleas. He is the just Judge who defends the fatherless and oppressed, ensuring that the wicked within us can no longer perpetuate its oppression. Integrity and uprightness serve as a shield, preserving those who place their hope in God. We called upon God to redeem us from all our troubles, recognizing His power to deliver us. The evil schemes of the wicked within us and coming against us lead to their own downfall, and those who harbor hatred for the righteous are left desolate. Yet, God redeems the souls of His servants, and we who trust in Him are given comfort and security. The salvation of the righteous comes solely from God; He becomes our strength during times of turmoil. With His deliverance, we are saved from the clutches of all that is wicked, no longer finding refuge in their unwavering trust. Throughout these verses, we witness the eternal nature of God's praise. The desires of the wicked eventually fade away, but His glory remains everlasting.

Our hearts' cries are for the knowledge of God's will and the power to carry it out. We long to be taught by His principle. Our lips overflow with praise as we meditate on His Word, for this principle of His is righteous. We seek His hand of assistance, having chosen to follow His ways. Our souls delight in His salvation, and we rely on His principle for sustenance. Despite moments of wandering, we d seek God, because we never forget His principle. We have been chasing God through these steps. We are Spirit chasers.

ק QUPH

This is the only time in our recovery that we see this principle. Building upon it, the "eye of the needle" offers valuable insights. In recovery, we focus upon His power. Each recovered Holy Ghost-filled believer has unique experiences that are utilized as building blocks for recovery, service, and ministry. Utilizing these existing elements is empowering during recovery. It involves redemption and repentance. It involves reevaluating our beliefs, faith, and efforts, and being open to evolving in our relationship with Jesus Christ.

Recovery benefits from a unified effort. This means seeking Jesus. We also seek support from various Holy Ghost-filled resources, including pastoral help, recovery communities, Holy Ghost-filled friends, and family. Unity in purpose helps foster a comprehensive approach to recovery.

The visual transformation of receiving with hands wide open toward the Holy Ghost creates a shift in perspective. Similarly, recovery requires recovered Holy Ghost-filled believers to reevaluate our attitudes towards ourselves, our struggles, and our daily repentance. Shifting perspectives open new possibilities and encourage Spirit-filled service and ministry.

The formation of the Holy Ghost coming upon us is wholeness, just as recovery aims to help us achieve a state of completeness by addressing physical, emotional, and spiritual aspects of our lives. It's a reminder that recovery is about admitting this Spirit into all parts of ourselves and integrating ourselves harmoniously under the umbrella of the Holy Ghost.

The flow of the Holy Ghost is continuous throughout recovery. Recovery is not a linear process; setbacks occur. However, the circular nature of the Holy Ghost's protection surrounding us reminds us that even in the face of difficulties, the journey continues, and that if we rely on God's power, recovery and salvation are granted. We remain in the eye of the storm. This guarantee is as dependable as the horizon.

The Holy Ghost experience is created through an anointing of our spirits in receptive mode, with arms wide open. In recovery, admitting repentance and being wide open to a new life is a requirement. This involves leaving behind old patterns of behavior and thought that no longer serve us and moving towards the healthier alternative, which is the Holy Ghost, Jesus within us.

By applying the experience of the Holy Spirit, being composed of receiving Him with arms wide open and the communion of the Word and our spirit to recovery, we gain insights into the nature of this journey. In holiness, we recognize service, ministry, and anointing! We understand the importance of unity, relying on God's power, and embracing repentance to achieve a fulfilling, purposeful, and recovered life. It's as if communion has been introduced into our lives and now it is spilling over unto others. The Spirit is the eye of the needle that we now thread.

Being recovered, we have experienced the breath of God and discovered its evidence as we did in *step six*. It is this breath of God that brought this new recovered Holy Ghost-filled life into existence. It was heard in the inhale of the inward movement of the Holy Spirit that manifested in our lives the moment we had that Name applied to us in baptism.

This revelation is an essential element of our lives today. In various spiritual practices, including prayer, fasting, meditation, and worship, focusing on this revelation is one way to commune with the Holy Spirit. Similarly, we are reminded of the Holy Ghost's presence within us and our communion with Him. God dwells among His people. We all feel God's immanence and closeness to us.

It behooves us to mention that speech is a powerful tool that can either elevate or lower one's spiritual state. Choosing words with intention and wisdom has a profound impact on ourselves and others, aligning our words with the breath of God. Contemplating the significance of the breath of God serves as a reminder to cultivate mindfulness and awareness of the Holy Ghost's presence in our lives. It encourages us to seek spiritual communion, practice gratitude, and approach this new life with a sense of awe and wonder.

The sound of this revelation is soft and gentle, arriving with an attitude of humility before the Father. Recognizing the breath of God within us leads to a deeper understanding of our place in the will of God and our role in the grand tapestry of His creation.

Overall, the concept of the breath of God offers a profound perspective on spirituality, creation, and our relationship with the Holy Ghost. It invites us to explore the wonderful mysteries of existence and seek the Holy Ghost's presence in every breath we take, as He gave up His breath for us on the cross.

ת TAV

The power of the Cross was first seen in the seed which was watered in *step one*. As the destination, sealing, completion, and fullness in recovery, the cross is the goal of achieving completeness in our new life. Recovery involves addressing various aspects of our well-being—physical, emotional, mental, and spiritual—to achieve a harmonious existence. The cross is also the place of new beginnings. In recovery, we undergo profound changes, leaving behind old patterns of behavior. This repentance marks the start of a new chapter in our lives, a new mindset.

The cross offers the Holy Spirit's protection, reminding us of God's safeguarding of His people. In recovery, the cross is the protection offered by the Father. In the Bible, Ezekiel describes the cross as being a mark of identification. In recovery, it is the Holy Ghost experience that marks our new identity in life, guiding us on the path to repentance, service, and ministry. The cross represents our daily sacrifice which is acceptance and surrender. We cannot experience the sacrifice of the cross without both. Recovery involves acknowledging our mistakes with honesty. Surrendering to the process of recovery and accepting the need for repentance are powerful steps in the journey toward healing and salvation. However, acceptance and surrender are not enough by themselves. They require more action. Therefore, we take up our cross.

The cross is the place where the kingdom of heaven manifested in this life. In recovery, this cross reminds us of our intimacy with God and our communion with the Holy Spirit which connects us to our purpose. The cross is His will.

Overall, the cross as a destination holds deep spiritual significance. When applied to recovery, it serves as a meaningful reminder of the redemptive journey toward completeness, the power of surrender and acceptance, and the communion with something greater than ourselves in the process of healing and salvation. We ally ourselves.

קהת KOHATH

In this measure of faith, we ally ourselves with others who have received liberation from the bondage of self. In recovery, the journey begins with recognizing and breaking free from the bondage of sins such as addictions and alcoholism, trauma, and all other negative influences that stand in the way of our usefulness to God and to other people. Like the Israelites' wilderness journey, the path to recovery is simple but not easy and is filled with unknowns. It involves navigating through challenging emotions, facing past traumas, and resisting temptations. The Israelites received guidance from God through Moses, and therefore we seek God and support from fellow brothers and sisters in Christ who have recovered and provide essential guidance during recovery. Those of us who have recovered now have the responsibility to carry this message to others, which further nurtures our recovery. This involves focusing on spiritual relationships, respecting God's boundaries, and loving our neighbor as ourselves.

This wilderness journey is a period of testing and preparation for those who are recovered, and this measure of faith is a time of service, ministry, and learning. It is an opportunity to develop biblical principles, rely on God's power, and gain insights into the Holy Spirit. Throughout recovery, trusting in the process, having faith in God, and believing in the power of the Holy Ghost are vital aspects of progress. Recovery is not an endpoint but a continuous process of service, ministry, and redemption. Reaching the "Promised Land" is achieving a fulfilling life, free from the chains of the emotional struggles of sins such as addictions and alcoholism.

We now journey together as a congregation, finding support within a recovery community, a network of recovered Holy Ghost-filled believers who understand and empathize with the challenges of recovery. We are encouraged to remember that recovery is a spiritual journey and that while each path is unique, the peril is common and we can unanimously agree that the solution is Jesus Christ. After all, recovery has a Name and it is Jesus.

The application of the principle in our lives here can be attributed to the fundamental value of humility. It served as the guiding principle from which three other principles emerged: the pursuit of peace, endurance in the face of persecution for the sake of righteousness, and Jesus. Initially, as we transitioned through this measure of faith which began during the seventh step of kneeling, this shift seemed uncomfortable and unattainable. However, with time, the promises embedded within these principles became evident in our lives.

The foremost promise was the inheritance of the life that God intended for us. In addition to this, there were further promises of being acknowledged as children of God, receiving the kingdom of heaven, and obtaining heavenly rewards. These promises unfolded as we admitted this humble principle and they began to shape our faithful journey.

In this fourth measure of faith, we journey into the benefit of the overarching promises and principles of the restoration *steps seven, eight*, and *nine*. Allying in restitution, we became Spiritual servants of Jesus Christ and His children (Matthew 25:40).

Step seven in recovery commenced this restoration. It emphasized the vital importance of humbly, on our knees, confessing our sins and God being faithful to forgive them and purifying us from all unrighteousness. This step was covered by Matthew 5:5, which aligns with this step and fourth measure of faith by highlighting the blessedness of those of us who are meek. It becomes the sincere desire built upon humility, confession, forgiveness, and spiritual purification.

Step eight focused on being willing to reconcile while also coming to believe that we have been given the kingdom of heaven. Matthew 5:5 covers this step by emphasizing the blessedness of those who are meek. It invites us to cultivate a deep longing for closer communion with the covenant-keeping God, seeking His guidance and aligning our lives with His will. Through humility, we develop a greater awareness of God's covenant, presence, and guidance in our lives, enhancing our communion with Him.

Step nine calls for us to be persecuted in the Name of Jesus. Matthew 5:5 covers this step and the fourth measure of faith by highlighting the blessedness of those who are meek. It emphasizes the fulfillment that comes from seeing God in His rebuilding of our lives based upon principles of recovery and practicing His righteousness in all areas of life. Through humility, we embody the message of being recovered and becoming a source of inspiration and guidance for others. We find ourselves doing what Jesus would do.

Moreover, Matthew 5:5 also conveys the promise that those who are humble shall receive the life that God intended for them. We are assured that we who actively pursue His righteousness and seek God's will experience a relationship with God, eternal hope, and peace. Matthew 5:5 covers *steps seven, eight*, and *nine* along with this fourth measure of faith in recovery. It emphasizes the blessedness of those who are humble, encouraging us to continue our service and ministry, seek a closer relationship with God, and live out the principles of recovery in all aspects of life. By reflecting on this, we who have recovered find love for others, share God's promises, and act as an inner witness of the Holy Spirit that our pursuit of His righteousness and commitment to recovery leads to a stronger relationship with God and a deeper sense of purpose in our journey of salvation.

These wonderful promises are only intensified by this *fourth measure* of faith. Again, in *step three*, we discovered that blessed are those who are meek: because they shall receive the life that God intended for them. *Step three* of the recovery process involved offering ourselves, establishing a vow through prayer, and repenting. The effectual fervent prayer of a righteous person avails much and acknowledges sins such as addictions and alcoholism in our backslidden lives. Now we see more and more how each step is intricately woven into the other. God is creating a new fabric for our lives, one of many colors.

In *step seven*, we recognized that blessed are the peacemakers. We seek God's peacemaking and are called the children of God. We realized our need for Jesus Christ and surrendered our will to God. *Step eight* declared that if we remember those who had something against us and become willing to first be reconciled to them all, ours is the kingdom of heaven. It speaks to the significance of the willingness to humbly pray for guidance, healing, recovery, and salvation.

In *step nine, we saw* where Matthew 5:11 and 12 states, "Blessed are those who are persecuted for my Name's sake; for their reward is in heaven." *Step nine* calls for us to do unto others as we also have them do to us except when to do so would injure them or others. Matthew 5:11 and 12 covers this step by highlighting the blessedness of those who are persecuted for His Name's sake, as rewards are laid up in heaven. We have been told time and time again that persecution for His Name's sake is often misunderstood as undue suffering, but in a spiritual sense, it refers to a gentle and humble reward God gives us and others. It involves surrendering our egos, pride, and self-will, and embracing an attitude of humility, teachability, and compassion. Being persecuted for His Name's sake enables us to see that God approaches us and others with empathy and a willingness to listen and support because we could not support ourselves.

In *step nine*, we who have experienced the Holy Spirit's anointing and have recovered were called to treat others as we would ourselves. This act requires persecution for His Name's sake to recognize that we are not superior or unique, but rather equal in our shared journey of healing. By embodying persecution for His Name's sake, we approach life with humility, offering support, encouragement, and guidance without judgment or superiority.

Furthermore, the promise in Matthew 5:11 and 12 that the persecuted for His Name's sake have rewards in heaven covers with the command of carrying the message of recovery. By living out the principles of recovery and practicing persecution of heart for His Name's sake, we contribute to the restoration and salvation of our recovery communities and society at large. We have rewards in heaven in the sense that His impact extends beyond ourselves, creating a more compassionate environment for all.

Outwardly, we learned that "Blessed are those who are persecuted for righteousness sake; for theirs is the kingdom of heaven" (Matthew 5:10). In the covering of the *fourth measure* of faith, the verse from Matthew 5:10 speaks of the importance of being persecuted for righteousness's sake. As we delve deeper into the principles and promises of faith, we come to understand the significance of this verse for our recovery, service, and ministry. In recovery, the mind plays a vital role in the process of healing and salvation. Renewing our minds allows us to break free from negative thought patterns and destructive behaviors, fostering a spiritual mindset. Matthew 5:10, which talks about being persecuted for righteousness's sake and receiving the kingdom of heaven, is connected to this process of mind renewal.

Being persecuted for righteousness's sake entails receiving compassion, forgiveness, and kindness towards both ourselves and others through prayer for the Holy Spirit. Admitting receipt of the Holy Spirit is vital because it enables us to live a life free from the bondage of sin and its guilt, shame, and self-condemnation that weighs us down in recovery. By submitting ourselves without reservation and receiving the Holy Spirit, we receive the kingdom of heaven. It is the will of God.

Moreover, being persecuted for righteousness's sake fosters healthy relationships and builds a supportive recovery community. When God removes the bondage of bitterness and judgment and offers the gift of the Holy Ghost and forgiveness, He opens the door to recovery and salvation, and we have received the kingdom of heaven. We are submitting to His will.

We look to serve others in faith. Covering this *fourth measure* of faith, Matthew 5:10 encourages us to have faith in the power of being persecuted for righteousness's sake. It assures us that by yielding to this persecution, we receive the kingdom of heaven. Having faith in being persecuted for righteousness's sake means trusting that the act of extending compassion and forgiveness is spiritually anointed by God. By embracing this, we invite the Holy Ghost, repentance, remission, healing, service, and ministry into our lives and the lives of others. This is fulfilling our once non-existent spirts. We discover that we have mental clarity and energy we never knew we had. The old man had to warn us to make time for rest because as the Spirit enlarges in our lives, our flesh was not designed to keep up with it. We had to schedule rest.

Throughout our recovery journey, we've learned the potency of being persecuted for righteousness's sake, especially in this fourth measure of faith. Admitting a persecution mindset and having faith in its anointed power allows us to experience the blessings of becoming persecuted for righteousness's sake. It frees our minds from bitterness and condemnation, strengthens our relationships, and fosters a compassionate environment for service and ministry.

Having become servants, we further see what Matthew meant when he said in 5:9, "Blessed are the peacemakers; for they shall be called sons of God." This verse relates to the mind and faith in the context of recovery. Therefore, we begin looking within.

Inwardly, in this measure of faith, the mind plays a crucial role in the healing and anointing process. It is through the renewal of the mind that we see God overcome our negative thought patterns, break free from destructive behaviors, and cultivate a spiritual mindset. Matthew 5:9 encourages us to embrace peacemaking as a fundamental aspect of our mindset.

A peacemaker's heart involves showing compassion, forgiveness, and kindness towards ourselves and others. It is an attitude that seeks to understand, empathize, and extend grace, even in the face of pain, hurt, or wrongdoing. Cultivating a peacemaking heart and mind is vital to this measure of faith.

First, peacemaking towards ourselves is essential in recovery. We understand that many of us in recovery carry feelings of guilt, shame, and self-condemnation due to past mistakes or the consequences of sins such as alcoholism and addictions. Admitting peacemaking involves admitting forgiveness, forgiving ourselves, and letting go of condemnation. It involves treating ourselves with kindness, understanding that recovery is a process, and being patient with the journey of healing and growth in ourselves and others.

Secondly, peacemaking towards others is crucial in building healthy relationships and fostering a supportive community in recovery. By extending peacemaking to others, we let go of bitterness, anger, and judgment. We offer understanding, empathy, and forgiveness to those who may have caused harm or have their struggles. Peacemaking opens the door to healing and salvation, both within ourselves and in our relationships with others.

In terms of faith, Matthew 5:9 encourages us to have faith in the power of peacemaking. It assures that those of us who practice peacemaking are called a child of God. Having faith in peacemaking means believing that the act of extending compassion and forgiveness has a Holy Spirit anointing. It means trusting that by admitting peacemaking, God creates healing, recovery, service, and ministry in our own lives and in the lives of others.

We learned the power of peacemaking from the seventh step. By embracing a peacemaking mindset and having faith in the power of peacemaking, we who have recovered experience the blessings of being a child of God. It allows us to free our minds from the burdens of bitterness and condemnation, cultivate healthier relationships, and create a compassionate environment for service, ministry, and anointing.

A measure of faith not only fosters the mind and faith, but it creates spiritual action from His promises and principles. This *fourth measure* draws these actions out of us. Recognizing the allying in restitution, we became Spiritual servants of Jesus Christ and His children (Matthew 25:40). We obtained this through spiritual action.

The allying of ourselves with God and His children is not a mere passing desire but a genuine yearning that propels us forward. It is more of His holiness that creates a love for others. We discover that seeking Him is daily bread for our souls, just as physical hunger prompts us to seek food.

We now know that true nourishment for our spirits is only found in His righteousness. We discover that while we have been preoccupied with the tiny morsels of these steps and measures of faith, Jesus has been preparing a buffet for us.

Guided by an inner alliance, we embark on a journey of spiritual action. Becoming spiritual servants of Jesus Christ and His children involves embodying the teachings of love, compassion, and service. There are many spiritual actions that ally us with restitution and help us fulfill this role. We engage in acts of kindness and compassion towards others, especially those in need. This involves volunteering at shelters, helping the homeless, supporting the sick and elderly, carrying the message to those sick and suffering from sins such as addictions and alcoholism, and helping those facing difficult circumstances.

Standing in this *fourth measure* of faith and looking back, we see it stated in *step ten* that we must continue to practice forgiveness and seek reconciliation with those we have conflicts or disagreements with. Now we can see how that drew upon the strength demonstrated through us from taking *step nine*. This whole recovery has been fostering healing and creating a harmonious environment within our recovery community. We continue to cultivate humility and empathy by putting ourselves in the shoes of others. We should seek to help them find God, who is the solution to their struggles, joys, and sorrows, and respond to them with empathy and support. We now stand up for recovery and advocate for the marginalized and oppressed needing salvation. Addressing recovery inequalities and working towards God-centered recovery is an important part of being a spiritual servant. We share the teachings of Jesus Christ and biblical truths with others in recovery. We do this through conversations, writings, and participating in recovery programs that promote the growth and effectiveness of God-centered recovery.

As discovered early in recovery, we dedicate time to prayer and meditation to seek guidance from God so that we know how best to serve others and fulfill His role for us as spiritual servants. We continuously ask Him to align our actions, intentions, and beliefs with His will. We work on growth and spiritual development, taking the prescribed action to align ourselves more closely with the values taught by Jesus Christ. We strive to be a source of support for those around us. Lifting others up with our words and actions fosters an atmosphere of spirituality and love. Being recovered, we demonstrate the values we hold dear through our new God-directed actions and choices. Leading by example inspires others to follow **RECOVERY 5:12's** path of service and compassion. In our recovery meetings, we foster an inclusive and welcoming environment, ensuring that everyone feels valued and accepted. Although repentance, baptism, and the gift of the Holy Ghost are our footing, we do want to create an environment where people want to stay. By incorporating these spiritual actions into our lives, we become more effective and compassionate servants of Jesus Christ and His children. Remember that the journey towards spiritual service is ongoing, and each small step taken with sincerity makes a significant impact on the lives of others and ourselves.

Recognizing the allying steps of restoration, we strengthen the spirit through our Lord, Jesus Christ. In the *fifth measure* of faith, we will bring the light God shines through us to Him and other believers. Our trust in faith overflows.

Meekness and Faith.

CHAPTER 22

FIFTH MEASURE OF FAITH

No longer walking in darkness, we now follow Jesus Christ.

"Then spake Jesus again unto them, saying, I am the light of the world: he that followeth me shall not walk in darkness, but shall have the light of life."
(John 8:12)

In the *fifth measure* of our journey, we wholeheartedly proclaim the marvelous works of God. Our rejoicing is directed towards Him as we sing praises to His Name, acknowledging Him as the Most High. We lift up our souls to God, placing our trust in Him as our Lord. We are determined to bless God at all times, and His praise will continually be on our lips. We choose not to fret or to envy evildoers, recognizing that they will, like we once were, be brought low like the grass and wither away like the green herb. With our whole hearts, we praise God and acknowledge the blessedness of those who Fear Him. We celebrate the blessings bestowed upon the recovered who walk in His ways and diligently keep His testimonies. We do not engage in iniquity but seek Him wholeheartedly. We are reminded of His command to diligently keep His principle, and we yearn for our ways to be directed according to His principle. By honoring His principle, we are not put to shame. We commit to praising Him with an upright heart as we continue to learn His righteousness. We faithfully keep His principle and His continuous guidance, knowing that He will not forsake us completely. We choose to enthusiastically praise God, the King, and we bless His Name for eternity.

The Lord is our keeper. In this fifth measure of faith, we have the assurance of protection of God's watchfulness. This intersects with new beginnings, renewal, and hope in this life with Christ. We begin to see the glory of the Lord in our daily lives, experiencing His presence.

We no longer walk in darkness. We recall that the fires of the tenth step still burn bright in our lives. Being poor in spirit, we hungered and thirsted after righteousness. He began shining His glorious Light through our lives. The ninth step showed us heavenly rewards as we committed to following Jesus Christ and were persecuted for His Name. This humility brought us the life that He had intended for us all along. He called us to be light bringers, bearing His marvelous Light to the world.

The eternal Lord has established His throne for judgment, and He will judge the world with His righteousness and administer justice with uprightness. We humbly ask to be led in His truth and to be taught by Him. When we looked to Him, we were enlightened, and our faces were not filled with shame. We let go of anger and forsake wrath. We no longer fret or are tempted to do evil, because we know how evildoers are cut off. But we who wait upon the Lord are inheriting the abundant life that God has intended for us. The Lord is gracious and full of compassion. In the house of the upright, there are spiritual wealth and riches. Teach us, O Lord, Your principle, and we will keep it until the end. Grant us understanding, and we will diligently observe Your principle with our whole heart. Guide us in the path of Your principle because it brings us delight. Incline our hearts to Your testimonies and guard us against covetousness. Turn our eyes away from vanity and revive us in Your way. We ask that God establish His Word to His servant, who is devoted to Fearing Him. We ask God to please remove the reproach we fear because His principle is good. We long for His principle; He revives us in His righteousness.

We speak of the majestic splendor of His glory and His wondrous works. As we delve deeper into prayer, we know that Jesus has seen it all. He beholds mischief and spite, ready to repay with a mighty hand. We who are poor entrust ourselves to Jesus; He is the helper of the fatherless. Consider our enemies within and without, because they are many, and they hate us with cruel hatred. Though the righteous face numerous afflictions, You, God, deliver us from them all. We have witnessed wickedness in great power, spreading itself like a green bay tree. Yet, in an instant, he passes away and cannot be found. The Fear of the Lord is the beginning of Wisdom. The wicked will see it and be grieved. Consider our affliction, Jesus, and deliver us, for we do not forget Your principle. Jesus, plead our cause and rescue us; He revives us according to His Word. Salvation is far from the wicked, for they do not seek His principle. His tender mercies are great, O Lord; He revives us according to His principle. Many are our persecutors and enemies, yet we do not turn away from Your testimonies. We are grieved by the transgressors who do not keep Your Word. Consider how we love Your principle; revive us, O Lord, according to Your lovingkindness. His Word is true from the beginning, and His righteous principle endures forever. He will fulfill the desires of those who Fear Him; He hears our cries and saves us.

God is a refuge for the oppressed, a haven in times of trouble. We who know Your Name put our trust in You, because You, God, have not forsaken those of us who seek You. You are the God of our salvation; we wait for You all day long. In just a little while, the wicked will cease to exist; their place is diligently considered, and it is no more. But the meek inherit the earth and delight in an abundance of peace. His righteousness endures forever.

We ask God to let His mercies come to us, O Lord, along with His salvation according to His Word. Then we have an answer for those who reproach us because we trust in His Word. We ask God to not take the Word of truth away from our mouths, because we have placed our hope in His principle. We make a covenant to keep His principle continually, forever, and ever. We walk in freedom because we seek His principle. We speak of His testimonies even before kings and are not ashamed. We find delight in His principle, which we have loved. We lift up our hands to His principle, which we have loved, and we meditate on His principle.

When we were in our wickedness, with our prideful demeanor, we did not seek God; He was absent from our thoughts. Our ways were always troublesome, and His principle was far from our sight. We scoffed at the mention of internal spiritual enemies. This thought brings us to the wonderful works of the Lord in the lives of those we now fellowship. It is a light shining brighter than any void.

This light of life no longer lets us who wait upon Him be put to shame; we once transgressed without cause and were ashamed. His light through our lives magnifies and exalts His Name. As light bringers, we commit our way to Him, trust in Him, and He makes His will happen. He brings forth our righteousness like the light and our justice like the noonday sun. The works of God are great. We who are called His children are mighty in this life. We find ourselves shining bright as long as we remain in Christ.

His Word is a lamp to guide our steps and a light for our paths. We have made a solemn vow to keep His righteous principle. We once were greatly afflicted; He revived us according to His Word. He accepted the willing praise from our mouths and is teaching us His principle through the light. Regardless of life's highs and lows, we experience the stability of His serenity. How could we ever forget His principle? Wickedness continues to set its little snare for us, but we will not stray from the light of His principle. We have taken His testimonies as our eternal heritage because they bring joy to our hearts and burn bright for others to see the greatness of our King. We are determined to keep His principle always, even to the end. God is great and greatly to be praised; His greatness is beyond comprehension. A light shut up in our bones is burning bright for His glory.

א ALEPH

Unity, Power, and the Creator. We have discovered the One who has all Power. That One is God and His Name is Jesus. Now, this Power has become the light in our recovery. Jesus is the Light that guides us on our journey towards healing and wholeness. It is the communion with the Holy Ghost and the source of wisdom that illuminates the path to recovery and salvation. Recovery involves discovering the true life and will that God has intended for us. Power, as the source of creation, is the return to our core, our spirit, and brings a reconnection with our spiritual roots during the recovery process. Recovery involves integrating different aspects of ourselves and achieving unity. There is power in unity, the process of bringing together fragmented parts of ourselves and finding harmony in Jesus Christ.

Power communes with redemption and the descent of the Holy Spirit into the material world. In recovery, this is the anointing power of the light that brings about a transformed mind. We are reminded that these are not just theories but are facts from our own experiences. Different people and spiritual traditions have their own unique interpretations of the significance of this Power which is God. Ultimately, this serves as a powerful tool for prayerful contemplation, inspiration, and finding meaning on our journey of holiness, service, and ministry.

ה HEY

Step six revealed that grace is the light in our recovery. The presence of the Lord is the aspect of God's breath that creates our new lives. It signifies the Power flowing into the world, sustaining life. In recovery, the revelation is that of the presence of the Power that breathes life into the recovery process, providing comfort. It is an open window. It is the sense of vision. In recovery, this revelation is gaining clarity on life, allowing us to see through the challenges that God has overcome in our lives.

Through recovery and salvation, we have been equipped. We have entered a state of completeness and are being armed with the tools needed for our race. Our lives appear solid, because of His strength and the support of the fellowship. In this race of holiness, this is a necessary reliance upon God's Power to overcome challenges and move toward healing and salvation.

We see the removal of barriers and the breaking through of obstacles in the recovery process, allowing ourselves to embrace our true selves and move forward with renewed energy. As with all revelations, interpretations vary based on individual beliefs, cultural context, and experiences. This revelation serves as a potent anointing for those of us seeking God in recovery, reminding us of the presence of light and possibilities for service, ministry, and healing.

ר RESH

We have discovered prayer and it being at the forefront of all our affairs. In recovery, prayer is the guiding light that leads us through challenges, illuminating the path to healing. Like a beacon of hope, prayer is a constant reminder for those of us on this journey of holiness that we are always only a prayer away from Him overcoming all of our problems.

Just as light reveals, prayer reveals the anointed power of examining the heart throughout recovery. Shedding light on our thoughts and behaviors leads to profound changes. It helps us gain new perspectives and bring about changed lives.

Prayer is the Holy Ghost's light shining upon those of us in recovery. It enables us to acknowledge the presence of the Holy Ghost, which is the source of our strength, providing comfort throughout this journey of holiness.

Prayer communes the spiritual and physical realms, emphasizing the unity between the material and the heavenly. This unity is the merging of the inner light within us and the Holy Ghost's light guiding us toward holiness, fostering a harmonious integration of mind, body, and spirit.

Prayer is how we observe God overcoming obstacles in our lives. In recovery, it represents the light that shines on the path to relying on God. It encourages us to rise above challenges, providing the courage needed to move forward. By incorporating light into our prayer, we emphasize the Holy Ghost's guidance throughout the journey of recovery and our identity in Christ.

וָו

Communion is the bridging element. It is the tent peg that we heard about from *step four* that links the spiritual and physical realms. In this sense, communion is a vessel through which the Holy Ghost's light flows into the material world, energizing creation. Communion satisfies our aspiration for His knowledge and Spirit. As a path leading upwards, communion is the journey toward greater understanding and the pursuit of His marvelous light.

Communion also connects concepts, bridging ideas together. In light, communion is the interconnectedness of all things and the unity of knowledge. It implies that different aspects of wisdom and understanding are interconnected, forming a cohesive whole, much like light illuminates and connects all that it touches.

Communion provides completion. Light, in a spiritual sense, is often associated with a sense of completeness. Thus, communion reaches a state of deepening our relationships with God and being encompassed by the attentiveness to the promptings of the Holy Ghost. It is the pathway that leads us towards greater revelation. It represents the light that shines upon the journey of learning, service, and ministry. It illuminates the way and dispels darkness.

Communion holds various connections to His light, representing the vessel through which His light flows into the world, the aspiration for spiritual revelation, the interconnectedness of His knowledge, the completeness that His light brings, and the guiding path of illumination. These associations emphasize the role of communion in bridging the spiritual and material realms, allowing the light of His wisdom and understanding to shine forth.

NUN

Final righteousness. In recovery and its relationship to His light, His righteousness is the pursuit of the anointing of our lives through the guidance of God's light. His righteousness is striving to live a life aligned with righteousness and the fruits of the spirit. It involves seeking forgiveness for past mistakes, making restitution with others, and watching God make positive changes in our behavior and character.

His Light is spiritually powerful throughout recovery. In the Bible, light represents God's truth, guidance, and presence (Psalm 119:105; John 1:5). In recovery, light is the path to healing and salvation. It represents the illumination of the truth about our struggles, the recognition of the need for repentance, and the hope found in God's redemptive power.

Righteousness in recovery is the decision to embrace God's light in the journey toward healing. As we seek His righteousness, we are led to confront our past ideas and attitudes with honesty, guided by the light of God's grace. Righteousness in recovery involves seeking God's wisdom as He overcomes our sins such as addictions and alcoholism. He overcomes our destructive patterns as we watch His light reveal areas that need a change of thinking.

The pursuit of righteousness in recovery means walking in the light of God's truth, acknowledging weaknesses, and surrendering to His redemptive power. This process brings about inner healing, service, and ministry as we come to terms with our struggles, take responsibility for our actions, and seek God as He overcomes our challenges.

In the recovery journey, being surrounded by a supportive community of recovered believers provides the accountability needed to stay on the path of His righteousness. Through this supportive network, we draw strength from God's light and find hope from others who have walked this path.

Righteousness in recovery is the pursuit of living in alignment with God's truth. As we embrace God's light and seek His righteousness, we experience repentance and remission of sins such as addictions and alcoholism in our lives, leading to a deeper connection with God and a path toward recovery. The combination of His righteousness and light highlights the journey of seeking God's truth, observing as His light illuminates the path of recovery, and experiencing the redemptive power of His grace and love in the process.

This final measure of faith brings great principles and promises. The overarching principles include the blessings that come with being meek and those that come with hungering and thirsting after righteousness. As we get into this final measure, we experience further blessings through more persecution for righteousness's sake and Jesus' Name. This does not deter us because we see clearly now the overarching promises that guarantee that we are living the life God had intended for us all along. This is coupled with more promises of being saturated with the Holy Spirit. The promises get even deeper for we now have the kingdom of heaven in our lives and our rewards are multiplying.

In this *fifth measure* of faith, we journey into the benefit of the overarching promises and principles of the transition steps from restoration to recovery. We now can see these transitional *steps in nine* and *ten*. We remember that "Blessed are the meek; for they shall inherit the earth" (Matthew 5:5) and "Blessed are those who hunger and thirst after righteousness sake; they shall be filled" (Matthew 5:6).

Step nine in the recovery process completes this initial restoration. It emphasized the vital importance of humbly making restitution and knowing God hears our prayers. God is faithful to forgive us our sins and purify us from all unrighteousness. Matthew 5:5 and Matthew 5:6 highlight the blessedness of those who are meek. It becomes the sincere desire to hunger and thirst after righteousness through humility, confession, forgiveness, and spiritual purification.

Step ten focuses on being willing to continue with a poor spirit to follow Christ while also knowing that we have been given the kingdom of heaven. Matthew 5:5 and Matthew 5:6 cover this step by emphasizing the blessedness of those who are meek. It invites us to cultivate a deep hunger and thirst for righteousness's sake. We seek a closer communion with the covenant-keeping God, seeking His guidance and aligning our lives with His will. Through hungering and thirsting for His righteousness in humility, we develop a greater awareness of God's covenant, presence, and guidance in our lives, enhancing our communion with Him.

Moreover, Matthew 5:5 and Matthew 5:6 also convey the promise that those who are humble and who hunger and thirst after righteousness shall receive the life that God intended for them and shall be fulfilled. We are assured that we who actively pursue salvation, complete recovery, seek God's will, and align our lives with His righteousness will experience a relationship with God's eternal hope, and peace. Matthew 5:5 and Matthew 5:6 cover *steps nine* and *ten* of the recovery process. It emphasizes the blessedness of those who are humble, encouraging us to hunger and thirst after righteousness. They encourage us to continue our service and ministry, seeking a closer relationship with God, and living out the principles of recovery in all our affairs. By reflecting on this, we in recovery find love for others, share God's promises, and act as an inner witness of the Holy Spirit. Our pursuit of His righteousness and commitment to recovery leads to complete liberation through a relationship with God and a deeper sense of purpose.

These wonderful promises only intensified in this *fifth measure* of faith. Again, in *step three*, we discovered that blessed are those who are meek: because they shall receive the life that God intended. *Step three* of the recovery process involved offering ourselves, establishing a vow through prayer, and repenting. The effectual fervent prayer of a righteous person avails much and acknowledges sins such as addictions and alcoholism in our backslidden lives.

In *step nine*, we recognized that blessed are those who are persecuted for the Name of Jesus. We are persecuted for His Name's sake and receive a reward in heaven. We realized our need for Jesus Christ and surrendered our will to God. *Step ten* declared that we are blessed when we realize we can't do anything from God, because only then will we submit to His will. This speaks to the significance of remembrance and willingness to humbly pray for guidance, healing, restoration, complete recovery, and salvation.

We first saw in *step nine* where Matthew 5:11 and 12 states, "Blessed are those who are persecuted for my Name's sake; for their reward is in heaven." *Step nine* called for us to do unto others as we also have them do to us except when to do so would injure them or others. Matthew 5:5 and 5:6 cover this measure of faith by highlighting the blessedness of those who are meek, hunger, and thirst after righteousness. We have been told time and time again that meekness is often misunderstood as undue suffering, but in a spiritual sense, it refers to a humble reward God gives us and others. It involves surrendering our egos and embracing an attitude of humility. Being meek, hungering, and thirsting for righteousness enables us to see that God approaches us and others with empathy.

In *step nine*, we who have experienced the Holy Spirit's anointing and have recovered are called to treat others as we would ourselves. This act requires the persecution for His Name's sake to recognize that we are not superior or unique, but rather equal in our shared journey of healing. By embodying persecution for His Name's sake, we approach life with humility, offering support, encouragement, and guidance without superiority.

Furthermore, the promise in Matthew 5:5 and 5:6 that the meek shall have the life that God intended for them and those who hunger and thirst after righteousness shall be filled aligns with the concept of carrying the message of recovery in this measure of faith. By living out the principles of recovery and practicing meekness, hungering, and thirsting after righteousness, we contribute to the complete recovery and salvation of our communities and society at large. We have received the life God intended for us and have been filled in the sense that His influence and impact extend beyond ourselves, creating a more supportive environment for all.

"Blessed are those who are persecuted for my Name's sake; for their reward is in heaven" (Matthew 5:11 and 12). In the context of the *fifth measure* of faith, the verse from Matthew 5:11 and 12 speaks of the importance of being persecuted for His Name's sake. As we delve deeper into the principles and promises of faith, we come to understand the significance of this verse for our recovery, service, and ministry. In recovery, the mind plays a vital role in the process of healing and salvation. Renewing our minds allows us to break free from negative thought patterns and destructive behaviors, fostering a spiritual and healthy mindset. Matthew 5:11 and 12, which talk about being persecuted for His Name's sake and receiving rewards in heaven, are connected to this process of mind renewal. We look to serve others in faith.

Being persecuted for His Name's sake entails being kind towards both ourselves and others through prayer. Admitting receipt of the Holy Spirit is vital because it enables us to live a life free from the bondage of sin and its guilt, shame, and remorse that weighs us down in recovery. By submitting ourselves without reservation and receiving the Holy Spirit, we receive rewards in heaven.

Moreover, being persecuted for His Name's sake fosters healthy relationships and builds a supportive community in recovery. When God removes the bondage of bitterness and judgment and offers the gift of the Holy Ghost and forgiveness, He opens the door to restoration, complete recovery, and salvation. These are our rewards in heaven.

In terms of faith, Matthew 5:11 and 12 encourage us to have faith in the power of being persecuted for His Name's sake. It assures us that by yielding to being persecuted for His Name's sake, we will have rewards in heaven. Having faith in being persecuted for His Name's sake means trusting that the act of extending compassion and forgiveness is spiritually anointed by God. By admitting being persecuted for His Name's sake, we invite the Holy Ghost into our lives and the lives of others.

Throughout recovery, we've learned the potency of being persecuted for His Name's sake, especially in the *fifth measure*. Embracing a persecution mindset and having faith in its anointed power allows us to experience the blessings of becoming persecuted for His Name's sake. It frees our minds from bitterness and condemnation, strengthens our relationships, and fosters a compassionate environment for recovery service and ministry.

Having become servants, we further see what Matthew meant when he said in 5:10, "Blessed are those who are persecuted for righteousness's sake; for theirs is the kingdom of heaven." This verse relates to the mind and faith in recovery. We must begin looking within.

In recovery, the mind plays a crucial role in the healing and anointing process. It is through the renewal of the mind that we see God overcome our negative thought patterns, break free from destructive behaviors, and cultivate a spiritual mindset. Matthew 5:10 encourages us to embrace persecution for righteousness's sake as a fundamental aspect of our mindset.

Being persecuted for righteousness's sake involves showing compassion, forgiveness, and kindness towards ourselves and others. It is an attitude that seeks to extend grace, even in the face of pain and hurt. Cultivating a persecuted heart and mind for righteousness's sake is vital.

First, persecution for righteousness's sake towards ourselves is essential in recovery. We understand that many of us in recovery carry feelings of guilt, shame, and remorse due to past the consequences of sins such as alcoholism and addictions. Admitting being persecuted for righteousness's sake involves embracing forgiveness. It involves treating ourselves with kindness, understanding that recovery is a process, and being patient with the journey of healing and growth in ourselves and others.

Secondly, being persecuted for righteousness's sake towards others is crucial in building healthy relationships and fostering a supportive recovery community. By extending being persecuted for righteousness's sake to others, we let go of bitterness, anger, and judgment. We offer forgiveness to those who caused harm or have their struggles. Being persecuted for righteousness's sake opens the door to healing and complete recovery, both within ourselves and in relationships with others.

In terms of faith, Matthew 5:10 encourages us to have faith in the power of being persecuted for righteousness's sake. It assures that those of us who practice being persecuted are called children of God. Having faith in being persecuted for righteousness's sake means believing that the act of extending compassion has a Holy Spirit anointing. It means trusting that by admitting being persecuted for righteousness's sake, God creates healing, complete recovery, service, and ministry in our own lives and in the lives of others.

We learned the power of being persecuted for righteousness's sake from the ninth step. By admitting this mindset and having faith in the power of being persecuted for righteousness's sake, we who have recovered experience the blessings of receiving the kingdom of heaven. It allows us to free our minds from the burdens of bitterness and condemnation, cultivate healthier relationships, and create a positive and compassionate environment. It allows for service, ministry, and anointing.

A measure of faith not only fosters the mind but also creates spiritual action from His promises and principles. This *fifth measure* of faith draws these actions out of us. Recognizing the transition from allying ourselves with Christ and His children to bringing His light into these steps of healing and complete recovery, we strengthen the spirit through the Name of our Lord, Jesus Christ. We obtain this through spiritual action.

No longer walking in darkness and now following Jesus Christ is not a mere passing desire but a genuine yearning that propels us forward. It is a holiness that creates a love for others. We discover that seeking Him is daily bread for our souls, just as physical hunger prompts us to seek food. We now know that true nourishment for our spirits can only be found in His righteousness.

Guided by this inner alliance, we embark on a journey of spiritual action. No longer walking in darkness and now following Jesus Christ involves embodying His teachings of love and service. There are spiritual actions that can facilitate this transition. We embrace Jesus Christ as our Savior and commit to following His teachings and example. We acknowledge past sins and seek God's forgiveness through sincere repentance. Letting go of the burdens of guilt and remorse, we see Christ's forgiveness renew our spirits. It never goes without saying that we establish a regular practice of prayer, as we foster a direct and personal communion with God. We seek guidance through prayer and meditative reflection. We are reminded once again to immerse ourselves in the teachings of Jesus Christ by studying the scriptures. We seek to practice His messages of love. We strive to live according to the commandments outlined by Jesus Christ. We always align our actions with His teachings, practicing kindness, honesty, and humility. Most of us engage in acts of service and selflessness, following Christ's example of love for others. Some look for opportunities to help those in need, both within our community and beyond. We all nurture a deep and abiding faith in God and Jesus Christ. We trust in His wisdom as we navigate life's challenges. We encourage you to join a recovery community of believers who support and encourage one another in our spiritual journeys. We look forward to participating in worship services and fellowship to strengthen our faith. We practice gratitude for the blessings and gifts in our lives. We recognize God's hand in every aspect of our existence. We become a spiritual influence in the world by watching our faith and love for Christ shine through our actions, words, and interactions with others.

Remember that the process of following Jesus Christ is a lifelong journey. We were told to be patient with ourselves and remain open to service, ministry, and being recovered. As we consistently engage in these spiritual actions, we find ourselves increasingly aligned with Christ's teachings and experiencing a deeper communion with God's love and salvation.

Recognizing the light bringing steps of complete recovery, we strengthen the spirit through our Lord, Jesus Christ. In this final measure of faith, our trust in Him is our guiding light.

The final reward is knowing and seeing His Power demonstrated through our lives as we give Him more praise and exaltation. Not only because of the wonderful principles and promises that have evolved with each step but with the retrospective review of the journey we have traveled thus far. All the steps and measures of faith have produced an abundance of thanksgiving, so much that we cannot simply contain it! We must do something about it. Therefore, we enter His gates with *this ice chest full of thanksgiving*.

Temperance and Meekness.

CHAPTER 23

FAITH IN ACTION

"What doth it profit, my brethren, though a man say he hath faith, and have not works? can faith save him? If a brother or sister be naked, and destitute of daily food, And one of you say unto them, Depart in peace, be ye warmed and filled; notwithstanding ye give them not those things which are needful to the body; what doth it profit? Even so faith, if it hath not works, is dead, being alone."
(James 2:14-17)

My dear friend,

It's good to see that you have journeyed along a beautiful path of righteousness. When you have arrived at this point, having taken these steps of righteousness, I must share some good news with you.

Just this morning, the break of this day finds us at Heaven's door, a place where grace abounds. We've been here before. Familiar words and phrases echo in our souls. Now we dare to venture where the Spirit's winds blow. Can I challenge you to recall the moment when you were found, in the arms of God's mercy, firmly and sound? I can see you now standing before the throne, filled with Holy Fire.

As a preacher, fueled by Holy Ghost pride, I declare that you have been called to proclaim the Gospel's truth, to guide lost souls back to the fountain of childlike faith. To speak in tongues of fire, with anointed speech, because in the rooms of recovery, God's grace we reach.

I preach of the Holy Spirit's power, the healing it brings as we surrender our sins such as alcoholism and addiction, and our hearts take wing. In the fellowship of **RECOVERY 5:12**, a family we've become, united by our struggles, and by God's grace we overcome. We've been invited, filled with the Holy Ghost, to witness miracles, to testify the most. To believe in supernatural transformations, in the Name of Jesus, we find our salvation.

So let us gather, as a recovered congregation, to seek the Spirit's guidance, to find freedom. In the power of the Cross, we find redemption's key, as preachers, we lead by example, you see.

Your brother,

    The Preacher

Greetings! We, who are bound by the love of God and the Lord Jesus, extend our heartfelt message to all those who have courageously embarked on their journey of recovery. We acknowledge the seeds of transformation that have been planted within each of us, and we write this letter to reach out to everyone who is taking steps toward healing and recovery.

Dear fellow believers,

We want to encourage you that even in the midst of difficulties and challenges in recovery, there is an opportunity for you to experience immense joy. It is during these moments that your faith is refined, and as you persevere, it activates a power within you that enables you to endure all things. With each trial, your endurance grows stronger, and it allows the perfection of the Holy Spirit to permeate every aspect of your being, leaving no area lacking. Admit these trials as a pathway to greater transformation.

When any of us find ourselves longing for wisdom, we can confidently ask God for it, knowing that He generously gives without condemning us for our past failures. He showers us with His grace and extends His open hand to us. However, it is important that we approach Him with unwavering faith, without doubting His ability to provide. The one who is unsure, believing one moment and doubting the next, is like a ship tossed in the rough seas, unstable and constantly shifting. Such a person experiences a life of ups and downs, never finding firm footing. In recovery, half measures avail us nothing. We must wholeheartedly commit ourselves and remain steadfast, for being indecisive and wavering only leads to irritability, restlessness, and discontentment. In that state, we cannot expect to receive anything from the Lord. Therefore, let us approach Him with resolute faith, trusting in His wisdom to guide us in recovery.

The believer who recognizes their poverty of spirit has every reason to boast, for they have been exalted by God. Those of us who were once consumed by pride now boast about how God has humbled us. We have learned that all earthly glory is fleeting, like a wildflower that withers under the scorching heat of the sun. The false pride we once held onto in our pursuit of worldly prosperity has lost its allure. We now understand that this world is transient, and our hope is anchored in things above. Despite the trials we face, our faith remains steadfast, and we continue to experience the abundant blessings of God. True happiness is found when our faith withstands the tests and trials, and we receive the victorious crown of life that God has promised to all who love Him. So let us rejoice in our humbled state, knowing that in our weakness, God's strength shines through.

When we face temptation in recovery, we must remember that God is not the one tempting us. It is our own desires and thoughts influenced by sins such as alcoholism and addictions that lead us towards selfishness, darkness, and destructive behaviors. We must be mindful that our sin-driven desires such as addictions and alcoholism lure us away from our path to recovery. These selfish desires give birth to actions that perpetuate our sins such as alcoholism and addictions, and we harm ourselves and others. We must not deceive ourselves by blaming external factors; instead, we take responsibility for our own actions. We acknowledge that God is pure and free from sin, and as we grow in our understanding of Him, we recognize His unwavering love. We strive to align our thoughts with His life-changing power, seeking His strength to overcome temptation which is true freedom in recovery.

Every gift that God freely bestows upon us in recovery is good and perfect. These gifts come from the Father of lights, overflowing with completeness, abundance, and sufficiency. Through our faith in Jesus, we are called to be the light of the world, shining brightly amidst the darkness of sins such as alcoholism and addictions. God, as our loving Father, has brought us into a new birth, transforming us from within. We are born from above, filled with the Holy Spirit, and destined to radiate the light of Christ. Jesus, the unchanging source of heavenly light, has called us to be born again, to experience a transformation of our hearts and minds. It is through God's pure desire that we are given this new birth, bringing Him glory, and breaking the cycle of sin and death. This new birth is brought about by the truth of God's infallible Word, the promises of the unbreakable new covenant in Christ. Through this birth, we fulfill God's chosen destiny for us, becoming a chosen people out of all His creation. We are like the first fruits of His creation, a symbol of the greater spiritual harvest yet to come. Our lives serve as a pledge for God's ongoing work of spiritual transformation in us and in the world around us.

Let these words sink deep into your heart: Be quick to listen and slow to speak. In recovery, it is crucial that we cultivate the art of listening. We must listen to one another, opening our hearts to truly empathize. We must listen for God's voice, seeking His wisdom in every step. And above all, we must listen to His Word, as it penetrates our souls and transforms us from within. God has given us the capacity to listen with compassion.

Let us also be slow to anger. We recognize that human anger is not a tool that promotes God's righteous purpose. When we find ourselves angry or disturbed, it is an invitation to examine our hearts. Where are we harboring selfishness, fear, dishonesty, and inconsideration? We are called to abandon all forms of morally impure, self-centered, and wicked conduct, as these are rooted in demonic activities. Instead, with gentle and meek hearts, we surrender ourselves to God's life-changing work.

With a sensitive spirit, we absorb God's Word, allowing it to take root in our hearts. The Word of Life, the power of God's truth, has been implanted within us, ready to deliver us and save our souls. It is through the power of God's Word that we experience salvation—a salvation that encompasses our entire being, including our personalities, emotions, and thoughts. It is a salvation that extends beyond this temporal life and reaches into eternity. May we cling to the Word of Life and seek it to guide us on the path of true and lasting salvation. We do not just listen to the Word of Truth and not respond to it, for that is the essence of self-delusion and self-deception. His Word is like poetry written and fulfilled by our lives! Be ye doers of the Word, and not hearers only, deceiving your own souls. Be a doer of the Word!

In our recovery, we listen intently to the Word of truth and let its message penetrate our hearts. It becomes like a mirror that reflects our true selves, showing us who we are meant to be. We examine the face we were born with, recognizing the potential that lies within us. Through the mirror of the Word, we see ourselves as God sees us, unblemished by the destructive effects of sins such as alcoholism and addictions.

As we step out into the world, we hold onto our true identity, remembering where we come from. We fix our gaze on the principles that bring freedom and healing. The principle of love reminds us to extend compassion to ourselves and others. The principle of liberty guides our words and actions, as we strive to live in alignment with recovery.

We are judged by the standard of freedom, and so we speak and act in ways that honor this principle. We let the truth we hear captivate us, strengthening our resolve and providing us with the blessing of new hope. The truth empowers us to navigate the challenges of sins such as alcoholism and addictions, equipping us with the tools and mindset needed for lasting recovery.

We hold fast to the truth that captivates our hearts and allows transformation to take place within us. As we immerse ourselves in the Word of God, may it provide us with the strength to overcome the challenges we face, the courage to embark on the healing process, and the joy of living a life liberated from the clutches of sins such as alcoholism and addictions.

In all that we do, let us remember the words of Jesus, who promises blessings for those who listen to the Word of God and diligently follow its guidance. We are attentive to His teachings, seeking wisdom and direction for recovery. By carefully obeying the truth we hear, we align ourselves with the divine plan for our lives and open the door to God's blessings which have life-changing power.

As we walk this path of recovery, the Word of God is our compass, guiding us towards freedom. We find comfort in its pages, drawing strength from the promises it holds. Let us embrace the blessings that come from listening and obeying, experiencing the abundant life that Jesus offers to all who trust in Him.

We continually seek the truth, listen attentively, and obey wholeheartedly, knowing that in doing so, we walk in the path of God's blessings and find lasting transformation. It is essential for us to not only believe in our relationship with God but also to actively guard His Words within our hearts. When we neglect to do so, our hearts start drifting away, causing our journey in faith to become devoid of true meaning. Merely claiming to be recovered without guarding our speech is self-deception, rendering our faith useless.

Recovery, true spirituality, and genuine ministry, which are pleasing to the Lord, involve making a tangible difference in the lives of those who are marginalized and suffering inside and outside the rooms of recovery. It means reaching out to the addict and alcoholic and offering them this solution. It means searching for the orphans, the lonely, the abandoned, and the widows, offering them comfort and support in their distress. Searching for those who have no recovery lineage who other self-help programs have not worked or who are considered to have never had recovery and for those who have been separated from recovery. It also means resisting the corrupting influences of the world and upholding values that are in alignment with God's teachings.

Guarding our words and engaging in compassionate action are integral aspects of our spiritual growth and the manifestation of our faith. By being mindful of our speech and using our words to build up, encourage, and bring healing, we demonstrate the transformation that God's grace has brought into our lives. Additionally, by actively seeking to alleviate the suffering of others, we embody the love and compassion of Christ, reflecting His character to the world.

Let us continually strive to align our words and actions with the teachings of God. We guard our hearts, speak words of life and encouragement, and engage in acts of kindness, especially towards those who are in need. In doing so, we embody true ministry that pleases our Lord and brings transformation to those around us.

Dear fellow servants in glorious recovery, we must confront the harsh reality that our faith in the Lord Jesus Christ cannot coexist with prejudice. It is a battle we must fight within ourselves to overcome selfish desires and judgmental attitudes.

In the depths of our sins such as addictions and alcoholism, we were often swayed by appearances and worldly standards. We were captivated by the allure of certain individuals who seemed to have it all while overlooking those who were broken and struggling. But now, as we walk this path of recovery, we must reject such biases and embrace a new mindset.

Picture this scene: A person of our specific type of addiction and belief enters our recovery meeting, adorned with "successful brand of recovery," while a fellow suffering with another form of hurt, habit, or hang-up, dressed in rags, also joins us. If we show preferential treatment to the "recovery" individual, offering them a place of honor while disregarding or demeaning the one in spiritual poverty, we reveal the ugliness of prejudice and the impact of our sin-driven judgment.

But let us not be discouraged, for our journey towards healing requires us to adopt a different perspective. The foundation of our recovery lies in the teachings and example of Jesus, who calls us to love one another unconditionally and without bias. We are challenged to look beyond the external trappings and see the humanity and worth in every person we encounter. That's the gold in us all.

As recovered addicts and alcoholics, we know the pain of being judged and marginalized. Let us use that knowledge to break the cycle of discrimination within ourselves, our churches, and our recovery community. Our experiences have taught us the power of empathy. Just as we received support, so must we extend the same to our fellow servants, regardless of their appearance, background, or social status.

In our pursuit of recovery, we must examine our hearts honestly and seek the guidance of our Lord and Savior. Recovery empowers us to eradicate any remnants of prejudice which is the source of favoritism. Let us stand united, servants against sin such as addictions and alcoholism, showing love and equality to all who join us on this challenging journey.

With the strength and grace bestowed upon us, let us break the chains of judgment and embrace a recovery community built on support and solidarity. Together, we inspire change through demonstration of the life-changing power of recovery.

Our faith in the recovery process ignites a passion within us to treat every individual, regardless of their outward appearance or past struggles, with dignity, respect, and fairness. As we stand shoulder to shoulder, we reject prejudice and selfish judgment, and instead radiate the unwavering love and compassion that comes from our shared experience of battling sins such as alcoholism and addictions.

In the fellowship of recovery, let us forge a path of healing, encouraging one another to rise above the stigmas that plagued our lives. Together, we create a haven where all are valued, regardless of their circumstances. Keep fighting, fellow servants, and let us extend a hand of compassion to all who seek refuge in our shared journey of recovery.

Listen closely, for the voice of God resounds with a powerful message to us, the broken and addicted. He has chosen the ones considered foolish by the world's standards to confound the wise. Scripture declares, "But God chose what is foolish in the world to shame the wise; God chose what is weak in the world to shame the strong; God chose what is low and despised in the world, even things that are not, to bring to nothing things that are" (1 Corinthians 1:27-28).

We, the chosen ones in recovery, are heirs to the kingdom that God has promised to those who love Him. Yet, in our pursuit to impress others and feed our ego, we have insulted and overlooked those who are broken in spirit. Scripture rebukes us, "Do you not have houses to eat and drink in? Or do you despise the church of God and humiliate those who have nothing? What shall I say to you? Shall I commend you? In this matter, I will not praise you" (1 Corinthians 11:22).

Ironically, it is the elite members of recovery who exploit us and drag us into the courtroom of addictions and alcoholism. They mock the Name of our Savior, the very Name that we now bear since our commitment to recovery. They seek to undermine our progress and defile the reputation of the One to whom we belong and who has all Power. They cry that sobriety is not enough, yet wave books promoting sobriety without salvation. Be ever watchful of these big book Pharisees and recovery Sadducees. Although their motives may be good.

Let us heed the Scriptures and align our actions with recovery and salvation. We must not be swayed by the allure of worldly pleasures or prioritize the prideful over those who are broken and struggling. Instead, let us honor the Name of our Lord by showing compassion to all, especially to our fellow alcoholics and addicts who are seeking healing. As heirs of God's kingdom, let us shine as beacons of hope in the darkness of sin such as alcoholism and addictions, defying the norms of society and standing up for the marginalized. Our lives are a living testament to the life-changing power of our faith in Jesus Christ, and we never waver in our commitment to uplift and encourage our brothers and sisters who are sick and suffering.

Let us embrace our calling and boldly proclaim the Name of our Lord, extending a helping hand to those who are lost and broken. Our actions reflect the grace and redemption found in the Scriptures, and we are a source of inspiration and strength to one another.

With hearts full of gratitude and humility, let us remember that our true wealth lies not in material possessions, but in the eternal inheritance promised to us by our loving God. Together, as a community of recovered addicts and alcoholics, let us live out our calling, united in purpose and devoted to serving others in the Name of our Lord. For there is no salvation in any other Name.

Our calling is to wholeheartedly embrace and embody the royal principle of love. This principle, bestowed upon us by our King, transforms us into His royal sons and daughters, heirs of His kingdom. It compels us to love unconditionally, treating others with genuine care. It permeates every aspect of our lives, guiding our decisions and interactions. As we walk in unity, supporting and uplifting one another, our love becomes a testimony to the life-changing power of God's grace. Let us be known for our unwavering commitment to this principle, reflecting the character of our King and making a lasting impact on the lives of those around us, bringing glory to His Name. The principle of Love as given to us in this Scripture: "You must love and value your neighbor as you love and value yourself!" This principle seen in recovery strongly resonates throughout the Scriptures:

> *"Thou shalt not avenge, nor bear any grudge against the children of thy people, but thou shalt love thy neighbor as thyself: I am the Lord"* (Leviticus 19:18).

> *"Honor thy father and thy mother: and, Thou shalt love thy neighbor as thyself"* (Matthew 19:19).

> *"And the second is like unto it, Thou shalt love thy neighbor as thyself."* (Matthew 22:39).

> *"And the second is like, namely this, Thou shalt love thy neighbor as thyself. There is none other commandment greater than these."* (Mark 12:31).

> *"And he answering said, Thou shalt love the Lord thy God with all thy heart, and with all thy soul, and with all thy strength, and with all thy mind; and thy neighbor as thyself"* (Luke 10:27).

> *"For this, Thou shalt not kill, thou shalt not steal, Thou shalt not bear false witness, Thou shalt not covet; and if there be any other commandment, it is briefly comprehended in this saying, namely, thou shalt love thy neighbor as thyself"* (Romans 13:9).

"For all the principle is fulfilled in one word, even in this; Thou shalt love thy neighbor as thyself" (Galatians 5:14).

Keeping the principle of love throughout recovery is not just a noble aspiration but an essential way of life. It is crucial to recognize that when we show prejudice, including favoritism and discrimination, we not only commit a sin but also violate the very foundation of this principle of love. It is a holistic principle that requires our unwavering obedience. Just as the one who tries to keep all the steps of recovery but fails in just one point is considered to have broken them all, so too, breaking the principle of love in any aspect renders our efforts incomplete. The same God who instructs us, "Do not commit adultery," also commands us, "Do not murder." These principles, along with the Ten Commandments of Scripture, such as "You shall not kill" and "You shall not commit adultery," emphasize the importance of upholding the principle of love in every aspect of our lives. Let us remember the weight and significance of this principle as we navigate recovery, seeking to embody it fully in our thoughts and actions.

It is essential to understand that adherence to one part of the principle while disregarding another still makes us guilty of breaking the overall principle. It is not enough to avoid committing adultery but engage in murder, for both actions violate the sacred principle we are called to uphold. Therefore, it is imperative that we align our speech and actions in every aspect, knowing that we are destined to be tested by the perfect principle of liberty. In recovery, we must exercise caution in passing judgment on others without extending mercy, for judgment without mercy invites severe judgment upon ourselves. By choosing to show mercy, we gain authority over judgment and seek the triumph of mercy over condemnation. Let us be mindful of the power of mercy as we navigate our recovery path, admitting it as a guiding principle in our interactions with others.

The power of faith is revealed through our actions. It is not enough to merely claim faith without demonstrating it through tangible good works. How can this kind of faith save anyone? Imagine if a fellow brother or sister in recovery is in desperate circumstances, lacking proper clothing and food, and we simply bid them farewell, offering empty words of warmth and sustenance without providing them with a coat or a cup of soup. What value does our faith hold in such a situation? Faith that remains idle and devoid of action is dead and bears no fruit. The Scriptures affirm, "Do you want to be shown, you foolish person, that faith apart from works is useless?" (James 2:20). Our faith must be alive and active. We cannot rely solely on empty declarations but must translate our faith into practical deeds. It is through our actions that we demonstrate the life-changing power of faith. Let us not deceive ourselves with mere words but engage in acts of compassion and tangible assistance. True faith is vibrant, intertwining with our actions to bring about real change in the lives of others. Our faith is alive and fruitful, inspiring hope and salvation on the path of recovery.

Some may raise objections, saying, "One person has faith, and another person has works." Well then, prove to us that you have faith without any evidence of transformation and recovery, and we will show you our faith through the tangible actions and steps we take in recovery. You can claim to believe in the existence of a higher power, a supreme authority. Scripture affirms, "Hear, O Israel: The Lord thy God is one Lord" (Deuteronomy 6:4). That's all well and good, but even the demons acknowledge this truth and tremble with fear before it. We once cowered in the depths of sins such as alcoholism and addictions yet remained unchanged—we remained enslaved to our demons of substance abuse.

O empty soul lost in the depths of sin, do you still question the undeniable truth that faith without the life-changing power of good works is void? It is through our actions, as we surrendered ourselves on the altar of the third step in recovery, that we found favor in the eyes of God. Our faith and our actions intertwined, harmonizing to create a symphony of transformation of mind. It is in this divine dance that the ancient Scripture was fulfilled:

> *"And he believed in the Lord, and he counted it to him for righteousness"* (Genesis 15:6)

Our belief in God became a currency, exchanged for His righteousness. Our faith, like a deposit, is credited to our account as righteousness. We have become passionate lovers of God, intimate friends bound together by a love that knows no bounds. Scriptures say:

> *"Art not thou our God, who didst drive out the inhabitants of this land before thy people Israel, and gavest it to the seed of Abraham thy friend forever?"* (2 Chron. 20:7)

> *"I will open rivers in high places, and fountains in the midst of valleys: I will make wilderness a pool of water, and the dry land springs of water"* (Isaiah 41:18).

Now, it's glaringly evident that our righteousness before God is not solely determined by faith alone, but by the life-changing power of our works. Let's take a look at the story of the former addict or alcoholic who through their courageous actions found favor in the eyes of God. They welcomed others into their broken life and helped them escape from the clutches of addictions and alcoholism. Just as a lifeless body, consumed by the ravages of substance abuse, is nothing more than a hollow shell, so too is faith without the active expression of good works. It is an empty and futile existence, devoid of the profound change and redemption that recovery brings.

We do not readily embrace the role of teachers on this journey, for we understand that those who instruct are held to a higher standard of scrutiny. We acknowledge our imperfections, particularly when it comes to our use of language. If we possess the ability to restrain the words we utter, we demonstrate mastery over ourselves in every aspect. This mastery indicates that our character is reaching for more spiritual maturity.

Just as horses have bits and bridles in their mouths, allowing us to control and direct their substantial bodies, so too do mighty ships, despite their enormity and propulsion by powerful winds. Yet, they are steered by a minuscule rudder, guided by the person at the helm.

The tongue, seemingly insignificant, wields an immense power that mirrors the grip of sins such as alcoholism and addictions. It boasts with arrogance and asserts dominance over our lives. Just like a small flame ignites a massive inferno, the tongue sets ablaze our souls with its unmanageable tendencies. It epitomizes self-centeredness, wickedness, and a realm of perpetual wrongdoing. This treacherous organ, the most dangerous within us, corrupts the very fabric of our recovery community, resembling a relentless fire spawned from the depths of sin such as addictions and alcoholism. It burns fiercely, fueled by the infernal flames of our addictive and alcoholic desires, consuming everything in its path. It engulfs our existence, persisting across generations, relentlessly spinning like the wheels of a destructive cycle.

Just as humans have successfully conquered every wild creature on this planet - from untamed beasts to soaring birds, slithering reptiles, and creatures of the sea and land - the tongue remains an untamed force. It embodies the essence of sin, an uncontrollable beast, spewing forth words laced with poisonous toxicity. It indulges in the evils of self-centeredness, devoid of restraint.

Ironically, we employ this very tongue to offer praises to our Lord God and Father, and yet in the next breath, we unleash curses upon those who are made in His own likeness. By cursing others, we presume to play God, exercising false authority. It is a disheartening reality: from the same mouth, we pour out words of worship, only to follow them with curses. Such a paradox should never be the case.

We do not search for olives on a fig tree or attempt to pluck figs from a grapevine. In the same vein, it is impossible for fresh, life-giving water to flow from a spring tainted with bitterness. Likewise, a bitter spring can never produce refreshing water.

Admitting the wisdom from above, those who consider themselves attuned to the ways of God should exemplify it through a beautiful, fruitful life guided by the gentle nature of wisdom. True wisdom does not seek to boast about its accomplishments. This humble demeanor is the true testament of genuine wisdom.

However, if we find a bitter or jealous spirit lurking within our hearts, we must not attempt to mask it through pretense. Such behavior is devoid of God's heavenly wisdom; instead, it aligns with the wisdom of this world, characterized by self-centeredness, wickedness, lack of spirituality, and behaving in a devilish manner, possessed of a demon. Whenever jealousy, which obsessively seeks self-promotion at the expense of others, and selfishness are uncovered, they pave the way for a multitude of troubles: chaos, instability, disorder, and all manner of malicious behavior. Wisdom possesses an unwavering purity, holiness, and an indescribable peace. It embodies profound consideration and an insatiable hunger for knowledge that only comes from the Lord. It thrives on correction, eagerly embracing the opportunity to refine itself. This wisdom is always open to persuasion, its foundations sturdy yet flexible, ready to yield to the insights of others.

In its essence, this wisdom is infused with a blend of love, captivating all who encounter it. It proudly shuns prejudice, refusing to don any form of disguise. Its authenticity shines through, radiating truth in all its forms. And from its depths springs forth a bountiful harvest of righteousness, a testament to its unwavering commitment to goodness.

The seeds of this wisdom are diligently sown through peaceful acts, nurtured by those who passionately embrace the art of forging harmony. These individuals cherish the pursuit of peace, tirelessly cultivating an environment where wisdom can bear fruit.

Living in close communion with God! The source of our quarrels with one another stems from the internal battle that rages within us as we strive to assert our own will, which is attempting to satisfy our selfish desires. Jealousy takes hold of our hearts, fueling a sense of superiority over others. Envy leads us down a treacherous path, where we plot to harm, driven by our insatiable cravings. This is why we find ourselves locked in quarrels, not just with others but also with ourselves and with God.

Sadly, we often fail to obtain what we desire because we neglect to seek God's provision. For our provision only comes from God through Christ Jesus. And even when we do ask, our motives are tainted by spiritual sickness. We are warned against offering prayers driven by selfishness. Some among us have become unfaithful, engaging in an unholy affair with the values of the world. Yet, we know that aligning ourselves with the world's ways puts us at odds with God. By choosing to befriend the world, we position ourselves as enemies of God.

Scripture teaches us that the Spirit God has breathed into our hearts is a fiercely devoted lover, craving an ever-deepening connection with us. The Holy Spirit pursues us relentlessly and takes it personally when we turn away from Him in pursuit of worldly friendships. Nevertheless, God continues to pour out His boundless grace upon us. His grace is a precious gift, even stronger and more powerful than before. As the Scripture proclaims, "He scorns the scornful but gives grace to the humble" (Proverbs 3:34).

We wholeheartedly surrender ourselves to God, standing resolute against the grip of the enemy as we resist his temptations. As we seek, we see God, and His divine presence embraces us, touching the depths of our beings. We are committed to cleansing our lives, acknowledging our flaws as sinners, and striving for purity, forsaking double-mindedness. The weight of our past actions weighs heavily upon us, evoking genuine sorrow and tears. Our once carefree laughter turns into mourning, and our joy is humbled into deep humility. With open hearts, we willingly embrace the path of humility before the Lord, and in His grace, He lifts us up, exalting our spirits and granting us salvation.

As part of God's family, we never speak against another family member, for when we slander someone, we violate and speak against God's principle of love. Our duty is not to make ourselves a judge of the principle of love. The Scriptures say:

> *"Thou shalt not avenge, nor bear any grudge against the children of thy people, but thou shalt love thy neighbor as thyself: I am the Lord"* (Lev. 19:18).

> *"Draw nigh to God, and he will draw nigh to you. Cleanse your hands, ye sinners; and purify your hearts, ye double-minded (James 4:8).*

We humbly recognize that we are not in a position to judge the principle that guides our healing process. Our duty lies in faithfully obeying this principle that aligns with our beliefs and values, trusting in the One who has all Power to save and transform lives. It is not our place to pass judgment on others, for we understand that we, too, have experienced the pain and struggles of sins such as addictions and alcoholism. Instead, we focus on our own spiritual growth, striving to live in accordance with the principles we hold dear, and extending compassion to fellow travelers on this path of recovery. In Jesus' Name, we seek humility, acknowledging our own vulnerabilities as we journey toward complete recovery and salvation.

We look back on the times when we used to make plans for worldly success, unaware of what the future held. We now understand that our lives are transient, like a fleeting breath visible in the cold, here one moment and gone the next. Instead, we now surrender our tomorrows into the hands of the Lord, recognizing His sovereignty over our lives. We seek to live each day to the fullest, following His guidance and admitting His will. Our past boasting was born out of ignorance, as it neglected the higher purpose and selfishly pursued our own desires. Through our recovery in Jesus' Name, we learn humility and acknowledge that true fulfillment comes from aligning our will with His divine plan.

If God reveals an opportunity to do the right thing today, yet we refrain from doing it, we are guilty of sin. Listen, as we reflect on our past, we realize the depth of our false pride and arrogance. The time eventually came when we were overcome by misery and tormented by demonic forces that manifest in sins such as addictions and alcoholism. Our pride, once so prominent, decayed into nothingness, our extravagant lifestyles crumbled, and our material possessions stood as corroded witnesses against us. We selfishly amassed treasures for our own gain, but they turned into flames that consumed our very beings.

Listen closely! We hear the anguished cries of those whose relationships we deceitfully withheld, those whose efforts we took advantage of. The pleas for justice from those we cheated have reached the ears of the Lord of hosts, the Almighty God. Jesus!

We confess that we indulged in every worldly luxury and pleasure, yet we were merely filling our hearts with temporary satisfaction, oblivious to the impending day of reckoning. We condemned and inflicted harm upon the innocent, those who lacked the power to defend themselves. Most grievously, we inflicted pain upon Jesus, the embodiment of righteousness.

Consequently, God resisted us, standing against our pride and sinful ways. We recognize the consequences of our actions and the divine intervention we face. In recovery, we seek repentance and strive to align ourselves with God's will beginning with the remission of sins such as addictions and alcoholism, seeking His forgiveness and salvation.

We have learned to cultivate patience, eagerly awaiting the glorious presence of our Lord. We long for each moment He manifests Himself and becomes visible, as He unveils His nearness that is and has always been by our side. Every day, we earnestly look forward to the return of our Lord Jesus Christ, and He appears in our lives through His creations.

We liken ourselves to farmers who patiently await the harvest, knowing that it will come in due time through the nourishment of both early and latter rains. Our hopes remain high, and we patiently endure, for we sense the imminent closeness of the Lord's presence. He draws near to us daily, taking us by the hands, guiding us in His divine providence. We find comfort in knowing that we are part of God's family, united in His love.

Amidst our journeys, we refrain from brainstorming or grumbling about one another. We do not place blame on others for our troubles, recognizing that true judgment rests with the Lord, who is near and stands ready to appear at any moment. We approach each other with love, understanding, and a spirit of unity, knowing that the ultimate Judge is at the gate, just waiting to reveal Himself and bring about divine justice.

We take and receive disciples as our mentors. They have prophesied in the Name of the Lord, by His authority. The Scripture says:

"Is any sick among you? Let him call for the elders of the church; and let him pray over him, anointing him with oil in the name of the Lord" (James 5:14)

The disciples of Jesus faced immense trials, yet they displayed remarkable patience in the face of adversity. We hold them in high honor as our heroes, recognizing their blessedness as they remained faithful throughout their sufferings.

Job's story is well-known to us, as we are acquainted with the tremendous challenges he endured. In hindsight, we now witness how the Lord demonstrated His incredible kindness towards Job, revealing His deep compassion. It serves as a reminder that even in the midst of great trials, God's loving care prevails.

"And the Lord passed by before him, and proclaimed, The Lord, The Lord God, merciful and gracious, longsuffering, and abundant in goodness and truth" (Ex. 34:6).

"But thou, O Lord, art a God full of compassion, and gracious, longsuffering, and plenteous in mercy and truth" (Ps. 86:15)

We embrace a lifestyle of unwavering integrity. We no longer feel the need to verify our words through swearing by the heavens, the earth, or any other oath. We have learned that true honesty comes from within, and our "Yes" or "No" holds undeniable credibility.

By staying committed to our recovery, we avoid falling into the trap of hypocrisy. As we seek God, our actions and words reflect our genuine transformation. In Christ, we are people of integrity, consistently honoring our commitments.

Through recovery, we have come to understand that being authentic is a crucial aspect of our healing process. By maintaining honesty in all areas of our lives, we build strong foundations for our recovery journey.

In this new chapter of our lives, we observe our integrity shining through, empowering us to live with authenticity. We embrace the teachings of recovery, knowing that our unwavering commitment to truthfulness strengthens our walk with Christ and His creation.

In times of great hardship among the believers in our fellowship, we wholeheartedly press them to turn to prayer at once, asking God to remove it. Prayer is the powerful tool that connects us with the divine, offering comfort and healing. We gather, lifting our voices in unity, interceding on behalf of those who are still sick and suffering.

Through prayer, we access power, guidance, and divine intervention for those facing physical, emotional, or spiritual maladies. We pour out our hearts, expressing our deepest concerns and placing our trust in God's loving care. In these moments of collective prayer, we find support, knowing that we are not alone in our struggles.

As a fellowship in recovery, we offer our love for the recovery and salvation of our brothers and sisters. We trust in the faithfulness of God, believing that He brings miraculous healing. Through the power of prayer, we stand together, united in our unwavering belief in God's mercy.

Our prayers access the source of power needed for the sick and suffering among us, reminding them of the healing power that flows through the grace of our Lord. Scripture says:

> *"And he spake a parable unto them to this end, that men ought always to pray, and not to faint"* (Luke 18:1)

> *"For if I pray in an unknown tongue, my spirit prayeth, but my understanding is unfruitful. What is it then? I will pray with the spirit, and I will pray with the understanding also: I will sing with the spirit, and I will sing with the understanding also"* (1 Cor. 14:14-15)

In recovery, we recognize the importance of fostering an uplifting ministry. When there are individuals among us who are experiencing joy in their recovery, we encourage them to express their gratitude and praise. Whether through music or singing we celebrate their progress and the joy that God has brought through their recovery.

On the other hand, when any member of our fellowship is grappling with sickness, which may include physical, emotional, or spiritual weariness, we call upon the elders of the church, many of whom are also in the recovery community. We humbly request their presence to pray over the sick and suffering individual and anoint them with oil in the Name of our Lord. Through prayer, we seek healing and salvation, believing in the power of faith and the support of our recovery community.

We understand that sins such as addictions, alcoholism, and the associated struggles are linked to underlying spiritual issues and past bonds. If there is sin and patterns of unhealthy actions that have contributed to the sickness or weakness, we acknowledge them and seek forgiveness and healing through the life-changing power of Christ. We have discovered God has been showing us this through recovery.

By offering prayers, anointing, and addressing the root of our troubles, we create a space for healing and salvation within our recovery community. We admit that true recovery goes beyond the physical, encompassing spiritual and emotional well-being. As we journey together, supporting one another with empathy, we trust in the Lord's ability to raise us up, restore us to health, and guide us toward a life of lasting recovery. Scripture says:

> *"For I have received of the Lord that which also I delivered unto you, That the Lord Jesus the same night in which he was betrayed took bread: And when he had given thanks, he brake it, and said, Take, eat: this is my body, which is broken for you: this do in remembrance of me. After the same manner also he took the cup, when he supped, saying, This cup is the new testament in my blood: this do ye, as oft as ye drink it, in remembrance of me. For as often as ye eat this bread, and drink this cup, ye do shew the Lord's death til he come" (1 Cor. 11:23-26).*

We find the Comforter as we search within the fellowship of believers. The old-timers who are in Christ recognize our struggle, extend forgiveness, and embrace us, understanding the battles we face. It is in this environment that we humbly acknowledge our wrongdoings, our faults, follies, and offenses, understanding the impact we have on others.

With contrite hearts, we confess our sins, laying bare our mistakes and seeking salvation. And in the presence of our fellow believers, we engage in the act of communal prayer. We intercede for one another, offering fervent supplications, knowing that within these heartfelt pleas lies the profound power waiting to be unleashed. If not special prayer meetings, we follow most of our recovery meetings with purposeful prayer among our willing members.

As individuals grappling with the realities of our humanity, we approach prayer with humility, recognizing our frailties. Yet, despite our imperfections, we pray with a resolute faith that surpasses our limitations. It is through this prayer intensity, this unwavering devotion, that we tap into the supernatural realm and witness divine intervention.

Within the sanctuary of prayer, a change of mind always occurs for those who refuse to leave this realm. We experience healing and salvation, not merely in the physical sense but also in the depths of our souls. The passionate prayers of godly believers reverberate with a tremendous force, evoking a response from a higher power. Miraculous answers manifest before our eyes, reminding us of the extraordinary possibilities that lie within the realm of faith.

So, in our pursuit of recovery, we find ourselves enveloped in a community that offers unwavering support. Within the context of prayer, we discover a source of strength that transcends our limitations, empowering us to overcome the challenges that beset us.

As members of God's beloved family, we go after the one who wanders from the truth and bring them back. When we restore the sinner back to God from the error of their way, we give back to their soul and save their soul from death. They are returned to spiritual life from spiritual death. We cover over countless sins, bringing about forgiveness through restoring the person back to God. To cover sin is atonement. This is our demonstration of love!

Welcome to the family.

CHAPTER 24

THE FELLOWSHIP OF PRAYER

*"And let us consider one another to provoke unto love
and to good works: Not forsaking the assembling of
ourselves together, as the manner of some is;
but exhorting one another: and so much the more,
as ye see the day approaching."*
(Hebrews 10:24-25)

With our newfound power of faith, we now discover unwavering support within the recovery fellowship of those who understand our struggles. The compassionate embrace of fellow recovered addicts and alcoholics, who have faced similar battles, offers forgiveness and acknowledges the profound challenges we endure. In this sacred space, we humbly confront our wrongdoings, recognizing the destructive nature of our offenses that have harmed both ourselves and others. With courageous vulnerability, we lay bare our sins, seeking salvation and healing. Within the collective prayers of our companions, we find the strength to intercede for one another, fervently pleading for divine intervention.

Despite our human frailties, we approach prayer with humility, recognizing our limitations while nurturing a steadfast faith that transcends our struggles. It is within the raw intensity of our prayers that we tap into Power, witnessing miraculous transformations within our souls and permanent recovery. The power of communal prayer resounds with an undeniable force, releasing a torrent of mercy, peace, and love upon our broken selves. Together, bound by our shared experiences and the unwavering support of our fellow recovered addicts and alcoholics, we embark on a life-changing journey of recovery, knowing that within the sacred realm of prayer, hope and recovery await us.

Our original intention was to share with you the remarkable psychic change and deliverance we have experienced throughout our recovery. However, we feel compelled to challenge you instead, urging you to fiercely defend your newfound freedom, persistently contend against the grip of sins such as addictions and alcoholism, and wholeheartedly engage in the ongoing race for salvation. It is on behalf of faith we embrace the beliefs that guide us, and it is through the life-changing power of being recovered that we address you. We do not merely speak of faith as a passive belief in a higher power; rather, it encompasses the profound body of truth we receive from the inspired Word of God. It is through this divine wisdom that God, in His infinite love, has entrusted us, His dedicated servants in recovery, with the tools and teachings that empower us to walk the path of lasting freedom which only comes from salvation in Jesus' Name. We were encouraged to fervently hold onto these truths, defend them against the onslaught of the lies of sins such as addictions and alcoholism, and continually add to our arsenal of recovery tools. Remember, these sacred truths have been entrusted to us, and it is our calling to honor and protect them, not only for our own recovery but also for the benefit of others who may embark on the same journey.

There have been some who have sneaked in among us unnoticed.

> *"For I know this, that after my departing shall grievous wolves enter among you, not sparing the flock. Also of your own selves shall men*

arise, speaking perverse things, to draw away disciples after them"(Acts 20:29-30).

"But there were false prophets also among the people, even as there shall be false teachers among us, who privily shall bring in damnable heresies, even denying the Lord that bought them, and bring upon themselves swift destruction"(2 Peter 2:1).

They are depraved people whose judgment was prophesied and written in Scripture a long time ago. They have perverted the message of God's grace into a license to commit immorality and debauchery even in recovery. The Scriptures say:

"What shall we say then? Shall we continue in sin (<u>such as addictions and alcoholism</u>), that grace may abound?" (Rom. 6:1).

"For the grace of God that bringeth salvation hath appeared to all men. Teaching us that, denying ungodliness and wordly lusts, we should live soberly, righteously, and godly, in this present world; Looking for that blessed hope, and the glorious appearing of the great God and our Savior Jesus Christ; Who gave himself for us, that he might redeem us from all iniquity, and purify unto himself a peculiar people, zealous of good works" (Titus 2:11-14).

The gospel of grace resounds as a symphony of beauty, captivating our hearts and souls. It is through the life-changing power of God's grace that we are strengthened and equipped to embrace an elevated existence beyond recovery, no longer entangled or swayed by the chains of our past sinful lives. We refuse to turn against or deny our one true and absolute Master, the Sovereign God. In our former state, we lived in denial of the authority, glory, and sovereignty of our Master and Lord Jesus Christ. However, through the immeasurable grace bestowed upon us, we now recognize Jesus Christ as our Lord and Savior, yielding to His divine authority and surrendering our lives to His loving guidance. We not only seek recovery but eternal salvation.

We feel compelled to emphasize, especially within recovery, that the saving grace of the Lord Jesus has rescued us from the grip of sins such as addictions and alcoholism. However, it is essential to acknowledge that those among us who clung to unbelief faced the consequences of their actions. In the journey of recovery, we draw strength from these reminders, understanding the importance of steadfast faith and aligning ourselves with the truth that leads to lasting freedom which is only found in salvation. We admit the life-changing power of God's grace, as it guides us in overcoming our struggles and reclaiming our true purpose.

In our former lives, marked by sins such as addictions and alcoholism, we regrettably resorted to belittling anything that eluded our comprehension. We mishandled sarcasm in a feeble attempt to cover our deceit. We slashed at the confidence of others with total disregard for the truth that lay gnawing at our own spirits. This inappropriate speech increased in brutality as other insensitive people joined in these barbaric verbal attacks of sarcasm. It is a spirit of delusion that cloaks those who practice it labeled as wittiness. Sarcasm is the brutal weapon used to assassinate other people's characters. It is pure murder. We acted in a manner akin to irrational beasts, driven solely by our impulsive instincts. Like animals consumed by the heat of passion, we blindly followed our natural inclinations, heedless of the consequences. It was through these unchecked animalistic instincts that we wrought corruption upon ourselves, leading to our own self-destruction. The weight of our actions was overwhelming, and we were ensnared in the grip of a curse that afflicted us deeply. Oh, how grievous it was for us to bear the burden of such a destructive path.

In our pasts, we unwittingly mirrored the footsteps of Cain, who turned away from the acceptable sacrifice desired by God and instead offered the fruit of his own efforts. Similarly, we too, in our sins such as addictions and alcoholism, sought salvation through our own accomplishments and self-made offerings. However, it is crucial to be aware of the danger posed by false teachers who attempt to distort the purity of true recovery and salvation through the gospel. These individuals insist on incorporating human works and additions to the message of grace and calling it "recovery," thus polluting its essence. We must remain vigilant, guarding the integrity of the gospel, knowing that there is more than just recovery, as salvation is a gift of divine grace, unmerited by our own works or achievements.

In our sins such as addictions and alcoholism, we mirrored the rebellious nature of others who were trapped in the same destructive patterns. As a result, we faced a similar fate, spiraling toward our own demise. The enticing allure of worldly pleasures seduced us, and we were consumed by our insatiable cravings.

False teachers and the temptations of this world lured us further into darkness, leading us away from the path of recovery to salvation. These spiritually disconnected "old-timers" become like dangerous hidden reefs, lurking within the fellowship of recovery communities and recovery ministries. Instead of embracing the love, unity, and healing that these gatherings are intended to provide, they bring harm. Their presence lacks reverence, as they disregard the guidance of a wise mentor or disciple of Jesus Christ. They resemble clouds that promise relief but fail to deliver, driven aimlessly by the turbulent winds of their own desires. Their lives resembled barren trees in the late stages of autumn, devoid of fruitfulness and uprooted from the foundation of recovery. Like tumultuous waves, they crash and fling forth the foamy remnants of their shame and disgrace. They are like wandering stars, leading themselves and others astray, destined to dwell in the darkness of their sin unless they choose the path of recovery and seek the light of salvation.

Within our midst, we encounter individuals who are incessantly discontented, perpetually finding fault with everyone around them. Their hearts are driven by their own wicked desires, and their words dripped with scandalous remarks and profanities. They take pleasure in employing seductive flattery to manipulate and control others. These individuals are characterized by a toxic combination of dissatisfaction and deceit, seeking to fulfill their own selfish agenda at the expense of those they interact with.

But you, our fellow travelers and friends in recovery, we urge you to recall the teachings of those who have walked before us in the life-saving gospel of Jesus Christ. They have warned us that in our journey, there will always be those who mock and ridicule, driven by their own ungodly desires. These individuals sow seeds of division and discord, adhering solely to their natural instincts without tapping into the life-changing Power of the Holy Spirit as He reveals Himself throughout the recovery process and the support of the fellowship. Let us remain steadfast in our recovery, united in our pursuit of the gospel of Jesus Christ and salvation, guided by the wisdom of those who have triumphed over the bondage of sins such as alcoholism and addictions. We are not swayed by the negativity and temptations that may arise, but instead, rely on God's strength as He displays it through those who have recovered and the empowering presence of the Holy Spirit to guide us along our path toward eternal salvation.

Continue to build yourselves up on the foundation of your most holy faith, nurturing it constantly. It's about progress, not perfection. Let your prayers be a constant expression of communion with the Spirit, as you seek guidance, strength, and renewal in recovery. Anchor your hearts firmly to the love of God, embracing His boundless mercy through our Lord Jesus Christ, who grants us the gift of eternal life. We are responsible. When anyone, anywhere, reaches out for help, we place their hand into the hand of God. And for that, we are responsible. In our interactions with others who still harbor doubts, we let compassion be our guiding principle. We extend a helping hand to those who are in danger of being consumed by the flames of sins such as alcoholism and addictions, striving to rescue them from their perilous situation.

We are to show mercy repeatedly, yet never forget the reverence and awe of God that should accompany our acts of kindness. We remain vigilant in keeping ourselves untainted from the temptations of the flesh that hinder our own recovery process.

We continue to grow in faith, showered with God's love and mercy, and His compassion inspires others to embark on the path of healing and freedom from the bondage of sin such as addictions and alcoholism.

Now, to the One who holds immeasurable power, shielding us from the pitfalls of sins such as addictions and alcoholism, enabling us to stand blameless in His glorious presence, overflowing with ecstatic delight, we lift our voices to the only God, our Savior, through our Lord Jesus Christ, giving Him eternal praise and honoring His majestic splendor. His unmatched power and authority extend beyond the boundaries of time, encompassing every moment of our recovery journey, and will continue to do so throughout all the ages to come. Let us unite in heartfelt gratitude and declare, "Amen!" to affirm our unwavering faith in His life-changing work in our recovered lives. In Jesus' Name.

CHAPTER 25

RECOVERY 5:12

"Two are better than one; because they have a good reward for their labor. For if they fall, the one will lift up his fellow: but woe to him that is alone when he falleth; for he hath not another to help him up. Again, if two lie together, then they have heat: but how can one be warm alone? And if one prevail against him, two shall withstand him; and a threefold cord is not quickly broken." (Ecclesiastes 4:9-12)

The core of **RECOVERY 5:12** lies in the communion of individuals who have experienced profound recovery through Jesus' Name from sins such as alcoholism and addictions. It is a remarkable revelation, defying the beliefs of conventional medicine, modern psychiatry, and even conventional recovery programs, which deemed a cure for alcoholism and addictions unattainable. Yet, within this fellowship, members have not only achieved complete recovery but have also supported and guided one another on their paths to salvation through the gospel of Jesus Christ.

Their extraordinary metamorphosis hinges on their united embrace of a "spiritual way of life," bolstered by the reciprocal aid and guidance they offer each other. Through their shared dedication and support, they have shattered the concept of incurability, forging a path toward genuine recovery.

Alcoholism and addictions are spiritual diseases, devoid of moral condemnation. We who have grappled with these self-driven conditions do not consciously choose substance use; rather, we were driven by a taskmaster of sin who utilized an irresistible compulsion. We were carnal and sold under this sin. Its bounds were shameless. This powerlessness over sins such as addictions and alcoholism tragically leads some to contemplate suicide. Even after treatment ends, relapses often occur immediately upon discharge for many of us. The temptation of substances even ensnares us at the funerals of friends who lost the battle against the sins of alcoholism or addictions. Despite genuine efforts to abstain for prolonged periods, we suddenly find ourselves entangled once again in self-destructive patterns. Witnessing these heart-wrenching scenarios reveals the overwhelming hold that sins such as alcohol and drugs have on our lives, disregarding the dire consequences we face.

Being recovered means that we have been delivered from a spiritual condition which resulted in a seemingly hopeless state of mind and body. The path to recovery commences with the complete exhaustion of our ideas and the realization that interventions of medical institutions and treatment centers alone cannot heal us. We come to recognize the fatal nature of our disease and its grip on our bodies, minds, and souls. This realization paves the way for admitting that God delivers us if we wholeheartedly seek Him. Here are the steps we took.

RECOVERY 5:12 provides a clear elucidation of the physical ailment endured by alcoholics and addicts through the knowledge we have attained through our intimate connection with God. We have comprehended that we who have been afflicted with this spiritual condition exhibit an exaggerated physical response to sins such as addictions and alcoholism, surpassing that of the average person. The mere deed or, in our case, the consumption of a single drink or drug instigates a pernicious craving that can solely be assuaged by further indulgence in the same deed or substance. Hence, once the initial deed is performed, such as when a drink or drug is consumed, the alcoholic or addict forfeits their ability to halt their progression along a ruinous trajectory.

RECOVERY 5:12 recognizes a compelling psychiatric theory that carries remarkable simplicity. It declares that only an alcoholic or addict possesses genuine insight into the mental intricacies and state of another alcoholic or addict. Additionally, we have cultivated a straightforward, albeit unconventional, comprehension of how people perceive God. Through our journeys, we have arrived at the realization that our previous understanding of a Higher Power lacked the requisite potency and capability to liberate us from sin such as addictions and alcoholism. Regardless of our conception, even if it is "J-e-s-u-s" and we receive our conception from the Bible, it still does not hold the necessary Power to deliver us – that Power is God and not who we think He is. As we focus on Him, we pour out our conception in light of His Holiness.

Undeniably, **RECOVERY 5:12**, the extraordinary fellowship of individuals who have overcome insurmountable sins such as addictions and alcoholism, incorporates a profound religious aspect. Within this recovery community, members have personally witnessed authentic healing, openly acknowledging God as the source of their recovery. Each recovered member of **RECOVERY 5:12** acknowledges that their journey to recovery manifested through wholeheartedly surrendering their struggles to Jesus Christ, surpassing their preconceived notions, and embracing a deep and effective experience of Him.

With steadfast certainty, we have acknowledged that science in isolation cannot bestow upon us a cure. We have come to understand our powerlessness to govern the unyielding sinful obsession with alcohol or drugs through our own efforts. The prayers, admonitions, and pleas from our dear ones, employers, or friends, although valued and needed, have proven incapable of affecting our healing. Our recovery requires a life-changing encounter with the Holy Spirit. We have wholeheartedly embraced the indispensable need for divine intervention. Humbly, we have surrendered ourselves utterly to a profound purification of our barred spirits.

RECOVERY 5:12 thrives as an entirely informal recovery community, fostering an atmosphere of inclusivity in all aspects, with one notable exception. It advocates a simple yet rigorous spiritual practice that demands unwavering commitment daily. Its agenda is to make this Jesus' Name recovery available to every church and gathering of followers of Jesus Christ throughout the globe. The intricate details of this practice are extensively expounded upon in this book, offering precise instructions.

The notion of complete deliverance within the **RECOVERY 5:12** community initially pose a challenge for the average alcoholic or addict to accept, regardless of the extent of their despair. The resistance towards affiliating with any church is understandable, considering the loss of faith or lack thereof in the efficacy of religion to offer genuine help. Nevertheless, each cure accomplished within the **RECOVERY 5:12** community signifies a profound spiritual awakening created by the Holy Spirit. Those of us who have recovered from the clutches of the bondage of sins such as addictions and alcoholism have wholeheartedly embraced what we term "a spiritual way of life."

RECOVERY 5:12 sets itself apart from other prominent religious and 12-step recovery movements through its distinct approach to breaking free from sins such as addictions and alcoholism. While it recognizes the profound impact of faith, it places a particular emphasis on the individual's experience of offering themselves to Jesus Christ as the path to deliverance from the lethal grip of sin.

RECOVERY 5:12 members are urged to maintain an open mind regarding their understanding of God. While individuals hold diverse interpretations, they have collectively recognized the inadequacy of their conceptions of God in effecting the required transformation in their lives. They have come to grasp that it is the Power of God, irrespective of individual conceptions, which possesses the capability to shift them from a state of pain in addiction and alcoholism into one of enduring healing.

Through embracing the Holy Spirit that surpasses individual conceptions, members of **RECOVERY 5:12** converge in our acknowledgment of a singular source of omnipotent power capable of liberating us from the clutches of sins and leading us towards enduring healing. We attribute this life-changing power to Jesus, who personifies recovery and salvation. Some of us entered with pre-existing religious or spiritual beliefs, which served as a framework for our *understanding* of a higher power. However, it is also recognized that not everyone possesses a well-defined belief system in the beginning, and that is perfectly acceptable, as it has minimal bearing on the awesome nature of experiencing the One True God.

In **RECOVERY 5:12**, the crucial element lies in the complete willingness of the individual to seek assistance from a power beyond themselves, irrespective of their conception of that Power. What holds utmost significance is the recognition that we require help surpassing human capabilities to surmount our challenges and the acceptance that there is One who has all Power in heaven and earth and His Name is Jesus. We challenge you to find Him now.

The recovery fellowship values the prayers, literature, and teachings of established religions, as they are essential in providing valuable guidance. However, **RECOVERY 5:12** emphasizes that the crucial factor is the individual's sincere open-mindedness to accepting aid through experiencing this Power which is Jesus Christ. Through this humble approach, individuals in **RECOVERY 5:12** embark on a journey of seeking God, experiencing the life-changing power of Jesus Christ, and finding the cure from sins such as addictions and alcoholism.

Indeed, within the fellowship of **RECOVERY 5:12,** individuals have encountered a wide range of religious experiences that have been life-changing and life-saving. These experiences encompass the full spectrum of religious psychology. Some have had profoundly powerful encounters, akin to the dramatic moment when Saul was struck down on the road to Damascus. Others have not yet reached a complete intellectual conviction, but they have witnessed the undeniable evidence in their lives that living by biblical principles has led to their recovery from a deadly spiritual disease. Even when we can't see it, He is working.

Having spent years trapped in the cycle of sins such as addictions and alcoholism, unable to overcome the compulsion to drink or use drugs, we have now reached a point where the desire to engage in self-destructive behaviors no longer arises within us. The shift we have experienced is something we only attribute to a higher power, which is God, whose Name we now know is Jesus. It is the surrender to this Power and the willingness to embrace a spiritual way of life that sets the stage for the life-changing work of the Holy Ghost leading us to salvation.

Through this process, we found complete recovery from our sins such as addictions and alcoholism. The precise mechanism behind this transformation cannot be comprehended, but the profound changes experienced are unmistakable. The power of God, working through the Holy Ghost, brings about complete freedom from the grip of sin. The collective testimony of diverse religious experiences testifies to the life-saving nature of spiritual help it has on individuals who, in other circumstances, have been resistant to accepting such assistance.

It is encouraging to hear that many members of **RECOVERY 5:12** are discovering increased support within the church. Engaging in family devotions, participating in **RECOVERY 5:12** step and Bible studies, or simply reflecting on God in the quietude of our minds have proven to be valuable sources of strength. However, it remains a collective acknowledgment among the members that the recovery experienced within **RECOVERY 5:12** are made possible through the shoulder-to-shoulder assistance of our fellow recovery travelers who have also struggled with sins such as addictions and alcoholism and have been delivered by

God. The Lord uses the shared experiences from those who have walked a similar path to play a crucial role in the recovery process.

The potency of mutual compassion within the recovery fellowship stands as a testament to the healing that emerges when God's children unite, sharing common aspirations. Because where two or three are gathered in Jesus' Name, there He is in the midst of them. The Lord our God in the midst of us is mighty; He saves, He rejoices over us with joy; He rests in His love, He joys over us with singing. Through the profound connection formed among those who have battled sins such as addictions and alcoholism, the Holy Spirit manifests Himself through our collective endeavors, catalyzing profound transformations and fostering enduring recovery. While formal religion and individual spiritual practices are vital to the overall well-being and growth of the members, the understanding remains that it is the power of fellowship and the support of one another that have been instrumental in our recovery. Together, we have experienced the life-changing work of the Holy Spirit, finding a new life in the recovery process.

The members of **RECOVERY 5:12**, who have experienced the Lord's deliverance from our medically incurable sins such as alcoholism and addictions, comprehend that a vital aspect of sustaining recovery lies in actively aiding others who are grappling with similar difficulties. By extending a helping hand to fellow pathological alcoholics and addicts, offering support, guidance, and empathy, we not only contribute to the recovery of those individuals but also strengthen our own dedication to maintaining our paths of salvation in Jesus Christ.

The fellowship of **RECOVERY 5:12** was originally founded on this principle. The members recognized the life-changing power of the Holy Spirit as He manifests Himself through the mutual support and assistance of others. By sharing our experiences, providing encouragement, and initiating new prospects toward complete deliverance in Jesus' Name, we create a cycle of recovery and renewal within the fellowship.

We have firsthand experience with the various unsuccessful methods of control we attempted in the past. We have tried different strategies and self-made rules to manage the sins of drinking and drug use, but always find ourselves ineffective in achieving lasting recovery. It is through recovery fellowship and the act of helping others that we have discovered a more sustainable and life-changing approach.

By actively engaging in the recovery of others, we reinforce our own commitment to Jesus Christ's example of serving others and deepening our understanding of the principles and practices that have led to our own deliverance by the Holy Spirit's guidance. The process of reaching out to others and offering support becomes a constant reminder of the importance of our own ongoing race.

In this way, we of **RECOVERY 5:12** have found a path to sustained recovery by admitting the responsibility of helping fellow alcoholics and addicts and initiating new prospects toward the cure, which is salvation in Jesus' Name. It is through these acts of service and fellowship that we reinforce our commitment to the race of life and prevent backsliding.

Many of us have attempted numerous methods to control our drinking and drug use, only to find that none of them work. These self-invented devices and external control strategies often prove ineffective and leave us feeling trapped in a cycle of insanity. This realization, born out of experience and repeated failures, becomes a turning point that opens the door to seeking a different approach. For those of us of **RECOVERY 5:12**, this shift led us to embrace a spiritual way of life and seek total surrender to the Holy Spirit. He became the sole manager of our will and lives. By surrendering our self-reliance and acknowledging our powerlessness over sins such as alcoholism and addictions, we find hope within the fellowship of others who have experienced similar struggles. Through this collective journey, we discover a solution that goes beyond mere manageability— a life-changing spiritual experience that can only be brought by salvation in Jesus' Name.

There is a unique understanding that arises when one alcoholic or addict speaks to another. No amount of knowledge about the disease, medical treatments, or psychological theories can replicate the deep understanding that comes from experience. Many of us have tried countless methods to control sins such as alcoholism and addictions, seeking comfort in science and professional help, but often found ourselves defeated and trapped in a cycle of shame and despair. We have witnessed the futility of these attempts, and the looming specters of death or psychiatric confinement have haunted us. It is within the fellowship of **RECOVERY 5:12** that we have discovered a life-changing power that transcends conventional wisdom. Through sharing our stories, supporting one another, and embracing the way, truth, and life, we have found a cure that eluded us through orthodox methods alone.

Those of us in **RECOVERY 5:12** who have been delivered through Jesus' Name have a special inclination to reach out to others when they find them at the lowest point of their lives. It's when they come to themselves, consumed by regret and wishing they were dead, that they are most receptive to hearing about where we have been and what we have done. In those moments of self-doubt, when they whisper to themselves, questioning their sanity, the resounding answer seems to be "yes." It's even in those moments when they feel the physical sensations of withdrawal, like bright-eyed snakes and insects crawling up their arms, that the doors of hope are opened wider. In those moments, the pathological drinker or drug addict becomes willing, even eager, to open up and have a conversation with someone who truly understands, based on our own firsthand experience, what it means to say, "I can't understand myself." It is through this shared understanding of the depths of despair and self-confusion that a deep connection is formed, and the path to Jesus' Name recovery and salvation begins to take shape.

Indeed, what often strikes the pathological drinker or drug user who has reached such a desperate state is the realization that the recovered alcoholic or addict not only comprehends the unique struggles and experiences that only another alcoholic or addict can truly understand, but that we also possess a profound understanding of many aspects that the lost individual believes to be known only to themselves. This discovery creates a sense of astonishment, as they come to recognize that their escapades are not exclusive to their own history but are shared by others who have walked a similar path of addiction and recovery.

It is a common belief among alcoholics and addicts to perceive our experience of addiction as somehow different from others. We think we are unique little snowflakes. While we are informed in treatment centers, by therapists, or physicians that alcoholism or addictions is a disease, there is often a tendency to view our own version of the disease as distinct and, perhaps, less severe than others'. To no fault of treatment centers, this perception leads many of us to believe that our condition has not yet reached an incurable stage, maintaining a glimmer of hope that we can still exert control over it on our own terms. This sense of individuality and the illusion of control are formidable barriers to seeking help for a solution that extends beyond our own efforts.

During interactions with treatment centers, therapists, and family physicians, alcoholics and addicts often receive stark warnings regarding the dire consequences of relapse. Treatment center leaders emphasize the high probability of falling back into the same destructive patterns upon resuming alcohol or drug consumption. Therapists explore psychological explanations, attributing the addictions to unresolved emotional issues or deep-seated resentments towards family members. Family physicians, recognizing the gravity of the situation, underscore the life-or-death stakes, urging the individual to quit their substance abuse to avert a fatal outcome. These are all very true.

Initial treatment comes to an end, and therefore there is a tremendous need for further recovery-based treatment continuum. One thing we have learned is that treatment is not recovery and recovery is not treatment. One working with the other provides the most optimum launch pad from which to begin. Treatment explanations or warnings from physicians alone, while providing true warnings and explanations aiming to underscore the seriousness of the situation, are often perplexed when they discover that somehow, they inadvertently contribute to the alcoholic or addict's perception of our own uniqueness and the belief that we they somehow exert control or manage their addiction without fully surrendering to a solution that surpasses their individual understanding. It's a precarious position and requires unity of recovery and treatment in this spiritual disease.

Presbyters, ministers, business partners, employers, parents, and spouses often play supportive roles in listening to confessions and offering understanding. However, their responses can vary. Often times a clergyman unaware of **RECOVERY 5:12** and missing the need for physical detoxification, may look past the excessive drinking and focus initially on the spiritual aspect of the sin, while a partner or employer may issue an ultimatum, demanding the cessation of such behavior or the termination of the relationship without the spiritual recovery resources of **RECOVERY 5:12**. Spouses or parents may disregard any consideration of **RECOVERY 5:12,** feeling that their expression of deep emotional pain caused by the drinking or drug use will help. Others oblivious to the principle of recovery may suggest exercising willpower and taking responsibility for one's actions to overcome the addictions. Yet, in the depths of our beings, the alcoholic or addict recognizes that our compulsions to drink or use drugs stems from an overwhelming spiritual suffering that no one else can fully comprehend unless they suffer the same malady. We once believed that the only way to cope with this unbearable spiritual pain is through the temporary relief provided by sins such as addictions and alcoholism. This profound sense of isolation and the desperate need for escape made it challenging for us to find comfort in the well-intentioned advice and admonishments of others.

Those under the bondage of alcoholism and addiction present a range of excuses to those of us who are recovered. These excuses include their inability to sleep without the aid of liquor or drugs, constant worries, troubles in business, mounting debt, physical discomfort or pains, overwhelming workload, excessively frayed nerves, grief, disappointment, intense and irrational fears, fatigue, conflicts within the family, and profound feelings of loneliness. We smile at such a sally knowing that these manifestations scream of the carnality prison they are being held captive in. However, we know of a solution.

In their desperation to justify their drinking or drug use, the sick and suffering individual seeks comfort in these explanations, hoping that they will understand the underlying reasons for their sinful bondage of alcoholism and addiction. They believe that these external factors contribute to their need for substance abuse and serve as a temporary escape from their internal struggles.

We of **RECOVERY 5:12** dismiss the excuses presented by the suffering alcoholic addict with a swift rebuttal. We declare, "Don't try those alibis on me. I have used them all myself." By doing so, we assert our deep understanding of the justifications that the individual is attempting to rely on. Having personally employed these very same excuses in our own struggles, we who have been recovered by Jesus Christ recognize them as mere attempts to rationalize and perpetuate destructive ungodly behavior.

We share our own history of sins such as alcoholism and drug addictions, often revealing experiences that are as bad, if not worse, than those of the person seeking help. It is one of the few times that we advocate sharing a drunk-a-log or dope-awards. As we exchange stories, a sense of camaraderie and understanding builds between us. In this informal yet effective communication, our willingness to disclose our own struggles encourages the new convert to open up and admit things they have never acknowledged even to themselves. It is through these testimonial meetings and frequent gatherings that we of **RECOVERY 5:12** provide each other with encouragement, replacing the social and emotional void left by our former drinking and drug use. We now understand that a practicing alcoholic or addict is profoundly spiritually ill and emphasize the importance of recognizing this reality. We are aware that even within the medical community, there can be a tendency to view failure to recover as a physical or mental failing rather than a symptom of a spiritual disease. Comparing it to other serious illnesses like cancer or psychosis, they stress the need for compassion and proactive measures, urging individuals to seek appropriate treatments before it is too late. We do the same while knowing that recovery has a Name and it is Jesus.

Those of us who have recovered speak honestly and directly to our uncured fellows, acknowledging the gravity of their condition. We emphasize that the person is not only physically sick, suffering from an exaggerated response to alcohol or drugs that requires medical detoxification, but also mentally and spiritually sick. We offer reassurance that there is a spiritual path to recovery for each aspect of our sins. Through our own experiences and the principles of **RECOVERY 5:12**, we provide hope and guidance, showing that there is a way to overcome the physical, mental, and spiritual afflictions of alcoholism and addictions.

To heal from our spiritual illnesses, it was necessary to embrace the presence of God, regardless of our previous conception of Him. If you truly have a sincere desire to do whatever it takes to recover and acknowledge the reality that you continue to drink or use drugs even against your own will and without comprehending why, it becomes vital to cease deceiving yourself and embrace a spiritual way of life. Are you ready to accept the assistance that is being extended to you?

It is truly a miraculous phenomenon that such a straightforward approach yields such profound transformations for alcoholics and addicts who were bound together by desperate circumstances. By admitting our powerlessness, seeking God, cleaning house, and connecting with a community of individuals who share similar struggles, incredible healing takes place. Recovery is simple but not easy. Through the power of the Holy Spirit, shared experiences, and a genuine willingness to change, what once seemed impossible becomes attainable in Christ.

We of **RECOVERY 5:12**, having all experienced the devastating effects of sins such as alcoholism and addictions firsthand, do not advocate for sole reliance on prohibition, aversion, or abstinence. Our primary focus is on the understanding that for individuals afflicted with the spiritual disease of alcoholism and addiction, the use of substances is incompatible with a fulfilling life. Through our own transformations and the success stories of countless others, we have witnessed the power of our recovery fellowship and our reliance on the Holy Spirit in conquering what was once deemed an incurable condition. Our aim is to share this message of recovery and salvation with those who are still suffering, offering them a new life free from the grip of sins such as alcoholism and addictions. After all, recovery has a Name and it is Jesus.

RECOVERY 5:12 is solely dedicated to guiding alcoholics and addicts toward finding a connection with this Higher Power. The group meetings are informal and inclusive where, as members, we gather in various locations that can accommodate our gatherings. Although our local churches are the preferred soul surgery centers for our meetings, our meeting locations include many diverse places where alcoholics or addicts are present, as well as places where individuals are supportive of the recovery fellowship's mission, even if they do not personally struggle with addictions. The primary purpose of these meetings is to create a Jesus' Name environment for those seeking recovery. If we successfully see people want to come back, repent, get baptized in Jesus' Name, and receive the Holy Spirit, then we can consider it a good meeting indeed. Any meeting with God in the middle is a successful meeting.

The publication of **RECOVERY 5:12** marks a significant milestone for Jesus' Name recovery. This book, available for purchase, provides a comprehensive account of **RECOVERY 5:12**'s spiritual path of recovery through these twelve recovery steps and five measures of faith. It serves as a testament to the effectiveness of Jesus' Name recovery and the fellowship's methods. It offers hope and inspiration to those seeking God's deliverance and complete recovery. We pray that it becomes an invaluable resource for individuals, families, medical professionals, and psychotherapists, shedding light on the power of mutual support, spirituality, and transformation in overcoming the spiritual bondage of sins such as alcoholism and addictions.

The sufferer of sin truly comprehends the depths of the problem. **RECOVERY 5:12** provides a unique perspective that allows readers, whether they are struggling individuals, friends and family, or professionals in various fields to grasp the true nature of the alcoholic or addict's struggle.

From the vantage point of experiences and the collective wisdom of the recovery fellowship, this book offers insights that cannot be gleaned from external observations. Like the intricate details of an Old Testament Tabernacle visible only from within, the intricacies of sins such as addictions and alcoholism become clearer when seen through the eyes of those who have been completely delivered. This book provides an inside view, shedding light on the complexities, challenges, and the hope of recovery and salvation through the gospel of Jesus Christ.

For victims of the bondage of sins such as alcoholism and addictions, **RECOVERY 5:12** offers a source of guidance pointing to Jesus' Name for recovery. It enables friends, family members, physicians, clergymen, psychiatrists, and social workers to deepen their understanding of the spiritual disease and the biblical path to recovery. By delving into the pages of this book, readers gain profound insights into the life-changing power of this Tabernacle pattern of recovery and the recovery fellowship that grows up around those who have been recovered by Jesus Christ as He guides us through His principle. This is more than recovery; it is eternal salvation in Jesus' Name.

CHAPTER 26

THE CALL

*"Therefore if any man be in Christ, he is a new creature:
old things are passed away; behold,
all things are become new."
(2 Corinthians 5:17)*

Throughout this recovery process, we are asking and receiving, we are seeking and finding, we are taking action and revealing the open door. Through this relationship with Jesus Christ, we have become devoted servants of God and faithful followers of Him. He personally chooses us and sends us forth to support and uplift the faith of others, leading them toward the life-transforming gospel of Jesus. This truth is founded on the profound hope for lasting, eternal freedom from the chains of sins such as addictions and alcoholism. Jesus, who is always faithful and true, made this promise to us even before time began, and in His perfect timing, He unveiled it through His powerful message. This sacred trust has been bestowed upon us, and with the authority of Jesus Christ, our Savior, we declare it courageously, sharing the message of hope, healing, and recovery to all who are willing to listen. We write to you, our true family in the faith of that which we have in common.

Dear family in faith and recovery,

May God the Father and Christ Jesus, our Savior, abundantly bestow upon you the gift of grace and the serenity of peace. It is by the divine arrangement of Jesus that we have been called to this purpose, to bring order and recovery to the areas that still require attention, and to celebrate the healing and recovery happening in every recovery community we encounter. Through the empowering presence of God and the guidance of Jesus, let us faithfully continue our mission of facilitating spiritual connectedness, recovery, and the pursuit of Holy Ghost joy in every place we go.

Let us remember and adhere to the instructions we have been given for effective facilitation and support in our recovery work:

> (1) Being recovered, it is vital that we maintain a blameless character. We must cultivate healthy relationships, demonstrate our faith through our actions, and not be known for reckless or disobedient behavior.

> (2) As recovery group facilitators, we are entrusted with the work of God. Therefore, we must strive to lead by example and maintain a faultless demeanor. We should avoid arrogance, quick-temperedness, altered minds, violence, and greed. Instead, let us cultivate a spirit of hospitality, love for what is good, self-control, uprightness, holiness, and discipline. Our unwavering commitment to the trustworthy and doctrinally sound message enables us to encourage others and refute the false teachings of those who oppose it.

We must be aware that there are individuals, including some from traditional recovery groups, who rebel against the truth and deceive others with nonsensical ideas. It is our responsibility to put an end to their harmful rhetoric, as they disrupt entire groups by teaching things they ought not to teach. Their motives are driven by the desire for power and recognition, which is truly shameful.

Therefore, let us stand firm in our commitment to upholding the principles of recovery, promoting unity, and guiding others toward a life of healing and freedom. Keep our words and actions aligned with the truth, bringing hope and recovery to those who seek it.

We understand the struggles of being ensnared in traditional recovery programs ourselves, having once functioned as sponsors within those fellowships. It is with honesty that we acknowledge the pervasive presence of deceit, unscrupulous individuals, and those who lacked discipline and self-control hidden in the name of recovery.

Considering this, it becomes our responsibility to provide clear guidance and correction, so that individuals develop a healthy and genuine recovery, relinquishing reliance on the myths and human principles that stem from those who have turned away from the truth.

Through our own experiences, we have come to recognize that purity is attainable for those who strive for it. However, during our past states of defilement and unbelief, nothing appeared pure to us. Our minds and consciences were contaminated, leading us to make claims of knowing God while our actions blatantly contradicted such knowledge. We were filled with animosity and disobedience, rendering us incapable of producing anything truly good.

With humility, we now seek to guide others toward true recovery, which is a path of purity, faith, and genuine transformation. Let us continue to shed the falsehoods of our pasts and embrace the truth that sets us free, equipping ourselves to lead recovered lives characterized by righteousness and goodness.

It is imperative we now acknowledge that this whole journey in recovery was always pointing toward the sound gospel message in each step and measure along the way. As guides on the path of recovery, we strive to lead others in the gospel salvation plan. We demonstrate how to cultivate a faith that is grounded, love that is genuine, and endurance that is unwavering. Moreover, we model behavior befitting those who live a holy and righteous life.

Let us be vigilant in avoiding slanderous speech and the enslavement to substances. Instead, we are called to exemplify the path to goodness, encouraging others to love one another, maintain purity, and engage in sincere worship as we fully submit ourselves to Jesus. By doing so, we ensure that no one discredits the message that originates from God.

Furthermore, we exhort others to embrace seeking God in all aspects of their lives. It is crucial that we become living examples of good conduct, demonstrating sincerity and seriousness in our teaching. Our words should be sound and unassailable, leaving no room for criticism, so that even our adversaries find no basis for speaking ill of us.

Our lives reflect the life-changing power of the gospel, as we lead others on the journey of recovery with unwavering commitment to the truth. We who have recovered willingly surrender ourselves to our Lord and Savior, Jesus Christ, recognizing Him as our ultimate authority. Our utmost desire is to please Him in all of our affairs. We acknowledge the destructive nature of engaging in behaviors that steal our focus from His life-changing power. Instead, we strive to embody faithfulness, seeking His grace to shape our thoughts, words, and actions.

In all that we do, our aim is to bring glory to God by reflecting the teachings of our Savior. Through our transformed lives, we exemplify the life-changing impact of Christ's love. We wholeheartedly embrace the opportunity to honor God through recovery, understanding that our testimonies inspire others who are still sick and struggling both inside and outside of the recovery community.

By relying on Christ's strength, we navigate the path of recovery with humility. We continually seek His wisdom to walk in His ways. In doing so, we proclaim His power and demonstrate the freedom that comes from surrendering our lives to Him.

The boundless grace of Jesus Christ shines upon us, granting deliverance and hope to every recovering soul. In the radiant light of this grace, we receive divine instructions to turn away from the destructive clutches of sins such as addictions, alcoholism, and the allure of worldly desires. With unyielding determination, God causes us to embrace a life transformed by discipline, moral uprightness, and an unwavering commitment to His Spirit. Each step and measure of faith are infused with the anticipation of the triumphant return of our Savior, Jesus Christ, who we now know walks beside us, guiding our every move and revealing His presence in the miraculous unfolding of our recovered lives.

In the depths of our sins such as addictions and alcoholism, Jesus selflessly surrendered Himself for our sake, breaking the chains that bound us to the darkness of our sins. Through His redemptive sacrifice, we are set free to pursue lives marked by recovery, righteousness, and continuous spiritual growth in His life-changing power. As beloved members of His chosen family, we are divinely called to embrace a purpose-driven existence, actively engaging in acts of kindness and selfless service. It is our sacred duty to impart these life-giving truths, wielding the authority bestowed upon us by the Holy Ghost. As we walk alongside fellow travelers on the path of recovery, we serve as beacons of hope, providing unwavering support, encouragement, and guidance. Empowered by the Holy Spirit, we utilize God's unique gifts to uplift others, fostering a community of recovery.

Let us rise above attempts to diminish our progress, but instead, let us steadfastly embrace the undeniable truth we declare. By embodying this principle, we bring honor to the divine. We consistently depend on His boundless mercy as we navigate together this path of renewal.

As Christ's disciples, we must emphasize the significance of urging others to be obedient to governing powers and be always prepared to engage in virtuous deeds. Let us promote the avoidance of the destruction of others' character, instead fostering an environment of compassionate demeanor towards all people.

Let us never forget that we too were once ensnared in ignorance, disobedience, and transgression. We were enslaved by our own desires, indulging in fleeting pleasures. Our existences were marred by hostility, envy, and resentment towards others, and we were also recipients of such negativity. However, it was solely by the immeasurable grace and love of our Savior, Jesus Christ, that we were rescued. Our deliverance was not the result of any righteous acts we performed, but solely due to the limitless compassion of God. Through the Holy Spirit, we underwent a profound transformation, experiencing a new birth and receiving a new life.

In His boundless mercy, God graciously bestowed upon us the abundant outpouring of the Holy Spirit through our Savior, Jesus Christ. Through His grace, we have been declared righteous and recovered our relationship with Him, receiving the blessed assurance of everlasting life. These words hold true, serving as a poignant reminder that our salvation is an extraordinary gift from God, firmly rooted in His unfailing mercy.

As we engage with others, let us embody these teachings by boldly proclaiming the life-changing power of God's love. Our conduct should stand as a testament to the radical change He has brought into our lives as we wholeheartedly embrace His abundant grace and steadfastly walk in the hope of eternal salvation. Let us emphasize these matters of utmost importance so that all who are recovered are driven to dedicate their time and energy to impactful acts of goodness that benefit and uplift others. We must actively reject futile arguments, endless debates about spiritual lineage, religious conflicts, and battles over methods of godless recovery steps and programs. These distractions hold no value. It is our earnest recommendation to issue two clear warnings to those who sow division, and thereafter sever ties with them. We understand that those who foster division are corrupted, and their evident sins expose the falsehood of their ways.

In our unwavering commitment to obedience to our Lord and the pursuit of service, we wholeheartedly devote ourselves to uplifting those who are on their journey of recovery. We earnestly desire to provide unwavering support, ensuring that they have all the resources and assistance required to embark on this life-changing path of healing in Jesus' Name. The call is to actively engage in acts of compassionate service, diligently addressing authentic needs and shunning a life of apathy.

As we conclude, let us extend warm greetings to all. We send our heartfelt greetings to our recovery family, as well as those who are on the verge of becoming friends in the faith. Together, we continue to walk in obedience, supporting and uplifting one another on this life-changing journey of recovery.

God's grace be with us all.

CHAPTER 27

THE POWER OF DISCIPLESHIP

"But ye shall receive power, after that the Holy Ghost is come upon you: and ye shall be witnesses unto me both in Jerusalem, and in all Judaea, and in Samaria, and unto the uttermost part of the earth."
(Acts 1:8)

We, who have experienced deliverance from the grip of sins such as addictions and alcoholism, have become devoted servants of the One who possesses limitless power—Jesus. He has called us to be His disciples and has bestowed upon us a unique purpose of sharing this incredible message. Therefore, we have written you a letter in hopes of emboldening you in your efforts to seek Him.

Dear fellow traveler,

This letter is addressed to all who find themselves on a similar journey of recovery, for you have been specifically chosen to embrace holiness in His sight. May you be enveloped in abundant and joyful grace, as well as the complete well-being that emanates from our Father, the Lord Jesus Christ, starting from this very day in your recovery journey.

Our purpose is to proclaim the Good News. Although it is not entirely new, it is, in fact, new to recovery and the fulfillment of the long-awaited hope that was promised to us through numerous prophecies recorded in the sacred Scriptures. This Good News revolves around the person of Jesus. He descended from a lineage of royalty as a human being, but through the mighty power of God, He was raised from the dead and uniquely anointed by the Holy Spirit, He has been exalted. Now, Jesus is not only our Lord but also our Deliverer. Our minds are set on Him.

Through Jesus, a grace-filled joy overflows within us, enabling us to embrace the calling of discipleship in recovery. Our mission is to reach people in recovery from all walks of life and guide them into a faithful commitment to Jesus, bringing honor to His Name. It is a privilege to inform you that you are among the chosen ones who have received the divine call to belong to Jesus!

We give thanks to Jesus for all of you because it's through your Christ-centered recovery and conversion to Jesus that the testimony of your strong recovery and faith is spreading throughout the world. God knows that we pray for you continually, for we passionately serve and worship Him with our spirits in the name of Christ-centered recovery and the Good News of Jesus.

Our heartfelt desire and ongoing prayer are to have the opportunity to visit every one of you as we walk this happy road of destiny, in accordance with God's perfect plan and timing. We eagerly yearn for the chance to meet you face-to-face in recovery communities and ministries to build a connection. Our intention is to share with you the precious gift of the Holy Spirit, which empowers us to remain steadfast in our faith.

When we gather for the purpose of recovery, something truly extraordinary takes place. We experience a profound sense of unity, and a beautiful spiritual exchange occurs. We are mutually comforted by the unwavering recovery of one another. These recovery gatherings bring forth a powerful synergy that supports us in our recovery from sins such as addictions and alcoholism.

Driven by our profound love and deep sense of compassion, we feel compelled to share the message of hope and recovery with all individuals, regardless of their struggles and past mistakes. We are filled with anticipation as we bring you the incredible news of the life-changing Power of Jesus in recovery.

This is the Good News of Jesus Christ! We proudly admit the extraordinary message of God's liberating Power that breaks the chains of sins such as addictions and alcoholism through Jesus. We refuse to be ashamed of it. Our hearts overflow with excitement as we declare that everyone who believes in Jesus experiences true freedom from the grip of sin.

This Good News unveils a continual revelation of God's unwavering honesty—a perfect honesty given to us when we surrender to His healing embrace. It leads us from merely existing through sins such as addictions and alcoholism to the Power of living a life of fulfillment through faith-filled recovery in Him. It is a life-changing journey that empowers us to walk in the victory that comes from trusting in God's unfailing promises.

This is what the Scripture means when it says:

"The just shall live by faith!"

God's redemption is revealed! Through recovery, we have come to witness the life-changing power of God's love. In His wisdom, God unveils His compassionate response to our brokenness. He is not indifferent; instead, He extends His healing touch to recover every aspect of our uncovered lives.

In the depths of sins such as addictions and alcoholism, we often suppressed the truth and refused to acknowledge our need for help. Our spiritually misguided choices separated us from the truth about ourselves and God. Even in our darkest moments, God's love was at work, gently calling us to embrace His healing and salvation.

As we embarked on the path of recovery, we discovered that God's truth and life-changing power are not elusive. Rather, they are intimately woven into the fabric of our being. From the very beginning, God designed us with an innate awareness of His love and a longing for recovery.

Through the process of recovery, we have come to realize that God's healing is not limited to physical and emotional recovery. It encompasses the fullness of our being, addressing the deep-seated wounds within us. God's love penetrates the hidden corners of our hearts, exposing the root causes of sins such as addictions and alcoholism and offering true freedom.

In the face of our past mistakes, we find comfort in the understanding that God's grace is abundant and His redemption is boundless. His healing touch mends the broken pieces of our lives, giving us the strength to overcome sin. His salvation allows us to live victoriously.

Throughout our recovery, we have come to recognize the fingerprints of God upon our lives. His presence was, is, and shall always be there, even when we turn away from Him. In the depths of our sins such as addictions and alcoholism, we failed to honor God.

Instead, we allowed ourselves to be consumed by foolish thoughts, distorting our understanding of who God truly is. Therefore, we would create our own conceptions of Him. We would even use his name and draw our own interpretations from the Word to create our conception without understanding that any conception is not the One they call Jesus of Nazareth. Our hearts became clouded with moral and philosophical darkness, leading us further into the depths of our sins such as addictions and alcoholism. We thought we were wise, relying on our own intelligence, but we were shallow fools. For the clay does not mold the Potter.

We traded the everlasting glory of the eternal God for temporary pleasures and fleeting idols such as alcohol and drugs. We worshipped people, places, and things that could never truly satisfy our souls. It was a foolish exchange that left us empty and trapped in the cycle of sin.

However, through the process of recovery, we have come to realize the magnitude of our folly. We have experienced firsthand the life-changing power of God's love. His unfading splendor far surpasses anything this world can offer.

As we reflect on the darkness we once embraced, we are humbled by God's enduring patience and unwavering love. Our recovery stands as a testament to His faithfulness of hope for those still trapped in the grip of sins such as addictions and alcoholism.

Today, we choose to honor God as our true source of fulfillment. We express gratitude for His mercy, recognizing that His love is the only path to recovery and true salvation. We have learned that the pursuit of temporary pleasures leads to emptiness, while a life centered on God brings everlasting joy.

Our lives serve as a testimony to the life-changing power of God's love and a reminder that no one is beyond His reach. In His divine plan, our recovery becomes a beacon of hope, illuminating the path to redemption for all who are searching for more than mere freedom from alcohol and drugs.

This is why God lifted off His restraining hand and let us have full expression of our sinful and shameful desires. We were given over to moral depravity, dishonoring our bodies by sexual perversion among ourselves—all because we traded the truth of God for a lie. We worshiped and served the things God made rather than the God who made all things—glory and praises to Him for eternity of eternities!

In our pasts, we allowed ourselves to be consumed by disgraceful passions. We strayed from the natural order of things and engaged in behaviors that deviated from God's intended design. Lustful desires blinded us, leading us to exchange the beauty of healthy relationships for the pursuit of distorted worldly views. These choices carried consequences, and we experienced the due penalty for our deviation from God's plan. Our troubles were of our own making.

However, as we reflect on recovery, we recognize the life-changing power of God's love. Through His mercy, we have found healing and salvation. We have come to understand that true, genuine relationships are only found in alignment with God's design.

Today, we embrace the truth that God's plan for our lives is rooted in Him who love. We seek to honor Him by admitting God-honoring relationships. We strive to walk in obedience to His commands, knowing that His ways lead to true fulfillment.

We share this perspective not to judge others, but to testify to the redemptive work of God in our own lives. We offer our recovery experiences as a testament to His transforming power, acknowledging that He brings healing and salvation to anyone who turns to Him. To whosoever will. Our words and actions reflect the love that we have received, and they serve as a beacon of hope for others who are seeking healing from any form of unhealthy behavior.

In our pasts, we foolishly disregarded the true knowledge of God and were ruled by a mindset that led us astray. God, in His righteous judgment, allowed us to be consumed by a worthless way of thinking, resulting in a complete abandonment of proper conduct.

Our lives were characterized by sinfulness in its various forms. We became self-centered and driven by evil desires. Greed consumed us, and our hearts were filled with jealousy that led to hateful arguments. Deception defined our interactions, and we took pleasure in spreading malicious gossip. Our egos were inflated, and we arrogantly insulted God without any basis. We rebelled against authority, including our own parents, and our behavior was immoral. We were completely devoid of faith, lacking any sense of compassion. Despite being fully aware of God's principle and the proper order of things, we willfully chose to immerse ourselves in darkness. Furthermore, we encouraged others to do the same and even celebrated their participation in sinful acts.

We share these aspects of our pasts not to boast or glorify our previous actions, but rather to highlight the life-changing power of God's grace. In His mercy, He reached out to us in our brokenness and offered us recovery, salvation, and forgiveness through Jesus Christ.

As we stand on the other side of sinful lifestyles such as alcoholism and addiction, we recognize the depth of our wrongdoing and the immense grace extended to us in recovery. We now strive to live according to God's principle, acknowledging our need for His guidance and surrendering our desires to His will. Through His transforming work, we seek to walk in humility, reflecting His character and extending mercy to others. Our lives serve as a testament to the power of God's forgiveness, and we continually point others toward the path of righteousness and the true life found in Him.

God alone judges sin! In recovery, it is important for us to humbly acknowledge our own shortcomings and past sins before passing judgment on others. We cannot claim exemption from God's righteous judgment, for we ourselves have been guilty of similar offenses. When we engage in judgment and yet participate in the same sinful behaviors, we bring condemnation upon ourselves.

We must recognize that God's judgment is based on absolute truth, as He possesses perfect knowledge. Regardless of our perceived status, we cannot escape His judgment by hypocritically condemning others while engaging in the same transgressions.

Instead of focusing on judging others, let us turn our attention inward and seek forgiveness for our own wrongdoings. We approach God with contrite hearts, acknowledging our need for His mercy. In humility, we should strive to live in accordance with His principle, treating others with love, compassion, and understanding.

Our actions reflect genuine recovery, repentance, and a desire to walk in righteousness, knowing that it is only through God's forgiveness and life-changing work in our lives that we have truly be set free from the chains of sins such as addictions and alcoholism.

In recovery from alcoholism and addictions, we came to recognize how we had taken God's extraordinary kindness for granted and even despised Him for it. Through our experiences, we have encountered His unwavering understanding in our lives. However, it became evident that we must not mistake His tolerance as acceptance of the destructive behaviors associated with alcoholism and addictions.

The richness of His extravagant kindness was meant to touch our hearts, leading us to a place of genuine recovery, repentance, and transformation. We discovered that His kindness was an invitation to change our ways as He aligned them with His will. Sadly, our hearts were calloused and resistant to redirection, and we unknowingly accumulated judgment and wrath for ourselves.

It is essential to understand that each of us receives the appropriate consequences for our actions. God, in His righteous judgment, will respond accordingly to what we have done. This realization serves as a reminder that choices and behaviors have repercussions, and we must take responsibility for our actions.

Therefore, as individuals who have found recovery, let us not underestimate God's kindness. Instead, let us be deeply moved by His mercy, allowing it to transform us from the inside out. We fully embrace the path of repentance and wholeheartedly seek a lasting change, knowing that God's desire is our salvation. We mourn.

In our recovered state, we have learned that when we choose to live a life rooted in pleasing God, we find freedom from fear of what lies ahead. However, there was a time when our lives were governed by selfishness. Our hearts were unresponsive to the truth of God, and we were prone to embracing dishonesty. It was during that time that we experienced the consequences of our actions, facing the full weight of divine wrath.

Those of us who have journeyed through the depths of alcoholism and addiction know firsthand the turmoil that accompanies such a lifestyle. We were ensnared in a cycle of selfishness, causing us to experience immense distress.

But as we surrendered ourselves to a higher power and made the courageous decision to walk the path of recovery, a remarkable transformation took place. Instead of embracing the darkness of our pasts, we began to seek goodness and live in accordance with God's will. This shift in our mindset and actions brought about a profound change in our lives.

In the midst of our recovery, we discovered a newfound sense of purpose. We witnessed the unfading glory of healing and salvation unfolding within us. Our lives became adorned with true honor as we walked with integrity.

No longer enslaved by the chains of sins such as addictions and alcoholism, we experienced a continual peace that surpassed all understanding. Our peace came from knowing we are no longer controlled by substances but rather guided by a higher power who grants us strength. Our recovery serves as a testament to God's mercy. He saw us in our brokenness and extended His hand to lift us out of the depths of despair. In His impartial love, He lavishes us with His blessings, regardless of our past struggles.

As we continue to walk the path of recovery, we embrace a life of gratitude, cherishing each day as a precious gift. We share our stories with others, offering hope and encouragement to those still trapped in the grip of sins such as addictions and alcoholism.

Regardless of our exposure to the scriptures, the wages of sin remained the same - we faced inevitable ruin for our actions. Similarly, when we embarked on the life-changing journey of taking these recovery steps and measures of faith but failed to obey His principle, we found ourselves condemned by our own lack of adherence. It was not mere knowledge of the steps and measures that justified us before God, but the wholehearted commitment to faithfully carrying out their instructions, which led to the source of our exoneration.

Even in recovery from addictions and alcoholism, we have come to understand that there is a principle at work in our hearts. When we take these steps and abstain from our harmful habits, this principle is reinforced and becomes a guiding force in our lives. We do not have traditional steps to follow, but the principle is still present and governs us. Our conscience bears witness to what is right and wrong, and our thoughts either validate or correct us. This recovery is something that is revealed on the day when God, through Jesus, exposes the hidden secrets of our hearts. Our response to the Good News of the Gospel is the standard by which our recovery is judged. When we embrace the truth and follow it, we experience true freedom from our sins such as alcoholism and addictions.

Relying solely on the steps was not enough to save us. We have proudly identified as being in recovery, finding comfort in our faith and relationship with God. We have believed that we possessed superior knowledge and understanding of God's will through the traditional recovery programs. In our arrogance, we saw ourselves as guides for the blind, shining lights in the darkness, and teachers of the foolish and immature, all because we possessed the treasury of truth found in recovery. However, we were confronted with a sobering question: Do we practice what we preach? We admonish others not to steal, but have we stolen? We quickly condemn adultery, but have we ourselves been guilty of it? We proclaim our disdain for idolatry and false gods, but do we withhold from the true God what is rightfully His? Our boasting in recovery was rendered meaningless when we dishonored God by breaking His principle. Our actions aligned with the very words that state, "Because of you, God's precious Name is cursed."

It became evident that our reliance on the steps alone, without true adherence and transformation, led to hypocrisy and dishonor towards God. We realized the importance of aligning our actions with our beliefs, of living out the principle we professed. True recovery goes beyond mere words or knowledge; it requires a genuine transformation of the heart and mind followed by a covenant to honor and follow God's will.

We place our trust in the symbolic "working" of the steps, yet we recognize that true value lies in faithfully living out the teachings they impart. If we violate the principle of the steps, we render our taking all of them meaningless. Furthermore, if those who have not formally taken all of the steps wholeheartedly embrace the underlying principle, will not their obedience bring them greater contentment than the mere act of taking the steps? And will not those who have never gone through the steps but exhibit spiritual integrity serve as judges when we fail to live up to their principle? Our satisfaction does not come from superficial adherence, for it is not the outward working of a step that brings contentment. Instead, we find contentment in the inward transformation that comes through a profound and impactful spiritual experience—a radical change that lays our hearts bare. It is not the steps themselves that hold power, but the life-changing work of the Holy Spirit. Therefore, our praise does not arise from our own accomplishments, but from the recognition that it is God Himself who deserves all the glory.

Taking the steps holds significance in recovery, and there are indeed various advantages to finding contentment as we take them. Above all, it sets us apart in God's eyes, as we are entrusted with the revelation of His prophetic promises. However, what happens if some of us experience a relapse? Does our relapse diminish God's faithfulness? Absolutely not! God's faithfulness remains unwavering, while our own shortcomings and failures are exposed. This serves to fulfill what has been written in Scripture:

> *"Your words will always be proven true, and you will emerge victorious when you are tested by your critics!"*

But what if our relapse shows how right God is? Doesn't our relapse serve the purpose of making God look good? Of course, we are only speaking from a human viewpoint. Would that infer that God is unfair when He displays His anger against wrongdoing? Absolutely not! For if that were the case, how could God be the honest deliverer of all?

So, if recovery from sins such as addictions and alcoholism brings into sharp contrast the power of God's healing and redemption, and if our testimonies highlight His grace and salvation, then why should we be condemned as sinners? Is it right for us to continue sinful behaviors such as alcoholism and addiction just so we can experience His forgiveness and deliverance? Absolutely not! Let it be clear that our message is one of hope and freedom from the grip of sin, not an endorsement of sinful lifestyles. Anyone who misrepresents our message in such a way is distorting the truth and undermining the life-changing work of God.

Universal sinfulness. Are we then claiming that those of us who have taken the steps are inherently superior to others? Absolutely not! We have already acknowledged that both those who follow the traditional recovery programs and those who embrace an alternative method like the biblical-based **RECOVERY 5:12** are all subject to the bondage of sins such as addictions and alcoholism. The Scriptures confirm this truth, as it is written:

> *"No one consistently does what is right, not even one! No one possesses true spiritual insight, and no one naturally seeks after God. All have deliberately strayed from God's ways. All have become corrupt and unworthy. Kindness is absent among them, and not a single person is truly good. Their words emit a putrid stench, akin to the smell of death—repulsive and vile! Deceitful lies flow effortlessly from their tongues. Venomous poison drips from their lips. They spew bitter profanity, aiming to wound and harm. They are consumed by violence and murder, leaving destruction and sorrow in their wake. They have never experienced the path of peace. They willingly turn their eyes away from the awe-inspiring presence of God."*

Now, we come to a profound understanding that every instruction outlined in **RECOVERY 5:12** is intended for those of us who have lived under its authority. This serves two significant purposes: first, it silences every excuse and eliminates any possibility of boasting about our supposed innocence. And second, it holds each one of us accountable to the divine standard set by God. It is crucial to recognize that no one can attain a state of righteousness before God merely by adhering to the steps. On the contrary, it is through these steps that the true nature of sins such as addictions and alcoholism is fully exposed and revealed, leaving no room for deception.

The Good News unveils freedom from sin. But now, apart from the steps, the liberating power of God's honesty is revealed through Jesus, the Anointed One. This is the long-awaited promise foretold in the Scriptures. It is through the faithfulness of Jesus that we, who have struggled with sin, experience the tangible manifestation of God's honesty. In His great compassion, God extends His grace to all of us, regardless of our pasts. We were all once trapped in the chains of sins such as addictions and alcoholism, desperately in need of God's glory. Yet, through His powerful declaration of freedom, God lavishly pours out His love and favor upon us. This incredible gift of freedom flows abundantly, breaking the bondage of self and releasing us from its grip. It is through Jesus, the Anointed One, that we find true deliverance from the guilt, shame, and remorse of sin.

Christ's redemption breaks us free from the chains of sins such as addictions and alcoholism. His purpose was to offer Himself as the sacrificial lamb, taking upon Himself the weight of our sins. Through His death on the cross, He became our source of hope and the ultimate means of finding forgiveness and freedom from the grip of sin. Jesus is our refuge, our place of mercy and grace, where we can find comfort by placing our faith in Him. His sacrifice is a profound testament to God's deliverance, as He patiently bore the burden of our sins such as alcoholism and addictions, and held back the full consequences of our actions. Christ's love covered over our mistakes until the appointed time. When the moment was right, God, in His perfect balance of justice and mercy, made the ultimate sacrifice—giving Himself. Through Jesus' sacrifice, we now have a pathway to something beyond recovery - salvation. As we anchor ourselves in the faithfulness of Jesus through these steps and measures of faith, we are distracted as God made it possible and declares us righteous and worthy of His love. Our past struggles with sins such as addictions and alcoholism no longer define us; instead, we are set free by His boundless mercy. In Christ, we find the strength to overcome, the power to break free, and the hope of a new life filled with joy.

Where, then, is there room for boasting? Can we take credit for our own recovery? Absolutely not! It is not our own efforts, our adherence to the steps, or our willpower that brings us acceptance from God. Our righteousness and freedom from sins such as addictions and alcoholism do not come from our works but from our faith in the life-changing power of Jesus. Somehow, as we took these steps, we did not see that God was giving us a new attitude toward sin without any thought or effort on our part. We find that He has placed us in a position of neutrality. He removed our problem.

So, let us make it clear, God's declaration that we are righteous and recovered in His sight can only come through our faith in Jesus, the One who sets us free from the bondage of sin. It is through our surrender to Him and His work on the cross that we find true freedom and new life. Our faith in Jesus, not the steps alone, is what truly matters and brings us into a recovered relationship with God. And we could not arrive at this point of our journeys if it were not for the steps and measures we take.

In recovery, we humbly acknowledge that it is the grace of God working in us that brings about the needed mental and spiritual transformation. We recognize that without His intervention, we would still be trapped in the grip of sins such as addictions and alcoholism. It is through His mercy and love that we have found healing and freedom.

So, let us never boast of our own accomplishments. Instead, let us give all the glory to God, who, in His infinite grace, has rescued us from the darkness of sin and brought us into the light of His love. Our faith in Jesus is our anchor, our source of hope, and the foundation of our recovery.

Is God exclusively for those who follow the twelve steps, or does He embrace all humanity equally? He is the God of all! One God, treating everyone the same, forgiving our guilt, and making us right with Him through faith, regardless of who we are. Does faith diminish the steps' significance? Not at all. Faith establishes the steps' rightful role, like the life-changing **RECOVERY 5:12**. God's inclusivity extends to all, not favoring any group. Faith harmonizes with the steps, guiding us toward recovery. **RECOVERY 5:12** steps and measures are rooted in faith and facilitate true healing.

We now recognize faith, steps, and measures as allies. Through faith, we receive God's grace, and the steps become practical tools for our recovery journey in righteousness. They align with God's principle for wholeness, and He provides each of them with a measure of faith. So, faith, steps, and measures synergize. God's love and mercy empower us to overcome sins such as alcoholism and addictions as we find lasting recovery. We admit the inclusive God, who welcomes all on the path to recovery.

Our faith and salvation. Let us consider our own struggles with sin. It is evident that we have embraced traditional recovery as part of our journey. However, it is crucial to understand that our deliverance and being recovered are not a result of our adherence to these steps alone. If our recovery and salvation depended on our own efforts, we would have reason to boast, but in reality, no one can boast before God. Instead, let us reflect on the profound truth revealed in the Scriptures: It is through our unwavering faith in God's grace that we find true salvation.

Our battle with sins such as addictions and alcoholism is a testament to our powerlessness and need for spiritual connectedness. The steps alone cannot save us; they serve as tools to guide us, but it is our faith that unlocks the life-changing power of God. When we come to a place of surrender, acknowledging our inability to overcome our problems on our own and placing our trust in God's mercy, a profound shift occurs.

Through our faith, we invite God into the depths of our struggles, allowing Him to work through us. It is not our completion of the steps that grants us recovery or salvation, but rather our unwavering belief in God's ability to heal and save. Our faith becomes the conduit through which God's redemptive love flows into our lives, washing away our guilt and shame.

Let us humbly testify that our recovery is not the result of our own achievements, but rather a divine intervention. Our faith acts as a bridge, connecting us to God's boundless grace and transforming power. We find comfort in knowing that our recovery and salvation are rooted in His faithfulness, not in our own works.

Therefore, as we navigate recovery, let us do so with a deep sense of gratitude and dependency on God's grace. It is through our faith, not the steps alone, that we experience true freedom and find purpose in our lives. Our faith in God's saving power empowers us to walk in the fullness of His love.

We come to understand that while people work, they receive wages that are rightfully earned. These wages cannot be deemed as a gift since they are a result of our efforts. However, God's honesty operates differently. It cannot be acquired through our own works; rather, it is received when we place our faith in the One who has the power to transform the deceitful into the honest in His divine perspective. It is through our unwavering belief that God's honesty is credited to our account, enabling our recovery and salvation.

In recovery, we understand that true healing comes when we surrender our struggles and trust in God's intervention. It is not our own striving that brings about lasting change, but rather the work of God's grace in our lives. The Scriptures affirm this truth, reminding us of the immeasurable joy that accompanies the forgiveness of our rebellious actions and the covering of our sins including alcoholism and addiction through the cleansing power of Jesus' blood.

As we hear the Lord speak His words of love and mercy over us, declaring, "I will never hold your sins against you," we experience a profound sense of happiness. This divine proclamation marks a turning point, a renewed hope that propels us forward on the path of recovery. In God's unwavering forgiveness, we find the strength needed to overcome sin.

Reflect on this: Does this profound sense of fulfillment only manifest in those who successfully complete each step of the recovery process, or is it attainable for all who embrace faith? Our answer is clear: It is through faith that we are credited with God's life-changing power in the journey of recovery. And faith without works is dead.

How did we come to receive this precious gift of righteousness and align ourselves with God's will? It is important to note that we had not yet completed the 12-step program when God accepted us. In fact, we were still powerless and unable to manage our lives. It was crystal clear that we lacked the ability to overcome our struggles when God made this declaration about us. However, it was later, even in our state of powerlessness, that we received an outward sign of spiritual awakening. This sign served as a seal, confirming that God had already transferred His righteousness and that He was aligning us with His will through faith.

This divine act of transferring righteousness and aligning with His will is not limited to us alone. It qualifies us to share this message of recovery with others who believe, even those who do not follow the traditional 12-step approach. Just as we have experienced, God extends His righteousness to them through faith as they align with His will. We recognize that we not only follow the authentic principles of faith, but we also provide guidance to those who have both completed the twelve steps and those who choose to embrace the path of faith, as we did prior to completing the steps.

The contrasting nature of faith and the step-by-step process is evident when it comes to the promise we receive. God has assured us, as well as all others who embark on this path, that we will be connected to a spiritual heir who will overcome all our character flaws. This promise is not fulfilled by merely completing the required steps, but rather through the righteousness that is transferred to us by faith as He aligns us with His will.

If the fulfillment of this promise were dependent on taking the steps alone, then faith would lose its power, and the promise itself would be rendered useless. **RECOVERY 5:12's** steps and measures of faith serve as catalysts for individual spiritual development, but they should not overshadow the life-changing power of faith. It is essential to recognize that adhering to 12-step programs can sometimes lead to a sense of guilt, whereas faith brings about freedom from such burdens.

Furthermore, it is important to acknowledge that where no steps exist, there cannot be a violation of those steps. Faith transcends the limitations of a prescribed process and opens up the possibility of a direct connection to the divine, unencumbered by the shortcomings or missteps associated with a structured system.

In essence, the promise of victory over our flaws is not contingent solely upon taking the steps, but rather on the righteousness that is transferred to us through unwavering faith as He aligns us with His will. By admitting faith and His aligning us with His will, we plug into its inherent power, allowing us to experience the fullness of God's promise flowing through our lives and into others.

The promise depends on faith, extending to all who follow this path of spiritual recovery. It is not limited to those obedient to the steps, but also to those who embrace the faith of fellow travelers. Some of us serve as living examples, as in the presence of God, we held firm in our belief that He has the power to resurrect the dead and bring into existence things that have not yet come to be. Even in the face of seemingly insurmountable obstacles, we clung to our faith in the promise and anticipated its fulfillment. We chose to trust in God's word, and as a result, we became dedicated followers of this spiritual path.

Despite the timing of the promise being made later, our faith remained unwavering and resilient as He aligned us with His will. We were not discouraged by our own inability to generate such steadfast faith. Our belief in God's promise never wavered; instead, it grew stronger and fortified our determination to follow **RECOVERY 5:12** steps and measures. We were filled with a mighty faith, fully convinced that God possessed all the power necessary to bring His promises to fruition. With hearts filled with gratitude, we glorify God for the faithfulness He bestowed upon us.

Now we understand the reason why our faith is counted as righteousness before God and is the driving force aligning us with His will. This declaration of righteousness and spiritual alignment was not exclusively spoken over us but is also available to all. When we wholeheartedly believe in and admit the One who possesses all power and knowledge, we too receive the imputation of perfect righteousness flowing from Him through our lives. This aligns us with His will. Jesus willingly surrendered Himself to be crucified, bearing the weight of our sins such as addictions and alcoholism, and through His resurrection, He demonstrated that He has reconciled us with God, making us righteous in His sight. In Jesus, we are aligned with His will.

Through our faith in Jesus, God's righteousness is credited to us, declaring us righteous in His sight. This grants us true and lasting peace with God, all thanks to the work of our Lord Jesus. Our faith guarantees us continual access to God's marvelous kindness, establishing a perfect relationship with Him. This fills us with incredible joy as we celebrate our hope and experience the glorious presence of God.

That's not all! Even in times of trouble, we have joyful confidence, knowing that our pressures develop in us patience. And patience refines our character, and proven character leads us back to hope. This hope is not a disappointing fantasy, because we now experience the endless love of God cascading into our hearts through the Holy Spirit who we are absolutely certain has entered our hearts and lives in us! He is truly accomplishing things in our lives that we could not have even imagined by aligning with His will.

When the time was right, Jesus came and died, showcasing His love for us sinners who were utterly helpless. It is rare for someone to die for the sake of a self-centered person. We can grasp the concept of someone sacrificing their life for a truly noble individual. However, Jesus displayed His fervent love for us by laying down His life while we were still in the depths of drugs and alcohol, lost and ungodly.

The depths of His unfailing love for us are boundless! Through the precious blood of Jesus, we have heard the powerful declaration, "You are now righteous in My sight." As a result of Christ's sacrificial offering, we are spared from ever experiencing the wrath of God. Even when we were once enemies, God, in His immense grace, fully reconciled us to Himself through the death of Jesus. This extraordinary act of salvation goes beyond mere friendship; it bestows upon us something greater.

Now that we have found peace with God and share in His resurrected life, we are not only rescued from the dominion of sins such as addictions and alcoholism but freed from its grip altogether. It is a profound deliverance that has set us free. And even beyond that, our hearts overflow with triumphant joy in our newfound relationship with God—all because of Jesus! His love, sacrifice, and resurrection have brought us into a state of unparalleled joy and eternal communion with Him.

The gift of grace surpasses the magnitude of sin – even alcoholism and addictions. When we succumb to sin, its effects permeate our entire being. Sins such as addictions and alcoholism once infiltrated our human experience, resulting in spiritual death. The shadow of spiritual death loomed over every aspect of our lives.

Even before the steps of recovery were laid out, sins such as addictions and alcoholism resided within us. However, where there were no specific steps, the weight of sin was not held against us. Nonetheless, spiritual death exerted its dominion from the beginning, even though we did not transgress in the same manner as others. The initial encounter with powerlessness and unmanageability served as a foretaste of the Deliverer who was to come, providing a glimpse of the redemption that awaited us.

In recovery, there is simply no comparison between the gravity of our past transgressions and the overflowing grace we now experience. The gift of grace surpasses the magnitude of our crimes in sin. While it is true that our actions cause harm to ourselves and others, the abundance of God's grace and His gracious gift of acceptance reaches far and wide, touching the lives of many. All of this is made possible because of what Jesus, our Deliverer, has done for us.

This gift of grace goes beyond recovering what was lost or, better yet, what we gave away. It offers us so much more than we could ever imagine. Our transgressions such as drinking and using drugs had left us facing a spiritual death sentence, with the verdict of "Guilty!" echoing in our hearts. However, this gracious gift sets us free from the chains of our past failures such as addictions and alcoholism, and it brings us into the perfect righteousness of God. We stand acquitted, with the resounding words of "Not guilty!" declared over us.

This gift of grace becomes our lifeline, our source of hope and recovery. It is through this gift that we find healing, redemption, and a new beginning. It is a reminder that no matter how deep our sins or how far we may have fallen, God's grace is greater. It is a beacon of light in our darkest moments, offering us a fresh start and the opportunity to live a life of freedom and purpose.

Once trapped in the clutches of spiritual death, our blunders allowed it to reign as the supreme ruler over our lives. However, now we are embraced even more firmly by the unyielding grip of grace. As a result, we not only continue to reign as royalty in life but also revel in our majestic freedom, bestowed upon us through the gift of His perfect righteousness found in Jesus. We have been delivered.

In other words, just as condemnation came upon us through transgression, so through one righteous act of Jesus' sacrifice, His perfect righteousness that makes us right with God and leads us to a victorious life is now available. Our disobedience opened the door for us to become sinners, but our obedience opened the door for us to be made perfectly right with God and acceptable to Him. We have a new Master!

Then, **RECOVERY 5:12** steps and measures of faith were introduced into God's plan to bring the reality of our sinfulness out of hiding. And yet, wherever sins such as addictions and alcoholism increased, there was more than enough of God's grace to triumph over it all. And just as all that which blocks us from Jesus reigned through spiritual death, so also is it conquered by grace reigning as King through righteousness, imparting eternal life through Jesus, our Lord and Savior.

The triumph of grace over sin. What then shall we do? Shall we continue in the grip of sins such as addictions and alcoholism so that God's grace may abound even more? Certainly not! We have died to the power of sin once and for all, just as a dead person passes away from this life. How, then, can we continue to live under its destructive rule any longer?

Let us not forget that all of us who have been baptized in Jesus' Name have also been baptized with His death. Through our baptism, we have been buried and entombed with Him, so that just as Glory raised Jesus from the dead, we too have been raised with Him. This resurrection empowers us to walk in the freshness of new life, free from the chains of sins such as addictions and alcoholism.

As we are permanently grafted onto Him, we not only experience a death like His but also a resurrection like His, which imparts new life to us. This new life breaks the grip of sin and fills us with the power to overcome its hold. Through the grace of Jesus, we are set free to live a life of victory.

In Jesus' Name, we admit the triumph of grace over sin, knowing that we are no longer bound by its chains. We walk in the newness of life that His resurrection brings, forever grateful for His transforming power in recovery.

Could it be any clearer that our former identities are now and forever deprived of their power? We were crucified with Him to dismantle the stronghold of sins such as addictions and alcoholism within us so that we would not continue to live one moment longer submitted to sin's power.

Indeed, a dead person is incapable of sinning. Therefore, if we have been crucified with Jesus, we understand that we also share in the fullness of His life. We recognize that just as Jesus has been raised from the dead and will never die again, His resurrection life has triumphed over spiritual death and its power has been completely defeated. Therefore, we never have to drink or use drugs again.

Through His surrender, Jesus died to the power of sin once and for all, but now He lives continuously. And in the same way, as we are joined with Him, we no longer identify ourselves as slaves to sin. Instead, we see ourselves as having been disconnected from its influence and unresponsive to its appeal. We choose to live in a daily relationship with Jesus, seeking to please God and walking in alignment with His will.

Through this intimate connection with Jesus, we find strength to resist the pull of sins such as addictions and alcoholism and live a life that brings pleasure to God. It is through this ongoing relationship and surrender to Him that we experience freedom from the power of sin and the abundant life that He offers.

We hold onto the truth that we are in a relationship with Jesus, and we continually align our lives with His example through His teachings. Through His Spirit, we are empowered to overcome the grip of sins such as alcoholism and addictions and live in the fullness of His life, walking in righteousness and freedom for the glory of God.

Sin's reign is over! It no longer has power over us. We refuse to let sins such as addictions and alcoholism control our lives and dictate our actions. Instead, we who are recovered surrender ourselves to God, embracing the resurrected life He has given us. Our focus is on living for His pleasure and advancing His kingdom.

It's important to remember sins such as addictions and alcoholism do not conquer us. God has conquered us and is now our Lord. Our recovery from sin is not defined by a set of steps but by the life-changing grace of God. His grace empowers us to resist temptation and break free from our chains.

Under God's grace, we experience true victory. We are no longer enslaved by our past struggles. Our lives are marked by righteousness, joy, and purpose. In alignment with His will, we continue to surrender to God's guidance. His grace works in us, renewing our minds and transforming our hearts. In recovery, we rely on God's grace to overcome challenges and walk in His perfect will. Through His grace, we are empowered to live a life of fulfillment.

Grace liberates us for God's service! So, what should our response be? Shall we indulge in sins such as addictions and alcoholism without restraint because there are no longer steps to condemn us? Absolutely not! Such a notion is repulsive to us. We comprehend that grace grants us the freedom to select our master. However, we choose with great care, for we willingly yield ourselves as devoted servants, committed to the one we opt to obey. That One is God, may you find Him now.

If we choose to embrace sin such as addictions and alcoholism, it assumes authority over us, taking ownership of our lives and immediately rewarding us with spiritual death. But when we choose to obey God, He leads us into the realm of His perfect righteousness. His divine guidance directs our path as He aligns us with His will.

In recovery, we are no longer enslaved to the destructive allure of sin. Instead, we serve God wholeheartedly, offering ourselves as instruments of His righteousness. By the empowering grace bestowed upon us by God, we are freed from the chains of sins such as addictions and alcoholism and equipped to live triumphant lives in alignment with His will. Our choices reflect our surrender to His lordship, and we discover profound joy and fulfillment as we follow His path of perfect righteousness.

We find comfort in the fact that God is pleased with our recovery transformation. Once upon a time, we were enslaved to the power of sin, but now our obedience runs deep within our hearts. Our lives are shaped by the truth we admit and the teachings we wholeheartedly devote ourselves to.

Today, we joyfully celebrate our freedom from our former master—sins such as addictions and alcoholism. Whether it be alcoholism, addictions, hurts, habits, or hang-ups, we have broken free from the chains of self-centeredness and entered into a new realm where God's perfect righteousness reigns over us. We willingly submit ourselves as loving servants to His divine will, seeking His life-changing power to guide our every step.

This surrender to God's righteousness grants us a sense of freedom that we never experienced while under the dominion of sin. Our lives are no longer defined by the bondage of our past but by the liberation found in our devotion to God's truth. We embrace this new identity as His beloved servants, walking in the light of His love.

In recovery, we have often used the language of "servant" and "master" to help us grasp the concepts of surrender and obedience. In the past, our bodies and souls were subjected to impurity, leading to further turmoil in our lives. However, a remarkable transformation has taken place within us.

Now, we willingly yield ourselves as servants of righteousness. This act of surrender takes us deeper into the realm of true holiness that we experience each time we pass through the west side of the Tabernacle journey, where we are set apart for God's purposes. In our former state, when we were bound as servants to sin, we had no obligation to righteousness. We lived our lives without any regard for moral principles. We did not care about the next right thing even if we could have performed it.

But now, as we embrace the path of recovery, we have experienced a profound shift. We have willingly submitted ourselves to the authority of righteousness, recognizing its power to lead us toward recovery and salvation. Our lives are no longer characterized by the destructive patterns of sins such as addictions and alcoholism but by a sincere devotion to the pursuit of righteousness.

This surrender to righteousness sets us apart, transforming our thoughts, actions, and desires. It guides us on a path of true holiness, where we align ourselves with God's will and seek to live according to His standard. It is through this surrender that we find a new way of life, untethered from the chains. We are now bound to the life-changing power of righteousness.

What advantage is there in engaging in these shame-inducing behaviors? They only leave us burdened with a legacy of shame and immediately lead to spiritual death. However, a remarkable transformation has taken place.

As God's devoted servants, we now live in freedom from the power of sin. It's essential to reflect on the incredible benefits we now experience. We are brought deeper into the realm of true holiness, a journey that culminates in eternal life. The meager wage that sins such as addictions and alcoholism offer is spiritual death, a consequence that is separation from God.

In contrast, God bestows upon us His extravagant gift of eternal life, which is found through our relationship with our Lord Jesus. This gift far surpasses anything that sins such as addictions and alcoholism could ever offer. It is a manifestation of His boundless love towards us.

With recovery being the focus, let us rejoice in our new identity as God's beloved servants, freed from the power of sin. Through our relationship with Jesus, we experience the promise of a recovered life. Let's live in gratitude, fully embracing the abundant life that God has provided for us.

Now, let's consider the concept of freedom from the steps. For those familiar with them, we understand that when we die, our obligation to the steps comes to an end. It's similar to a married couple who vow to stay together until death separates them. If one spouse passes away, the surviving partner is released from the marriage bond.

Likewise, in our journey of recovery, our death with Christ signifies the end of our old life controlled by sin and the rules of the steps. Through His grace, we are set free from the burdens of our past. It's not about adhering to strict guidelines but being joined to Jesus, our source of strength.

In this new life, we no longer need to rely solely on steps. Instead, we rely on our relationship with Jesus to guide us on the path to recovery and salvation. Let us admit this truth and walk confidently in the freedom that comes from a life surrendered to God's power.

We can apply the same principle to our relationship with God. Through our spiritual awakening and identification with the body of Christ, we have died to our former "husband," the steps. This death and resurrection experience enables us to enter into a new union with the One who was raised from the dead.

Now, we are free to "marry" this new partner, who is Jesus Christ, our Savior. In this divine union, we are empowered to bear spiritual fruit for God. We are no longer bound by the limitations of the steps but are called to a deeper, more intimate relationship with our Heavenly Father. Let us embrace this new covenant and seek the life-changing power of God's love to flow through us, producing lasting change.

In our previous existence, the steps served as a guide, shedding light on our powerlessness and unmanageability. They revealed our character defects, leading to the manifestation of a spiritual malady. However, since our liberation from the steps, we have died to their influence. We are no longer driven by the approach of following a prescribed path.

Now, we are free to serve God in a new way, guided by the freshness of a transformed life empowered by the Holy Spirit. Our motivation stems from a deeper connection with God rather than adherence to a set of steps. Let us embrace this freedom and seek the Holy Spirit to lead us on a journey of spiritual fulfillment.

What, then, is the purpose of the steps? Are we suggesting that they are sinful? Certainly not! In fact, the steps serve a vital role in recovery. They provide a clear definition of our powerlessness and unmanageability in the face of sins such as addictions and alcoholism. For instance, when the steps encourage us to avoid self-seeking behavior, they serve as a catalyst for us to recognize the wrongness of our desire for attention that rightfully belongs to others.

It is through the guidance of God's principle that sins such as addictions and alcoholism are awakened within us and find a foothold to stir up various wrong desires. Without the steps, the powerlessness and unmanageability of sin remain dormant, hidden beneath the surface. Therefore, we acknowledge the significance of the steps in helping us confront our weaknesses and facilitating our paths to recovery. They bring awareness to the destructive nature of sin and provide a framework for lasting transformation.

In our former life, we lived without a clear understanding of the problems of addictions, alcoholism, hurt, habits, and hang-ups. As a result, we were unaware of the powerlessness and unmanageability of the sins that resided within us. However, when we heard of the **RECOVERY 5:12** steps and measures of faith, the true nature of our sins became apparent, and their destructive consequences became evident, leading to a spiritual death sentence.

It is important to note that drugs and alcohol themselves are not the problem. The issue lies in our own fallen nature and our susceptibility to sin such as addictions and alcoholism's influence. **RECOVERY 5:12's** steps and measures, when understood and followed correctly, are designed to bring life and freedom. It is our misinterpretation or misapplication of them that can lead to negative outcomes.

Therefore, we acknowledge the importance of the correctness of the steps and measures. They serve as a valuable tool for individual spiritual growth and transformation when approached with humility and a sincere desire for recovery.

Life under the steps. Did something meant to be good become spiritual death to us? Certainly not! It was the powerlessness and unmanageability of unmasked sins such as addictions and alcoholism that produced our spiritual death. The steps and measures merely uncovered the selfishness and evil of our sins so they could be seen for what they are. We know that the steps and measures are divinely inspired and come from the spiritual realm, but we are human beings made of flesh and trafficked as a slave under sin's authority.

As individuals in the grip of sin, we often find ourselves in a perplexing state. Despite our genuine desire to do what is right, we continually fall into behaviors that go against our moral compasses. Even when our actions contradict our intentions, our consciences affirm the importance of the steps that guide us toward recovery.

In this journey, we come to recognize that it is not our true selves who are engaging in these destructive behaviors, but rather the unwelcome intruder of sin that has infiltrated our humanity. We acknowledge that our fallen nature harbors nothing good, and our own willpower alone is insufficient to bring about lasting change. Our noble aspirations to do good are often thwarted when we succumb to the very things we strive to avoid. This dissonance between our desires and actions reveals the influence of sin, hindering us from fully embracing our identities in Christ.

Through our experiences, we come to understand the ongoing struggle within us. While we genuinely desire to please God, we discern another power at work in our humanity, constantly waging war against our consciences and taking us captive to the principle of sin. It is an agonizing situation, leaving us trapped and helpless.

But thanks be to God! He alone possesses the Power to rescue us from this miserable state of alcoholism and addiction. Through our Lord Jesus, a way out is provided. When we rely on Him, our renewed minds become focused on God's righteous principles.

In this realization, we find hope. Though our flesh is aligned with the principle of sin, our transformed thinking allows God to align our spirits with His ways. We recognize that our deliverance is not of our own doing, but that it is through the mighty Power of God that we are set free from the grip of sins such as addictions and alcoholism and eternal spiritual death. With gratitude, we surrender to God's Power, relying on His guidance to lead us on the path of recovery.

Living by the empowering presence of the Holy Spirit, we find freedom. The case against us is closed, and there is no longer any condemning voice haunting those of us who are united with Jesus in life. The powerful principle of Jesus Christ, made possible through the anointing of His Name, has set us free.

We recognize that God has accomplished what the steps alone could never achieve. The steps, while valuable, are constrained by the limitations of human nature. But through the Holy Spirit, we experience a supernatural transformation that transcends our weaknesses and brings about true freedom. It is through the power of God's Spirit that we are empowered to overcome the chains of sin and walk in the fullness of life that Jesus has secured for us.

Yet God through Jesus identifies with human weakness. Clothed with humanity, God gave His body to be an offering so that He could once and for all condemn the guilt and power of sins such as addictions and alcoholism. Now we see how every righteous requirement of the **RECOVERY 5:12** steps and measures are fulfilled through Jesus living His life in us. We are free to live, not according to our flesh, but by the dynamic Power of the Holy Spirit!

When we allowed our fleshly desires to dictate our actions, our focus was solely on our own self-interests. However, as we surrender to the leading of the Holy Spirit, our motivations are aligned with spiritual realities. We come to understand that a life governed by self-will is spiritual death, but when we yield our will to the control of the Spirit, we find true life and peace.

It's important to recognize that our self-will, driven by the desires of the flesh, opposes God's plan for our lives and refuses to submit to His guidance. No matter how hard we may try, our fleshly nature cannot please God. However, when we seek the Holy Spirit, He guides our lives, and we are no longer under the dominion of the flesh but under the authority of the Spirit. This connection to the Holy Spirit is a vital indication of our belonging to Him and experiencing the transforming work He desires to do within us.

Now Jesus lives His life in us! And even though our bodies are spiritually dead because of the effects of sins such as addictions and alcoholism, His life-giving Spirit imparts life to us because we are fully accepted by God. Yes, God raised Jesus to life! And since God's Spirit of Resurrection lives in us, He raises our spiritually dead body to spiritual life by the same Spirit that breathes life into us!

We are no longer bound to the desires and demands of the flesh. We have been set free from its control, and we are under no obligation to live according to its dictates. When we allow ourselves to be driven by the flesh, we are spiritually dead. However, when we embrace the life of the Spirit, we experience a transformation that leads to the death of the corrupt ways of the flesh. In this surrender to the Spirit's guidance, we taste and partake in the abundant life that God has in store for us.

As spiritually mature children of God, we are guided by the promptings of the Holy Spirit. We no longer operate from a place of religious duty, which breeds fear and a sense of never measuring up. Instead, we have received the Spirit of complete acceptance, embracing us as members of God's family. We never feel abandoned or alone, for the Spirit rises within us, and together with our spirits, we cry out with heartfelt affection, addressing God as our beloved Father. The Holy Spirit continually reminds us of our identities as cherished children of God, speaking intimately to our innermost being, assuring us, "You are God's beloved child!" In **RECOVERY 5:12**, this is what our journey through the southside of the Tabernacle revealed along with the holiness of the *third measure of faith*.

As genuine children of God, we are entitled to partake in all His riches, including our deliverance from sin. We are heirs of God Himself, and through our relationship with Jesus, we inherit the power to overcome the chains of sin. Just as we accept His sufferings as our own, we also embrace the process of recovery, knowing that it leads to transformation. In our journey, we experience His mercy, which empowers us to break free from the bondage of addiction and walk in the fullness of a new life. We are in Him, in His triumph over sins such as alcoholism and addictions, and His victory becomes our own.

A glorious destiny of freedom from sin awaits us! We firmly believe that the trials and struggles we face in recovery are insignificant compared to the immense glory that is to come. The entire universe eagerly anticipates the manifestation of God's glorious work in us, yearning to witness our transformation. The consequences of our past actions have brought bondage to creation, but now, there is a collective longing for salvation. Creation itself groans, like a woman in labor, waiting for the moment of deliverance. And we, who have tasted the first fruits of the Spirit, join in this yearning, eagerly desiring the fullness of our identity as God's children, including the transformation of our physical bodies. This hope fuels our perseverance as we patiently wait for its fulfillment, trusting in the unseen promises yet to be revealed. Our hope is not in vain, for we know that God is faithful and will bring about the complete manifestation of our glorious destiny.

In recovery, there are moments when we feel uncertain. We may not know how to pray or what to ask for, as the weight of our struggles can be too heavy to put into words. But in those vulnerable moments, the Holy Spirit comes alongside us, intimately acquainted with our human frailty. The Spirit becomes our advocate, interceding on our behalf before God, pleading for us with groanings that transcend language. This is a tongue that needs no human interpretation, for our hearts know that the Spirit is interpreting our needs into a heavenly language. The Holy Spirit understands the depths of our pain, the battles we face, and the healing we desperately need. When we are at a loss, the Spirit steps in, bridging the gap between our brokenness and God's perfect understanding. We can find comfort in knowing that the Holy Spirit is present, guiding our prayers through tongues and carrying our burdens, especially when we struggle to express ourselves. In recovery, the Holy Spirit is our constant companion, bringing divine intervention beyond what known words can convey. It is best to speak with Him alone than with someone who might misunderstand.

God, who intimately examines our hearts in *steps four* and *five* of **RECOVERY 5:12**, is fully aware of our deepest longings and desires. He understands the inner workings of the Holy Spirit within us, as the Spirit fervently intercedes for us, aligning our prayers through speaking in tongues with God's divine purpose and our unique destinies. We firmly believe that every intricate detail of our lives is intricately woven together by God to fulfill His perfect plan. As His beloved children, we have been called to live out His intended purpose for us. Even before we were born, God had intricate knowledge of us and ordained us to be conformed to the likeness of Jesus. We are part of a vast family of recovered people, and we are destined to become like Jesus in the way He loves others. In this beautiful design, we find our identity, as we grow in resemblance to our Savior and walk in unity with our fellow recovered believers.

God, in His divine wisdom, predestined our destiny and called us to Himself. Through His calling, He graciously imputed His perfect righteousness to all who responded. And as recipients of His righteousness, He has glorified us in Jesus. We are elevated to a position of honor and shared glory in Him. This is not our doing, but the marvelous work of God, who has chosen to bestow His glorification upon us. It is a testament to His life-changing power in our lives. We stand in awe of His marvelous plan and gratefully admit who we are in Him.

The demonstration of God's love is awe-inspiring. It leaves no room for doubt. If God Himself stands by our side, who can possibly overcome us? The evidence of His love is seen in His greatest gift to humanity, Jesus. God willingly offered Jesus as a perfect sacrifice, fully surrendering Him on our behalf. Through this act, God shows His complete devotion and holds nothing back from us. He lavishly pours out His love, offering us everything that He has to give. We can rest assured that God's love knows no limits and His provisions are abundant. In the face of such love, we are filled with confidence, knowing that we are secure in His embrace.

Who then can condemn us, those whom God has chosen to be His own in the midst of sin's struggles? It is God Himself, the judge, who has declared us "Not guilty!" He has demonstrated His love by giving us the greatest gift of all, Jesus, who offered Himself as a sacrifice for our surrender. Jesus not only laid down His life for us but also triumphed over death, rising again, and ascending to the very power of God's authority. How could He ever condemn us when He continually intercedes for our victory? In the face of sin such as addictions and alcoholism, we can find comfort in knowing that no accusations hold weight. Instead, we have a powerful advocate in Jesus, who prays for our freedom. With His unwavering support, we can confidently face our struggles, knowing that we are destined for triumph.

What can possibly separate us from the unfailing love of Jesus, especially in recovery? The answer is clear: nothing and no one. His love transcends all boundaries. No matter the problems we may face, His love remains unchanging. Even in the face of persecution, His love stands strong. We encounter challenges, but His love for us endures. We are not alone in our struggles, for Jesus walks beside us, providing comfort. His love empowers us to persevere, no matter the circumstances. So, let us take heart in the unbreakable bond of love between us and our Savior, knowing that His love will always prevail.

Yet even in the midst of all these challenges, we triumph over them all, for God has made us to be more than conquerors, and His demonstrated Love is our glorious victory over everything, even sins such as addictions and alcoholism!

We now stand firm with unwavering confidence, fully aware that no force in the universe can separate us from the relentless love of God. His love conquers all, prevailing over the grip of sin, the struggles we face, the temptations that arise, and the darkness that surrounds us. There is nothing in our pasts, presents, or futures that could weaken the powerful love God has for us. It is a love that extends beyond our shortcomings. It is a love that breaks the chains of addiction and sets us free to walk in victory. No matter how intense the battle is, we are assured that God's love is unchanging. It is a love that pursues us, strengthens us, and empowers us to overcome every obstacle. We can rest in the assurance that His love is greater than any sin, and with His love, we can experience true freedom and complete recovery.

We carry a burden of love for our fellow members of the recovery community. Our hearts are heavy with sorrow as we witness the struggles and pain you endure. We long for you to experience the life-changing power of faith in Jesus. Our conscience compels us to speak the truth, for our love for you is so deep that we would be willing to bear any sacrifice, even to be separated from Jesus, if it meant that you would come to know Him. Such is the intensity of our desire to see you find salvation and freedom in a relationship with our Savior.

You, our fellow members in recovery, are living testimonies of salvation, chosen by God and part of His divine plan. In your journey, you have access to God's glorious presence, the wisdom and guidance of the steps, the profound teachings found in this book, the supportive fellowship of the recovery community, and the life-changing promises of God. We recognize that our own recovery is intertwined with yours, as we share a common heritage. Together, we form a spiritual family, united by the Holy Spirit, who reigns over all things. Our voices join in eternal praise to Him, both now and forever. Amen!

Undoubtedly, God remains faithful in fulfilling His promises to the recovery community, and His faithfulness will never falter. However, it is important to understand that not everyone who has gone through the steps truly belongs to the spiritual awakening that they signify. Merely going through the motions and completing the steps does not guarantee a genuine transformation of the spirit. It is not the physical act of taking the steps that determines spiritual awakening; rather, it is through God's promise that we are truly counted as spiritually awakened. It is the children born of His promise who are recognized as experiencing true spiritual transformation.

God's grace in recovery! Does this mean that God is unfair in choosing whom to extend His grace to? Absolutely not! God's choice in the realm of recovery is not based on our efforts. It is not about how badly we want it. Instead, it is solely based on God's divine purpose. God has the right to show mercy to whomever He chooses and to extend His grace even to those who seem undeserving. It is His loving and merciful nature that guides His selection process. We must humbly accept that it is within God's authority to choose whom He wills to grant freedom from addictions and to transform lives.

The sovereignty of God in recovery! If someone questions God's authority and asks, "If God is fully in control, how can He hold us accountable? Who can resist His will?" Who are we, mere human beings formed from clay, to question the One who molded us? Shall we dare to say to the Potter, "Why did you create me like this?" Are we denying the Potter's right to shape and mold the clay according to His divine plan? Does not the Potter have the authority to create from the same lump of clay both vessels of great beauty and vessels of common use? We must submit to God's sovereignty in the process of recovery, trusting that He has the wisdom to shape us according to His purpose.

In the midst of God's righteous judgment and His rightful authority to display His power, He exhibits extraordinary patience towards us, even though we deserve His wrath. We, who were once vessels destined for destruction, now witness His mercy and the glorious manifestation of His presence. God has chosen us in advance to receive His glory, as we walk the path of **RECOVERY 5:12**. Let us remember the prophetic words spoken by God: "To those who were rejected and deemed not My people, I will declare, 'You are mine.' And to those who were unloved, I will proclaim, 'You are my beloved.'" In the very places where we were once considered insignificant, we will be known as "Children of the living God." We urge the recovery communities to take heed, for though their numbers are vast like the sands of the seashore, only a remnant will find salvation. The Lord, Yahweh, will fulfill His word without delay and bring about His plans on the earth.

What does this paradox teach us? It reveals a profound irony: Those who were not actively seeking recovery through **RECOVERY 5:12** were the ones who embraced it fully, receiving the gift of perfect righteousness through a measure of faith that aligned us to His will. On the other hand, those who diligently pursued recovery through the twelve steps did not attain the same level of transformation. Why did this happen? It was because they sought righteousness through their own efforts, relying on works instead of faith. They were unable to grasp that righteousness could only be obtained through faith, and they stumbled over the stumbling stone—the very concept that challenged their preconceived notions. As it was foretold, "Be cautious! I am placing a stumbling stone in their spiritual path, a rock of offense that will cause them to stumble. However, those who believe in Jesus will not be put to shame." We had free will after all. The freedom to give our thoughts over to Jesus Christ or not.

Our hearts are filled with a fervent desire and our prayers are ceaseless for our fellows in recovery programs to encounter the saving grace of God. We recognize their deep devotion to God, yet many remain in spiritual darkness. They have overlooked the righteousness that God freely offers, choosing instead to rely on their own conceptions and efforts to earn acceptance from Him. They have refused to surrender to the righteousness that comes from God alone. Let it be known that Jesus is in the culmination of the steps. Through Him, God has imparted His flawless righteousness to all who place their measure of faith in Him.

In the past, it was written that one must thoroughly and honestly follow every aspect of the steps to attain spiritual awakening. However, the faith and righteousness we now receive proclaim a different message. It tells us that we don't need to embark on an impossible journey to find the Messiah or bring Him back from the dead. The faith and righteousness we admit speak these words to us: God's living message is within our reach, as close as our own heartbeat and as near as the words on our lips.

So, what is this living message of God? It is the revelation of faith that leads beyond recovery unto salvation, the very message we proclaim. As we took these steps, openly declaring that Jesus is Lord and sincerely believing in our hearts that God raised Him from the dead, we experienced more than recovery. We experience salvation. Our believing hearts receive the precious gift of God's righteousness, and our mouths overflow with gratitude for this great salvation. The Scriptures encourage us with the assurance that everyone who puts their trust in Him will never be disappointed.

The Good News is for everyone, regardless of whether they follow a recovery program or **RECOVERY 5:12**, because our Lord Jehovah is the same for all. He is abundantly generous and ready to pour out His treasures upon all who call upon His Name. It is true that anyone who calls upon the Name of the Lord Yahweh will be rescued and experience new life through repentance and baptism in Jesus' Name for the remission of sins such as alcoholism and addiction.

How can someone call upon Him if they have not yet believed? And how can they believe in someone they have never heard of? And how can they hear without someone proclaiming the message of life? And how can the message be proclaimed if there are no messengers sent out? That is why the Scriptures declare the great importance of those who bring the joyful news of peace and good things to come. However, not everyone will welcome this good news, as it is written: "Lord, is there anyone who hears and believes our message?"

No, it is not that recovery programs haven't heard the message, for the voice proclaiming the message of Jesus has been heard throughout the world and has reached the ends of the earth. We have indeed heard the message. We understood that God's message was not only for ourselves but for others as well. It was even foretold that God would use those who are considered "nobodies" and those without understanding to provoke and stir up those who were seeking Him.

Fearless persons in recovery programs boldly proclaim that they have encountered the Power of God even when they were not actively seeking it. The manifestation of God's presence appeared before them, even though they were not consciously asking to know Jesus. Yet, regarding those in recovery programs, it can be said, "With love, God has persistently reached out His hands day after day, offering Himself to this unbelieving and stubborn people."

God's love and pursuit of those in recovery programs, and indeed of all people, are relentless. Despite any unbelief, God continues to extend His love and offer of salvation to us, always desiring for us to experience His life-changing grace.

God will not forget His promises to the recovery programs! We ask this question: Did God really push aside and reject anybody? Absolutely not! For we ourselves are in recovery, thoroughly following our path, from the strength given by God. God has not rejected those in recovery programs! We hear testimony in the rooms of recovery, and how we pray to God, agonizing over the steps? "Lord, they have assassinated the characters of the old-timers; they have demolished Your sacred places. Now we are the only ones left and they want to remove us!" The revelation God spoke to us in response: "You are not alone. For I have preserved a remnant for myself—thousands of others who are faithful and have refused to worship their own conceptions."

Indeed, God's work in this age of fulfillment is characterized by His abundant grace that empowers His chosen ones. It is important to understand that this grace is not earned through our good works; rather, it is a gift freely given by God. The striving of recovery programs or anyone else cannot achieve what only God's grace provides.

In His divine wisdom, some have been chosen to receive this grace and experience its transforming power, while others have been hardened and unable to receive the truth. As it was prophesied, God granted them a spirit of deep slumber, closing their eyes to the truth, and preventing their ears from hearing it, even until this present day.

Scripture also speaks of the consequences that befall those who resist God's grace and reject His truth. Their table, symbolizing their sources of satisfaction and happiness, becomes a snare and a trap that leads to their own ruin. They receive the retribution they deserve; their eyes are blindfolded from seeing the truth, and they remain stooped over in their spiritual blindness.

It is a sobering reminder that our response to God's grace is crucial. Those who humbly admit His grace and surrender to His will find transformation and salvation. However, those who reject His grace and harden their hearts miss out on the blessings and spiritual insight that come through a relationship with Him.

We are not saying that recovery programs have stumbled so badly that they never recover. On the contrary, their stumble and struggles have served a greater purpose in God's plan. The extension of salvation to all, including those following **RECOVERY 5:12**, is meant to provoke and awaken a sense of longing and desire in recovery programs. It is a reminder that the very things that God has freely given to some are available to all.

The world as a whole is being enriched through the failures and shortcomings of recovery programs. Their experiences serve as a catalyst for growth and spiritual wealth for those in the **RECOVERY 5:12** community. However, we only imagine the immense blessings and spiritual awakening that will come when recovery programs themselves fully embrace the truth and experience their own restoration.

The restoration of recovery programs holds the potential to bring about tremendous spiritual abundance, not only for themselves but for all who witness and partake in their journey. It is a testament to God's redemptive power and His ability to turn struggles into sources of inspiration and transformation.

Now, we address those who are walking the path of spiritual recovery through **RECOVERY 5:12**, as we are called to be disciples and reach out to those who are committed to giving themselves completely to and thoroughly following our path. We unintentionally bring attention to this ministry whenever we are in the presence of recovery programs, as they see hope in us which stirs up a sense of longing and desire within them. It is not our aim to make them envious of the abundant blessings that God has bestowed upon those who wholeheartedly embrace **RECOVERY 5:12** steps and measures, however, many are won over to the recovery found in our journey.

If the temporary rejection of recovery programs has already released the reconciling power of God's grace into the world, we can only imagine the incredible impact it will have when they are reinstated and reconciled to God. It will unleash resurrection power throughout every aspect of our lives. The restoration and reconciliation of recovery programs will bring about a life-changing and life-giving force that will permeate and rejuvenate our entire recovery existence.

We eagerly anticipate the day when recovery programs fully embrace the truth and experience the power of God's grace in their lives. It will be a testament to the boundless love and redemptive work of God, not only in their individual lives but also in the lives of all who witness and partake in their recovery.

A cautionary message to believers recovering through **RECOVERY 5:12**. Just as many who access God in recovery programs are dedicated and set apart for Him, those who faithfully follow our path are also set apart. Just as the roots of a tree are considered holy and devoted to God, so are the branches. However, it is important to note that some branches have been pruned and removed. And we, who were once outsiders and not part of this cultivated tree, have been graciously grafted in by God, becoming joint partners with the remaining branches to partake in the wonderful richness of the recovery culture that has been nurtured.

Let us not become proud or boastful, thinking that we are superior to the recovery programs. There is no reason for arrogance, as the new spiritual path we embrace does not support or sustain itself independently. Instead, we acknowledge and recognize that our very life and growth are dependent on the root from which we are nourished.

We humbly acknowledge our indebtedness to the root, which provides us with spiritual nourishment. Our place among the branches is a testament to the unmerited favor of God, who has chosen to graft us into this sacred journey of recovery. Let us approach our partnership with humility and a deep sense of reverence for the foundation that upholds us.

We must be cautious not to develop a sense of entitlement, thinking that recovery programs were removed just to make room for us. It is true that some programs have been pruned due to their lack of faith. However, we must remember that our attachment to this path of recovery is solely based on our faith in God.

We should never take our position for granted. Instead, let us approach our journey with a deep sense of awe. Just as God did not spare those recovery programs that fell into unbelief, we should be aware that we too are accountable to God. We must fix our gaze on the simultaneous kindness and strict justice of God.

God's treatment of those who fell into unbelief was severe, the consequences of turning away from faith. Yet, His relationship with us is characterized by tenderness. It is imperative that we continue to trust in His kindness. Otherwise, we risk also being cut off from the life-giving source of His grace. Let us remain steadfast, cultivating a deep reverence for the God who guides the recovery journey.

Indeed, God is always willing to extend His mercy to those who turn from unbelief to embrace faith. Just as God brought us into this path of recovery, even though we were once part of a recovery program, He is more than capable of reconnecting the recovery programs by guiding them back from their own cultivated conceptions of a higher power.

God's desire is for all people, regardless of their background or previous paths, to come to faith and experience His life-changing power. He longs for reconciliation and recovery, and He works in the lives of individuals and programs alike.

As we continue our own recovery journeys, let us hold onto hope and pray for the reconnection and renewal of the recovery programs. May they turn from unbelief to faith, rediscovering their own unique paths to healing and growth. And may we, as beneficiaries of God's grace, extend love and support to those who are still on their own journey of recovery.

The mystery of the Gospel and how **RECOVERY 5:12** constantly points towards it is profound and awe-inspiring. It is important for us to approach it with a willingness to learn, rather than assuming we already have all the answers. We need to recognize that there is a temporary resistance to the Gospel within the recovery community, but this hardening is not permanent.

God's plan includes individuals who will embrace the **RECOVERY 5:12** path and experience more than recovery but be pointed to salvation. These people are being reached and incorporated into God's family; His redemptive work is extending to encompass all recovery programs. This demonstrates God's unfathomable grace and His desire for the salvation of all.

As we contemplate this mystery, let us maintain a posture of humility, seeking discernment from God. Let us continue to share the message of salvation with the recovery community, trusting that God's timing for their salvation will ultimately be fulfilled.

Indeed, it is true that there is opposition to the Gospel within some recovery programs. However, it is important to remember that God's love extends to all people, including those who currently oppose the Gospel. The initial calling and choosing by God of individuals within these programs is a testament to His divine plan and purpose.

Once God chooses someone and bestows His gifts upon them, His calling and gifts are irrevocable. His love is not easily withdrawn. While some individuals may currently be resistant to the Gospel, it does not mean that God has abandoned His love for them. Instead, we can trust in God's faithfulness and His ongoing work in the lives of those within the recovery programs.

Being recovered among those of **RECOVERY 5:12**, it is essential that we embody the love and compassion of God as we interact with the recovery community. Our responsibility is to extend a helping hand, offer support, and share the message of God's grace and redemption.

By demonstrating love and acceptance, we create a safe and welcoming environment for individuals in the recovery community to explore and embrace the life-changing power of the Gospel. Our words and actions should align with the principles of **RECOVERY 5:12**, reflecting the love, forgiveness, and recovery that God offers.

Through genuine relationships, we provide a living testimony of the positive changes that come from embracing faith and following the path of **RECOVERY 5:12**. Our goal should be to inspire hope, provide encouragement, and ultimately lead others to experience God's love and His plan for their lives.

Remember, our mission is not to impose our beliefs upon others, but rather to serve as living examples of the life-changing power of the Gospel. Through our love and kindness, we can make a significant impact and create opportunities for others to encounter God's grace and find permanent recovery in their lives.

Indeed, being recovered in **RECOVERY 5:12**, we can attest to the life-changing power of God's tender mercies in our own lives. We were once rebels and big book Pharisees, going against God's will and pursuing our own conceptions. However, through His lovingkindness and mercy, we have experienced a profound change.

Having personally tasted God's tender mercies, we are now called to extend those same mercies to others, including those in the recovery community. We understand the doubts that can arise on the journey to recovery and spiritual awakening. Therefore, we can empathize with their experiences and offer them a compassionate approach.

Rather than judging recovery programs for their unbelief, we open the door to share the abundant blessings and grace that God has poured out on us. We recognize that all of humanity, regardless of their background, can find themselves imprisoned by unbelief. But God, in His infinite love, unlocks our hearts and extends His tender mercies to all who are willing to take steps and measures toward Him.

Our role is to be conduits of God's love and mercy, inviting others to experience the recovery and salvation that comes from embracing faith and surrendering to God's plan. Through our actions and testimonies, we can demonstrate the reality of God's tender mercies and inspire others to seek His grace and forgiveness. In essence, by sharing our own stories of redemption and extending God's tender mercies, we can help others in the recovery community find healing and salvation in their lives.

Regardless of our conceptions, we can never wrap our minds around the riches of God, the depth of His wisdom, and the marvel of His perfect knowledge! We can never search out the mysterious way He carries out His plans! We can never discover how the Lord thinks! Or: "Who has ever first given something to God that obligates God to owe him something in return?" Because God is the source and sustainer of everything, everything finds fulfillment in Him. All praise and honor are given to Him forever! In Jesus' Name, Amen!

The transforming power of the Gospel calls for a wholehearted response from us following the recovery path of **RECOVERY 5:12**. We are called to surrender ourselves completely to God, offering our lives as living sacrifices dedicated to His purposes. This act of surrender is a sacred commitment and an expression of our genuine worship.

Living in holiness becomes our aim as we seek to align our lives with what delights God's heart. We understand that our lives are no longer conforming to the opinions of the culture around us but are being inwardly transformed by the Holy Spirit. This transformation involves a complete reformation of our thinking patterns.

Through the work of the Holy Spirit, our minds are renewed, enabling us to discern God's will for our lives. Our transformed thinking guides our actions and behaviors, leading us to live a beautiful life that is pleasing and perfect in God's eyes.

As we respond to God's marvelous mercies, we embrace a life of obedience. We seek to honor God in every area of our lives, seeking His truth to shape our character. Being recovered, our transformed lives become a testimony of the power of the Gospel, drawing others to experience the satisfaction found in a life surrendered to God.

RECOVERY 5:12 teaches us that our role in the body of Christ is characterized by humility which is selflessness. God's grace enables us to recognize and address the dangers of pride that hinder our spiritual growth and unity as believers.

Rather than being driven by selfish desires and seeking gain, we are called to empty ourselves of self-centeredness. This means shifting our focus from our own interests to the well-being and needs of others. We embrace a servant-hearted attitude, considering others as more important than ourselves.

In assessing our worth, we rely on the measure of faith that God has given us. Our self-esteem is not based on worldly standards, but on how God sees us. We recognize that our true worth comes from being created by God and from our identities as redeemed children of the highest King.

By admitting appropriate self-esteem in Christ, we find a balance in recognizing our strengths and weaknesses, celebrating our unique gifts and abilities while also acknowledging our dependence on God's grace and the contributions of others. This helps us maintain humility and a proper perspective of ourselves within the body of Christ.

As we walk in humility through the Holy Spirit, we contribute to the harmony of the body of Christ. We recognize that each member has a valuable role to play, and we celebrate the diversity of gifts and talents within the recovery community of believers.

In recovery, we recognize that each person has unique strengths and gifts given by the Spirit. Just as the Church and the human body are made up of many parts with different functions, so too is the recovery community. We are all interconnected and rely on each other for support.

Some of us have the gift of insight. We tap into our own experiences and share words of wisdom and guidance, offering hope to others in recovery.

Others have a natural inclination to serve. We find fulfillment in helping our fellow friends in recovery, whether it's through lending a helping hand, sharing resources, or simply being there to listen and support.

Some of us have a talent for teaching. We have a deep understanding of the principles and tools of recovery and are able to effectively communicate with others, empowering them to make positive changes in their lives.

The gift of encouragement is a powerful tool in recovery. Some have a knack for lifting others up and providing motivation during challenging times. Our words and actions bring comfort to those around us.

There are those among us who have a generous spirit. We give without expecting anything in return, freely offering our time, resources, and support to meet the needs of our fellow recovering individuals. Our generosity fosters an environment of compassion.

Leadership is another valuable gift in the recovery community. We take on roles of guidance and mentorship, using our experiences and knowledge to inspire and guide others on their recovery journeys. Through our leadership, we help create a sense of direction and unity.

Lastly, some of us possess a natural ability to show empathy and compassion. We understand the struggles and challenges faced by our peers and offer a non-judgmental space for them to share their experiences. Our compassion helps create a sense of belonging and connection within the recovery community.

In recovery, each person's unique gifts and talents are essential for collective healing and spiritual growth. By nurturing these gifts, we create a supportive environment where everyone can thrive. Together, we contribute to the recovery of the whole community, spreading hope, strength, and inspiration along the way.

In our transformed relationships, our hearts are guided by love and humility. We reject selfishness and embrace virtue. We treat our fellow recovering travelers as family, showing them tender respect. We continually strive to honor one another, surpassing ourselves in our regard for each other.

Our enthusiasm is directed toward serving Jesus Christ, and we keep our passion for Him alive. The Holy Spirit radiates through us, infusing us with joy as we dedicate ourselves to His service. In times of trouble, we maintain constant communion with God.

We actively care for the needs of our fellow believers, offering our support. We extend warm hospitality, welcoming others into our lives. Instead of speaking curses, we speak blessings over those who reject us. We share in the joys and sorrows of our recovery community.

Living harmoniously, we value others just as we value ourselves. We reject a self-centered attitude and willingly engage in humble service, identifying with those who are humbled as in **RECOVERY 5:12's** *fourth measure* of Faith. We remain humble, knowing that we do not possess all knowledge.

Forgiveness is ingrained in our hearts, and we hold no grudges as **RECOVERY 5:12's** *steps four* and five *along* with the *third measure* of faith has taught us. Instead, we plan our lives around benefiting others in the noblest ways possible as the **RECOVERY 5:12** *"Sick Person Prayer"* demonstrated. We strive to befriend everyone, never harboring ill will. We entrust matters of justice to God, knowing that He brings about righteousness.

The principle reminds us to respond to our enemies with surprising kindness. By doing so, we awaken their conscience and open the way for reconciliation. Our focus is on defeating evil with good, refusing to let darkness overpower us.

RECOVERY 5:12's *steps seven, eight,* and *nine* along with the *fourth measure* of faith have shown us that in our transformed relationships, we embody compassion, creating a supportive recovery community that reflects the life-changing power of recovery.

In our relationship with civil authorities, we honor the role they play in maintaining order. We submit to their authority and offer our support. We understand that all authority comes from God, and therefore, every governing body has been established by His appointment.

Resisting civil authority is seen as opposing the divine order established by God, and it carries serious consequences. However, as law-abiding citizens who do what is good, we need not fear those in authority. Our actions align with righteousness, and we commend ourselves for being responsible members of society.

We acknowledge that civil authorities serve as instruments of God for the well-being of society. They are entrusted with maintaining order. When we once acted unlawfully, these authorities had the responsibility to bring us to account. The presence of weapons in the hands of authorities is a symbol of their duty to protect society.

RECOVERY 5:12 compels us to obey civil authorities not merely out of fear of punishment, but because we desire to live with a clear conscience. We strive to uphold the principles of integrity in all our affairs, including our relationship with civil authorities. By doing so, we contribute to the overall well-being of society.

This is also the reason we pay our taxes, for governmental authorities are God's officials who oversee these things. It is our duty to pay all the taxes that we are required and to respect those who are worthy of respect, honoring them accordingly. We don't owe anything to anyone, except our outstanding debt to continually love one another, for the one who learns to love has fulfilled every requirement of the steps.

The steps and measures of **RECOVERY 5:12** align with Jesus' teachings, particularly the commandments to refrain from adultery, murder, stealing, and coveting. These commandments are rooted in the principle of loving one's neighbor as oneself. Love encompasses and fulfills all the requirements of the steps and measures. When we truly love others, it becomes impossible for us to cause harm or engage in actions that would hurt them. Love guides our thoughts, words, and actions, leading us to treat others with kindness, respect, and compassion. It motivates us to consider the well-being and needs of others before our own.

By admitting love as the guiding principle, the steps and measures of **RECOVERY 5:12** encourage us to live in harmony with Jesus' teaching. Love becomes the foundation upon which we build our relationships, make amends for past mistakes, and seek reconciliation with others. Through love, we strive to bring healing and recovery into our lives and the lives of those around us.

In the spirit of unity, we extend a warm invitation to all sincere believers, regardless of the maturity of their faith. We choose not to engage in fruitless debates that revolve around mere opinions, recognizing that our focus should be on the essentials of our shared faith. We are reminded that God has graciously welcomed us as His creation, regardless of our individual circumstances. Considering this, we strive to emulate His example by extending love and fellowship to all believers, recognizing that our unity is found in our similarities rather than in our differences.

By focusing on what unites us rather than what divides us, we foster an environment of love and support within the body of believers. Our goal is to walk together in unity, acknowledging that we are all works in progress, and allowing God's grace to transform us on our individual journeys of faith.

As believers, we recognize that it is not our place to sit in judgment of someone else's service or ministry. We understand that each person's service is accountable to their own master, who is God. It is God who determines the success or failure of one's endeavors.

We firmly believe that as God's servants, we are supported by His divine power. It is through His strength that we are able to stand and carry out the tasks He has entrusted to us. Our confidence lies in the fact that God equips us with the necessary resources to fulfill our unique callings.

Therefore, rather than passing judgment on others, we focus on faithfully carrying out our own service and ministry, seeking to honor God and follow His leading. We trust in His discernment, knowing that He alone has the authority to assess the fruitfulness of our endeavors.

In humility, we recognize that we are all servants of God, dependent on His mercy. We strive to support one another in our respective journeys, knowing that we are all part of the larger body of Christ. By embracing mutual respect, we create an environment where each person's service is appreciated, and where God's purposes are advanced collectively.

Indeed, within the body of Christ, there are different convictions and practices regarding certain matters, such as recovery, and observing specific methods of praying. It is important to recognize that having diverse approaches is not inherently wrong. For those who consider a certain way as more sacred, they do so with the intention of honoring the Lord. They approach these practices as acts of devotion to God. Similarly, those who do not hold the same convictions also do so with the intention of honoring the Lord. In matters where convictions differ, it is crucial to maintain a spirit of love towards one another. Rather than allowing such differences to create divisions, we should focus on the common goal of serving the Lord. What matters most is the posture of our hearts to God in all that we do. It is through this genuine devotion that we cultivate a deepening relationship with Him and foster a spirit of unity among believers.

Indeed, as followers of Jesus Christ, our lives are not lived in isolation, but rather in service to our Master. Whether we live or die, our purpose is to bring honor to Him. We recognize that we belong to our Master, both in life and in death. The significance of Jesus' death and resurrection lies in the fact that through His sacrifice and triumph over death, He became the Lord over all. He holds authority over both the spiritually dead and the living. His death and resurrection have profound implications for our lives, as it offers us the opportunity to experience spiritual life through reconciliation with God. Therefore, as we live out our faith, we do so with the understanding that our lives are dedicated to serving our Master. In all that we do, whether in life or death, we seek to align ourselves with His will. Our identity is found in our relationship with our Lord, Jesus Christ.

Why would we judge others because of how they approach their recovery, despising them for their methods? We all have our own journey to navigate, and it is not our place to pass judgment on others based on their recovery practices. We are each accountable for our own choices and actions. Just as it is written: "As surely as I am the Living God, I tell you: 'Every knee will bow before me and every tongue will confess the truth and glorify me!" Therefore, each one of us must take responsibility for our own salvation and give an account of our progress to Jesus Christ. We cannot control others' journeys, but we can focus on our own commitment to our recovery path. Rather than criticizing others, let us foster a spirit of support. We are all facing our own battles with sin such as addictions and alcoholism, and we each have unique approaches that work for us. Let us focus on recovery, treating others with compassion, and seeking salvation in Jesus' Name. In the end, it is accountability to Jesus that matters most.

Walking in love in recovery! We choose to release criticism towards others on their recovery journey. Instead, we commit ourselves to never intentionally causing others to stumble through our actions. We are convinced, through experience with God, that different approaches to recovery are valid. However, we also recognize that what is acceptable for us may not be the same for others. If someone finds certain practices to be unhelpful, we respect their perspective. We prioritize love over asserting our own convictions. We do not want to harm the progress of others, for whom our Lord and Savior Jesus Christ sacrificed so much. By choosing not to impose our conceptions on others, we prevent giving them a reason to speak ill of what we know to be good. The kingdom of heaven is not defined by rigid rules and conceptions, but by the presence of the Holy Spirit, which brings righteousness to our lives. As we admit these kingdom realities, we serve Jesus and earn the respect of those around us.

To commemorate the last discussion of conceptions, we feel it best if told in a story. Once, in a recovery community plagued by decreasing recovery rates and despair over increasing overdoses, a great recovery gathering took place and formed a convention. The people of the recovery community, weary and doubting, had assembled to witness a contest of faith and power. On one side stood a multitude of self-help gurus, followers of a deity they called "their conception," whom they believed to be the source of power. On the other side stood a solitary figure, a person who had recovered from a hopeless state of mind and body. They were the followers of the One who has all Power, a God unseen but believed by a faithful few.

This who was connected to the One who has all Power, raised his voice above the murmurs of the crowd. "How long will you waver between two opinions? If the One who has all Power is God, follow Him. But if 'your conception' is, then follow it."

The people remained silent, torn between their old beliefs and the hope that this person's words offered. This recovered individual, with the courage of unwavering faith, issued a challenge. "Let two altars be built, one for 'your conception' and one for the One who has all Power. The God who answers by complete recovery and salvation, He is God."

The followers of 'their own conception' eagerly accepted the challenge, confident that a god of their understanding would come to their aid. They built their altar, made sacrifices in their lives, and began their fervent self-help program of meditation. From morning till noon, they cried out to their conception to hear them!

But there was no answer. No Power came from the heavens to consume their offering. The crowd watched with growing doubt, wondering if they had put their faith in the wrong deity.

The one who had been saved by the One true God, with solemn determination, took their turn. They rebuilt the altar of the One who has all Power, carefully arranging things according to His will and their sacrifice. Then they did a most unusual thing. They dug themselves into a hole and ordered that anything that the others thought had Power could be removed, not once, but three times, until they began removing the measures of faith and implemented as much of their program as possible. They applied their arrangements over His, and the very path itself was barely recognizable.

As the sun descended toward the horizon, the person of salvation began to pray, "O Lord, God of Abraham, Isaac, and Israel, let it be known today that You are God in Israel and that I am Your servant. Answer me, O Lord, answer me, so these people will know that You, the One who has all Power, are God."

And then, as if in response to their fervent plea, fire fell from the heavens. It consumed not only the sacrifices and His arrangements but also licked up all the evidence of the self-help program applied to His way. The people of the self-help program fell to their knees, their faces filled with awe, for they had witnessed a miracle beyond any they had ever seen.

"God is the One who has all Power!" they cried out in unison.

The saved person turned to the prophets of 'their own conception' and said, "Don't leave! Do not one of you leave!" And the people remained captured by the One called Jesus of Nazareth, who revealed that they had been led astray with their empty beliefs.

That day, the people of the self-help group renounced 'their own conception' and turned their hearts to the One who has all Power. The decreasing recovery rates that had plagued them began to lift, and the recovery community once again bore fruit. It was a day of reckoning, a day of revelation, and a day when faith in the true God was restored.

From that day forward, the people of the recovery community remembered the contest as a lesson in the power of unwavering faith and the undeniable might of the One who has all Power. They knew that their true source of recovery and salvation lay not in their own conceptions but in the divine, unseen force that had answered with fire from the heavens. Recovery has a Name and it's Jesus.

In our interactions within the recovery community, we strive to embody love. We celebrate diversity, recognizing that we are all on a unique journey of healing. Through our actions and attitudes, we aim to create an atmosphere of acceptance, where individuals find comfort. We prioritize fostering uplifting relationships. We actively seek to support one another on our recovery journeys. We understand that insisting on our own opinions about someone else's practices undermine the work of healing that God is doing in their lives. While we have the freedom to hold our own convictions, we recognize that deliberately causing offense is not an act of love. Instead, we choose to refrain from pushing our own beliefs onto others. We understand that everyone's recovery path is unique, and we respect the individuality of recovery. We keep our convictions about these matters between ourselves and God, avoiding the imposition of our views on others. We find joy in living according to our conscience when it aligns with our faith. However, if we find ourselves doubting our own convictions, holding onto them leads to inner turmoil. We recognize the importance of trusting in the Holy Spirit's guidance. We understand that any actions we make that are not rooted in faith are considered sinful.

Love indeed serves as the key to fostering unity within the recovery community. As we mature spiritually in our faith, it becomes evident in our actions. We no longer live solely to please ourselves but have learned the value of patience with those who are still growing in their spiritual journey. Our purpose is to support others, empowering them to make choices that are beneficial for their own well-being and growth. Even Jesus, who possessed all power and authority, did not live to please Himself. He exemplified selflessness and sacrificial love. His life fulfilled the prophetic words that all the insults directed toward God's people would fall upon Him. This reminds us of the depth of His willingness to bear the burdens of others. In our interactions within the recovery community, we strive to embody the same spirit of selflessness. We seek to disciple others, helping them mature spiritually. By extending support, we create an environment where individuals thrive on their recovery journeys. We recognize that our own maturity enables us to better serve others and contribute to the unity and well-being of the recovery community.

The wisdom found in the Scriptures serves as a valuable resource for instructing us on how to live our lives. Through its teachings, we receive practical wisdom that enables us to endure difficult circumstances. The Scriptures provide us with a solid foundation upon which to build our lives.

We rely on God, who is the source of great comfort. His grace sustains us to navigate the ups and downs of life. Through our relationship with Jesus, we experience oneness with fellow believers. This unity is a gift from God, and it flows from our common bond in Christ.

When we come together with one voice, united in our mission, we bring glory to God. We honor Him when we admit one another as partners on this journey, just as Jesus fully received each one of us. Our acceptance of one another reflects the love of God. God's grace abounds in our lives, fostering harmony among us. Let us join in a unanimous rush of power, using our voices to glorify God. As we walk in unity, we become a powerful testimony of God's life-changing work in our lives and a beacon of hope to others. The message of salvation extends to all people, regardless of their background or ethnicity. In Jesus a new ruler emerges, one who brings unity to all.

As believers, we have the privilege to participate in the fulfillment of these prophecies. Through our testimony, we reflect on the hope found in Jesus. It is through Him that people from all walks of life discover the faithfulness of God. Let us admit our role as bearers of this message of hope, extending God's love to those around us. In doing so, we join the chorus of praise from the ends of the world, declaring the greatness of our God and inviting others to find their hope in Him.

Praise the Lord, everyone; let every person in recovery lift their voices in praise to Him. For great is His love toward us, and His faithfulness endures forever in recovery. It is prophesied that Jesus, the One who brings transformation, will rise up to rule over our lives, fulfilling our deepest desires for recovery which leads to eternal salvation.

Now, God, the wellspring of hope, fills you to overflowing with uncontainable joy as you place your trust in Him on your recovery path. The Power of the Holy Spirit surrounds your life with His superabundance, renewing your strength and empowering you to overcome every challenge. In the midst of sins such as addictions and alcoholism, there is a universal need for salvation. As you trust in God and seek His guidance, His Spirit empowers you to experience a joy that transcends circumstances. Your life becomes a beacon of hope, inspiring others on the journey of recovery. You will find comfort in God's faithfulness. Let your story of God overcoming sin become a testimony of His life-changing power. As you rely on His strength, you radiate hope to those who are still struggling, pointing them to the source of true freedom.

In God, there is hope for lasting recovery, for He is the One who can bring renewal to every aspect of our lives. Trust in Him seeking His guidance on the path to recovery and salvation. As people in recovery, we are fully convinced of our true spiritual worth. We know that we are full of goodness and that we have the power to overcome our sins such as addictions and alcoholism with the Holy Spirit managing our lives. Through this power, we share our experience, strength, and hope with others who are struggling with sins such as addictions and alcoholism.

The grace of God has made us servants of Jesus Christ on the **RECOVERY 5:12** path, and we are constantly doing the work of recovered alcoholics and addicts. We strive to make an acceptable offering to our Lord so that we are set apart and made whole by the Holy Spirit. Through our communion with Jesus Christ, we find confidence in recovery. We are not presumptuous to speak of anything except what our Lord and Savior has accomplished through us. Because many people are coming into **RECOVERY 5:12** by the Power of the Spirit, which is displayed through the amazing transformation we have undergone in our own lives. Starting from a place of repentance, we go from day to day fully embracing the path of **RECOVERY 5:12**. It is our constant passion to be pioneers in recovery, instead of relying on the foundation of someone else's program. Those who know nothing about recovery will clearly see it in our lives, and those who have not yet heard will respond to the message of hope and healing.

Our dedication to our mission has often prevented us from being able to visit everyone in person, but now with this book, there are no more obstacles standing in our way. As we travel to spread our message to others, we hope to make a stop and spend time with you. We cherish every fellowship we have the privilege to share in, and we are hopeful that you will assist us in our spiritual journey. Regardless of where our current path leads us, it will always be a place of peace, where we can offer encouragement and support to God's people in recovery. We are committed to ministering to their needs and providing them with the guidance and love they require.

We are thrilled to share with you the wonderful news that our fellows in **RECOVERY 5:12** are generously contributing to support those who are struggling with sins such as alcoholism and addictions among the recovery community. It fills our hearts with joy to have the opportunity to give back to our peers in peace, as they have expressed a sense of indebtedness for the guidance we have provided. Just as we have received help and found healing, it is only fitting that we extend our support to others who are still on the journey of recovery. As we continue our journey of **RECOVERY 5:12**, we plan to visit you on our way, bringing with us the encouragement we have gained through our own experiences. We are confident that when we come to you, we will bring an abundance of inspiration from our collective journey of recovery, as we are overflowing with the life-changing power of renewal.

In light of our shared journey of recovery, we earnestly appeal to you, our fellow brothers and sisters in Christ, to join us in prayer to God. Through our connection with our Lord Jesus Christ, let us come together and intercede for one another. We humbly ask the Father to protect us from the challenges we face from those who do not understand our recovery journey. Furthermore, we desire the well-being of the recovery community in peace and that it will be received with favor by God's holy people. It is our heart's desire that God would grant us the opportunity to bring this support to you with great joy, knowing that it aligns with His divine will. Your fellowship is a source of refreshing for us, and we long to be mutually uplifted in our shared pursuit of wholeness. God who graciously bestows His peace be present with you always. We wholeheartedly affirm this prayer, believing that it will come to fruition according to His perfect plan. Sending messages of love to all on the path of recovery! You will soon be introduced to our fellow companions, who have been transformed by the power of the Lord and are now dedicated ministers in this journey of **RECOVERY 5:12**. We ask that you warmly embrace them and extend your hospitality. Recognize their dedication to the Lord's work.

We are deeply grateful for our partners in recovery who have walked alongside us, risking their own well-being to help us find freedom. They are deserving of our utmost appreciation. We also send our warm greetings to all believers who have embraced the path of **RECOVERY 5:12** and are faithfully serving the Lord in their own recovery journeys.

Let us not forget to acknowledge our beloved family members who have been with us through thick and thin, sharing the struggles and victories of our recovery. Their unwavering support and love are cherished.

We extend our greetings to all our fellow travelers on this path, who are our fellow recovery servants who have fought their own battles and triumphed over sins such as addictions and alcoholism just as we have.

To the women who have shown great dedication in their ministry of recovery, we send our utmost admiration. We acknowledge the unique challenges they face. We also extend our greetings to those who have been chosen for a special purpose by the Lord, and to who have shown us a mother's love.

We cannot overlook our esteemed friends, mentors, and counselors, who have provided guidance throughout recovery. They have been beacons of truth. We also greet all those who gather with them, sharing in the journey of transformation.

In closing, we send our love and support, symbolized by the holy embrace of fellowship. All those in recovery across all recovery communities and fellowships, join us in extending warm greetings to one another.

As we conclude, we want to provide a final word of caution to all of you. Be vigilant, for there are individuals among you who may sow seeds of division. These individuals try to lure you away from the teachings you have received in your **RECOVERY 5:12** journey. Do not allow yourselves to be ensnared by their deceptive tactics. It is important to recognize that such individuals are not genuinely committed to serving the Lord Jesus. Instead, they are driven by their own selfish desires, seeking gain and influence. They may use persuasive words and present themselves as righteous and enlightened, but their true intentions are to deceive and manipulate the hearts of the innocent.

The Bible should never be replaced by any book and there is no book divinely inspired as the Word of God. Therefore, remain steadfast in the truth you have come to know. Lean on the teachings that have brought you healing and salvation. Seek wisdom and discernment from trusted mentors, counselors, and fellow believers who are aligned with the principle of recovery. Remember, recovery is sacred. Guard your hearts and minds against those who would lead you astray. Stay connected to the support and recovery community that uplifts you in your pursuit of lasting transformation. The Lord will continue to guide you, granting you discernment as you navigate the **RECOVERY 5:12** path with unwavering determination.

We rejoice when we think of those of you who are deeply committed to faith. Our desire for you is to become scholars of all that is good, continuously seeking wisdom that aligns with God's truth. Let your hearts remain innocent, guarded against the temptations of selfishness which is evil. Remember that the God of Peace is actively defeating Satan, empowering you to overcome any obstacles in your journey. The wonderful favor of our Lord Jesus surrounds you, enveloping you with His love. Our recovery ministry partners, who are dear to God, send their loving greetings, along with a message of recovery and salvation for our fellows. Our gracious hosts, whom we encounter in our journey of **RECOVERY 5:12**, extend our greetings, along with the entire congregation of our house and church. Additionally, the administrative team and our fellow companions on this path of healing send their warm regards.

Praise be to God! We give thanks and glory to the One who possesses all power to strengthen us and keep us firm in our **RECOVERY 5:12** journey, relying on the promises revealed in the life-changing message we share—the message of Jesus. This message unveils a mystery that was hidden for ages but is now made known through the eternal decree of God. It is a message that empowers us to take these steps and measures of faith in freedom. Now, let us give all glory and praise to God, the source of wisdom, for all eternity through our Lord Jesus Christ! Amen!

This chapter has been transcribed by a fellow traveler on the **RECOVERY 5:12** path of recovery, in a state of contentment, and is sent from this place of fulfillment. May it serve as a source of strength and illumination for all who receive it.

Sincerely,

A layman with a pen

APPENDIX: A

*"And the things that thou hast heard of me
among many witnesses,
the same commit thou to faithful men,
who shall be able to teach others also."*
(2 Timothy 2:2)

DISCIPLESHIP in **RECOVERY 5:12**:
FREQUENTLY ASKED QUESTIONS (FAQ)

These questions are many that have been asked by those battling with drugs and alcohol. Regardless of your hurt, habit or struggle, it is our expectation that you too will find nuggets of wisdom to use in your path through recovery to salvation.

When is it appropriate to avoid places where there is sin occurring such as drinking and drugging?

> "Abstain from all appearance of evil." - 1 Thessalonians 5:22

If you have not yet taken this path to ensure your spiritual growth and transformation, then it would be best to avoid these places until you have had a spiritual foundation established beneath you.

How do I handle people offering me drinks or drugs?

> "Wherefore come out from among them, and be ye separate, saith the Lord, and touch not the unclean thing; and I will receive you."
> - 2 Corinthians 6:17

It was not other people's drinking that "triggered" us or caused us to get drunk or high. We politely decline, wittingly saying something like, "Our life experience has clearly told us that we have exceeded our limit for this life and we can no longer safely drink alcohol or use drugs of any kind."

Can I have liquor or drugs of any kind in my home?

> "And if thy right hand offend thee, cut it off, and cast it from thee: for it is profitable for thee that one of thy members should perish, and not that thy whole body should be cast into hell." - Matthew 5:30

Do not keep them in your home unless you have good reason or motive to have them. We have discovered that those of us who have recovered very seldom have any reason to have liquor or drugs of any kind in our homes.

What is the **RECOVERY 5:12** position on drinking or using drugs?

> "Wine is a mocker, strong drink is raging: and whosoever is deceived thereby is not wise." - Proverbs 20:1

We have come to realize that if you are an alcoholic or addict of the hopeless and helpless variety, you have lost all choice in the matter of being able to drink or use drugs safely. Therefore, the moment we drink or use drugs, we disconnect spiritually, leading to a mental return to our vomit and eventually physical death by alcohol and drugs. For us to drink or use drugs is to die; therefore we don't drink or use drugs.

Is giving someone a ride to a recovery meeting considered sufficient service?

"Let every one of us please his neighbour for his good to edification." – Romans 15:2

Although giving a ride to a recovery meeting is an act of service, the motive behind the ride is the determining factor. Regardless, the service we speak of is being of maximum service to God and to our fellows. Merely providing a ride, although needed and appreciated, is not sufficient in light of providing maximum service to God. And there is no better service than trying to carry the Gospel Message.

What if the new prospect wants to call it off?

"And whosoever shall not receive you, nor hear your words, when ye depart out of that house or city, shake off the dust of your feet." - Matthew 10:14

Gently raise your face toward heaven and give thanks to God! This action has prevented countless hours of work and prayer that would have been null and void if the new prospect had gone along with the steps dishonestly. Remain open to the new prospect for they will come back around if they are one of us and do not die due to sins such as addictions and alcoholism. Move onto the next desperate person willing to do anything to escape the bondage of sin.

What are some ways that I can find out more about a prospect?

> "And they said, Believe on the Lord Jesus Christ, and thou shalt be saved, and thy house." - Acts 16:31

> Consult social media, friends, family, and pastor. Nothing counts more, however, than a good old-fashioned sit down and conversation with the prospect themselves. Jesus will reveal all that is needed.

What if they stick to the idea that they can still control their drinking and/or drug use?

> "Be ye not unequally yoked together with unbelievers: for what fellowship hath righteousness with unrighteousness? and what communion hath light with darkness?" - 2 Corinthians 6:14

> Leave the Bible and this book at their feet and let them know that should they discover that they can no longer control their drinking and drug use, to give you a call. There is a solution.

Can anyone diagnose someone as an alcoholic or addict?

> "Know ye not that ye are the temple of God, and that the Spirit of God dwelleth in you?" - 1 Corinthians 3:16

> Of course, the medical or treatment professional and the fellow alcoholic or addict may make such a determination. But none can diagnose as accurately as the alcoholic or addict themselves based upon the information provided and their own experience.

What if someone does not want to stop drinking or using drugs?

> "Give not that which is holy unto the dogs, neither cast ye your pearls before swine, lest they trample them under their feet, and turn again and rend you." - Matthew 7:6

Dust your sandals off at their door and move on to the next potential prospect who has exhausted all of their own efforts and wants to stop.

How do I handle ministers, physicians, and treatment centers?

"Where no counsel is, the people fall: but in the multitude of counselors there is safety." – Proverbs 11:14

View them as fellow servants in the battle for recovery. Be quick to see where each one is correct in their own knowledge and be quick to use what they have to offer. This is more than recovery, we are trying to see their souls saved.

How do I handle my passion for recovery?

"And every man that striveth for the mastery is temperate in all things. Now they do it to obtain a corruptible crown, but we an incorruptible." - 1 Corinthians 9:25

It must be given away to get it. It must be given away to keep it. It must be bridled as we take the steps and unleashed as we align with God's will through the measures.

How do I handle someone who is drunk or high?

"Be not among winebibbers; among riotous eaters of flesh." - Proverbs 23:20

Don't. Wait until they are not drinking or using drugs, even as early as when they are coming to or coming down. When they awake, they will seek it again so your window of opportunity to carry this message is narrow.

What if someone is still drinking or using drugs?

> "And the lord said unto the servant, go out into the highways and hedges, and compel them to come in, that my house may be filled." - Luke 14:23

> We never tell anyone at any time they cannot drink or use drugs. If they are as hopeless and helpless as we were, they will want to stop sooner than later and find that they can't on their own. They will know of the person who spoke of a solution and come calling. Be prepared.

What if they say they want to quit for good and they would go to any extreme to do so?

> "For whosoever shall call upon the name of the Lord shall be saved." - Romans 10:13

> Gently turn your face toward the heavens and thank God, for He has chosen to do business with another lost soul and has asked that you be in the room as a facilitator between Him and them. Time to give them the Bible this book and set an appointment following the tasks as outlined in the book.

What if they say they do not want to see you?

> "He that reproveth a scorner getteth to himself shame: and he that rebuketh a wicked man getteth himself a blot." - Proverbs 9:7

> Get the Bible and this book to them. If they wish, provide simple instructions, read these, and call if you ever need any help or just to talk.

Is there anything that can be done while someone is still in their cups or still high?

> "And he said unto them, This kind can come forth by nothing, but by prayer and fasting." - Mark 9:29

> The first thing that should always be done is to involve God in prayer, meditation, and fasting for them.

Should the loved ones be involved in approaching the prospect?

> "Wherefore receive ye one another, as Christ also received us to the glory of God." - Romans 15:7

> It is better to meet the prospect alone than with their loved ones around. It is good, however, to have a meeting with them all early on to gather information and outline the program of action as stated in this book so they will know what milestones to look for and the goal of recovery and salvation.

What is the best way to approach a prospect?

> "Preach the word; be instant in season, out of season; reprove, rebuke, exhort with all longsuffering and doctrine." - 2 Timothy 4:2

> God makes the way. We are to always be available to carry this message. The scenarios that He uses to bring people across our paths are marvelous in themselves. Don't be afraid to extend a friendly hand.

What if the prospect needs hospitalization?

> "They that are whole have no need of the physician, but they that are sick: I came not to call the righteous, but sinners to repentance." - Mark 2:17

Many do and that is okay. Alcohol and benzodiazepines cause the most dangerous detoxifications which should be administered under medical supervision. This is typically a four- or five-day process. Heroine and M.A.T. detoxification is grueling for some and best performed under nursing care because of the medications that can help with headaches, nausea, chills, sweats, GI symptoms, and overall discomfort, as well as mention linen changes and encouragement of liquids, food, and sunshine. Most other drug separations can be handled with a brief period of convalescence.

With all of the confidentiality rules, how can I visit the prospect while they are hospitalized?

"Bear ye one another's burdens, and so fulfil the law of Christ." - Galatians 6:2

The individual prospect can grant you access with proper signatures within their medical record. You may need to undergo certain sign-in procedures and be aware of visiting hours.

Should I always include the loved ones or those close to the prospect?

"Two are better than one; because they have a good reward for their labour." - Ecclesiastes 4:9

Once we and the prospect have embarked on their recovery journey, there is little reason for us to include their loved ones, unless they too are interested in their own recovery journey.

When is the best time to call on the new prospect?

"Boast not thyself of tomorrow; for thou knowest not what a day may bring forth." - Proverbs 27:1

Soon after their last debacle and while they are under the brutal heel of their consequences is when they are best able to receive such a life-saving message.

What if the prospect is depressed after a bout of drinking or drug use?

"The righteous cry, and the Lord heareth, and delivereth them out of all their troubles. The Lord is nigh unto them that are of a broken heart; and saveth such as be of a contrite spirit." - Psalm 34:17-18

As they should be. Let them know that you have a solution and that they never have to return down that road again. Otherwise, lovingly give them the familiar adage, "suffer you dog, suffer."

When do I tell the new prospect about my being a member of **RECOVERY 5:12**?

"But sanctify the Lord God in your hearts: and be ready always to give an answer to every man that asketh you a reason of the hope that is in you with meekness and fear." - 1 Peter 3:15

It's never our intention to announce that we are a member. As our relationship grows, we are sure to invite them to every recovery meeting we attend, and the reading of this book and taking the actions prescribed by it will all point towards the solution, which is God. They'll find themselves shoulder to shoulder with you as they discover they too are a member of **RECOVERY 5:12**.

What if the prospect does not want to follow the suggestions of **RECOVERY 5:12**, such as by not wanting to take a particular step?

"Give not that which is holy unto the dogs, neither cast ye your pearls before swine, lest they trample them under their feet, and turn again and rend you." - Matthew 7:6

Hopefully, you discover this sooner rather than later so as to not waste time that you could be spending with another hopeless and helpless addict or alcoholic. However, at some of these steps, many balk thinking they can find an easier or softer way. In this case, we gently tip our hats to them and go about our way while leaving the door of opportunity open to them should they want to try this way of living in the future.

My prospect is on fire and wants to get started on the next step at once! Is this ok?

"Also, that the soul be without knowledge, it is not good; and he that hasteth with his feet sinneth." - Proverbs 19:2

Although the prospect is not the one in charge of their transaction with God, it is always exciting to see a desperate, drowning person reach so solidly for this solution. Keep their motives at bay but, if possible, give them the solution as quickly as you're able to. For they did not delay in getting their drink or drug, why should they wait to get recovered and saved.

My prospect is not interested in taking the steps and only wants a handout. What do I do?

"For even when we were with you, this we commanded you, that if any would not work, neither should he eat." - 2 Thessalonians 3:10

We do not provide handouts but are sure to maintain adherence to the overall principle of loving another. Just as Jesus has and continues to love us, we also are to love one another. This is best materialized by offering solutions and pointing to resources rather than by giving handouts.

What if my prospect wants to try another method of recovery?

> There is a way which seemeth right unto a man, but the end thereof are the ways of death." - Proverbs 14:12

> We do not hold the corner of the market on recovery. What we offer is not only recovery but points toward salvation in Jesus' Name. Keep the door open, encouraging them to keep in contact and to return if they ever want to try this way of life.

I have not heard back from my prospect, what do I do?

> "And whosoever shall not receive you, nor hear your words, when ye depart out of that house or city, shake off the dust of your feet." - Matthew 10:14

> Ensure their safety and if they are not interested, move on to the next potential prospect.

I am failing with every one of my prospects; what am I doing wrong?

> "Trust in the Lord with all thine heart; and lean not unto thine own understanding. In all thy ways acknowledge him, and he shall direct thy paths." - Proverbs 3:5-6

> We chuckle at this one. It is common to begin proselytizing and when we do, the message becomes more important than the author. Before long, it is our program, our prospect, our, our, our. Should you find yourself here, we recommend getting back onto your face to focus on the Father.

My prospect wants to take the steps with someone else. What do I do?

> "And if one prevail against him, two shall withstand him; and a threefold cord is not quickly broken." - Ecclesiastes 4:12

No problem. Encourage them to seek God in all they do and these steps are how we seek God.

Everyone says not to get too involved, but what if my prospect is homeless and broke?

> "He that hath pity upon the poor lendeth unto the Lord; and that which he hath given will he pay him again." - Proverbs 19:17 (KJV):

> This is the perfect time to point them to resources and solutions that they can partake in. We let God handle the rest. We can offer them a solution which is contained in this book.

Should I allow a prospect into my home?

> "He that despiseth his neighbour sinneth: but he that hath mercy on the poor, happy is he." - Proverbs 14:21 (KJV):

> This is a difficult question we often face. This is not an ideal situation for you may pay for it with all sorts of consequences. With the resources available today, a couch in a sober living home is only a phone call away.

How is allowing a prospect to live with me harmful?

> "Make no friendship with an angry man; and with a furious man thou shalt not go." - Proverbs 22:24

> They may begin to see you as their counselor, parent, or higher power which shall derail their recovery. On the other hand, you may find that more of your time outside of their recovery is used up, thus making less time for others who desperately need this solution too.

Am I to avoid helping the prospect outside of step-work?

> "Bear ye one another's burdens, and so fulfil the law of Christ." - Galatians 6:2

> This is entirely dependent upon both of your motives. The simple rule is to not get in the way of their dependence upon a relationship with God. It is also important to remember the pitfall of expectations if our motives for helping are not checked.

What can I expect living the 12th Step life?

> "The thief cometh not, but for to steal, and to kill, and to destroy: I am come that they might have life, and that they might have it more abundantly." - John 10:10 (KJV)

> Expect that there is more. There is a measure of faith distributed to us and learning how to fully align ourselves with His will through this measure of faith brings about a life that you will not want to miss. Keep seeking Him.

How long do I allow a prospect to live in my home?

> "But if any provide not for his own, and specially for those of his own house, he hath denied the faith, and is worse than an infidel." - 1 Timothy 5:8 (KJV)

> Typically, more than 24 hours is an overstay. An overnight bed is enough time to get to the available resources during any working day.

What about the prospect's loved ones or those closest to them?

> "Think not that I am come to send peace on earth: I came not to send peace, but a sword. For I am come to set a man at variance against his father, and the daughter against her mother, and the

daughter-in-law against her mother-in-law. And a man's foes shall be they of his own household." - Matthew 10:34-36 (KJV)

We stay out of domestic affairs. They are best handled by God and the family.

What about lending money to a prospect?

"He that hath pity upon the poor lendeth unto the Lord; and that which he hath given will he pay him again." - Proverbs 19:17 (KJV)

We loan money to no one because it creates expectations which convert into resentments for us. We try not to give money away when it could be used to better serve God and others.

When and how do we give to the prospect?

"But when thou doest alms, let not thy left hand know what thy right hand doeth: That thine alms may be in secret: and thy Father which seeth in secret himself shall reward thee openly." - Matthew 6:3-4 (KJV)

We let God determine when and how we give to Him or His children.

What about the prospect who feels they cannot go on without their relationship?

"But seek ye first the kingdom of God, and his righteousness; and all these things shall be added unto you." - Matthew 6:33

Regardless of job, vehicle, or relationship, we must seek Him. Whatever we put first before our recovery will be the first thing we give away when we return to drugs and alcohol.

Does this process bring happiness back to my relationship?

> "Thou wilt shew me the path of life: in thy presence is fulness of joy; at thy right hand there are pleasures for evermore." - Psalm 16:11 (KJV)

> These steps will bring a smile back to your face. As far as all else, here are the steps we took.

What about the prospect's home?

> "Lay not up for yourselves treasures upon earth, where moth and rust doth corrupt, and where thieves break through and steal: But lay up for yourselves treasures in heaven, where neither moth nor rust doth corrupt, and where thieves do not break through nor steal." - Matthew 6:19-20

> There is nothing that should get in front of our seeking God.

When should the prospect begin practicing at home?

> "This book of the law shall not depart out of thy mouth; but thou shalt meditate therein day and night, that thou mayest observe to do according to all that is written therein: for then thou shalt make thy way prosperous, and then thou shalt have good success." - Joshua 1:8

> Immediately.

What if the prospect's loved ones are at fault?

> "Judge not, that ye be not judged. For with what judgment ye judge, ye shall be judged: and with what measure ye mete, it shall be measured to you again." - Matthew 7:1-2

That is not the message of **RECOVERY 5:12**. There is only one person who is responsible for pouring the alcohol down our throats, pushing the needle into our arms, crunching those pills, rolling the bowl, pigging out on calories, entering the relationship, exerting influence over others, or placing feeling before God, and that person is us.

How do you handle the loved ones' arguments and fault-finding?

"Wherefore, my beloved brethren, let every man be swift to hear, slow to speak, slow to wrath." - James 1:19

Every time a person is angry or disturbed, something is wrong with them, or if it us who is angry or disturbed then something is wrong with us. If we are offended by someone, we go to God. Seeing that they are a sick person, we ask God how we can be helpful. "God save me from being angry. Thy will not mine be done."

What if the prospect cannot avoid the loved ones' arguments?

"Wherefore, my beloved brethren, let every man be swift to hear, slow to speak, slow to wrath." - James 1:19

More than likely, they have been harmed by the many years of our poor actions. There are years of reconstruction ahead. We make amends where amends need to be made and then resolutely turn our thinking towards those we could help of His love, His Power, and His way of life.

What if there is a divorce or separation?

"For the Lord, the God of Israel, saith that he hateth putting away: for one covereth violence with his garment, saith the Lord of hosts:

therefore take heed to your spirit, that ye deal not treacherously."
- Malachi 2:16

Not all relationships are restored. However, through the principle of **RECOVERY 5:12** and these steps, there are ways to repair the damage we have done to relationships. Even in the face of divorce or separation, we can repair the damage we have done. God does the rest.

When is it best to move back in together?

"Trust in the Lord with all thine heart; and lean not unto thine own understanding. In all thy ways acknowledge him, and he shall direct thy paths." - Proverbs 3:5-6

We stay out of domestic disputes, but the answer is, "Here are the steps we took."

What is the danger of relationships being mended quickly?

"And be not conformed to this world: but be ye transformed by the renewing of your mind, that ye may prove what is that good, and acceptable, and perfect, will of God." - Romans 12:2

If we have not taken the steps, we have not had a spiritual awakening, and this happens in or out of a relationship.

What is the lifespan of the "Sponsor" and "Sponsee" relationship?

"A friend loveth at all times, and a brother is born for adversity."
- Proverbs 17:17

In traditional 12-step programs, the prospect is qualified and then takes the 12 steps as prescribed by a sponsor who has had a spiritual awakening as a result of taking these steps. While the prospect is taking the steps, if anyone were to ask if they are or have taken the steps, the sponsor is the one person who can sponsor them by saying, "they are or have taken these steps." If the prospect takes these steps thoroughly and honestly and they have had a spiritual awakening as a result of these steps, then they will have told the sponsor everything about them. The sponsor will know more about them than any other on this Earth. This qualifies them to be life-long friends, but that is a discussion best had once the prospect has had their spiritual awakening.

How involved should the sponsor be in a prospect's quarrels at home?

"He that passeth by, and meddleth with strife belonging not to him, is like one that taketh a dog by the ears." - Proverbs 26:17

Other than being a listening ear, we stay out of domestic disputes and refer back to "Here are the steps we took."

What advice can I give to a prospect's loved ones?

"Humble yourselves in the sight of the Lord, and he shall lift you up." - James 4:10

We do not give advice, for our advice to ourselves resulted in years of self-defeat and utter self-destruction. But we no longer have these effects in our lives, and if you were to ask us how, we would tell you, "Here are the steps we took."

APPENDIX B

> *"Two are better than one; because they have a good reward for their labour. For if they fall, the one will lift up his fellow: but woe to him that is alone when he falleth; for he hath not another to help him up. Again, if two lie together, then they have heat: but how can one be warm alone? And if one prevail against him, two shall withstand him; and a threefold cord is not quickly broken."*
> *(Ecclesiastes 4:9-12)*

GROUPS: HOW IT WORKS

MEETINGS

Welcome Message

Announcements of meeting/s time

Pass the basket, explaining that we are a supported ministry and that we like to try and pay our way

Readings of meeting guidelines etc

Describe how we help to perfect and enlarge each other's prayer lives through prayer requests

Receive prayer requests; if it is a large room then show prayer requests by a show of raised hands

Conduct prayer

Read a Bible Scripture

Read from the book

Share on what has been read or launch into a book study or begin a step study for 30-45 minutes.

Ask if there are any questions

Have a time for the Holy Spirit, repentance, and/or water baptism

Fellowship

APPENDIX C

*"I exhort therefore,
that, first of all,
supplications, prayers, intercessions,
and giving of thanks,
be made for all men."*
(1 Timothy 2:1)

PRAYER MEETING: HOW IT WORKS

Opening Worship:

> Begin the prayer meeting with praise and worship, singing uplifting and spiritual songs.
>
> Encourage participants to engage in heartfelt worship, expressing their devotion and adoration to God.

Welcome and Introduction:

> Start the meeting by welcoming everyone present and providing a brief introduction to the purpose and format of the prayer gathering.

Set a tone of reverence and anticipation for the movement of the Holy Spirit during the meeting.

Scripture Reading and Devotion:

Select a relevant Bible passage related to prayer, revival, or the work of the Holy Spirit.

Read the passage aloud, followed by a short devotion or reflection, highlighting key insights or lessons.

Sharing Testimonies:

Allow participants to share testimonies of answered prayers, spiritual experiences, or encounters with God's power and grace.

Encourage individuals to testify to the faithfulness and goodness of God in their lives.

Corporate Prayer:

Facilitate a time of collective prayer, inviting participants to pray aloud or silently as they feel led by the Holy Spirit.

Pray for specific needs within the community, church, nation, and global concerns, emphasizing intercession for spiritual revival and transformation.

Singing in the Spirit:

Create a space for participants to engage in spontaneous singing or singing in tongues under the guidance of the Holy Spirit.

This practice allows individuals to express their deep connection with God and seek spiritual edification.

Praying for Healing and Deliverance:

> Offer an opportunity for those in need of physical, emotional, or spiritual healing to come forward for prayer.

> Anointing with oil and the laying on of hands can be incorporated, following biblical practices for healing and deliverance.

Words of Prophecy and Spiritual Gifts:

> Create an atmosphere that welcomes the manifestation of spiritual gifts such as prophecy, tongues, interpretation of tongues, and words of knowledge.

> Encourage individuals who operate in these gifts to share inspired messages or words of encouragement for the edification of the body.

Closing Prayer:

> Conclude the prayer meeting with a final prayer, expressing gratitude for the time spent in God's presence and seeking His continued guidance and blessing.

> Offer a prayer of blessing and empowerment for all participants as they go forth from the meeting

APPENDIX D

"All scripture is given by inspiration of God, and is profitable for doctrine, for reproof, for correction, for instruction in righteousness: That the man of God may be perfect, thoroughly furnished unto all good works." (2 Timothy 3:16-17)

BIBLE STUDY

1. Opening Prayer:

   - Begin the Bible study with a prayer, asking the Holy Spirit to guide and illuminate the study, opening hearts and minds to receive divine insights and understanding.

   1 Corinthians 2:9-10:

   "But as it is written, Eye hath not seen, nor ear heard, neither have entered into the heart of man, the things which God hath prepared for them that love him. But God hath revealed them unto us by his Spirit: for the Spirit searcheth all things, yea, the deep things of God."

2. Worship and Praise:

   - Engage in a time of worship through singing hymns or worship songs that focus on exalting and glorifying God.

   - Encourage participants to enter into a spirit of worship, expressing their love and devotion to God.

   Psalm 95:1-2 (KJV):

   "O come, let us sing unto the Lord: let us make a joyful noise to the rock of our salvation. Let us come before his presence with thanksgiving, and make a joyful noise unto him with psalms."

3. Introduction and Icebreaker:

   - Welcome the participants and provide a brief introduction to the purpose and theme of the Bible study session.

   - Start with an icebreaker activity or question to help create a comfortable and engaging atmosphere, allowing participants to get to know one another.

   1 Peter 4:9 (KJV) encourages hospitality and welcoming others:

   "Use hospitality one to another without grudging."

4. Scripture Reading and Context:

   - Select a specific Bible passage study and read it aloud.

   - Provide a brief overview of the historical and cultural context, as well as any relevant background information, to aid in understanding the passage.

   Joshua 1:8 (KJV):

"This book of the law shall not depart out of thy mouth; but thou shalt meditate therein day and night, that thou mayest observe to do according to all that is written therein: for then thou shalt make thy way prosperous, and then thou shalt have good success."

5. Teaching and Discussion:

- Present a teaching or lesson based on the chosen Scripture, focusing on its meaning, theological significance, and practical application for the lives of believers.

- Encourage open dialogue and discussion among participants, inviting questions, insights, and reflections related to the study.

2 Timothy 2:15 (KJV):

"Study to shew thyself approved unto God, a workman that needeth not to be ashamed, rightly dividing the word of truth."

6. Application and Reflection:

- Facilitate a time for participants to reflect on how the scripture study applies to their own lives and spiritual journey.

- Encourage individuals to share stories, experiences, or challenges that relate to the scripture and discuss practical steps for applying the scripture.

James 1:22 (KJV):

"But be ye doers of the word, and not hearers only, deceiving your own selves."

7. Sharing and Testimonies:

- Invite participants to share testimonies, insights, or lessons they have learned from their own study of the scriptures or experiences with the scriptures under discussion.

- Encourage an atmosphere of encouragement and edification as individuals share their faith journeys.

Psalm 107:2 (KJV):

"Let the redeemed of the Lord say so, whom he hath redeemed from the hand of the enemy."

8. Closing Prayer and Benediction:

- Conclude the Bible study with a closing prayer, thanking God for His revelation and guidance throughout the session.

- Offer a benediction, seeking repentance, baptism, God's blessings, and the Holy Spirit for participants to live out the truths discovered in the study.

Psalm 119:18 (KJV):

"Open thou mine eyes, that I may behold wondrous things out of thy law."

APPENDIX E

"Draw nigh to God, and he will draw nigh to you.
Cleanse your hands, ye sinners; and purify your
hearts, ye double minded."
(James 4:8)

THE BEATTITUDES: PRINCIPLES, PROMISES, AND FRUIT

I. STEPS ONE, TWO, THREE:

   a. "Blessed are the poor in spirit; for theirs is the kingdom of heaven." (Matthew 5:3)
   - *i.* *STEP ONE* PRINCIPLE: Blessed are the poor in spirit.
   - *ii.* *STEP ONE* PROMISE: For theirs is the kingdom of heaven.
   - iii. EXPLANATION: Blessed are we when we realize we can't do anything from God. Only then will we submit to His will.
   - iv. FRUIT OF THE SPIRIT: Love.

II. STEPS FOUR, FIVE, SIX:

a. "Blessed are those who mourn; for they shall be comforted." (Matthew 5:4)

    i. *STEP TWO* PRINCIPLE: Blessed are those who mourn.
    ii. *STEP TWO* PROMISE: For they shall be comforted.
    iii. EXPLANATION: Blessed are those whose hearts grieve because they have sinned; the Lord will console and refresh us.
    iv. FRUIT OF THE SPIRIT: Joy.

III. STEPS SEVEN, EIGHT, NINE:

a. "Blessed are the meek; for they shall inherit the earth." (Matthew 5:5)

    i. *STEP THREE* PRINCIPLE: Blessed are the meek.
    ii. *STEP THREE* PROMISE: For they shall inherit the earth.
    iii. EXPLANATION: Blessed are you when you're humble enough to admit you don't know it all and you're willing to learn. It is you who will see God supply all your needs.
    iv. FRUIT OF THE SPIRIT: Peace.

IV. STEPS TEN, ELEVEN, TWELVE:

a. "Blessed are those who hunger and thirst after righteousness sake; they shall be filled." (Matthew 5:6)

    i. *STEP FOUR* PRINCIPLE: Blessed are those who hunger and thirst after righteousness sake.
    ii. *STEP FOUR* PROMISE: They shall be filled.
    iii. EXPLANATION: Blessed are you when you seek God's ways just as a starving and parched person seeks food and drink; if you seek God's will that much, you will always be satisfied.
    iv. FRUIT OF THE SPIRIT: Longsuffering.

(The above principles are the overarching beatitudes that cover the steps and measures as an umbrella)

V. *STEP ONE*: [Overarching beatitude: "Blessed are the poor in spirit; for theirs is the kingdom of heaven." (Matthew 5:3)]

   a. "Blessed are the poor in spirit; for theirs is the kingdom of heaven." (Matthew 5:3)

      i. *STEP ONE* PRINCIPLE: Blessed are the poor in spirit.
      ii. *STEP ONE* PROMISE: For theirs is the kingdom of heaven.
      iii. EXPLANATION: Blessed are we when we realize we can't do anything from God. Only then will we submit to His will.
      iv. FRUIT OF THE SPIRIT: Love.

VI. *STEP TWO*: [Overarching beatitude: "Blessed are the poor in spirit; for theirs is the kingdom of heaven." (Matthew 5:3)]

   a. "Blessed are those who mourn; for they shall be comforted." (Matthew 5:4)

      i. *STEP TWO* PRINCIPLE: Blessed are those who mourn.
      ii. *STEP TWO* PROMISE: For they shall be comforted.
      iii. EXPLANATION: Blessed are those whose hearts grieve because they have sinned; the Lord will console and refresh us.
      iv. FRUIT OF THE SPIRIT: Joy.

VII. *STEP THREE*: [Overarching beatitude: "Blessed are the poor in spirit; for theirs is the kingdom of heaven." (Matthew 5:3)]

   a. "Blessed are the meek; for they shall inherit the earth." (Matthew 5:5)

      i. *STEP THREE* PRINCIPLE: Blessed are the meek.
      ii. *STEP THREE* PROMISE: For they shall inherit the earth.

iii. EXPLANATION: Blessed are you when you're humble enough to admit you don't know it all and you're willing to learn. It is you who will see God supply all your needs.
iv. FRUIT OF THE SPIRIT: Peace.

VIII. STEP FOUR: [Overarching beatitude: "Blessed are those who mourn; for they shall be comforted." (Matthew 5:4)]

a. "Blessed are those who hunger and thirst after righteousness sake; they shall be filled." (Matthew 5:6)

   i. STEP FOUR PRINCIPLE: Blessed are those who hunger and thirst after righteousness sake.
   ii. STEP FOUR PROMISE: They shall be filled.
   iii. EXPLANATION: Blessed are you when you seek God's ways just as a starving and parched person seeks food and drink; if you seek God's will that much, you will always be satisfied.
   iv. FRUIT OF THE SPIRIT: Longsuffering.

IX. STEP FIVE: [Overarching beatitude: "Blessed are those who mourn; for they shall be comforted." (Matthew 5:4)]

a. "Blessed are the merciful; for they shall be shown mercy." (Matthew 5:7)

   i. STEP FIVE PRINCIPLE: Blessed are the merciful.
   ii. STEP FIVE PROMISE: For they shall be shown mercy.
   iii. EXPLANATION: Blessed are those who can show compassion toward others when they don't deserve it. Because of this, God will do the same for you.
   iv. FRUIT OF THE SPIRIT: Gentleness.

X. *STEP SIX*: [Overarching beatitude: "Blessed are those who mourn; for they shall be comforted." (Matthew 5:4)]

   a. "Blessed are the pure in heart; for they shall see God." (Matthew 5:8)

       i. *STEP SIX* PRINCIPLE: Blessed are the pure in heart.
       ii. *STEP SIX* PROMISE: For they shall see God.
       iii. EXPLANATION: Blessed are you when your motives are pure. It is you who will know God in all His fullness.
       iv. FRUIT OF THE SPIRIT: Goodness.

XI. *STEP SEVEN*: [Overarching beatitude: "Blessed are the meek; for they shall inherit the earth." (Matthew 5:5)]

   a. "Blessed are the peacemakers; for they shall be called sons of God." (Matthew 5:9)

       i. *STEP SEVEN* PRINCIPLE: Blessed are the peacemakers.
       ii. *STEP SEVEN* PROMISE: For they shall be called sons of God.
       iii. EXPLANATION: Blessed are those who seek peace with others, for you will have joy even when it isn't easy; you are truly acting like a child of God.
       iv. FRUIT OF THE SPIRIT: Faith.

XII. *STEP EIGHT*: [Overarching beatitude: "Blessed are the meek; for they shall inherit the earth." (Matthew 5:5)]

   a. "Blessed are those who are persecuted for righteousness sake; for theirs is the kingdom of heaven." (Matthew 5:10)

       i. *STEP EIGHT* PRINCIPLE: Blessed are those who are persecuted for righteousness sake.
       ii. *STEP EIGHT* PROMISE: For theirs is the kingdom of heaven.

       iii. EXPLANATION: Blessed are you when you are mistreated for doing what Jesus would do, for you are submitting to His will.

       iv. FRUIT OF THE SPIRIT: Meekness.

XIII. STEP NINE: [Overarching beatitude: "Blessed are the meek; for they shall inherit the earth." (Matthew 5:5)]

  a. "Blessed are those who are persecuted for my Name's sake; for their reward is in heaven." (Matthew 5:11 & 12)

       i. *STEP NINE* PRINCIPLE: Blessed are those who are persecuted for my Name's sake.

       ii. *STEP NINE* PROMISE: For their reward is in heaven.

       iii. EXPLANATION: Blessed are you when you are mistreated in the Name of Jesus, for your reward will be greater than anything you've experienced here on earth.

       iv. FRUIT OF THE SPIRIT: Temperance.

XIV. STEP TEN: [Overarching beatitude: "Blessed are those who hunger and thirst after righteousness sake; they shall be filled." (Matthew 5:6)]

  a. "Blessed are the poor in spirit; for theirs is the kingdom of heaven." (Matthew 5:3)

       i. *STEP TEN* PRINCIPLE: Blessed are the poor in spirit.

       ii. *STEP TEN* PROMISE: For theirs is the kingdom of heaven.

       iii. EXPLANATION: Blessed are we when we realize we can't do anything from God. Only then will we submit to His will.

       iv. FRUIT OF THE SPIRIT: Love.

XV. STEP ELEVEN: [Overarching beatitude: "Blessed are those who hunger and thirst after righteousness sake; they shall be filled." (Matthew 5:6)]

a. "Blessed are those who mourn; for they shall be comforted." (Matthew 5:4)

   i.   *STEP ELEVEN* PRINCIPLE: Blessed are those who mourn.
   ii. *STEP ELEVEN* PROMISE: For they shall be comforted.
   iii. EXPLANATION: Blessed are those whose hearts grieve because they have sinned; the Lord will console and refresh us.
   iv. FRUIT OF THE SPIRIT: Joy.

XVI. STEP TWELVE: [Overarching beatitude: "Blessed are those who hunger and thirst after righteousness sake; they shall be filled." (Matthew 5:6)]

a. "Blessed are the meek; for they shall inherit the earth." (Matthew 5:5)

   i.   *STEP TWELVE* PRINCIPLE: Blessed are the meek.
   ii. *STEP TWELVE* PROMISE: For they shall inherit the earth.
   iii. EXPLANATION: Blessed are you when you're humble enough to admit you don't know it all and you're willing to learn. It is you who will see God supply all your needs.
   iv. FRUIT OF THE SPIRIT: Peace.

XVII. FIRST MEASURE: [Overarching beatitudes: "Blessed are the poor in spirit; for theirs is the kingdom of heaven." (Matthew 5:3)] AND ["Blessed are those who hunger and thirst after righteousness sake; they shall be filled." (Matthew 5:6)]

a. [Covering beatitudes:

   i. "Blessed are the poor in spirit; for theirs is the kingdom of heaven." (Matthew 5:3)] AND

ii. "Blessed are the meek; for they shall inherit the earth." (Matthew 5:5)]

   1. *FIRST MEASURE*, BEATITUDE OF WITNESS: "Blessed are the merciful; for they shall be shown mercy." (Matthew 5:7)

   2. *FIRST MEASURE*, BEATITUDE OF PRAYER: "Blessed are those who hunger and thirst after righteousness sake; they shall be filled." (Matthew 5:6)

   3. SCRIPTURE & EXPLANATION: But grow in grace and the knowledge of our Lord and Saviour Jesus Christ. To him be glory both now and forever. Amen (2 Peter 3:18). Although we will never fully understand that which is God, we are encouraged as believers to continually grow in our understanding of God's grace and in our relationship with Christ.

   4. FRUITS OF THE SPIRIT: Gentleness and Longsuffering.

XVIII. SECOND MEASURE: [Overarching beatitude: "Blessed are the poor in spirit; for theirs is the kingdom of heaven." (Matthew 5:3)]

   a. [Covering beatitudes:
   i. "Blessed are the poor in spirit; for theirs is the kingdom of heaven." (Matthew 5:3)] AND
   ii. "Blessed are those who mourn; for they shall be comforted." (Matthew 5:4) AND
   iii. "Blessed are the meek; for they shall inherit the earth." (Matthew 5:5)]

      1. *SECOND MEASURE*, BEATITUDE OF WITNESS: "Blessed are the pure in heart; for they shall see God." (Matthew 5:8)

      2. *SECOND MEASURE*, BEATITUDE OF PRAYER:

"Blessed are the merciful; for they shall be shown mercy." (Matthew 5:7)

3. SCRIPTURE & EXPLANATION: (Psalm 51:17) The sacrifices of God are a broken spirit: a broken and contrite heart. O God, thou wilt not despise. We are reminded of the importance of having a contrite heart and a willingness to confess and repent of sins.

4. FRUITS OF THE SPIRIT: Goodness and Gentleness.

XIX. THIRD MEASURE: [Overarching beatitude: "Blessed are those who mourn; for they shall be comforted." (Matthew 5:4)]

a. [Covering beatitudes:
   i. "Blessed are those who hunger and thirst after righteousness sake; they shall be filled." (Matthew 5:6) AND
   ii. "Blessed are the merciful; for they shall be shown mercy." (Matthew 5:7) AND
   iii. "Blessed are the pure in heart; for they shall see God." (Matthew 5:8)]

   1. *THIRD MEASURE*, BEATITUDE OF WITNESS: "Blessed are the peacemakers; for they shall be called sons of God." (Matthew 5:9)
   2. *THIRD MEASURE*, BEATITUDE OF PRAYER: "Blessed are the pure in heart; for they shall see God." (Matthew 5:8)
   3. SCRIPTURE & EXPLANATION: (1 Peter 5:6 & 7) We humbled ourselves therefore under the mighty hand of God, that he may exalt us in due time. We cast all our care upon Him, because he cares for us. We are reminded that we have relinquished control and rely solely on God's provision and care as we embark on the path of faith through these measures.
   4. FRUITS OF THE SPIRIT: Faith and Goodness.

XX. *FOURTH MEASURE*: [Overarching beatitude: "Blessed are the meek; for they shall inherit the earth." (Matthew 5:5)]

   a. [Covering beatitudes:
   i. "Blessed are the peacemakers; for they shall be called sons of God." (Matthew 5:9) AND
   ii. "Blessed are those who are persecuted for righteousness sake; for theirs is the kingdom of heaven." (Matthew 5:10) AND
   iii. "Blessed are those who are persecuted for my Name's sake; for their reward is in heaven." (Matthew 5:11 & 12)]

   1. *FOURTH MEASURE*, BEATITUDE OF WITNESS: "Blessed are those who are persecuted for righteousness sake; for theirs is the kingdom of heaven." (Matthew 5:10)

   2. FOURTH MEASURE, BEATITUDE OF PRAYER: "Blessed are the peacemakers; for they shall be called sons of God." (Matthew 5:9)

   3. SCRIPTURE & EXPLANATION: (Matthew 25:40) And the King shall answer and say unto them, Verily I say unto you, Inasmuch as ye have done it unto one of the least of these my brethren, ye have done it unto me. We are reminded of the importance of showing compassion and kindness to others, especially to those who may be considered the least or most vulnerable in society. Jesus, the King, is speaking, and He emphasizes that when we extend love, help, and support to those in need, we are doing it unto Him.

   4. FRUITS OF THE SPIRIT: Meekness and Faith.

XXI. *FIFTH MEASURE*: [Overarching beatitudes: "Blessed are the meek; for they shall inherit the earth." (Matthew 5:5)] AND ["Blessed are those who hunger and thirst after righteousness sake; they shall be filled." (Matthew 5:6)]

a. [Covering beatitudes:
   i. "Blessed are those who are persecuted for my Name's sake; for their reward is in heaven." (Matthew 5:11 & 12) AND
   ii. "Blessed are the poor in spirit; for theirs is the kingdom of heaven." (Matthew 5:3)]
      1. *FIFTH MEASURE*, BEATITUDE OF WITNESS: "Blessed are those who are persecuted for my Name's sake; for their reward is in heaven." (Matthew 5:11 & 12)
      2. *FIFTH MEASURE* BEATITUDE OF PRAYER: "Blessed are those who are persecuted for righteousness sake; for theirs is the kingdom of heaven." (Matthew 5:10)
      3. SCRIPTURE & EXPLANATION: (John 8:12) Then spoke Jesus again unto them, saying, I am the light of the world: he that followeth me shall not walk in darkness, but shall have the light of life. We are reminded of the anointed power of following Jesus, the Light of the world, and how through Him, we find true meaning, purpose, and a path to eternal life. We emphasize the importance of having a relationship with Jesus as the source of spiritual illumination and guidance for our lives.
      4. FRUITS OF THE SPIRIT: Temperance and Meekness.

APPENDIX F

"Feed the flock of God which is among you, taking the oversight thereof, not by constraint, but willingly; not for filthy lucre, but of a ready mind; Neither as being lords over God's heritage, but being ensamples to the flock." (1 Peter 5:2-3)

WHAT IS A PASTOR?

If you are as fresh to this new way of living as we were, you are going to have some questions that most people would have but seldom think it is appropriate to ask. But we are living with a different plan now and we must subject ourselves to a spiritual leader who can assist us in our journey down this path. The most basic need is a pastor. At one point, we all needed one and didn't know it.

As Holy Ghost-filled recovered believers, we would advise you to find a pastor, a spiritual leader, and a shepherd who plays a crucial role in this new way of life and community. The term "pastor" is derived from the Latin word for "shepherd," and in the context of recovery and faith, it signifies someone who guides, nurtures, and cares for the members of a congregation. Here are some common offices the pastor fulfills in our lives:

1. Spiritual Leader: A pastor is considered the spiritual head of a church, responsible for providing biblical teachings, guidance, and counsel to the congregation. They are seen as anointed individuals who are called by God to lead and serve His people. Hebrews 13:7 - "Remember them which have the rule over you, who have spoken unto you the word of God: whose faith follow, considering the end of their conversation."

2. Preacher and Teacher: One of the primary roles of a pastor is to preach and teach the Word of God. They deliver sermons and lead Bible studies, helping the congregation understand the Scriptures and how they apply to daily life. 2 Timothy 4:2 - "Preach the word; be instant in season, out of season; reprove, rebuke, exhort with all longsuffering and doctrine."

3. Shepherd: The pastor is often likened to a shepherd who cares for the flock. They are expected to be attentive to the needs of their congregants, providing spiritual care, counseling, and support during difficult times. 1 Peter 5:2-3 - "Feed the flock of God which is among you, taking the oversight thereof, not by constraint, but willingly; not for filthy lucre, but of a ready mind; Neither as being lords over God's heritage, but being ensamples to the flock."

4. Worship Leader: The pastor often leads the congregation in worship, creating an atmosphere for the Holy Spirit to move and work among the people. Psalm 100:2 - "Serve the Lord with gladness: come before his presence with singing."

5. Administrator: Beyond the spiritual aspects, a pastor also takes on administrative responsibilities within the church, overseeing the church's activities, managing staff and volunteers, and coordinating various programs and events. 1 Corinthians 14:40 - "Let all things be done decently and in order."

6. Intercessor: Pastors are intercessors who pray for the needs of the congregation and the community, seeking God's guidance and intervention in various situations. 1 Timothy 2:1 - "I exhort therefore, that, first of all, supplications, prayers, intercessions, and giving of thanks, be made for all men."

7. Community Involvement: Pastors are encouraged to actively engage with their local communities, promoting outreach and missions, and demonstrating God's love through acts of service and compassion. Galatians 6:10 - "As we have therefore opportunity, let us do good unto all men, especially unto them who are of the household of faith."

8. Spiritual Gifts: Pastors are empowered by the Holy Spirit and may demonstrate spiritual gifts such as healing, prophecy, and speaking in tongues, as described in the New Testament. 1 Corinthians 12:7-11 (KJV) - "But the manifestation of the Spirit is given to every man to profit withal. For to one is given by the Spirit the word of wisdom; to another the word of knowledge by the same Spirit; To another faith by the same Spirit; to another the gifts of healing by the same Spirit; To another the working of miracles; to another prophecy; to another discerning of spirits; to another divers kinds of tongues; to another the interpretation of tongues: But all these worketh that one and the selfsame Spirit, dividing to every man severally as he will."

In recovery, the role of a pastor is considered a divine calling, and their service is highly respected and valued within the church community. The pastor's primary mission is to lead people to a deeper relationship with God, to encourage spiritual growth, and to equip the congregation to live according to biblical principles and values. A pastor is a good thing.

APPENDIX G

"Now, therefore, ye are no more strangers and foreigners, but fellow citizens with the saints, and of the household of God." (Ephesians 2:19)

WHAT IS A CHURCH FAMILY?

Since we were already asking what a pastor is, we should also ask what a church family is. We found that a good church family is sometimes closer than our real families. We spend more time with them during the week than we do with our own families at times. This church family brings a new way of living to a community of people that we would otherwise not normally mix with.

As Holy Ghost-filled recovered believers, we believe that the church family is not just a group of people who gather for religious activities but a deeply connected and spiritually bonded community. The church family is a group of people who share a common faith in Jesus Christ, are filled with the Holy Spirit, and strive to live according to biblical principles and teachings.

1. Unity and Love: In the church family, there is a sense of unity and love among our members. We are encouraged to love one another as Christ

loved us, supporting and caring for each other in both times of joy and times of struggle.

2. Worship and Praise: The church family comes together to worship and praise God, lifting our voices in song, prayer, and thanksgiving. Worship is not just a ritual; it is a heartfelt expression of our love and adoration for the Lord.

3. Spiritual Growth: Within the church family, there is an emphasis on spiritual growth and maturity. We encourage each other to study the Bible, seek a deeper relationship with God, and develop the gifts and talents that the Holy Spirit has bestowed upon us.

4. Prayer and Intercession: The church family is a place where prayer is fervently practiced. We believe in the power of prayer and intercede on behalf of one another, our community, and the world.

5. Discipleship and Mentoring: More mature believers in the church family take on the role of mentors and discipleship, guiding and nurturing younger or newer Christians in their faith journey.

6. Outreach and Evangelism: The church family is mission-minded, seeking to share the love and message of Christ with others. We actively engage in outreach and evangelism to make a positive impact on our community and beyond.

7. Spiritual Gifts in Action: In the church family, we recognize and encourage the operation of spiritual gifts. Each member has unique gifts given by the Holy Spirit, and we value the diversity and contributions of every person.

8. Fellowship and Support: The church family provides a place of fellowship and support, where believers can find encouragement, comfort, and accountability in our walks with God.

9. Communion and Baptism: The church family partakes in communion as a symbolic remembrance of Christ's sacrifice, and baptism is celebrated as an outward expression of faith and new life in Christ.

10. Family Bonds: In a church family, there is a sense of close-knit family bonds. We refer to each other as brothers and sisters in Christ, acknowledging our shared spiritual heritage and relationship as children of God.

Overall, the church family is a place where believers can grow in faith, experience the presence of the Holy Spirit, and find a loving and supportive community to walk alongside in their journeys of following Christ.

APPENDIX H

"But the fruit of the Spirit is love, joy, peace, longsuffering, gentleness, goodness, faith, meekness, temperance: against such there is no law."
(Galatians 5:22-23)

GIFTS OF THE SPIRIT

Administration:

1 Corinthians 12:28 (KJV):

"And God hath set some in the church, first apostles, secondarily prophets, thirdly teachers, after that miracles, then gifts of healings, helps, governments, diversities of tongues."

Apostle:

Ephesians 4:11 (KJV):

"And he gave some, apostles; and some, prophets; and some, evangelists; and some, pastors and teachers."

Counsel:

Proverbs 11:14 (KJV):

"Where no counsel is, the people fall: but in the multitude of counsellors there is safety."

Distinguishing Between Spirits:

1 Corinthians 12:10 (KJV):

"To another the working of miracles; to another prophecy; to another discerning of spirits; to another divers kinds of tongues; to another the interpretation of tongues."

Evangelists:

Ephesians 4:11 (KJV):

"And he gave some, apostles; and some, prophets; and some, evangelists; and some, pastors and teachers."

Exhortation:

Romans 12:8 (KJV):

"Or he that exhorteth, on exhortation: he that giveth, let him do it with simplicity; he that ruleth, with diligence; he that sheweth mercy, with cheerfulness."

Faith:

1 Corinthians 12:9 (KJV):

"To another faith by the same Spirit; to another the gifts of healing by the same Spirit."

Faithfulness:

1 Corinthians 4:2 (KJV):

"Moreover it is required in stewards, that a man be found faithful."

Fear of the Lord:

Proverbs 1:7 (KJV):

"The fear of the Lord is the beginning of knowledge: but fools despise wisdom and instruction."

Fortitude (Might):

Ephesians 6:10 (KJV):

"Finally, my brethren, be strong in the Lord, and in the power of his might."

Gentleness:

Galatians 5:22-23 (KJV):

"But the fruit of the Spirit is love, joy, peace, longsuffering, gentleness, goodness, faith, meekness, temperance: against such there is no law."

Gifts of Healing:

1 Corinthians 12:9 (KJV):

"To another faith by the same Spirit; to another the gifts of healing by the same Spirit."

Giving:

Romans 12:8 (KJV):

"Or he that exhorteth, on exhortation: he that giveth, let him do it with simplicity; he that ruleth, with diligence; he that sheweth mercy, with cheerfulness."

Goodness:

Galatians 5:22-23 (KJV):

"But the fruit of the Spirit is love, joy, peace, longsuffering, gentleness, goodness, faith, meekness, temperance: against such there is no law."

Helps:

1 Corinthians 12:28 (KJV):

"And God hath set some in the church, first apostles, secondarily prophets, thirdly teachers, after that miracles, then gifts of healings, helps, governments, diversities of tongues."

Interpretation of Tongues:

1 Corinthians 12:10 (KJV):

"To another the working of miracles; to another prophecy; to another discerning of spirits; to another divers kinds of tongues; to another the interpretation of tongues."

Joy:

Galatians 5:22-23 (KJV):

"But the fruit of the Spirit is love, joy, peace, longsuffering, gentleness, goodness, faith, meekness, temperance: against such there is no law."

Kindness:

Galatians 5:22-23 (KJV):

"But the fruit of the Spirit is love, joy, peace, longsuffering, gentleness, goodness, faith, meekness, temperance: against such there is no law."

Knowledge:

1 Corinthians 12:8 (KJV):

"For to one is given by the Spirit the word of wisdom; to another the word of knowledge by the same Spirit;"

Leadership:

Romans 12:8 (KJV):

"Or he that exhorteth, on exhortation: he that giveth, let him do it with simplicity; he that ruleth, with diligence; he that sheweth mercy, with cheerfulness."

Love:

1 Corinthians 13:13 (KJV):

"And now abideth faith, hope, charity (love), these three; but the greatest of these is charity."

Mercy:

Romans 12:8 (KJV):

"Or he that exhorteth, on exhortation: he that giveth, let him do it with simplicity; he that ruleth, with diligence; he that sheweth mercy, with cheerfulness."

Miracles:

1 Corinthians 12:10 (KJV):

"To another the working of miracles; to another prophecy; to another discerning of spirits; to another divers kinds of tongues; to another the interpretation of tongues."

Patience:

Galatians 5:22-23 (KJV):

"But the fruit of the Spirit is love, joy, peace, longsuffering, gentleness, goodness, faith, meekness, temperance: against such there is no law."

Peace:

Galatians 5:22-23 (KJV):

"But the fruit of the Spirit is love, joy, peace, longsuffering, gentleness, goodness, faith, meekness, temperance: against such there is no law."

Piety (Devotion - Delight in the Lord):

Psalm 37:4 (KJV):

"Delight thyself also in the Lord: and he shall give thee the desires of thine heart."

Prophecy:

1 Corinthians 12:10 (KJV):

"To another the working of miracles; to another prophecy; to another discerning of spirits; to another divers kinds of tongues; to another the interpretation of tongues."

Prophet:

Ephesians 4:11 (KJV):

"And he gave some, apostles; and some, prophets; and some, evangelists; and some, pastors and teachers."

Self-Control:

Galatians 5:22-23 (KJV):

"But the fruit of the Spirit is love, joy, peace, longsuffering, gentleness, goodness, faith, meekness, temperance: against such there is no law."

Serving:

Romans 12:7 (KJV):

"Or ministry, let us wait on our ministering: or he that teacheth, on teaching;"

Shepherds:

Ephesians 4:11 (KJV):

"And he gave some, apostles; and some, prophets; and some, evangelists; and some, pastors and teachers."

Speaking:

1 Corinthians 12:10 (KJV):

"To another the working of miracles; to another prophecy; to another discerning of spirits; to another divers kinds of tongues; to another the interpretation of tongues."

Teacher:

Romans 12:7 (KJV):

"Or ministry, let us wait on our ministering: or he that teacheth, on teaching;"

Teaching:

Romans 12:7 (KJV):

"Or ministry, let us wait on our ministering: or he that teacheth, on teaching;"

Tongues:

1 Corinthians 12:10 (KJV):

"To another the working of miracles; to another prophecy; to another discerning of spirits; to another divers kinds of tongues; to another the interpretation of tongues."

Understanding:

1 Corinthians 12:8 (KJV):

"For to one is given by the Spirit the word of wisdom; to another the word of knowledge by the same Spirit;"

Wisdom:

1 Corinthians 12:8 (KJV):

"For to one is given by the Spirit the word of wisdom; to another the word of knowledge by the same Spirit;"

Word of Knowledge:

1 Corinthians 12:8 (KJV):

"For to one is given by the Spirit the word of wisdom; to another the word of knowledge by the same Spirit;"

Word of Wisdom:

1 Corinthians 12:8 (KJV):

"For to one is given by the Spirit the word of wisdom; to another the word of knowledge by the same Spirit;"

www.ingramcontent.com/pod-product-compliance
Lightning Source LLC
Chambersburg PA
CBHW070743060526
44119CB00099B/472/J